The Origins and Foundations of Music Education

Second Edition

Also available from Bloomsbury

Activating Diverse Musical Creativities, edited by Pamela Burnard and Elizabeth Haddon

MasterClass in Music Education, edited by John Finney

Music Education with Digital Technology, edited by John Finney

The Origins and Foundations of Music Education

International Perspectives

Gordon Cox and Robin Stevens

Bloomsbury Academic
An imprint of Bloomsbury Publishing Plc

BLOOMSBURY

LONDON · OXFORD · NEW YORK · NEW DELHI · SYDNEY

Bloomsbury Academic

An imprint of Bloomsbury Publishing Plc

50 Bedford Square	1385 Broadway
London	New York
WC1B 3DP	NY 10018
UK	USA

www.bloomsbury.com

BLOOMSBURY and the Diana logo are trademarks of Bloomsbury Publishing Plc

First published 2017

British Library Cataloguing-in-Publication Data
A catalogue record for this book is available from the British Library.

ISBN:	HB:	978-1-4742-2909-8
	PB:	978-1-4742-2908-1
	ePDF:	978-1-4742-2911-1
	ePub:	978-1-4742-2912-8

Library of Congress Cataloging-in-Publication Data
Names: Cox, Gordon, 1942- | Stevens, Robin Sydney, 1947-.
Title: The origins and foundations of music education : international
 perspectives / edited by Gordon Cox and Robin Stevens.
Description: London ; New York : Bloomsbury Academic, 2016.
Identifiers: LCCN 2016012089 (print) | LCCN 2016013244 (ebook) | ISBN
 9781474229098 (hardback) | ISBN 9781474229081 (pbk.) | ISBN 9781474229111
 (epdf) | ISBN 9781474229128 (epub)
Subjects: LCSH: Music--Instruction and study. | Music--Instruction and
 study--History.
Classification: LCC MT1 .O75 2016 (print) | LCC MT1 (ebook) | DDC 780.71--dc23 LC record available
at http://lccn.loc.gov/2016012089

Typeset by Fakenham Prepress Solutions, Fakenham, Norfolk NR21 8NN
Printed and bound in India

Contents

Part I Europe

Part IV Africa and Asia-Pacific

       Robin Stevens and Jane Southcott   **223**

17   China: A socio-political perspective on the introduction and
       development of school music
       Wai-Chung Ho   **240**

18   South Africa: Indigenous roots, cultural imposition and an
       emerging national identity
       Robin Stevens and Eric Akrofi   **256**

       Conclusion
       Gordon Cox and Robin Stevens   **271**

       Index   **281**

List of Figures

List of Tables

List of Contributors

Eric Akrofi holds an EdD degree from the University of Illinois at Urbana-Champaign, USA, and was formerly Professor of Music Education at Walter Sisulu University, Mthatha, South Africa. His teaching career has been in universities in Ghana and South Africa. Aside from numerous conference presentations and published articles, he is the author of *Sharing Knowledge and Experience: A Profile of Kwabena Nketia, Scholar and Music Educator* (Afram Publications 2002).

Fred Ola Bjørnstad was Senior Lecturer in Music Education at Stord/Haugesund University College, Norway, until his retirement. He was one of three co-editors of *Med sang! Perspektiver på norske skolesangbøker etter 1814* (Oslo 2014), an anthology describing ideas and ideologies in Norwegian songbooks for schools after 1814. This was a result of the national inter-institutional project *Ideoskosa*, of which he was the leader.

Dilek Göktürk Cary served as an associate professor and founding head of the Music Department at Karabük University in Karabük, Turkey. She currently is an Associate Professor at Ipek University's Conservatory in Ankara, Turkey. As a widely published scholar, her main research interests include string pedagogy and teaching methods, the history of music education, ethnomusicological studies in Turkish music and music education in the twenty-first century.

Alicia Cristina de Couve graduated from the National Conservatoire of Music (Argentina), holds a bachelor's degree in History from the Argentine Catholic University and a post-degree certificate in Educational Research. She teaches Educational Policy, Didactics and Teaching Practice at Buenos Aires Astor Piazzolla Conservatoire of Music. She has published articles in *The Bulletin of Historical Research in Music Education*, *Arts Education Policy Review* and the *International Journal of Music Education*, among others.

Gordon Cox was, until his retirement, senior lecturer in Music Education at the University of Reading. He writes extensively on the history of music education and is a past co-editor of the *British Journal of Music Education*. He is currently Chair of the History Standing Committee of the International Society for Music Education. His most recent book is *The Musical Salvationist* (Boydell Press 2011).

Magne Espeland is Professor of Music and Education at Stord/Haugesund University

College in Western Norway. He has written extensively on the development of different aspects of music as a curriculum subject in schools nationally and internationally, especially on music listening and music composition. He is currently chairing Music West, a network of higher music education institutions in Western Norway, and leads a research programme on Culture and Creativity Pedagogy.

Ana Lucía Frega, currently Head of the Centro de Pedagogía Musical (CePeM) at the Music Department of the Universidad Nacional de las Artes in Buenos Aires, Argentina, is an ISME honorary life member. Author of many books in Spanish, some translated into English, she is co-author with Wayne Bowman of *The Oxford Handbook of the Philosophy of Music Education*, and is editor of the Spanish version as a compendium published in mid-2016.

Rūta Girdzijauskien is Head of the Department of Music Education and a Professor at Klaipėda University, Lithuania, President of the Lithuanian Music Teachers' Association and a board member of the European Association for Music in Schools (EAS). Her main research interests include teacher education and the development of creativity through musical activity. She has published monographs, books of applied pedagogy, numerous articles and a music textbook series for schools.

Wilfried Gruhn is Professor Emeritus of Music Education at the Music Academy Freiburg, Germany. He has served as co-editor of several journals. He was President of the International Research Alliance of Institutes for Music Education (RAIME) (1995–7), an ISME board member (2000–4), Director of the Gordon Institute, Freiburg (2003–9) and served as President of the International Leo Kestenberg Society (2009–12). His research areas include historical and empirical research.

Wai-Chung Ho is a professor in the Department of Music, Hong Kong Baptist University, Hong Kong, China. She is a specialist in music education with particular focus on curriculum studies and sociology of music/music education. Her main research areas include the sociology of music and the comparative study of East Asian music education. Her most recent book is *School Music Education and Social Change in Mainland China, Hong Kong and Taiwan* (Brill 2011).

Jere T. Humphreys, Professor of Music at Arizona State University, USA, is an award-winning researcher and dissertation advisor, Fulbright Scholar, and international keynote speaker and teacher. He was editor of the *Journal of Historical Research in Music Education*, section editor for the *Oxford Handbook of Music Education* and contributing editor for the *Grove Dictionary of American Music* (2nd edn). He engages in extensive hands-on and board-level service with community organizations.

Lia Laor is a musicologist and music educator. She is the former Chair of the Music Education Graduate Programme at Levinsky College of Education, Israel, and currently the Dean of the Faculty of Education. Professor Laor founded and edited *Mafteah*, a journal for Israeli music educators, and coordinated the curriculum committee that was responsible for the preparation of the new national music curriculum. Her research interests include the history and philosophy of music education, music teacher education, and the development of professional identity and leadership among music educators.

Lisa Lorenzino has served as Music Education Chair at the Schulich School of Music, McGill University, Montreal, Canada, since 2007. Her research interests focus on cross-cultural approaches to music teaching in formal and informal settings. Dr Lorenzino's publications range from articles and book chapters on the Cuban conservatory system to *El Sistema*, the history of jazz flute and teacher identity. She is actively involved as a jazz/Latin flautist.

Besa Luzha, a classical pianist undergraduate (1994), studied music education in Kosovo and at the Institute of Education, University of London (2014). She works as Assistant Professor at the Music Department, School of Arts, University of Prishtina, Kosovo. She is also a national coordinator of the music education curriculum for the Ministry of Education in Kosovo (since 2000). Her research interest is in the sociology and history of music education.

Marie McCarthy is Professor of Music Education at the University of Michigan, USA. She has published numerous historical studies, including two books: *Passing It On: The Transmission of Music in Irish Culture* and *Toward a Global Community: A History of the International Society for Music Education, 1953–2003*. She is editor of the *Journal of Historical Research in Music Education* and serves on the ISME History Standing Committee.

François Madurell is Professor of Musicology at the University Paris-Sorbonne, France. He is a member of the Joint Research Unit of the Institut de Recherche en Musicologie, which is part of the French National Centre for Scientific Research (IReMus CNRS-UMR 8223). He is also director of the *Journal de Recherche en Education Musicale*. His other fields of research include musicology, music education and twentieth-century music.

Claudia Dal Pino graduated from the National Conservatoire of Music, Argentina, completed a master's degree in Music Didactics at CAECE University, Argentina and a post-degree certificate in Educational Research. She is Vice-Principal at Buenos Aires' Astor Piazzolla Conservatoire of Music, Argentina, and teaches research methodology at the Universidad Nacional del Artes, Argentina. She has published articles in *The Bulletin of Historical Research in Music Education*, *Arts Education Policy Review* and the *International Journal of Music Education*, among others.

Gabriel Rusinek is Associate Professor in the Faculty of Education, Complutense University of Madrid, Spain. Dr Rusinek edits the peer-reviewed open-access research journal *Revista Electrónica Complutense de Investigación en Educación Musical* and is a member of the editorial boards of ISME's *International Journal of Music Education*

– Practice and *Revista Internacional de Educación Musical*, and of the advisory boards of the *International Journal of Education and the Arts* and *Music Education Research*. He is a commissioner of ISME's Music in Schools and Teacher Education Commission.

Emilija Sakadolskis is an associate professor at the Lithuanian University of Educational Sciences in Vilnius, Lithuania. A graduate of the University of Maryland College Park in the USA, she has been working with Lithuanian educators on educational reform since the fall of the Soviet Union in the early 1990s. Her academic interests include music teacher education, curriculum and learning theories, educational research methodologies and educational policy.

Susana Sarfson is an associate professor, Faculty of Human Sciences, University of Zaragoza, Spain. Her research interests lie in the areas of history of music education in Spain and Latin America, the links between music and literature, and Spanish Baroque music. Dr Sarfson supervises many postgraduate research students in multidisciplinary fields of music, education and literature.

Jane Southcott is an associate professor in the Faculty of Education at Monash University, Australia. She researches the history of the music curriculum in Australia, America and Europe, and community engagement with music and cultural identity focusing on positive ageing. Dr Southcott supervises many postgraduate research students. She is president of the Australian and New Zealand Association for Research in Music Education and an editorial board member of internationally refereed journals.

Jusamara Souza completed her PhD in Music Education at the Universität Bremen, Germany. She is a Professor of Music Education in the Institute of Arts at the Universidade Federal do Rio Grande do Sul (UFRGS), Brazil, working at the undergraduate and graduate levels and supervising MA and PhD students. Her research interests include formal and informal music education, mass media and music education, and the history and sociology of music education.

Robin Stevens was formerly associate professor of Music Education at Deakin University, Melbourne, Australia, and is now a Principal Fellow in the Melbourne Conservatorium of Music at The University of Melbourne. He has a long-standing interest in historical research in music education, particularly the development and propagation of the tonic sol-fa method and notation in England and its dissemination to Australia, South Africa and Asia-Pacific countries.

Nancy F. Vogan is Music Research Professor Emerita, Mount Allison University, Sackville, New Brunswick, Canada. Her publications include *Music Education in Canada: A Historical Account* (1991) (co-author with J. Paul Green) as well as numerous articles in books, journals and encyclopedias. She is currently preparing a book on the history of singing schools and tunebooks in the Maritime provinces of Canada and researching the history of music teaching at Mount Allison.

Preface and Acknowledgements

In this second edition we have incorporated five new chapters, which extend the reach of the book. They deal with the following countries: Brazil, Israel, Kosovo, Lithuania and Turkey. In addition, a substantial Conclusion has been added. Previous chapters have been updated where necessary to take account of recent developments in music education. Furthermore, in order to increase the accessibility of the book, questions for each chapter have been devised in order to facilitate discussion and reflection.

Our thanks go in particular to Alison Baker at Bloomsbury Publishing for her support and encouragement from the inception of the book to the publication of this revised and expanded second edition. We also thank our colleague, Marie McCarthy, editor of the *Journal of Historical Research in Music Education*, for her advice and ideas that have contributed so much to the scope and coverage of the book, and to the anonymous reviewers for their probing and critical responses to our original proposal and to the book's subsequent revision and expansion. The editorial process has been enlivened by the commitment and good humour of our authors, including those new colleagues who have joined us in this second edition. Finally we thank Sheila Woodward, President of the International Society for Music Education, for agreeing so readily to contribute a foreword.

Gordon Cox and Robin Stevens

Foreword

This distinctive volume traces music education in the compulsory schooling systems of eighteen countries through a historical and contextual lens that is breathtaking in its scope. Across varying times and shores, it is seen emerging from beneath the rolling tides, riding the crest of the wave, then struggling beneath the surface, only to reappear again reshaped and moulded by powerful forces.

We read the vivid stories of school music education echoing or defying the political, economic, religious and social ideologies of the day. The distinguished authors provide authoritative perspectives that are appropriate in today's era, where social justice is often paramount in the thinking of educators. They portray the existence and nature of school music education against backdrops of colonial rule, the founding of nations, civil revolutions, dictatorships and democratic processes. We are guided through influences of nationalism, racial discrimination and religious fundamentalism, among others, carving their indelible imprint on music in schools.

In a fascinating world tour, we encounter uncanny similarities crossing cultural and geographical borders. At other times, we witness the complexities of a particular struggle or triumph rendering unique and distinctive features. Educational philosophies wax and wane, in certain places firmly planting school music within the essential curricular core, but in others relegating it to shelter under the umbrella of arts education. We learn of the striking challenges of addressing traditional and innovative philosophies, approaches and methodologies for the teaching of music. The vital role of music educators in needing to advocate vocally for the survival of quality school music is sobering. In days gone by, it might have been enough for music teachers to impress policy-makers by simply doing an excellent job of facilitating student success. Instead, there are today many examples where the efforts of teachers and professional associations like the International Society for Music Education (ISME) have impacted upon policy decisions to keep music alive in schools.

ISME is indebted to the authors of each chapter and to the editors, Gordon Cox and Robin Stevens, for this invaluable contribution to the literature. This second edition of *The Origins and Foundations of Music Education* (as did the first) reflects the values of ISME in promoting music education for all across the lifespan and fostering global understanding and cooperation among music educators across the world.

Sheila C. Woodward, ISME President,
Department of Music, Eastern Washington University, USA

The International Society for Music Education (ISME) was founded in 1953 under the auspices of UNESCO. The mission of the Society is to build a worldwide community of music educators, foster intercultural understanding and cooperation, and to nurture and promote music education worldwide. Its seven Commissions, one Forum and nine Special Interest Groups embrace a comprehensive view of music education.

Website address: www.isme.org

Introduction

Gordon Cox and Robin Stevens

The idea for this book arose from a concern that for too long historians of music education have been overly constrained by the national boundaries within which they work. Yet today we observe musical practices and musical tastes in music classrooms that draw on a wide variety of cultures across the world.

Melissa Cain (2015: 463) illustrates the trend:

> Over the past 25 years, school music programs across the globe have increasingly aimed at being more diverse and culturally inclusive. This has been an outcome of policy makers, theorists, and practitioners responding to changes in contemporary school populations and societies, decolonization, economic migration, and other aspects of globalization.

It seemed to us that one way of coming to understand such momentous changes was to uncover the roots of our present national practices and to compare and contrast them with those of music educators working within different cultures around the world. We hoped that the undertaking of such a study would deepen our understanding of music as a powerful educational force, and also question our taken-for-granted pedagogies and our assumptions about the place of music in compulsory schooling. However, we realized that our shared knowledge of this historical phenomenon is currently fragmentary, and accordingly we identified as a first step the publication of a series of studies to provide more comprehensive documentation and analysis of this foundational aspect of school music from a variety of international perspectives.

This is no straightforward a matter: music education is a somewhat complex and problematic field for investigation. A British music education journalist recollected in 2004 'trying years ago to explain to a Minister how instrumental, ensemble, curriculum and extended-curriculum music were separate (but connected) and different (but complementary), and sympathising as his expression became not less but more puzzled' (cited in Rainbow with Cox 2006: 325). Furthermore, music education, like most educational policy, is primarily a national concern: 'each country grapples with its didactic traditions, educational folkways and institutional constraints that require integration into the larger educational agenda of the country' (Lehmann 2012: 641). When it then comes to dealing with music education internationally, the problem is magnified, as 'what counts as music education in one national context may be very different from what is practised elsewhere'

(Fautley and Murphy 2015: 119). For example, in many European countries, there are essentially two paths to follow: school music (for all) and specialist music schools (or conservatoires) that operate after school and at weekends as an additional option, for which parents may have to pay (see Hennessy 2015). In order to keep this study within bounds, we have to a large extent focused upon what might be called 'generalist classroom music' for all, rather than on specialist music schools, or on electives.

In this opening section we trace the historical background of the introduction of compulsory schooling and follow this with a concise survey of work regarding inter-national and comparative historical studies of music's place in the school curriculum. Finally, an account is provided of the genesis and subsequent development of the book right through to the present edition, together with some remarks concerning historical research.

The social origins of formal education go back many centuries, and in most settings derive from the initiatives of religious groups. Towards the end of the eighteenth century in Europe, and later in other parts of the world, revolutionary convulsions created a new ideal – to educate large numbers of the body public – and to arrange this education in a series of levels. Cummings (1997) has proposed six core patterns of 'modern' education, including the French, Prussian, English, American, Japanese and Russian. In each instance, these nation-states created empires that included an educational dimension. They were to have a profound impact on global mass education.

Williams (1997: 120) provides us with a helpful chronology of compulsory schooling:

> Compulsory schooling began in the early 1700s in Europe … [It] was initiated in the more peripheral European states, beginning in the various German states and in Austria, then in Denmark, Greece, and Spain. By the mid-1800s, states outside Europe began to institute compulsory schooling – Haiti, Argentina, Massachusetts in the United States, then Japan. European nations continued to enact compulsory schooling statutes – Norway and Sweden, then finally in the late 1800s, the industrial leaders – France, The Netherlands, and Britain.

In recent times, considerable progress has been made in the provision of universal primary education, a development enshrined as Goal 2 of the United Nations' Millennium Development Goals, whose target was to 'ensure that, by 2015, children everywhere, boys and girls alike, will be able to complete a full course of primary schooling' (United Nations [UN] 2008: section 2: 10). However, the UN report states that in 2006 there were still some seventy-five million children not receiving a school education. By the start of 2015, considerable progress had been made, so that enrolment in primary education in developing regions reached 90 per cent of the child population. However, fifty-eight million children remain out of school (UN 2015).

The potential for utilizing compulsory schooling as a research focus is considerable, both for its contemporary relevance and for its historical underpinning. In particular, it is a subject that lends itself readily to a composite analytical approach, and which, according to J. A. Mangan (1994: vii), is 'concerned comparatively with a historical phenomenon that is of direct relevance to anthropologists, sociologists, educationists and historians of various persuasions'. In the context of the present study we identify more specifically those curriculum historians who are concerned principally with what should be taught in schools, which brings with it the age-old question of 'what knowledge is of most worth?' (see Holmes and McLean 1989: vii).

Since the beginnings of music education in public schooling in the nineteenth century, it has been common to search for successful music education practice in various countries. In 1837 Lowell Mason, the pioneer of American music education, visited Europe to observe methods of teaching music and search for materials to assist him in the development of his singing curriculum for the Boston school system (see Broyles 1990; Tate 2001). Ten years later Mason's compatriot William Batchelor Bradbury spent several weeks in Switzerland and eighteen months in Germany and compiled vivid accounts of good practice in music classrooms (see Karpf 2002). Between 1879 and 1901, two distinguished British music educators, John Hullah and John Spencer Curwen, made separate efforts to investigate the true situation regarding music instruction in Western Europe (and America in the case of Curwen) (see Hullah 1879; Curwen 1901). Both men were eager to assess the truth of the legendary German supremacy in school music. In this aspect they were disappointed in what they found (Rainbow 1985; Kertz-Welzel 2015).

In the twentieth century, Kemp and Lepherd (1992) traced the beginnings of serious work in the fields of international and comparative music education to the 1953 UNESCO Conference in Brussels, which considered the 'Role and Place of Music in the Education of Youth and Adults'. One of the principal outcomes of the Brussels conference was the formation of the International Society for Music Education (ISME) under the auspices of the International Music Council, itself under the aegis of UNESCO (see McCarthy 2004, 2012, 2015). To date, ISME operates in over eighty countries. It affirms its core values as follows:

- there is a need for music education in all cultures;
- effective music education depends on suitably qualified teachers who are respected and compensated properly for their work;
- all teacher education curricula should provide skills in and understandings of a selection of both local and international musics;
- formal and informal music education programs should serve the individual needs of all learners, including those with special needs and exceptional competencies; and
- music education programs should take as a point of departure the existence of a wide variety of musics, all of which are worthy of understanding and study. (ISME 2015)

Stephanie Horsley (2014) points out that ISME's work in collecting information on music education in various nation states has largely focused on international education rather than comparative education. In spite of sharing common roots, however, comparative education research and international education research are not the same. Horsley cites the Danish scholar Frede N. Neilsen (2006) who concluded that international education is concerned with issues of practice and implementation, while comparative education aims to provide historical, philosophical or otherwise interpretative explanations of how two or more educational systems have developed, responded to and/or influenced societal change.

A significant contribution to comparative studies of music education has been made by Laurence Lepherd with his pioneering work on comparisons of the systemic provision of music education from a variety of international perspectives (Lepherd 1988, 1994, 1995; also see Kemp and Lepherd 1992). However, while amply describing systemic aspects such as the current state of and provision for music in schools, there is little about the underlying historical processes involved in establishing music as a curriculum subject. Some other contributions to the comparison of systemic music education provision include Campbell's *Lessons from the World: A Cross-Cultural Guide to Music Teaching and Learning* (1991), Hargreaves and North's *Musical Development and Learning: The International Perspective* (2001), Rodríguez-Quiles and Dogani's survey of school music across Europe (2011) and most recently a comparative study of Estonian and Finnish general music education (Sepp et al. 2015).

Addressing the importance of historical perspectives in such approaches, Keith Watson (2001: 24) makes the point that 'there is a real need for comparative education to re-establish its unique role in providing comparative historical insights for future policy action'. With regard to music education, Kertz-Welzel (2008, 2013, 2015) argues that while comparative music education is a necessity, dealing as it should with issues of internationalization and globalization, at the same time it can relate to other research fields, including music education history and philosophy.

As a first step in developing ideas for this book, the two editors put a proposal to the meeting of the History Standing Committee of the International Society for Music Education in Kuala Lumpur in 2006 for such a project. In preparation for the subsequent ISME World Conference in Bologna in 2008, we contacted prominent scholars from eight different countries to contribute to a symposium. All this culminated in the publication of the first edition of *The Origins and Foundations of Music Education* in 2010. It contained separate chapters on fourteen countries based upon three main areas: Africa and the Asia-Pacific region, the Americas and Europe. We decided to start the book with Europe simply because, first, that was the region where compulsory schooling began (Williams 1997) and, second, it became apparent that, through colonialism and missionary and military influences, it was European ideas that were the most influential in the pioneering days of mass compulsory schooling across the countries we selected.

Among our priorities for future action was the extension of the geographical and cultural scope of the study, to include some of Russia's former satellite states, where music education had been a powerful force, in addition to countries that manifest Jewish and Muslim cultures. As a result the following countries make their appearance in this revised and expanded second edition: Israel, Kosovo (a state still awaiting full recognition internationally), Lithuania and Turkey. In addition, we have included a new chapter on Brazil, in order to present a fuller coverage of music education in South America. Furthermore, we requested that chapters from the first edition should be updated where necessary to take account of significant recent developments. The resulting eighteen chapters have been organized into the following geographical groupings: Africa and the Asia-Pacific region, the Americas, Europe,[1] and the Middle East. In order to ensure that there was some coherence between the different chapters, we asked contributors to explore the following core issues concerning the introduction of music as a mandated part of the curriculum in compulsory schooling[2]:

- historical and political contexts;
- aims and content of music as a compulsory subject;
- teaching methods;
- training of teachers;
- experiences of pupils; and
- reflections on the present state of music education in the light of past developments.

However, we became strongly aware that too tight a focus would unnecessarily force the great diversity of historical factors into a straitjacket. Such matters as federal-versus-centralized nation-states, the unequal treatment of minorities and the influences of colonialism, revolution and war have all meant that there were as many differences as similarities and as many discontinuities as continuities in the progress of music as a curriculum subject. Accordingly, readers will notice that different writers have placed different emphases on these core issues according to the historical contexts they have been researching.

A new Conclusion has also been written for this second edition, which draws the threads of the core issues together, linked tightly to the political, sociological and educational trends of the past and the present.

A further innovation is a series of 'Reflective questions' placed at the end of each chapter, designed for either individuals or groups. The questions can also be used as springboards to problematize the different approaches to the writing of history evident in the eighteen accounts. We have been keen throughout the editorial process to encourage authors to retain their own personal voices, so that there is a wide range of different approaches to telling the story of the rise of music education in a variety of national settings. After all, there is never only one such story – rather, there is room for multiple interpretations and narratives.

Notes

1. Of the eight European countries represented in this collection, at the time of writing (2015) six are present members of the European Union (EU), in addition to Kosovo as a potential candidate for membership. Norway is not a member, but has close links through its membership of the European Free Trade Association (EFTA).
2. As a caveat, it should be emphasized that we do not dismiss the importance of other less-formal modes of learning music, including informal, non-formal and semi-formal settings (see Campell 1991; Green 2011). Far from it: in fact, the boundaries between these different modes are becoming increasingly porous.

References

Broyles, M. (ed.) (1990), *A Yankee Musician in Europe: The 1837 Journals of Lowell Mason*, Ann Arbor, MI: UMI Research Press.

Cain, M. (2015), 'Celebrating Musical Diversity: Training Culturally Responsive Music Educators in Multiracial Singapore', *International Journal of Music Education* 33 (4): 463–75.

Campbell, P. S. (1991), *Lessons from the World: A Cross-Cultural Guide to Music Teaching and Learning*, New York: Schirmer.

Cummings, W. K. (1997), 'Patterns of modern education' in W. K. Cummings and N. F. McGinn (eds), *International Handbook of Education and Development: Preparing Schools, Students and Nations for the Twenty-First Century*, Oxford: Pergamon, pp. 63–86.

Curwen, J. S. (1901), *School Music Abroad: A Series of Reports on Visits to Schools … During the Years 1882 to 1901*, London: J. Curwen. [Reproduced as a Classic Text in Music Education #5, Boethius Press, now available from Boydell Press, Woodbridge, Suffolk, UK.]

Fautley, M. and R. Murphy (2015), Editorial: 'Difficult Questions in Music Education', *British Journal of Music Education* 32 (2) 119–22.

Green, L. (2011), 'Musical Identities: Learning and Education: Some Cross-cultural Issues' in C. Bernd (ed.), *Vergleich in der musikpädagogischen Forschung*, Essen: Die Blaue Eule, pp. 11–34.

Hargreaves, D. J. and A. North (eds) (2001), *Musical Development and Learning: The International Perspective*, London: Continuum.

Hennessy, S. (2015), 'O jardín o erial: contradicciones entre políticas educativas y prácticas escolares en educación musical' ['Garden or desert: the contradictions of policy and practice in music education'], *Revista internacional de Educatión musical* 3, 39–47

Holmes, B. and M. McLean (eds) (1989), *The Curriculum: A Comparative Perspective*, London: Routledge.

Horsley, S. (2014), 'A Comparative Analysis of Neoliberal Education Reform and Music Education in England and Ontario, Canada', University of Western Ontario, Electronic Thesis and Dissertation Repository. Paper 1873.

Hullah, J. (1879), *Report on Musical Instruction in Elementary Schools on the Continent*, London: HMSO. [Reproduced as a Classic Text in Music Education #5, Boethius Press, now available from Boydell Press, Woodbridge, Suffolk, UK.]

International Society for Music Education [ISME] (2015), 'Leading and Supporting Music Education Worldwide', www.isme.org/general-information/29-isme-vision-and-mission (accessed 11 December 2015).

Karpf, J. (2002), '"Would that it were so in America": William Bradbury's Observations of European Music Educators, 1847–9', *Journal of Historical Research in Music Education* 24 (1): 5–38.

Kemp, A. E. and L. Lepherd (1992), 'Research methods in international and comparative music education' in R. Colwell (ed.), *Handbook of Research on Music Teaching and Learning*, New York: Schirmer, pp. 773–88.

Kertz-Welzel, A. (2008), 'Music Education in the Twenty-first Century: A Cross-Cultural comparison of German and American Music Education Towards a New Concept of International Dialogue', *Music Education Research* 10 (4): 439–49.

Kertz-Welzel, A. (2013), '"Two souls, alas, reside within my breast": Reflections on German and American Music Education Regarding the Internationalization of Music Education', *Philosophy of Music Education Review* 21 (1): 52–65.

Kertz-Welzel, A. (2015), 'Lessons from elsewhere? Comparative music education in times of globalization', *Philosophy of Music Education Review* 23 (1): 48–66.

Lehmann, A. (2012), 'Internationalizing music education' in G. E. McPherson and G. Welch (eds), *The Oxford Handbook of Music Education Vol. 2*, Oxford: Oxford University Press, pp. 641–3.

Lepherd, L. (1988), *Music Education in International Perspective: The People's Republic of China*, Darling Heights, Queensland: Music International.

Lepherd, L. (1994), *Music Education in International Perspective: Australia*, Toowoomba, Queensland: University of South Queensland.

Lepherd, L. (1995), *Music Education in International Perspective – National Systems: England, Namibia, Argentina, Russia, Hungary, Portugal, Singapore, Sweden, the United States of America*, Toowoomba, Queensland: University of Southern Queensland.

Mangan, J. A. (ed.) (1994), *A Significant Social Revolution: Cross-Cultural Aspects of the Evolution of Compulsory Education*, London: Woburn Press.

McCarthy, M. (2004), *Toward a Global Community: The International Society for Music Education 1953–2003*, Nedlands, Western Australia: ISME.

McCarthy, M. (2012), 'International Perspectives' in G. E. McPherson and G. Welch (eds), *The Oxford Handbook of Music Education, Vol. 1,* Oxford: Oxford University Press, pp. 40–62.

McCarthy, M. (in press), 'Marking the Passage of Time (2003–2013): Reflections on ISME at its Sixtieth Anniversary', *International Journal of Music Education*.

Neilsen, F. N. (2006), 'A View of the Future of an International Philosophy of Education: A Plea for a Comparative Strategy', *Philosophy of Music Education Review* 14 (1): 7–14.

Rainbow, B. (1985), 'Introduction', J. Curwen and J. Hullah, *School Music Abroad (1879–1901)*, Kilkenny: Boethius Press, pp. v–xii. [Now available from Boydell Press, Woodbridge, Suffolk, UK.]

Rainbow, B. with G. Cox (2006), *Music in Educational Thought and Practice: A Survey from 800 BC*, Woodbridge: Boydell Press.

Rodríguez-Quiles y García, J. A. and K. Dogani (2011), 'Music in Schools Across Europe: Analysis, Interpretation and Guidelines for Music Education in the Framework of the European Union' in L. Airi and M. Marit (eds), *Music Inside and Outside the School*, Frankfurt am Main: Baltische Studien zur Erziehungs und Sozialwissenschaft vol. 21, pp. 95–122.

Sepp, A., Roukonen, I. and H. Ruismäki (2015), 'Musical Practices and Methods in Music Lessons: A Comparative Study of Estonian and Finnish General Music Education', *Music Education Research* 17 (3), 340–58.

Tate, P. (2001), 'Comparative Perspectives' in C. Philpott and C. Plummeridge (eds), *Issues in Music Teaching*, London: Routledge/Falmer, pp. 224–37.

United Nations (2008), *The Millennium Development Goals*, New York: United Nations.

United Nations (2015), 'United Nations Millennium Goal 2 – Achieve Universal Primary Education', www.un.org/millenniumgoals/education.shtml (accessed 3 March 2015).

Watson, K. (ed.) (2001), *Doing Comparative Educational Research: Issues and Problems*, Wallingford, UK: Symposium.

Williams, J. H. (1997), 'The diffusion of the modern school' in W. K. Cummings and N. F. McGinn (eds), *International Handbook of Education and Development: Preparing Schools, Students and Nations for the Twenty-First Century*, Oxford: Pergamon, pp. 119–36.

PART I: EUROPE

Chapter 1

Britain: Opportunities and threats equally balanced

Gordon Cox

In the following account I trace chronologically the development of music as a compulsory subject in British schools. Readers will note that this is not a triumphalist account of unalloyed progress, but is rather a narrative that chronicles a continuing struggle to establish music as a valued and powerful subject for school pupils to encounter and experience. The main focus of the chapter is on the English scene, bearing in mind that for much of the time England, Wales, Scotland and Northern Ireland have shared in many aspects of a common educational history. However, their educational patterns have never been identical, and differences, particularly with devolutionary pressures, are becoming sharper with the passage of time.

Historical context for the introduction of music into the school curriculum

From the 1840s Britain witnessed what Rainbow (1967: 13) referred to as the 'phenomenal growth of school music'. This coincided with a sight-singing mania that so gripped the country that the nineteenth century became known as the 'Sight Singing Century' (Scholes 1947: 1). Two men were to dominate this movement and came to influence profoundly the direction of compulsory musical instruction in schools after 1870: John Hullah (1812–84) and John Curwen (1816–80).

In his early days, John Hullah was much influenced by his mother's musical gifts and his father's democratic tendencies (F. Hullah 1886). His education linked this connection between art and democracy. After studying at the Royal Academy of Music in London, the idea formed in him of developing schools for popular instruction in vocal music. He visited Paris to see for himself the work of the German musician Joseph Mainzer, who had established singing classes for working men, but in the end Hullah allied himself with the French music educator G. L. B. Wilhem, who had written a music manual for use in the monitorial system of schools (which had large classes split into small groups, each under a monitor). As well as holding classes in schools, Wilhem was committed to spreading musical skills to as wide a spectrum of adults as possible, and particularly to working people (Rainbow 1967).

By 1840, Hullah had been taken up by the educational reformer James Kay (Secretary to the Committee of Council on Education), who requested that Hullah translate Wilhem's method into English for school use. This became known as *Hullah's Manual* (1842) and was the basic text for his singing schools, which spread like wildfire throughout the country. When Hullah's teaching method is considered, it is necessary to note that his vehicle for such sight singing was the fixed-doh method, where 'doh' is always 'C'. Unfortunately, the method encapsulated in *Hullah's Manual* was not a success, with one critic calling it 'diffuse, circumlocutory, confused and superficial' (Barnett 1842: 6): few pupils got further than the end of the first book, as its later stages proved to be impenetrable.

John Curwen became the great promoter and evangelist of the tonic sol-fa method, whose foundation lay on the 'movable doh': the tonic of the new key was always 'doh' (see Rainbow 1980; McGuire 2009). His book *Singing for Schools and Congregations* (1843) heralded the start of a new era: Curwen's tonic sol-fa swept the country and the Empire under its banner 'Cheap, Easy and True' (see Rainbow 1980). Curwen's method was based on the work of Sarah Glover (1786–1867), which he synthesized and publicized. In 1867 he founded the Tonic Sol-fa College, which provided the home of his movement and was to provide generations of teachers with opportunities to develop their sight-singing skills through its part-time and vacation courses.

The introduction of music into schools: music inspectors

The Elementary Education Act of 1870 made both free and compulsory education possible (Lawson and Silver 1973). Schools at this time were subject to payment by results, introduced in the 1862 Revised Code. Briefly, annual financial grants to schools became conditional on the proficiency of the children as tested by the inspectors. Music education was at a low ebb; in fact, in 1871, it was omitted from the government code. Pressure was placed on the government to reinstate it and, in 1872, it was announced that the grant to day schools would be reduced by one shilling per scholar unless inspectors were satisfied that vocal music was part of the ordinary course of instruction. But in order to earn the grant, schools could simply teach a few songs by ear. This was a clearly unsatisfactory and negative state of affairs, so as a result of further pressure the

Code of 1874 provided that one shilling per scholar should be paid if singing was taught satisfactorily. In order to police this, a music inspector – none other than John Hullah – was appointed by the government. It was his job, and that of his immediate successor, John Stainer, to monitor standards of musical teaching principally in the training colleges of England, Wales and Scotland as well as providing crucial advice on policy matters and documentation (see Cox 1993, 2005).

Increasingly, however, school inspectors were complaining of the deterioration of music standards in public elementary schools. It appeared that most pupils were being taught to sing by ear rather than by note. Hullah was dispatched to the continent to investigate musical instruction in elementary schools between April and July 1879. Significantly, Rainbow (1985) has pointed out that Hullah omitted to visit France, and this might have been a quite conscious decision, as it would have exploded the fact that the Wilhem system had been abandoned in the 1840s and that cipher notation was gaining ground. One of the outcomes of Hullah's journey was his recommendation that, after 1882, no financial award would be made for singing unless it was taught by note (although this was never to be fully implemented). The problem was that his system obfuscated the process of sight singing, rather than clarifying it.

Hullah's successor as inspector, in 1882, was John Stainer (1840–1901), who was a musician of considerable stature (see Dibble 2007) – he was one of the finest organists and improvisers in the country, organist at St Paul's Cathedral and Professor of Music at Oxford. However, he had little (if any) experience of teaching in schools. He solved this by appointing as his assistant W. G. McNaught (1849–1918), who had considerable experience as a teacher and was also a keen advocate of the ideas of John Curwen and the tonic sol-fa method.

The partnership between Stainer and McNaught flowered into a period of consolidation for music in schools. They had developed a theoretical position into a practical outcome, well researched and suited to 'payment by results'. The situation now was that schools teaching singing 'by ear' would only receive six pence per pupil per annum, whereas those teaching 'by note' received one shilling. The payment-by-results system was withdrawn in 1901.

There was a feeling of optimism in the air. McNaught pointed out that 1,504,675 children had gained the grant for singing by note in one previous year (Browne 1885–6). It led him to claim somewhat extravagantly that 'So far as the elementary musical education of the children in our schools is concerned we are accomplishing more than any other nation in the world' (ibid.: 19).

On Stainer's death, it was expected that McNaught would be his successor as music inspector, but instead the appointment of Arthur Somervell (1863–1937) was announced in 1901. There was an outcry: although Somervell was establishing himself as a composer, he had little experience of schools. His thirty years in office coincided with a profound shift away from utilitarian traditions towards an artistic and educational liberalism (see Cox 2003). Somervell's contribution, as we shall see, lay in the introduction of national songs into schools and the development of an idealist justification for the teaching of music.

Justifications for music's place in the school curriculum

What values impelled this quest to spread musical instruction into the school curriculum? John Hullah was particularly influenced by the Victorian Christian Socialists, who believed that social suffering might be alleviated by Christian works of charity and the elevating consequences of popular education. First, he believed that music could refine and civilize, principally through the process of sight singing. Individuals could be fashioned into productive members of the community by reconciling 'cotton spinning and counterpoint, husbandry and harmony' (Hullah 1846: 20). Hullah became known as someone who could transform popular amusement into valuable instruction. He believed that music encouraged positive moral values – 'patience, temperance, power of attention, presence of mind, self-denial, obedience and punctuality' (Hullah 1854: 15). He admitted that there might not be a direct connection, but performers could never manage without acquiring such qualities. Here the extrinsic values that music might serve are stated. The results of such an education would be seen in a socially redemptive context, but it should be noted that the redemptive power of music was linked by Hullah to its activity, with no mention of its content.

Both Stainer and McNaught were practical men – we might describe them as conviction politicians who acted within a narrow sphere most effectively and became almost populist figures. As a result, they tended to dismiss high-flown claims for the educative power of music. Nevertheless, Stainer had no doubt there was a connection with the beautiful and the good. He believed that listening became a creative process in which art, thought, action and the moral were energized. This led him to the practical conclusion that 'our real want in England at this moment is not professional performers or even composers, but intelligent hearers' (Stainer 1892: 57–8). McNaught concurred and declared he was wary of making exorbitant claims for the subject (*School Music Review*, October 1896, 96). His musical friends were no better ethically than his non-musical acquaintances. Of course, he conceded, there may be an indirect moral influence through the emotions, and there certainly was intellectual value, but music did not get rid of Original Sin! Both men talked of music's extrinsic values cautiously. The danger was that music could suffer a narrowing of interests and a concentration on methods and techniques for their own sakes.

Arthur Somervell was an idealist – a key phrase in his writings is the 'Whole of Things', and he subscribed to the Platonic notion of 'the True, the Good and the Beautiful'. There was a need for balance between science, art and moral ideas, and such a unity of experience could heal divisions in society. Care should be taken not to limit the aim of music education to the creation of greater numbers of singers and instrumentalists – music might build up the Ideal Citizen. It was simply Somervell's belief that 'your only really practical man is the one with a trained and cultivated imagination' (Somervell 1905:

151). The arts provided such a sure foundation. By seeking a theory based on Plato and Aristotle, Somervell was placing his formulation of music education within the tradition of Matthew Arnold, who had revived the old humanist notion of the centrality of literature as an energizing moral force (ibid.). For Somervell, like Arnold, art took over many of the functions of religion.

Content and methods

It is hard to recreate what went on in an elementary school singing class. We have to rely on the writings of the inspectors. Hullah carried out an experiment in 1876 in which he taught sixty-five infants for twenty minutes daily for a fortnight and occasionally for five minutes in odd periods of recreation. By the end of this time he claimed the children could name notes correctly and give utterance to diatonic scale notes. They could beat time with their hands, distribute notes in measures, and touch on their hands (using the hand as a manual stave) a tune that they sang accurately. Moreover, they could sing at sight from the blackboard, were intensely interested and had 'sympathy of ear and eye' (Hullah 1878: 6). He concluded that these children reached a better standard than two-thirds of teacher training college candidates.

Both Stainer and McNaught had to work under the payment-by-results scheme, with schools receiving a greater grant if singing 'by note' was taught rather than singing 'by ear'. There was a tendency for this to encourage mechanical teaching. However, McNaught believed fervently that true tonic sol-fa teaching could be invested with feeling. How was this to be achieved in practice? One of the chief means of disseminating ideas to music teachers was the monthly periodical, the *School Music Review*. McNaught wrote three series of articles that considered three crucial questions:

1 What were the necessary steps to enable effective note singing to take place?
2 What was the relationship of tonic sol-fa to staff notation?
3 How could tonic sol-fa cultivate the power of observing sounds and mentally hold them for analysis?

He believed that teaching had to illuminate the relationship between tones and he vividly outlined how the theory of mental effect could be approached through the 'doh' chord:

> Demonstrate (not merely assert) the firm repose of 'doh', the bold cheerfulness of 'soh', the plaintiveness of 'me', the exultation ('hurrah' would be a better word for children) of the high 'doh' ... Make a great deal of each note, so that the impression is vivid. Suppose the keen, bright, eager expectancy of 'te' and the meeker expectancy of 'ray' have been amply demonstrated, and that 'fah' is to be introduced. You have got somehow to build up in your pupils' minds an impression of gravity, sternness, dignity and expectancy. You must make them feel it by a variety of well-chosen illustrations. (McNaught 1894–5: 23–4)

As with everything else he touched, McNaught produced a simple practical scheme. As a start, he concentrated on the teaching of a timeless tune; next, he dealt with the teaching of time and rhythm. It was only when regular pulse, variety of accent and the distribution of sounds over or in a pulse were mastered that notation should be introduced. But this skill was crucial, because McNaught believed the only rational test of such teaching lay in the ability of pupils to perform rhythms from signs and to write down signs on hearing musical patterns.

The relation between music and national feeling permeated popular music education during the latter half of the nineteenth century. The culmination of this relationship was reached with the publication of *The National Song Book* (Stanford 1906) – its influence was so widespread that by 1917 it could be boasted that there was hardly a school in the country that did not possess a copy. National songs were supposed to express the emotions of a people; they were long established and were individually composed, frequently by esteemed musicians. The national song was 'popular by destination' (Greene 1935: xcviii). As far back as 1842 the relationship between music and national feeling had been reckoned to be important from an educational perspective: as many legends were expressed in songs, the teaching of singing could fix the words in children's minds (Hullah 1842: iv).

National songs were at the peak of their popularity around the turn of the century. But how do we know which songs were actually sung in school? For the purposes of this chapter, I shall note the number of times a song was reprinted in six major collections of songs published between 1884 and 1906 (see Farmer 1895; Hadow 1903; Nicholson 1903; Sharp 1902; Stanford 1884, 1906). There were eight songs common to all: 'The British Grenadiers', 'Early One Morning', 'The Roast Beef of Old England', 'Come Lasses and Lads', 'The Mermaid', 'Here's a Health unto His Majesty', 'Hearts of Oak' and 'Rule, Britannia!'. The values these songs encapsulate are clear – the need to respect authority, contempt for one's enemies, superiority over others and a looking back to rural life and the values of the past. As for the musical qualities, the songs are all in the major key, and all but two are in simple duple or quadruple time. The vocal range, however, varies considerably.

The principal resistance to the hegemony of the national song in schools was the folksong. This was generally reckoned to have been communally composed expressing the feelings of the collective soul, springing from the oral tradition: 'popular by origin' (Greene 1935: xcviii).

The oral tradition that promulgated folksong without the aid of notation understandably threatened music educators, whose main aim was to encourage the ability to sing at sight from notation. The two traditions collided in the controversy of 1905, when the Board of Education (1905) published a list of 'national or folksongs'. Cecil Sharp (1859–1924), the great folksong collector, was furious about the bracketing together of the two categories (see Cox 2003). He maintained that the list contained 'scarcely a single genuine peasant-made folk song' (*School Music Review*, June 1906: 1). He was to wage the battle for a genuine folksong repertoire in schools for the next twenty years. It is ironic that folksongs eventually became part of a rigid orthodoxy that linked them inseparably with the values of national songs.

But whatever the pros and contras of folksongs compared with national songs, everyone agreed that music education had to fight the pernicious effects of popular culture – in particular, this meant music-hall songs. Somervell's position was that national songs were morally superior and that popular music vulgarized and exerted a harmful influence on character. Bad music was popular because it was attractive.

Music in teacher training

From their earliest days, training colleges instructed all their students to teach singing and, by the end of the nineteenth century, many were also providing facilities for practising instrumental music. But none trained specialists. The annual inspection of individual students included a note test, a time test, an ear test and the performance of a solo song. In addition, the students presented a choral performance and were required to sit a theory examination. Stainer and McNaught had to submit detailed reports (Committee of Council on Education Reports 1883–1899, hereinafter referred to simply by date), and these provide details concerning musical training (see Cox 2005).

In his first report, Stainer (1883) drew attention to the lack of musical training of most students. No great change would come, he believed, until elementary schools were able to produce teacher candidates with a musical ear. He estimated that this might take ten or fifteen years to achieve. He praised the college teachers for working against the odds, when students arrived with untried voices, untrained ears and ignorant of any musical notation. In spite of this, he witnessed that much valuable work was being carried out; in fact, he declared that wonders were performed. Indeed, throughout his inspectorship, Stainer found 'proof of the upward tendency of musical taste among students in training colleges' (1897: 354). One of the actions Stainer took was to remove the study of harmony from the requirements in 1885. He felt too much time was devoted to it and the majority of candidates took it to be a technical puzzle. This was all part of a general strategy on his part, to discourage the thinking that theory was more important than practice.   .

Ideally, Stainer wished he could observe students giving music lessons in a practising school, but this was not practically feasible (1886). In McNaught's opinion, students should leave college with the code requirements: a dozen or so songs and fruitful lessons of time, tune and expression. Stainer, however, cautioned against expecting too much from training colleges. It was unrealistic to expect them to turn out cultivated and practical musicians.

A critique (Board of Education 1928) of the teaching of music in training colleges during the Victorian era, however, pointed to some of the drawbacks of the system for which Stainer and McNaught had been responsible. It concluded that what had been provided had been essentially non-cultural, cramped by its close dependence on the requirements of the elementary school and by its adherence to a syllabus framed in an ad hoc fashion: 'it inspired no love of music and failed to impart any understanding of it' (ibid.: 6).

From 'singing' to 'music'

The change in nomenclature from 'singing' to 'music' was officially confirmed in the Board of Education's publication *Handbook of Suggestions for Teachers* (1927). It signalled an enlargement of scope of the subject and included two new sections – melody training (in which children were encouraged to make tunes of their own) and appreciation (regarded as the climax of 'ear training'). By 1933 it was reported that the class teacher of music was suffering an *'embarras de richesses'*, including appreciation of music, community singing, the gramophone, the school orchestra, the percussion band, rhythmic work and wireless (radio) lessons (Board of Education 1933). The report finished on a triumphant note: 'The whole history of musical England from 1850 onwards is one of emergence from darkness to light, and undoubtedly the treatment of music in the schools has played a great part in the gradual transformation' (ibid.: 7).

After 1945 there was a further expansion in secondary school music-making, with choirs, orchestras, madrigal groups, brass bands and operatic ventures. Instrumental teaching in schools was encouraged and the methods of Kodály and Orff gained some prominence. The 1960s witnessed a growing interest in the use of contemporary music in the classroom, with children as both performers and composers. In this connection, a key figure was the distinguished composer Peter Maxwell Davies (see Davies 2013: 104–5).

The ascendency of a child-centred curriculum model encompassing experiment, creativity and contemporary musical styles was confirmed with the publication of the highly influential text *Sound and Silence: Classroom Projects in Creative Music* (Paynter and Aston 1970). This was in essence a manifesto justifying the place of music within a liberal education. However, a division could be discerned between those who upheld music as a creative art and those who advocated a subject-centred curriculum model focusing on skills, literacy and the Western musical tradition (see Cox 2002). Much of the debate between the two groups came to a head in the 1980s and 1990s with the introduction of the National Curriculum.

Towards the present and future

The most significant event in recent history regarding music as a school subject has been the development for the first time in England, Wales and Northern Ireland of a National Curriculum.

As a result of the publication of the Great Education Reform Bill in November 1987, all pupils aged five to fourteen were to be taught the new National Curriculum core subjects

(English, mathematics, science [and Welsh in Welsh-speaking schools in Wales]) by September 1989 and the foundation subjects, including music, by September 1992. The inclusion of music should not be regarded as having been automatic. There had been talk of not making it compulsory (see Barber 1996). Integral to the reforms was the creation of the Office for Standards in Education (Ofsted), which was to carry out regular detailed inspections of schools and their teaching in order to maintain and improve standards. As far as the music curriculum was concerned, there was a focus on composing and performing, listening and appraising. This practical, hands-on approach owed much to the pioneering efforts of John Paynter and Keith Swanwick.

Around the time that the National Curriculum in music was becoming established in schools, an influential justification for the subject came to prominence: the notion of the transfer of learning. Scientific research, according to Everitt (1998), demonstrated that music played a key role in the functioning of the brain. Behavioural psychologists had demonstrated how music could aid the learning process. Consequently, it was argued that giving more time to 'the 3 Rs' (writing, reading and arithmetic) was counter-productive if it led to fewer music classes. The notion that music could help children improve their learning in a number of areas such as literacy and numeracy appealed to politicians such as David Blunkett, then Minister of Education, who declared that while his priority lay in the raising of standards in 'the 3 Rs', if music could contribute to this, all the better (*The Times Educational Supplement* 22 May 1998).

Within music education a number of encouraging developments took place between 2004 and 2014. *The Music Manifesto* (DfES 2004) promised a new 'joined-up' policy for music education. The Schools Standards Minister, David Miliband, reiterated the government's commitment that over time any primary school pupils who wanted to would be able to learn a musical instrument. The government's commitment to music was based on five key resources: the vital foundation of the Music National Curriculum; professional collaboration; new flexibilities so that schools could work together; creativity and innovation in music charting new directions; and financial resources. In 2007, the government announced a £32 million settlement for music education, followed by an additional £18 million in 2014 'to help thousands of extra children to enjoy music'.

Three initiatives in particular have received substantial government funding: the Wider Opportunities Scheme, introduced in 2006, enabling all children within specific age groups in primary education to receive tuition on a musical instrument as part of a group, often the whole class; the Sing Up Campaign, from 2007–11, which aimed to put singing at the heart of every primary school (see Welch et al. 2010); and pilot projects in Scotland from 2008 and in England from 2009, based broadly on the principles of *El Sistema*, the programme of music and social education in Venezuela, using music to change the lives of children in disadvantaged areas (see Creech et al. 2013; Baker 2014). This is not to mention the highly influential Musical Futures Initiative, funded by the Paul Hamlyn Foundation, which aims to devise new and imaginative ways of engaging young people in music activities in the reality of twenty-first-century schools (see *Musical Futures*

Initiative). More specifically, it brings together formal education and informal learning (see Green 2008, 2014).

With regard to developments in teacher education, in 2009 it was reported that nearly a quarter of new teachers received their training in schools rather than in universities (*The Economist* 11 April 2009). Subsequently, this trend away from university- to school-based teacher training has continued, and, controversially, certain categories of schools, including Academies and Free Schools, can employ teachers without a training qualification.

In 2010 the government commissioned an independent review of music education in England. *The Henley Review* was published the following year, and after the conclusion of the survey the government published *The Importance of Music: A National Plan for Music Education* (DfE and DCMS 2011). Specifically, it called for the development of 'hubs' to deliver music education in partnership, building on the work of local authority Music Services and schools' collaborations with the music profession. It professed an ambition for every child to learn a musical instrument, and to improve the qualifications of those concerned with music education (see Stevens 2013: 125–6 for a critique of aspects of the National Plan).

In 2013 it was confirmed that music would remain as an essential part of the National Curriculum. The latest version of the Curriculum, which came into operation in September 2014, includes a specific requirement to introduce conventional musical notation to pupils in the final stage of primary school, together with a focus upon the so-called 'Great Composers'. It perhaps represents something of an ideological shift in curriculum emphasis (see DfE 2013).

In his concluding comments concerning recent developments, John Stevens (2013) imagines future generations of music educators looking back at the first decade of the millennium and seeing a move away from a stress on curriculum matters to a preoccupation with systems and structures, and from developing the imagination and creativity to meeting prescribed targets. The lesson he takes from this apparent distancing from the music itself is succinct and timely: 'stay close to the music' (ibid.: 126).

Conclusion

In this historical study there are correspondences between the past and the present. They include: the place awarded to music in the school curriculum – always there, but somehow conditional; the diversity of justifications for the subject, ranging from the severely practical to the high-flown; the fierce debate about pedagogy and about the musical content of the curriculum; arguments about whether the training of music teachers should follow the practice in schools or seek to change it.

The present health of the subject is best summed up by Katherine Zeserson, author of the report *Inspiring Music for All*: 'It is certainly the best and the worst of times for music education in England, with opportunities and threats equally balanced' (Zeserson

2014: 3). There is perhaps room for at least some cautious hope that the threats can be countered, and the opportunities celebrated, so that music does indeed become an energizing educational force in our schools.

Acknowledgement

I am indebted to Gary Spruce for updating me about recent developments.

Reflective questions

1 Hullah, Stainer and Somervell justified music's place in the school curriculum in very different ways. How convincing do you find their arguments?

2 To what extent do you believe that the content of a nation's music curriculum should reflect national pride, as was evident in the compilation of *The National Songbook*?

3 Discuss Somervell's view that 'bad music was popular because it was attractive' and the implications of holding such a view for music teachers.

4 The requirements in the 2013 National Curriculum document to introduce conventional notation to pupils in the final stage of primary school, together with a focus upon so-called Great Composers, represents a shift in emphasis. To what extent is this shift justified?

References

Baker, G. (2014), *El Sistema – Orchestrating Venezuela's Youth*, Oxford: Oxford University Press.

Barber, M. (1996), *The National Curriculum: A Study in Policy*, London: Keele University Press.

Barnett, J. (1842), *Systems and Singing Masters: An Analytical Comment Upon the Wilhem System as Taught in England with Letters, Authenticated Anecdotes and Critical Remarks Upon Mr John Hullah's Manual and Prefatory Minutes of the Council in Education*, London: W. S. Orr.

Board of Education (1905), *Suggestions for the Consideration of Teachers and Others Concerned in the work of Public Elementary Schools*, London: HMSO.

Board of Education (1927), *Handbook of Suggestions for Teachers*, London: HMSO.

Board of Education (1928), *Report on Music, Arts and Crafts and Drama in Training Colleges*, London: HMSO.

Board of Education (1933), *Recent Developments in School Music*, Educational Pamphlets No. 95, London: HMSO.

Browne, M. E. (1885–6), 'Music in Elementary Schools', *Proceedings of the Musical Association* 12: 1–22.

Committee of Council on Education (1873–99), *Reports of the Committee of Council on Education*, London: HMSO.

Cox, G. (1993), *A History of Music Education in England (1872–1928)*, Aldershot: Scolar Press.

Cox, G. (2002), *Living Music in Schools 1923–1999: Studies in the History of Music Education in England*, Aldershot: Ashgate.

Cox, G. (ed.) (2003), *Sir Arthur Somervell on Music Education: His Writings, Speeches and Letters*, Woodbridge: Boydell Press.

Cox, G. (2005), 'Inspecting the Teaching of Singing in the Teacher Training Colleges of England, Wales and Scotland 1883–1899', *Research Studies in Music Education* 24: 17–27.

Creech, A., P. Gonzalez-Moreno, L. Lorenzino and G. Waitman (2013), *El Sistema and Sistema-Inspired Programmes: A Literature Review of Research Evaluation and Critical Debates*, San Diego: Sistema Global.

Curwen, J. (1843), *Singing for Schools and Congregations*, London: Curwen.

Davies, P. M. (2013), 'Will Serious Music Become Extinct?' in P. Dickinson (ed.), *Music Education in Crisis: The Bernarr Rainbow Lectures and Other Assessments*, Woodbridge: Boydell, pp. 99–114.

Department for Education (2013), *National Curriculum in England; Music Programmes of Study*, London: DfE.

Department for Education and Skills (DfES) (2004), *The Music Manifesto*, London: DfES.

Department for Education and Department of Culture, Media and Sport (2011), *The Importance of Music: A National Plan for Music*, London: DfE and DCMS.

Dibble, J. (2007), *John Stainer*, Woodbridge: Boydell & Brewer.

Economist, The, 'Not so loony', 11 April 2009.

Everitt, A. (1998), 'Cerebral software', *Times Educational Supplement*, 24 April.

Farmer, J. (1895), *Gaudeamus: A Selection of Songs for Schools and Colleges*, London: Cassell.

Green, L. (2008), *Music, Informal Learning and the School: A New Classroom Pedagogy*, Aldershot: Ashgate.

Green, L. (2014), *Hear, Listen, Play! How to Free your Students' Aural, Improvisation and Performance Skills*, New York: Oxford University Press.

Greene, R. L. (1935), *The Early English Carols*, Oxford: Clarendon Press.

Hadow, W. H. (1903), *Songs of the British Islands: One Hundred National Melodies Selected and Edited for the Use of Schools*, London: Curwen.

Hullah, F. (1886), *Life of John Hullah LLD*, London: Longmans Green.

Hullah, J. (1842), *Wilhem's Method of Teaching Singing Adapted to the English Use Under the Superintendence of the Committee of Council on Education*, London: John W. Parker.

Hullah, J. (1846), *The Duty and Advantages of Being Able to Sing: A Lecture Delivered at the Leeds Church Institution*, London: John W. Parker.

Hullah, J. (1854), *Music as an Element of Education: Being One of a Series of Lectures Delivered at St Martin's Hall, in Connexion with the Educational Exhibition of the Society of Arts, July 24, 1854*, London: John W. Parker.

Hullah, J. (1878), *How Can a Sound Knowledge of Music be Best and Most Generally Disseminated? A Paper Read at the Twenty-Second Congress of the National Association for the Promotion of Social Science*, London: Longmans Green.

Lawson, J. and H. Silver (1973), *A Social History of Education in England*, London: Methuen; repr. Routledge, 2007.

McGuire, C. E. (2009), *Music and Philanthropy: The Tonic Sol-fa Movement,* Cambridge: Cambridge University Press.

McNaught, W. G. (1894–5), 'How to Teach Note Singing Pleasantly and Expeditiously', *School Music Review* 3: 15–6, 23–4, 61–2.

Musical Futures Initiative, www.musicalfutures.org.uk (accessed 7 September 2015).

Nicholson, S. H. (1903), *British Songs for British Boys: A Collection of One Hundred National Songs – Designed for the Use of Boys in Schools and Choirs*, London: Macmillan.

Paynter, J. and P. Aston (1970), *Sound and Silence: Classroom Projects in Creative Music*, Cambridge: Cambridge University Press.

Rainbow, B. (1967), *The Land without Music: Musical Education in England 1800–1860 and its Continental Antecedents*, Borough Green: Novello; repr. Boydell, 1997.

Rainbow, B. (1980), *John Curwen: A Short Critical Biography*, Borough Green: Novello; repr. in *Bernarr Rainbow on Music: Memoirs and Selected Writings*, Woodbridge: Boydell Press, 2010, pp. 93–138.

Rainbow, B. (1985), 'The Land with Music: Reality and Myth in Music Education', in A. E. Kemp (ed.), *Research in Music Education: A Festschrift for Arnold Bentley,* Reading: ISME Research Commission, pp. 19–32.

Scholes, P. (1947), *The Mirror of Music 1844–1944: A Century of Musical Life in Britain as Reflected in the Pages of the Musical Times*, London: Novello and Oxford University Press.

School Music Review, October 1896, June 1906.

Sharp, C. (1902), *A Book of British Song for Home and School*, London: John Murray.

Somervell, A. (1905), 'The Basis of the Claims of Music in Education', *Proceedings of the Musical Association* 31: 149–66.

Stainer, J. (1892), *Music in its Relation to the Intellect and the Emotions*, London: Novello, Ewer.

Stanford, C. V. (ed.) (1884), *Song-Book for Schools (being a Graduated Collection of Sixty-four Songs in One, Two and Three Parts Adapted for the Use of Children)*, London: National Society's Depository.

Stanford, C. V. (ed.) (1906), *The National Song Book*, London: Boosey.

Stevens, J. (2013), 'What Happened to the Music?' in P. Dickinson (ed.), *Music Education in Crisis: The Bernarr Rainbow Lectures and Other Assessments*, Woodbridge: Boydell, pp. 117–26.

Times Educational Supplement, The, 22 May 1998.

Welch, G., E. Himonides, J. Saunders and I. Papageorgi (2010), *Researching the Impact of the National Singing Programme 'Sing Up' in England: Main Findings from the First Three Years*, London: IMERC.

Zeserson, K. (2014), *Inspiring Music for All: Next Steps in Innovation, Improvement and Integration*, London: Paul Hamlyn.

Chapter 2

France: An uncertain and unequal combat

François Madurell

In his landmark article devoted to 'L'enseignement musical à l'école' ('The teaching of music in the school'), Maurice Chevais (1880–1943) offered an in-depth analysis of the situation in France and gave voice to the following hope:

> May we one day show esteem in France both for popular musical education and for those who assume the task of propagating it, and at last become aware of everything that can be asked of music and of choral singing in the aim of furthering [the] harmonious development of the child. (Chevais 1931: 3683)

His wish has never been fully realized. This observation points to a structural difficulty with incorporating music education into schools and reveals deep-seated, longstanding disagreement about methods, goals and curricula. The causes of this situation include the historical circumstances, the power of patriotic sentiment, the virulence of pedagogical disputes and the problem of teacher training. These are inextricably bound up with different perspectives on the functions of music education in school. To offer musical instruction to all children was to go against the ideology of 'the gift', strongly rooted in French musical culture. Possessing a gift for music was most often seen to be an advantage received from God or from nature, not as a matter of education or training.

The focus of this chapter will be on the years between 1870 and 1940, more specifically on tracing the origins of music as a school subject in France, the relationship of music education to patriotism, two pedagogical issues relating to cipher notation and to pitch, and the training of music teachers. Finally, after a consideration of the significant influence that Maurice Chevais had on French school music education, there will be some observations about the present situation.

The introduction of music as a subject in the school curriculum

Music was introduced to primary schools in Paris as early as 1819. As a subject, it enjoyed a high degree of prominence due to Guillaume Louis Bocquillon, known as Wilhem (1781–1842), a staunch advocate of choral singing, who became director of this branch of instruction in the schools of Paris in 1835. Wilhem had compiled a singing manual (1836) for use in the monitorial system of teaching (large classes split into small groups, each under a monitor). In his textbook, Wilhem broke down the rudiments of music into a series of easy steps, following a carefully planned sequence. His preparatory vocal exercises were based on the 'vocal staircase', which visually represented the diatonic scale as a set of stairs, with the semitones as appropriately smaller steps. At a later stage he used *phonomimie*, in which the hand was used as a stave. Exercises could be pointed out one note at a time on the hand. Wilhem's method aimed at overall musical instruction stretching into adulthood with his adult classes bringing together mechanics and labourers and their employers. The method nevertheless clearly established the fundamental principles for musical progression at the first level in schools. Wilhem insisted on a systematic course of ear training for children as well as a reliance on *solfège* (he employed the traditional French 'fixed-doh' sol-fa). Around 1841 it was estimated that some 12,000 children were receiving singing lessons using his method in the schools of Paris and that his adult classes included 1,500 students (see Rainbow 1967).

However, what has been called the 'Parisian exception' (Fijalkow 2003) cannot conceal the difficulty that music education had in becoming an integral part of French education and acquiring full status as a school subject. Although the Guizot Law (1833) required each town to open a school for boys and stipulated a place for music, by 1836, girls' schools were also required by law, but although the 'practice of singing' became mandatory for girls, it was to be merely optional for boys. This discrimination reflects the power of social roles and their influence on the school. Far from being a sanctuary, the school, which claimed to be a source of values, remained subject to prevailing traditions. In 1850, the Falloux Law – at once regressive and inconclusive – saw music return to being optional in status for all pupils. The law, furthermore, saw the status of music in schools to be subjected to the whims of the governing authority.

The matter came up again in 1881. Following a series of seven reports by educational experts (Alten 1995), the official syllabus issued as 'Programmes du 27 juillet 1882' did away with any and all sex discrimination and set out a clear political intention that singing (*chant*) would be mandatory for all children within compulsory primary instruction. It had therefore taken until 27 July 1882 for singing to claim its rightful place in primary education, within the framework of non-parochial schooling. Nevertheless, *chant* remained at the end of the subject list. Because musical instruction was based on singing, the teaching gradually came to incorporate the fundamental principles of the *solfège* method. The 1882 syllabus remained in force until 1923, when a mandatory test in singing was prescribed for the granting of the Primary Studies Certificate (*Programmes et instructions* 1923). This measure was put into effect from 1924. But many primary school teachers did not have sufficient training in music to implement the syllabus leading to the mandatory test. Aside from the crucial issue of adequate training for school teachers in music, introduction of the mandatory test epitomized the complex nature of the problem presented by music education in the schools of the Republic.

On the one hand, there was the problem of the comparatively unambitious requirements for music together with limited scheduling of class time (most often one hour weekly) and, on the other hand, the significant socio-cultural and political expectation that music should be provided for in the education of all citizens and that music should serve as a means of promoting patriotism. There was also the ongoing debate about the subject matter to be taught and the goals to be achieved, which were aggravated by conflicting opinions within the music profession – for some teachers, recommendations given by conservatories tended to emerge as a point of reference (Gédalge 1926), whereas other teachers who considered these recommendations unrealistic supported a music education approach best suited to the school context, thus taking into account school teachers' sometimes limited musical skills. Vançon (2004) has further elaborated on this ongoing issue.

Music education and patriotism

The disastrous Franco-Prussian War resulted in the fall of Napoleon III and the proclamation of the Republic. Bismarck demanded Alsace-Lorraine (under the Treaty of Frankfurt of 1871), which would only be returned to France at the Treaty of Versailles in 1919. Thus, according to the *Tribune des Instituteurs*, the attempt in schools at 'making sincere patriots' (Ferro 2003: 10) was seen as a benchmark for success in achieving a sense of national pride (see Pasler 2009).

It comes as no surprise, therefore, that patriotic songs have had a significant place in the repertoire of school songs, especially in the context of an increasingly threatening international climate. Michèle Alten (1995) has analysed the rise of patriotic fervour in school music and has revealed remnants of it up to the beginning of the 1920s. In the two decades preceding the First World War, the return of Alsace-Lorraine to France and the surge for revenge permeated a 'pro-Republican' focus in the teaching of morals and citizenship. Children were imbued with a growing patriotic spirit in which military heroism was glorified. Thus an entire generation was unobtrusively prepared for immense sacrifices to follow.

After the First World War – although the cult of the *patrie* or fatherland was maintained through ceremonies commemorating the Great War in which school teachers and students took a major role – the songs taught in classrooms focused more on the folklore of the regions of France, for example *Chansons populaires du val-de-Loire* (*Traditional songs from the Loire Valley*) (Chevais 1925), *Chansons populaires des provinces de France* (*Traditional songs from French provinces*) (Société française l'art à l'école 1925) and the first part of *Anthologie du chant scolaire et post-scolaire* (*Anthology of school and after-school songs*) (Société française l'art à l'école 1925). Gradually, school teachers forsook nationalist ideals as pacifism gained ground (particularly with the emergence of the trade union movement) and a new social perspective emerged.

This patriotic focus was not the only social imperative at the time. The incorporation of music education into the school curriculum came about in a period in which France – then still essentially a rural society – was undergoing massive industrialization. Many children from rural areas were to swell the ranks of workers tethered to exhaustingly repetitive tasks in the new factories. There was a growing realization that singing could also be beneficial for adult workers in such circumstances (Alten 1995: 38).

Music education in schools had survived major political and social changes, but, despite recognition of these extra-musical benefits, its status in the curriculum remained tenuous and its methods and practices lacked universal acceptance.

Pedagogical issues: cipher notation and the debate over absolute and relative pitch

It was a member of an influential educational committee, Amand Chevé, who, in 1882, pointed out the hurdle represented by the learning of music reading within the limited time allotted for musical instruction in schools (see Alten 1995; Vançon 2004: 42). Accordingly, he made a case for the use of the Galin–Paris–Chevé method (see Chevé 1852, 1862; Lee-Forbes 1977), which was based on Galin's (1818) cipher notation (*méthode chiffrée*), which, in turn, built on the principles set out by Rousseau in his *Projet concernant de nouveaux signes pour la musique* (1742). Put simply, in cipher notation, the degrees of the major scale are represented by the numerals 1 to 7, where the numeral 1 refers to the keynote of a major key. It was intended to be used as the initial stage in learning to sing at sight, making it possible to forgo the learning of conventional staff notation, although it was intended to facilitate this at a later stage. Although the official 1882 texts recommended no particular method, the ministerial decree of 23 July 1883 did authorize the use of cipher notation in schools (see Chevais 1931: 3648). Following the later ministerial decree of 4 August 1905 (Article 119), cipher notation was included in the curriculum of teachers' colleges and finally appeared in the *Manuel Général* in 1905.

Although 'Galinism' (the Galin–Paris–Chevé method) represents only one of many possibilities tried up to and including the 1920s, it fed one of those paralyzing polemical bouts of which France is so fond. Galinism certainly made the learning of simple melodies much faster than other approaches and offered certain advantages within a curriculum that had singing as its focus. With this in mind, the official texts based on this approach were introduced to teachers' colleges (*écoles normales*). Even Chevais, who was hardly well disposed toward this method, admitted that it had certain pedagogical merits, in particular the simplification of pitch and duration signs and the reduction of all major and minor keys to two scales: C for the major mode and A for the minor mode. Chevais (1931: 3648) considered that simplified methods were useful 'as temporary means of musical instruction', but that staff notation became necessary whenever more complex types of music were likely to be encountered.

The use of cipher notation gave rise to an extended debate over a period of some thirty years. Cipher notation was not suited to instrumental learning and therefore opposed by specialist music teachers. Accordingly, from 1923, it was no longer included in official syllabi.

Another key pedagogical issue was the French preference for the fixed-doh as opposed to the movable-doh method. France, like other Latin countries, saw considerable discussion about the merits of relative solmization and 'absolute' *solfège*. These methodological disputes poisoned the debate over music in schools. Eventually, the 1859 ministerial decree determining standard pitch (435 Hertz at a temperature of 18˚C), followed by the international congress of 1885, had unexpected consequences in France, something that, at the outset, was no more than the adoption of a mere convention. However, this gradually led to a music instructional approach based exclusively on actual (fixed as opposed to relative) pitch and misgivings about whatever methods employed a relative pitch approach, such as those devised by Curwen, Ward, Kodály and Gédalge. This unfortunate orientation to fixed pitch has prevailed to this day. The focus on an absolute pitch approach was opposed by the musicologist Jacques Chailley who, after a period of hesitation, finally acknowledged the need for a large-scale reform of music teaching methods and pointed out the negative effect of this methodological standoff (Chailley 1980, 1983). Other more concrete attempts, such as the French adaptation of the Kodály method put forward by Jacquotte Ribière-Raverlat (1975, 1978), did not meet with sufficient support to enable this innovation to flourish.

The excessive prominence given to perfect pitch as a benchmark of musical acumen, the excessive importance accorded to *solfège*-orientated skills and the dichotomy in focus presented by specialized musical instruction and more general classroom music education in schools were counterproductive to the development of music in schools. Furthermore, many generalist teachers felt that their training did not provide them with sufficient confidence to hold their own in music.

The training of music teachers

The relationship of generalist teachers to musical knowledge depends essentially on two factors: prior experiences in practical music-making at a personal level and the amount of specific musical training included in a course of teacher education. Some among the schoolteachers trained during the period of the Third Republic (1870–1940) had prior experience as singers or instrumentalists. This at least gave them a degree of self-confidence to take on musical activities in the classroom. A few even played their instruments in class, which was not the norm in the then-highly rationalist educational context. Music, as the 'last subject of instruction' in the curriculum, was deemed to be associated with emotional and bodily engagement, which frequently aroused misgivings among teachers. The exception to this view was that of those certain favourably disposed inspectors who were themselves musicians. In most cases, however, schoolteachers were ill at ease with music.

Despite official directives, the quality of teacher training in music varied considerably. Singing in tune, possessing an elementary knowledge of music and – in the best of cases – the rudiments of *solfège* placed considerable demands on teachers who were expected to devote most of their time and energy to teaching French children to read, write and count. It was not until the period between the two world wars that a 'teaching aptitude certificate' for voice, at two levels, was instituted and gave recognition to the competencies of musician–teachers, enabling them to teach in the higher grade (*école primaire supérieure*) and in teachers' colleges. Alten (1995) has noted that the situation in many regions remained so difficult that in 1933 André Ferré, Inspector for Primary Instruction, was seriously considering establishing ongoing professional training for teachers, with classes being organized at the various levels of France's administrative system (national, department-level and even inter-canton sessions). However, teacher training programmes are still inconsistently applied across France, and only Paris, with its intense cultural life and more highly specialized teachers, provides a high degree of consistency in its training of teachers in music.

Maurice Chevais

As a centralized state equipped with an educational system long considered to be exemplary, France has never satisfactorily resolved the problem of music education in the primary schools, whereas specialized musical training in music conservatoires and music schools has made spectacular progress.[1] The lack of a hard-headed approach, the absence of strong political will and fruitless conflicts hardly conducive to dispassionate reflection have all overshadowed the basic pragmatism that a handful of more insightful pedagogues were able to implement at an early stage. The pioneering efforts of Wilhem have already been discussed, but the work of another highly influential musical pedagogue, all too readily forgotten today, Maurice Chevais, is also important.

Between the two world wars Maurice Chevais was the dominant figure in the development of a suitable musical pedagogy for schools (see Fijalkow 2004). His thinking, in its epistemological breadth, overlooked none of the many aspects associated with music education. Based on actual knowledge about the child, it embraced the kinds of knowledge to be taught, teaching curricula, goals, pedagogical strategies, the training of schoolteachers and, more generally, the purposes of school music instruction. By focusing on the contribution of Chevais, we can discover more about the prevailing thought concerning musical pedagogy in the interwar period.

From the start, Chevais was keen to move towards a subject that had greater breadth and scope, so he preferred to talk about *enseignement musical* or *éducation musicale* rather than the more restricted *chant* (see Chevais 1925). He asserted the primacy of a sensory approach over any theoretical endeavour. At the first level, from 6 to 9 years of age, abstraction was avoided: the instruction was oral and relied primarily on singing. The aim was to educate the voice, the ear and musical taste. Singing thus was no longer the mere illustrative phase of a previously propounded theoretical approach but the main vehicle for music education. Chevais envisaged activities in terms of play, rhythm and physical exercise, being pleasurable and being able to instil lasting motivation for learning in children.

At the second level, from nine to twelve years, music education continued with the gradual introduction of musical signs and recourse to its visual representation. This was the beginning of musical instruction that should not impede the process of education in vocal, listening or aesthetic skills commenced in the previous level, a pitfall which many teachers did not know how to avoid. The rudiments of *solfège* were incorporated into the active and empathic environment of the classroom in which the teacher was constantly relating to the children. Chevais grounded his instructional system in a broad repertory of folksongs and mimed songs, intended for school festivals, which Chevais had collected. In 1909, Chevais had published a collection entitled *Chansons avec gestes* (*Songs with gestures*) that later was to become *Chants scolaires avec gestes* (*School songs with gestures*) (n.d.), in which the link between text, music and body movement came to the fore. Chevais did not reject previous methods such as *phonomimie*, an ingenious system of representing the C major scale and highlighting the notes of the common chord to the left of the vertical axis, with the remaining notes being located to the right.

The instruction carried out at the third level, from twelve years onwards, was essentially based on choral singing in both harmonic and polyphonic styles. Chevais was convinced of the effectiveness of choral activity outside the school to supplement classroom music and as a social activity of considerable civic and artistic value in adult life.

The models and progression advocated by Chevais may be debated, particularly the choices resulting from his belief in the innate nature of tonal feeling. But the humanitarian underpinning of his work should also be acknowledged, as should his concern for making the child, under the guidance of the teacher, a fully fledged participant in the co-construction of his or her musical skills. Within the context of French education, Chevais' method is indisputably the first of those identified as 'action-based'. Moreover, it is now well established that his approach influenced music learning outside the school setting, particularly within the movement advocating popular education (see Andrieux, in Pistone 1983).

In hindsight, the contribution of Chevais to music education is considerable (see Mialaret, in Fijalkow 2004), particularly in changing the focus from a theoretical to a sensory approach. By bringing the sensory approach to the fore and identifying the impediments to learning, Chevais became part of a major pedagogical innovation that, together with the work of Montessori and Dalcroze, informed research into child psychology. Chevais became interested in the work of Alfred Binet (1857–1911), who at the turn of the century had directed the *Société pour l'étude psychologique de l'enfant* (see Avanzini 1974; Binet and Simon 1908). Binet's influence on Chevais can be seen in his application of Binet's work on the psychological functioning of the child and his incorporation of a developmental perspective in his pedagogical procedures.

Without undertaking an in-depth exposé of the 'progressive' method advocated by Chevais (see Mialaret 1978), it is quite possible to grasp the significant psychological principles using present-day research tools. As opposed to most of his predecessors, for whom learning to read notes remained a prime issue, Chevais' psycho-pedagogical approach did not rely initially on the visual mode of learning, but on the combining of listening and singing (see Drake and Rochez 2003). This enlightened decision bypassed the prevailing practices in instrumental training in France, where visual-semantic and visual-motor combinations occupied a pre-eminent position. The priority granted to practice and the refusal to include abstract prerequisites brought Chevais considerably closer to the later methodologies of Jaques-Dalcroze, Kodály and Orff. Again, due recognition should be given to Chevais' intuition in making singing the most important part of music education. Today it is well established that singing contributes greatly to the transfer of knowledge and skills from one area of music to another (see Drake, McAdams and Berthoz 1999; Drake, Rochez, McAdams and Berthoz 2002).

The introduction of music into the school and its somewhat difficult integration into a centralized education system have provided the opportunity for an ongoing and fruitful discussion about musical pedagogy. Faced with a milieu that was anything but hospitable, music pedagogues attempted in successive stages to adapt to the structures of the school as an institution. The evolution of practices and manuals (see Augé 1889; Bouchor 1895; Marmontel 1886) demonstrates that classroom music education has broken loose, albeit slowly, from the prevailing model of musical instruction intended primarily for instrumentalists and singers. Hence recognition of a specific status for music education in the school and the hard-won acknowledgement of music as a specialism within the school system forms a common thread throughout the first two periods in the history of musical education in France (1833–82 and 1882–1923).

But what meaning should be attributed to school music education? Successively and at times simultaneously, the benefits of music – such as its promotion of social harmony, the encouragement of patriotic pride and the enhancement of aesthetic sensitivity – were recognized for this latecomer to the mandated school curriculum. This was achieved largely through Chevais, who saw music as a necessary means of personal expression for the development of the child and a pathway towards the increasing of human sensitivity. Herein lies the 'great lesson' offered by the last in a line of music education pioneers.

The present

In 1984 Annie Labussière, in a short study of music in general education, presented a damning critique of the situation in schools (emphases by Labussière):

> Musical education in the contemporary school, despite its apparent renewal and flourishing, is tainted and shackled by a certain number of external problems (economical, political, social), but more still by internal ones (methods, repertory, pedagogical orientation) which may not be solved empirically but by a constant give-and-take between *scientific procedure* (musicology, experimental psychology, psycho-pedagogy) and *curricula* and *teaching modes*. Furthermore, since the beginning of the century it has been possible to observe a succession of reforms, projects, amendments and sub-amendments whose

practical application (often short-lived or insufficient, and sometimes open to criticism) fails or else founders on the shoals of indifference, essentially in a country in which music has never been fully integrated into the overall school curriculum. (Labussière 1984: 440–1)

Today, while the psychological underpinnings of music education are generally acknowledged, the same does not apply in the case of discipline-based content within the school system that has recently been promoted under the guise of 'artistic education' (*Bulletin Officiel* 3 February 2005) and placed in competition with other artistic practices. Thus music education has lost its former clarity of definition. Its survival as a readily identifiable school discipline is no longer assured. It is striking to note the contemporary significance of the major questions raised by the pioneers of school music. A comparison of past and present – a painful one indeed – shows a persistence of problems for which no convincing solution has been offered. The lack of confidence often felt by generalist teachers in teaching music has not subsided (see Jahier 2006). It is recurring at a time when very severe restrictions are weakening the musical training of future generalist teachers, within institutes where teachers are supposed to receive adequate training to carry out their mission. The credibility of the generalist teacher in the area of music – a difficulty brought to light early on by the pioneers of music education – remains as an unresolved problem. Music, having entered the relative sanctuary of the schools of Third Republic through the back door, eventually became more firmly entrenched in specialized structures determined by locally controlled governmental entities (*collectivités territoriales*) such as music schools and conservatories. The gap between these two types of instruction has widened considerably, although the 'action-based' methods used in general education have ultimately contributed to the evolution of more innovative practices in the initial phases of specialized music teaching. The larger historical perspective is that the effort required today in order to set up a partnership between the primary school and specialist musicians, while laudable in itself, will only achieve positive results if the teacher in charge of the class is capable of following up the work of these artists. The effective training of teachers is an indispensable prerequisite to maintaining the status quo in music education and remains a very sensitive issue.

Pressed into service at the beginning of the twentieth century on behalf of extra-musical aims (most often social or political), school music education – today as in the past – is forced to justify its existence through arguments beyond the purely musical. In this respect, it is emphasized that music represents an indisputable contribution to the socialization of children and the transfer of more or less closely related competences, or, at the very least, an enhancement in other spheres of learning from a study of music. Research in this area (see Drake and Rochez 2003) has been carried out on populations for whom the amount of time spent in music practice is considerably more than that of French children in primary schools. This is the reason why this argument – potentially a double-edged sword – may only be used in the context of French school instruction with caution.

The first defenders of what today we call 'music education' were committed musicians who were fully aware that music had no need to hide behind an external justification, however laudable, in order to justify its presence in the school curriculum. The obligation to place their discipline at the service of other competencies or other educational aims has only been in response to the stubbornness of education authorities to recognize fully the intrinsic values of music. The place of music in the hierarchy of knowledge and skills that is represented in the curriculum remains fragile.

Ultimately, the difficulties of music education in schools mirror the ambiguities of the status of music in French society, which sometimes has been distorted to the point of caricature. Although highly valued by the social elite whenever it is associated with prestigious music training institutions, music is restricted to its function as entertainment for the lower and upper middle classes – in education, the practice of music is well regarded as long it is not to the detriment of basic subjects that are considered to be more important. As for the musical activities of the majority of students, these fail to connect with life outside the school. In other words, there is a disjunction between didactic action and social knowledge so that musical activities in school rarely attain the status of 'referent social practices' (see Martinand 1981). The introduction of music education to the school curriculum has brought with it the legitimacy accorded to other disciplines. As set out in the official regulations – for example, *Bulletin Officiel*, 9 March 1995 – governments will still adhere to the rhetoric of supporting school music, but this is not the case in reality. A plan for the inclusion of music in teacher training, at once ambitious and systematic, is indispensable if a major change is to be effected. Moreover, recognition of music education as an active ingredient in forming the child will necessarily entail a major curriculum reform that can be applied to all schools. This change has only been partial and hesitant attitudes have never fully disappeared.

Thus, pedagogues who devote their efforts to music education and expend considerable energy to convince a rather sceptical public opinion also struggle within the school system to have their ideas accepted. The efforts expended by these music educators, often in very restrictive environments, cannot but result in only modest results that are barely perceptible to political decision makers and to their hierarchy. Yet it is this basic work, made up of unceasing efforts and small victories, that should have deserved the overwhelming support of government agencies. Failure to perceive the benefits of school music education has remained a major obstacle to the development of a discipline that is prisoner to a reticent educational hierarchy and a hard-to-convince public opinion.

In hindsight, the interaction between society and the school system seems to have made music education a 'hot spot' around which a consensus has never been truly established. School music education turns out to be something of a litmus test of significant trends in French society with regard to perceptions about the art of music. This is manifest in a fascination with high-level musical practice that provides reassurance about the primacy of the cultural power of France as a breeding ground for great performers and composers, as opposed to music education for the masses that is crucial to any education of the wider population, which is treated condescendingly. High-profile manifestations of excellence have led to a neglect in building solid foundations within the school milieu. The continuum that spans the entire range from school music practice to the most sublime performances of great musicians has never succeeded in firmly establishing itself, despite the best intentions and efforts of numerous music teachers, composers and other enlightened minds.

These particular socio-historical conditions set France apart from other European countries such as Germany or Hungary. French musical life is affected by a division between elitists and those who favour a musical education for the majority of children. One cannot delve into the introduction of music education in the French school system without thorny socio-cultural questions being asked, or at least puzzling over the attitudes of government, one prone to legislating, but which, when it comes to matters of musical education, has shown itself to be rather weak willed than assertive. It is with self-sacrificing devotion that the most motivated teachers have striven to provide their students with a music education adapted as best they might to the unfavourable conditions in which teachers and students alike find themselves. This has brought about great diversity in pedagogical approaches and with it perhaps a lack of a clear focus.

Conclusion

The inroads made by music education into school curricula represent a succession of advances and retreats, of enthusiasms and abandonments. At the end of this brief overview, the overriding impression may well be one of an uncertain and unequal combat – the history of music education in schools seems to be marking time. Yet, within the course of a century, music has gradually managed to clarify its goals and content, adjusting them to the rather paltry means that were allotted to it within schools. Music has also shown itself to be capable of incorporating contributions from child psychology and has been receptive to the great psychological debates. The official regulations and successive programmes reveal the drawn-out changes that have caused music to proceed from being an entertainment to a decoration and more recently to being recognized as a discipline essential for the development of personality. However, it still remains for the true worth of music education to be felt by all those within the education community and for its significance to be clearly formulated to those authorities entrusted with oversight of the school curriculum. Today, as in the era of the pioneers, these conditions have not been met.

The situation to the present day remains very inconsistent, juxtaposing admirable successes – often inadequately acknowledged by schools and given little or no media exposure – with serious shortcomings. The current orientation of French school curricula as set out in the *Bulletin Officiel* 29 (20 July 2006) is to emphasize the 'basics' and to relegate music to the larger framework of artistic education. These measures are part of a conception of teaching in which utilitarian preoccupations merge with criteria of scientific and technological efficiency. In this context, the convictions and commitments of the pioneers of music education need to be recalled and forcefully reasserted, so that music educators may find a path to renewal and may become aware of how to adapt to the demands of a world that is now constantly on the move.[2]

Reflective questions

1 What are the roots of the problems that musical education has faced in establishing a place in the French system?
2 Is the strong rationalist school of thought in France responsible for the marginalization of musical education?
3 Has this reluctance observed in France also been present in many other countries?
4 Activities based around singing are the foundation of musical education. The introduction of instrumental activities has often been successful, yet is it really viable in the context of educating children on a national scale?

Notes

1. As far as secondary schools were concerned, music was taught to girls at the end of the nineteenth century, but it was only in 1937 that it was also taught to boys. The situation was not really improved until the 'plan Landowski' in 1969 (see Landowski 1979).
2. The following additional references should prove helpful for researchers wishing to explore further the historical development of music education in France: Chailley (1965, 1966); Chevais (1937, 1939, 1941); Dauphin (2004); Genet-Delacroix (1992); Kleinman (1974); Lescat (2001); Prost (1968); Roy (2002).

References

Alten, M. (1995), *La musique dans l'école de Jules Ferry à nos jours*, Issy-les-Moulineaux: EAP.

Augé, C. (1889), *Le Livre de musique*, Paris: Vve P. Larousse.

Avanzini, G. (ed.) (1974), *Binet: Écrits psychologiques et pédagogiques. Choisis et présentés par Guy Avanzini*, Toulouse: Privat.

Binet, A. and T. Simon (1908/2004), *Le développement de l'intelligence chez les enfants* [Reprod. en fac-sim. de l'édition de 1908, Paris: Masson], Paris: l'Harmattan.

Bouchor, M. (1895), *Chants populaires pour les écoles, Poésies de Maurice Bouchor*, Paris: Hachette.

Buisson, F. (1887), *Dictionnaire de pédagogie*, Tome 2, Paris: Hachette.

Bulletin Officiel n 5, 9 March 1995, 'Nouveaux programmes de l'école primaire'.

Bulletin Officiel n 5, 3 February 2005, 'Circulaire d'orientations sur la politique d'éducation artistique et culturelle (...)'.

Bulletin Officiel n 29, 20 July 2006, 'Socle commun de connaissances et de compétences'.

Bulletin Officiel hors-série n 3 du 19 Juin 2008.

Chailley, J. (1965), 'Solmisation relative ou solfège absolu', *L'éducation musicale* 21 (123), 26–7.

Chailley, J. (1966), 'Solmisation relative ou solfège absolu', *L'éducation musicale* 21 (125), 18.

Chailley, J. (1980), 'Hauteur absolue, hauteur relative' in H. P. M. Lithens and G. M. Steinschulte (eds), *Divini cultu splendori, studia musicae sacrae necnon et musico-paedagogiae: Liber festivus in honorem Joseph Lennards*, Rome, pp. 125–30.

Chailley, J. (1983), 'La solmisation Kodály, révélateur des problèmes de hauteur absolue et de hauteur relative dans les pays latins', *L'Éducation musicale* 40 (295), 7–10.

Chevais, M. (1909), *Chanson avec gestes*, Paris: A. Leduc.

Chevais, M. (1925), *Chansons populaires du Val-de-Loire: Orléans-Blois-Tours et des pays avoisinants*, Paris: Heugel.

Chevais, M. (1931), 'L'enseignement musical à l'école' in A. Lavignac and L. De Laurencie (eds), *Encyclopédie de la musique et Dictionnaire du Conservatoire* Part II, vol. 6, Paris: Delagrave, pp. 3631–83.

Chevais, M. (1937), *L'éducation musicale de l'enfance*. Vol. 1: *L'enfant et la musique*, Paris: A. Leduc.

Chevais, M. (1939), *L'éducation musicale de l'enfance*. Vol. 2: *L'art d'enseigner*, Paris: A. Leduc.

Chevais, M. (1941), *L'éducation musicale de l'enfance*. Vol. 3: *Méthode active et directe*, Paris: A. Leduc.

Chevais, M. (n.d.), *Chants scolaires avec gestes sur des mélodies recueillies ou composées par Maurice Chevais (...) 1er recueil*, Paris: A. Leduc.

Chevé, E. (1852), *La routine et le bon sens ou les conservatoires et la méthode Galin-Paris-Chevé*, Paris: Chez l'auteur.

Chevé, E. (ed.) (1862), *Galin, P., Exposition d'une nouvelle méthode pour l'enseignement de la musique*, Paris: E. Chevé.

Dauphin, C. (2004), 'Les grandes méthodes pédagogiques du XXe siècle', in J.-J. Nattiez (ed.), *Musiques: Une encyclopédie pour le XXIe siècle*. Vol. 2: *Les savoirs musicaux*, Arles: Actes Sud, pp. 833–53.

Drake, C. and C. Rochez (2003), 'Développement et apprentissage des activités et perceptions musicales' in M. Kail and M. Fayol (eds), *Les sciences cognitives et l'école*, Paris: PUF, pp. 443–79.

Drake, C., S. McAdams and A. Berthoz (1999), 'Learning to Sing a Novel Piece of Music Facilitates Playing it on the Violin but not the Other Way Round: Evidence from Performance Segmentations', *Journal of the Acoustical Society of America* 106 (4): 2285.

Drake, C., C. Rochez, S. McAdams and A. Berthoz (2002), 'Sing First, Play Later: Singing a Novel Piece of Music Facilitates Playing it on an Instrument but not the Other Way Round', *7th International Conference for Music Perception and Cognition (ICMPC) Proceedings*, Sydney: ICMPC. CD-ROM.

Ferro, M. (2003), *Histoire de France*, Paris: Odile Jacob.

Fijalkow, C. (2003), *Deux siècles de musique a` l'école: chroniques de l'exception parisienne, 1819–2002*, Paris: L'Harmattan.

Fijalkow, C. (ed.) (2004), *Maurice Chevais (1880–1943): un grand pédagogue de la musique*, Paris: L'Harmattan.

Galin, P. (1818), *Exposition d'une nouvelle méthode pour l'enseignement de la musique*, Paris: Rey et Gravier.

Gédalge, A. (1926), *L'enseignement de la musique par l'éducation méthodique de l'oreille* (*The teaching of music by the methodical education of the ear*, English trans. by Anna Mary Mealand), Paris: Libr. Gédalge.

Genet-Delacroix, M.-C. (1992), *Art et état sous la IIIe république: le système des beaux-arts, 1870–1940*, Paris: Publications de la Sorbonne.

Jahier, S. (2006), 'L'éducation musicale à l'école: les pratiques pédagogiques et le rapport au savoir musical des enseignants du primaire' (unpublished PhD thesis, University of Paris X-Nanterre).

Kleinman, S. (1974), *La solmisation mobile: de Jean-Jacques Rousseau à John Curwen*, Paris: Heugel.

Labussiére, A. (1984), 'Pédagogie et éducation musicale' in J. Chailley (ed.), *Précis de musicologie,* Paris: PUF, pp. 431–42.

Landowski, M. (1979), *Batailles pour la musique*, Paris: Le Seuil.

Lee-Forbes, W. (1977), 'The Galin-Paris-Chevé Method of Rhythmic Instruction: A History', London: University Microfilms International.

Lescat, P. (2001), *L'enseignement musical en France de 529 à 1972: 71 plans, chronologie, lieux, élèves, maîtres, études, emploi du temps, classes, manuels*, Courlay: J. M. Fuzeau.

Manuel général de l'instruction primaire (1905), Paris: Hachette.

Marmontel, A. (1886), *La première année de musique. Solfège et chants à l'usage de l'enseignement élémentaire*, Paris: A. Colin.

Martinand, J.-L. (1981), 'Pratiques sociales de référence et compétences techniques. Á propos d'un projet d'initiation aux techniques de fabrication mécanique en classe de quatrième' in A. Giordan (ed.), *Diffusion et appropriation du savoir scientifique: enseignement et vulgarisation. Actes des Troisièmes Journées Internationales sur l'Education Scientifique*, Paris: University of Paris (Paris 7), pp. 149–54.

Mialaret, J.-P. (1978), *Pédagogie de la musique et enseignement programmé*, Paris: EAP.

Pasler, J. (2009), *Composing the Citizen: Music as Public Utility in Third Republic France*, Berkeley: University of California Press.

Pistone, D. (ed.) (1983), *L'éducation musicale en France. Histoire et méthodes. Actes du colloque de l'Institut de recherches sur les civilisations de l'Occident moderne, 13 March 1982*, Paris: Presses de l'Université de Paris-Sorbonne (Paris IV), p. 8.

Programmes du 27 juillet 1882, *Bulletin administratif du ministère de l'Instruction publique*, Paris: Imprimerie Nationale.

Programmes et instructions de l'enseignement élémentaire (1923), Chambéry: Éditions Scolaires.

Prost, A. (1968), *Histoire de l'enseignement en France*, Paris: A. Colin.

Rainbow, B. (1967), *The Land without Music: Musical Education in England 1800–1860 and its Continental Antecedents*, London: Novello.

Ribière-Raverlat, J. (1975), *Chant-Musique. Adaptation française de la méthode Kodály: Livre du maître. Classes élémentaires, 1re Année,* Book 1, Paris: A. Leduc.

Ribière-Raverlat, J. (1978), *Chant-Musique. Adaptation française de la méthode Kodály: Livre du maître,* Book 2, Paris: A. Leduc.

Rousseau J. J. (1781), *Projet concernant de nouveaux signes pour la musique, lu par l'auteur à l'Académie des sciences le 22 août 1742,* Geneva.

Roy, J. (ed.) (2002), *La formation des professeurs des écoles en éducation musicale*, Paris: University of Paris-Sorbonne, Documents de Recherche OMF, Série Didactique de la Musique 31.

Société Française L'art à l'école (ed.) (1925), *Anthologie du chant scolaire et post-scolaire (Anthology of school and after-school songs)*, 1re série, *Chansons populaires des provinces de France (Traditional songs from French provinces)*, Paris: Heugel.

Vançon, J. C. (2004), 'De la polémique galiniste (1882–1883) au conflit Chevais/Gédalge (1917–1923): l'histoire de la musique à l'école à la lumière de ses querelles pédagogiques' in C. Fijalkow (ed.), *Maurice Chevais (1880–1943)*, Paris: L'Harmattan, pp. 39–56.

Wilhem, G. B. (1836), *Manuel de lecture musicale et de chant élémentaire á l'usage des collèges des institutions, des écoles et des cours de chant (...)*, Paris: Perrotin.

Chapter 3

Germany: Educational goals, curricular structure, political principles

Wilfried Gruhn

Introduction

Music instruction in public schools in Germany has a rather long history (for review see Braun 1957; Ehrenforth 1995, 1997; Gruhn 2003; Günther 1967; Nolte 1982, 1991; Schmidt 1986; Sowa 1973). However, when considering the development of music education, it is necessary to bear in mind that as a political unit Germany has changed many times and has existed in its present form only since 1990. The long history of the *Heilige Römische Reich Deutscher Nation* united various smaller states and local tribes (for example, Saxons, Prussians, Bavarians, Franks, Kelts etc.) and lasted from the Middle Ages until 1806. During the seventeenth and eighteenth centuries, Germany was scattered into innumerable kingdoms, duchies, archduchies, counties and principalities, so could not be thought of as a homogeneous political entity; rather it was a culturally and linguistically related assemblage of member states.

During the nineteenth century the House of Hohenzollern in Prussia became the most influential and powerful counterpart to the House of Habsburg in Austria. Therefore, Prussia will be taken as a model for music education in Germany, because the other states followed in adopting its educational policies. After the Second World War, Germany became a Federal Republic of ten states; since reunification in 1990, it has consisted of sixteen states that are culturally autonomous – the so-called *Kulturhoheit der Länder*. This caused and still causes many differences in school organization, curricula and educational policies in particular states that correspond to the ruling parties and their political agendas. The history of these divergent developments will not be addressed in this chapter; rather, some general principles that initially determined and then emerged from compulsory schooling and mandatory music learning will be discussed.

Figure 3.1 Latin school (*Lateinschule*) in the sixteenth century. The board with notation on the wall indicates that choral singing was part of schooling. (Woodcut from 1592; © H. Schiffler and R. Winkler (1991), *Tausend Jahre Schule*, Stuttgart: Belser Verlag, p. 67.)

Historical premises

Singing of Gregorian chant 'by ear' and later from notation had been part of the education in monastic schools since the Middle Ages (see Figure 3.1). But this form of education cannot be thought of as schooling in the modern sense. Only the very few students who were seen as having the potential to take over clerical or governmental positions were introduced to reading and writing. Formal education as such did not exist. The Augustinian monk Martin Luther (1483–1546), who was the first to codify a common German language (as distinct from the many dialects of the different Germanic tribes), recognized the importance of congregational singing in building and unifying a community. Accordingly, singing came to be widely taught in monastic and Latin schools and was no longer confined to its original liturgical function.

Through an edict of King Friedrich the Great (*Generallandschulreglement*), Prussia became the first state to introduce compulsory schooling in 1763. However, it took a long time before this law could be applied to the whole country. It has only been since the

Figure 3.2 Cartoon by J. Nussbiegel (1825) reflecting the situation of teaching during the seventeenth and eighteenth centuries. (Reproduced with permission of Germanisches Nationalmuseum Nürnberg.)

end of the eighteenth century that compulsory schooling in the German states and in the German kingdoms (e.g. Saxonia and Bavaria) came into being, albeit with limited effect. Teachers were not recognized in society as professionals, many of them being disabled soldiers who had adequate literacy and numeracy skills and a knowledge of Bible stories. They were poorly paid by parents, so needed additional income to maintain their daily lives. Therefore, it was not uncommon that pupils came to the teachers' homes and were taught all together by the teacher and his wife, who also had to perform household duties in between their teaching (see Figure 3.2).

Although great differences occurred between city and country schools, singing (or 'singing instruction') was always included in compulsory schooling. However, there was neither methodical teaching of singing and other subjects nor formal teacher training in place. Contemporary illustrations of singing masters depict teachers as lacking enthusiasm and being lethargic and indicate a feeling of depression and resignation to a poor lot in life (see Figure 3.3). Moreover, music journals of the time include complaints and reports about desperate conditions in schools, poor discipline and numerous calls for pupils to be excused from singing. By the same token, musical life flourished at the aristocratic courts – for example, at Köthen, Dresden, Mannheim, Munich etc. – and in cities such as Berlin and Leipzig. All this set a standard of musical excellence in performance and composition that spread to the rest of Europe. The dichotomy presented by the gap between educational and artistic standards is very characteristic of this period.

At the turn of the nineteenth century the educational reforms of the Swiss philanthropist Johann Heinrich Pestalozzi (1746–1827) profoundly influenced education on the Continent. Teachers travelled to Switzerland to meet with and learn from him and the German poet Johann Wolfgang von Goethe reflected and transfigured Pestalozzi's educational philosophy in his novel *Wilhelm Meisters Wanderjahre* (1821–9/1981), referring to this as *Pädagogische Provinz*. The interest aroused by Pestalozzi's ideas and their profound influence on early nineteenth-century education in Europe and the USA (see Gruhn 1993; Pemberton 1985)[1] were probably due to a desire for a clearly defined, formalized general teaching method. Pestalozzi's friends Michael Traugott Pfeiffer (1771–1849) and Hans Georg Nägeli (1773–1836) applied his ideas to singing in schools and edited the first instructional method book for singing according to Pestalozzi's principles (*Gesangbildungslehre* 1810).

However, their strict and highly systematized method was a misinterpretation of Pestalozzi's new understanding of the psychology of learning and the educational philosophy that aimed to follow children's natural development by supporting sensual experiences before introducing formal (verbal) knowledge. Unfortunately, Pestalozzi had never enunciated a psychologically grounded learning theory, but in essence this was

Figure 3.3 A typical music teacher of the nineteenth century. The violin was the standard instrument for the accompaniment of singing; the bow served as a pointer and often for punishment as well. (Print by Kauffmann 'Der Herr Cantor'; © H. Schiffler and R. Winkler, 1991, *Tausend Jahre Schule*, Stuttgart: Belser Verlag; reproduced with permission of Horst Schiffler.)

reflected in his published works. Nevertheless, Pfeiffer's and Nägeli's formalized instructional approach became more successful and influential than any other contemporary method book and made Pestalozzi famous all over Europe.

Singing during the nineteenth century was always part of the school curriculum in elementary education but was dominated by the debate about the optimal teaching method to employ. Formal aspects of a methodical approach to teaching – as reflected in *Formalstufen* (formal stages of teaching) by Johann Friedrich Herbart (1776–1841) – became the principal educational idea of that century and overshadowed all other aspects.

Philosophical and socio-cultural contexts: Four paradigms

In reflecting on compulsory music in school education and on how and why it was set up, four overarching paradigms can be identified: singing under the supervision and for the benefit of the church; singing as serving and promoting the values of the state; music (not specifically singing) as a component of general public education (*Volksbildung*)[2]; and music learning based on, and as a component of, the developmental growth of the child/pupil. Each of these paradigms will now be discussed in turn.

Singing as liturgical support

From the early Middle Ages, singing had been an integral part of the religious education of the German people. Even after the Royal Edict of 1763, singing remained under the control of the church. The main purpose of singing as a mandatory subject for all children in schools was to learn and commit to memory the melodies and words of hymns and chorales, with the aim of enhancing church services with the tuneful singing of children that would elevate the spirit of the community and enlighten the mind. Indeed, this idea of elevation and enlightenment gained through singing and listening to liturgical songs was fundamental to the teaching of singing in schools. This liturgical context also determined the song repertoire and curriculum content of music as a school subject – namely, congregational songs and music notation. Accordingly, the issue that dominated the music curriculum during the course of the nineteenth century was that of teaching methodology. This is reflected in the countless singing instructions that were published in each region by numerous singing teachers and supervisors (Abs 1811; Hientzsch 1829/1830; Hohmann 1838; Kübler 1826; Natorp 1813, 1820; Pfeiffer and Nägeli 1810; Schulz 1816; Zeller 1810; also see Gruhn 2003: 66–88).

Interestingly, solmization – whether using the movable- or fixed-doh approach – was never a matter of contention, as cipher notation, where numerals indicate the position of tones in a scale, was introduced through Pfeiffer's and Nägeli's *Gesangbildungslehre* (1810) and then more systematically through Natorp's *Anleitung* (1813) (see Figure 3.4).

B. Ch. L. Natorp: *Anleitung zur Unterweisung im Singen*, 2. Cursus, Essen ²1834, S. 54.

Figure 3.4 Notation with numbers according to Bernhard Christoph Ludwig Natorp's 'Anleitung zur Unterweisung im Singen' ('Introduction to singing instruction'), Essen, 1813, p. 52.

Singing in the service of the state and its values

In 1809 Wilhelm von Humboldt (1767–1835) became the Prussian Minister of Culture with control over the school system for the entire kingdom. He developed a new way of thinking about school education. The basis of his educational reforms (known as *Preußische Schulreformen*) was set out in his proposals for the schools in Königsberg (Prussia) and in Lithuania (*Königsberger und Litauischer Schulplan*) (Humboldt 1964, *Werke*, Vol. IV: 168–95). He maintained that each student should have the opportunity to develop individually according to his/her potential (*Kraft*). Humboldt deliberately chose to use the term *Bildung* (formation), which stems from the reflexive verb *sich bilden* (to grow, form) in the sense that the goal of schooling and teaching is to support the growth of the potential of every individual. The function of the state, he maintained, should be to guarantee academic freedom for the learning and growth of the individual. Accordingly, the main purpose of the state was to establish boundaries for school education within which teaching and learning could develop without state control or prescription (see Humboldt 1964, *Werke*, Vol. I: 56–233). The idea of academic freedom and general education (*Allgemeinbildung*), as opposed to occupational training (*Berufsbildung*), was at the core of Humboldt's conception of a university where learning was based on the apprenticeship model and students formed a research group and learnt by assisting their professor in his research. During his short period as Prussian Minister, Humboldt framed a broad set of philosophical ideals for education and outlined more general structures for schools. For the practical applications of teaching and learning, Humboldt specifically referred to Pestalozzi's principles, and sent Prussian teacher trainees to Switzerland for instruction in methods of teaching.

Humboldt's conception of education was obviously not aligned to the official view and appeared somewhat subversive to state officials, with the result that Humboldt resigned after ten months in office. Some decades later another educational model came to the fore. During the time of *Kulturkampf* (cultural conflict) from 1866, Reichskanzler Otto von Bismarck (1815–1898) broke the nexus between church and state, and the school system became controlled by government (see Figure 3.5). This was part of the development of a new national identity in Germany (Prussia) during the nineteenth century. Given the emergence of a new nationalism, the singing of patriotic songs was employed to establish a sense of national identity among students and to imbue them with feelings of patriotism and loyalty and, as such, was made an obligatory part of what was by then a system of compulsory schooling for young people (Lemmermann 1984). Accordingly, the music curriculum for each administrative district consisted of a mandated repertoire

Figure 3.5 A school prior to the transfer of educational authority from church to state. In his (1858) print, Adolf Menzel depicts King Friedrich Wilhelm I of Prussia (1688–1740) visiting a typical village school. (© H. Schiffler and R. Winkler (1991), *Tausend Jahre Schule*, Stuttgart: Belser Verlag, reproduced with permission of Horst Schiffler.)

of songs that had to be memorized as well as a prescribed syllabus involving voice training (*Stimmbildung*), sight reading and music theory (scales and intervals) (Nolte 1975). However, singing was recognized as neither an artistic nor an academic subject, but rather as belonging to technical subjects such as calligraphy (*Schönschreiben*) and drawing.

The change in the function of music in schools from serving the church to serving the state effectively saw only a change in repertoire – namely from liturgical to patriotic and folksongs – and a change in purpose – singing at church services and on church holidays was replaced by singing at celebrations of national commemoration days. Otherwise, there were no significant changes in teaching and learning, which were mainly based on the materials of the particular subject matter (*materiale Bildung*) and the memorization of verbal knowledge such as music theory and song texts. Although the structural change in school policy affected the function and the content of music in schools, it did not impinge on the methods of teaching singing.

Music as part of general education

In 1924 the subject called 'singing' was redesignated as 'music' by the Prussian school reforms of Leo Kestenberg (1882–1962). Kestenberg was preoccupied by his belief in the power of a general public education (*Volksbildung*). As a Jewish musician who had studied with the pianist and composer Ferruccio Busoni (1866–1924), Kestenberg began his career as a brilliant pianist, but soon became deeply involved in educational and political issues associated with the Social-Democratic Party. He organized working-class concerts, designed cultural programmes in Berlin and was appointed in 1918 after the First World War as an Official Adviser for Music (*Musikreferent*) in the Prussian Ministry of Culture. From this position, he initiated a significant reform of music education that was outlined in a new policy for schooling in general and for music in particular when the subject was mandated as part of the curriculum.[3] When 'singing' was replaced by 'music' in the school curriculum, the intrinsic aesthetic aspects of music as an art form came to the fore. Consequently, the various musical genres available at that time (which, for the want of other forms of media, could only be performed on a piano) were incorporated into the curriculum and singing as such was no longer seen as the most appropriate form of musical expression to promote creative experience and intellectual understanding within the new educational order.

The new subject of 'music' continued to be mandated as part of the state-supported school system, although its function, content and methods were continually revised. In general, however, the fundamentals of school music in Germany were still based on Kestenberg's principles: (i) music was an artistic (as opposed to technical) subject; (ii) music was taught by an academically trained professional school music teacher who was also trained in a second academic subject (as opposed to a singing master only able to provide singing lessons); (iii) music teachers undertook training in artistic, scientific and pedagogic aspects of a comprehensive course of music teacher education. Kestenberg can therefore be accorded the status of founder of modern school music development in Germany[4] (see Gruhn 2004, 2015; Kestenberg 1921).

From an international perspective, it is surprising that neither the pedagogical methods of Carl Orff (1895–1982) nor those of Zoltán Kodály (1882–1967) had any direct influence on German music education. Although school music teachers make use of the Orff-type classroom instruments, the pedagogical *Orff Schulwerk* approach has never been formally introduced into German schools probably because the basic ideas under-pinning Orff's conception of musicianship were seen as being at odds with the innovative reform initiatives of the progressive education.

The implementation of the Kestenberg reforms in German schools slowed and finally ceased during the years of the Third Reich – the twelve years of Nazism did not witness any new educational paradigm. Because of a demarcation of responsibility for school education between the Ministry of Culture and the Nazi Party (NSDAP), the old syllabi continued to remain in place for some time under the authority of the Ministry of Culture. However, there were comparatively few teachers who were trained during the period of educational reforms who were able to implement classroom teaching according to Kestenberg's ideas (see Gruhn 2003: 259ff.) Although new curricula were issued between 1937 and 1942 (Gruhn 2003; Nolte 1975), it was only after the Second World War that the reform process could be renewed. This process was aided by the philosopher and sociologist Theodor W. Adorno (1903–1969), who, from his exiled home in America, addressed the main representatives of the old '*musische*' ideology in his *Thesen gegen die musikpädagogische Musik* (*Theses against pedagogical music*) (Adorno 1954/1973), in which he strongly criticized the aesthetic foundations of their educational philosophy and, by this, opened a general debate about music education and initiated an educational change in the 1960s.

Music and child-centred learning

Based on the ideas of *The Century of the Child (Barnets århundrade)* (Key 1900) and motivated by the challenge of the launch of Sputnik 1 by the Russians in 1957, a new model of child- and student-centred learning and teaching emerged as a result of innovative theories to emerge from cognitive developmental psychology. With regard to curriculum reform, the selection of the musical content and its relation to appropriate teaching methods had to be organized into a systematic teaching progression – a sequential and developmental curriculum as opposed to a canon of mandatory objects or contents. The development of new curricula – different in each of the German states – caused a radical change in the way that teaching was perceived as a legitimate profes-sional discipline. The focus on the development of the child's potential as an individual represented a totally new perspective and resulted in new materials, new textbooks and new pedagogical approaches (Gruhn 2003: 327ff.). As a consequence, new trends of youth culture, pop, rock and jazz, contemporary music, film music, music for use in commercials etc. as well as many possibilities of music production and perception were included in the curriculum. This changed the way music was recognized in schools. It was now predicated on enabling all students to participate in the broad variety of musical forms and practices within a democratic society. This has strongly influenced the principle of general music as an educational right offered to everybody as a compulsory subject in school.

Teacher training

It seems both reasonable and obvious that the various phases of music as part of a compulsory school education should be reflected in different models of teacher training. When the function of school music (then singing) was to serve church liturgical purposes, the teacher in elementary schools and the church organist (*Kantor*) were often one and the same person especially in smaller villages. It was common that the 'teacher–Kantor' who taught pupils in the school at the same time was organist and choir director in the church, especially in Saxonia.[5]

When the state took control of schools and the development of education became the responsibility of the Ministry of Culture, new training institutions were established, so-called teacher seminars (*Lehrerseminare*), where graduates from the so-called *Volksschule* (comprehensive elementary school) continued their education and were trained to teach all subjects, including singing. All teacher trainees were required to play an instrument (the organ for church services and the violin as a portable instrument for classroom teaching). They also received tuition in vocal music within teacher training programmes. The convention of a generalist elementary (primary) teacher who teaches all school subjects originates from this early model of teacher training.

With the broadening of curriculum content associated with the move from 'singing' to 'music', together with a further expansion to include the new challenge of 'arts education', additional demands were put on teacher training programmes. Today, music teachers – specifically those in secondary schools (so-called *Gymnasien*) – need to be trained as musicians first and then to specialize in music pedagogy. The requirement that secondary teachers should be highly trained musicians resulted from the intro-duction to the school curriculum of music from across a broad span of historical periods and incorporating a wide variety of genres. This approach also called for 'symphony concerts for children'[6] through which students were introduced to symphonic music. In order to prepare their students for these concerts, teachers were required to demon-strate the pieces by playing them from a piano score. Accordingly, secondary music teacher education programmes were established at music academies, which then became academic institutions (*Musikhochschulen*), equivalent to universities in status. Teachers in elementary schools were trained in new academies for teacher training (*Pädagogische Akademien*) where music was included as an elective study within the generalist training course. Later, these institutions became pedagogical universities (*Pädagogische Hochschulen*), which were then integrated into universities during the 1970s in most German states. It is not surprising, therefore, that a change of paradigm relating to the purpose, function and structure of music education in schools caused changes in teacher training courses. Music education as part of the general educational system has a strong social dimension and is therefore reflective of the prevailing social, political and socio-cultural context in Germany.

However, underlying the development of music in schools and in the social life of Germany, there is a common belief in the emotional power of music. This can be traced back to the late eighteenth century when, with the prevailing aesthetic of *Empfindsamkeit* (sensitive style), music was evaluated in terms of its emotional and affective power. Music was understood as a *language du coeur* (Rousseau 1782) or in Hegel's (1835) terms as *tönende Innerlichkeit* (sounding intimacy), which is still deeply engraved on the popular understanding of music and has resulted in the widely held belief that music in schools has an effect on *Charakterbildung* (formation of mind and personality). This has its origins in eighteenth-century aesthetics and perpetuates a belief in the earlier doctrine of embellishment and elevation as the main power of music that marks it as an indispensable part of a human being's physical and psychic endowment.

New directions in compulsory music education

Music as a compulsory school subject for all children became the new imperative and this brought with it new challenges and difficulties for educators. Several compelling questions arise:

- How can we understand the culture of the new generation?

- How can this youth culture be integrated into a school curriculum?

- How can music educators deal with questions of the divergent musical cultures in a globalized world that are reflected in contemporary classrooms?

It is not only a question of being able to motivate students, but also of connecting music in school with their individual life worlds (*Lebenswelt*), a term introduced by the philosopher Edmund Husserl (1859–1938). The dichotomy between the musical experience of everyday life and the demands of music as an art form collide in the classroom and result in a clash of contradictory cultures, a challenge that has to be met by the teacher. There are many inspiring and persuasive new ideas as to how students might be involved in music-making, but there are nevertheless significant problems in dealing with the demands of different cultures and the experiences of students in a methodically cogent manner.

Therefore, it must be noted that each model or paradigm creates its own problems, difficulties and challenges that must be solved within the environment of particular social, cultural and educational contexts. Mandatory classroom music as part of compulsory schooling produces a multitude of educational questions and demands because obligatory class music teaching is different from individual and presumably optional instrumental lessons. The two different but equivalent demands call for didactic solutions based on clearer insights into teaching and learning procedures that are nowadays being informed by the findings from ongoing brain research (see Gruhn and Rauscher 2008).

Conclusions and prospects

The review of music in compulsory education from a German perspective shows that curricular decisions and educational concepts are always embedded in a socio-cultural and historical context. The four dominant paradigms discussed in this chapter provide a broad perspective for music in compulsory schooling, but they do not offer one single convincing model of how music should be introduced into schools.

The present-day situation in Germany demonstrates a rather broad variety of educational policies, school structures and training programmes because of the cultural autonomy of the sixteen federal states. Generally, music in elementary education is compulsory either as a discrete subject or as part of a subject group (*Fächerverbund*) such as aesthetic education. It is normally taught by the generalist classroom teacher whose training will usually include some specialized music education input. However, although music is in principle a compulsory subject, in practice this is not always the case, due to the higher priority often afforded to a more generalist focus on curriculum implementation. In secondary education, the situation is even more confusing. There are several competing types of secondary schools (*Gymnasium* and many different types of so-called middle schools or *Realschulen*). The school structure and school curricula differ from state to state. Teacher training programmes are offered at various institutions: at Universities of Music (*Musikhochschulen*) as well as at Educational Universities (*Pädagogische Hochschulen*), or at regular universities. Each type of higher education institution offers a different focus with a result that artistically well-educated music teachers work side by side with teachers who received a more pedagogically based training. They all implement music as a compulsory subject and aim to provide a set of rich musical experiences for students both within and outside formal schooling. Therefore one can state that music still belongs to the core curriculum, which is mandatory at least until Grade (or Year) 10 in all types of secondary school in the various German states.[7]

Accordingly, music is present in all schools and every pupil receives a music education for at least several years in general music classes. School choirs, bands, orchestras are supplementary and may be chosen by the students according to their interests and abilities. String and wind classes have become very popular in recent times. This reflects a new trend toward practical music-making of all genres (classical, pop, folk, non-Western etc.) in the core curriculum. Additionally, a growing interest in early childhood music education (*Musikalische Früherziehung* or *Elementare Musikpädagogik*) is highly influential on pedagogical theory and practice. New practical materials, in-service training courses and extra-curricular activities have been established (Busch and Henzel 2012; Dartsch 2014; Ribke 2010). In connection with the focus on an early and practical introduction to Western musical culture, an increasing emphasis has been placed on pedagogical concepts as far as concerts for children are concerned (so-called *Konzert-Pädagogik*; see Stiller 2008).

During recent decades, there has been a discussion in some states about whether music should be integrated into the wider context of aesthetic education or alternatively could make a new subject area that relates to life sciences (biology, nature, culture). It is clear that such notions weaken the function of music as a compulsory subject. Where these ideas have been implemented as a result of 'political' decisions, the effect has been to reduce the number of specialist music teachers in elementary schools. This follows an all-too-common belief that one art form may be replaced by any other because all of them promote aesthetic development. There have been signs that this trend might be countered by the growing recognition of the powerful relationships between music education, brain functions and human development. However, it should be noted that this vision of neurodidactics (brain-based learning) is challenged by a critical neuroscience, which recognizes the limits of an understanding of learning in terms of neuronal activities.

What is needed in school music above all is genuine music learning. Perhaps the provision of practical experience in all genres of contemporary music is one way forward in the development of a powerful and sustainable programme of music in compulsory schooling.

Reflective questions

1 What has been the rationale for including singing in the school curriculum? What was its function within compulsory schooling in Germany in the eighteenth and nineteenth centuries? What do the four images presented in this chapter (Figures 3.1, 3.2, 3.3, 3.5) indicate regarding the role of singing in school life?

2 What can you identify as being the most important paradigm shift in compulsory music education in Germany during the early twentieth century?

3 Discuss the three fundamentals of school music that are based on Kestenberg's principles. How relevant are they today?

4 Music Education as Aesthetic Education; Music Education or Aesthetic Education? Discuss the aims of music education in the context of present-day philosophies of education.

Notes

1. As a matter of interest, it was a more or less literal translation of a local German singing instruction book by J. G. Kübler (1826) that laid the foundation for Lowell Mason's famous *Manual of the Boston Academy of Music* (1834). For further details, see Gruhn (1993) and Pemberton (1985).
2. The term *Volksbildung* is difficult to translate. It refers to the social aim of providing everybody, including those of the lower social classes, with the opportunity to participate in the values of education. The principle of *Volksbildung* is embedded in the ideals and mission of education within the labour movement during the late nineteenth and early twentieth centuries.
3. Because of the importance of Kestenberg as a leading figure in Prussian/German music education, his complete literary works are to be published in a four-volume edition. For volume 1, see Gruhn 2009.
4. Kestenberg expended the same effort in developing music education in Israel when he immigrated to Tel Aviv in 1938 and became an Israeli citizen immediately after the proclamation of the state of Israel in 1948.
5. One of the most prominent examples was Johann Sebastian Bach, who taught at the Thomas Schule and was music director at the four main churches in Leipzig.
6. Similar to the initiatives of Robert Mayer in England and Walter Damrosch in the USA, Richard Barth started his first *Volksschülerkonzerte* (concerts for pupils of elementary schools) in Hamburg 1899/1900 (see Gruhn 2003: 211).
7. As mentioned earlier, it is extremely difficult to present a general overview of the German school system and of music education as part of it because of the many differences resulting from the cultural sovereignty (*Kulturhoheit*) of the federal states. In general, there is the policy of a three-tiered school system consisting of the elementary school (*Grundschule*), which then divides into main (*Hauptschule*), middle (*Realschule*) and high school (*Gymnasium*), all of which offer different qualifications. However, there are other models in some states where main and middle schools are merged into a regional school (*Regionalschule*), or where a four-tiered system is established in which an integrative comprehensive school (*integrierte Gesamtschule*) parallels the *Gymnasium*.

References

Abs, T. (1811), *Darstellung meiner Anwendung der Pestalozzischen Bildungsmethode*, Halberstadt: Bureau für Literatur und Kunst.

Adorno, T. W. (1973), 'Thesen gegen die musikpädagogische Musik [1954]' in R. Tiedemann (ed.), *Gesammelte Schriften*, vol. 14, Frankfurt am Main: Suhrkamp, pp. 437–40. [First unauthorized publication *Junge Musik*, 1953/54, 111–13.]

Braun, G. (1957), *Die Schulmusikerziehung in Preußen*, Kassel: Bärenreiter.

Busch, B. and Ch. Henzel (eds) (2012), *Kindheit im Spiegel der Musikkultur* (Forum Musikpädagogik, Bd. 112), Augsburg: Wißner.

Dartsch, M. (ed.) (2014), *Musik im Vorschulalter*, Dokumentation. Kassel: Bosse.

Ehrenforth, K. H. (1995), *Geschichte der musikalischen Bildung: Eine Kultur-, Sozial- und Ideengeschichte in 40 Stationen von den antiken Hochkulturen bis zur Gegenwart*, Mainz: Schott.

Ehrenforth, K. H. (1997), 'Geschichte der Musikerziehung' in L. Finscher (ed.), *Die Musik in Geschichte und Gegenwart. Allgemeine Enzyklopädie der Musik*, vol. 6, Kassel and Stuttgart: Bärenreiter and Metzler, columns 1473–99.

Goethe, J. W. von (1821–9/1981), *Wilhelm Meisters Wanderjahre* in *Werke Hamburger Ausgabe*, vol. 8, Munich: Beck.

Gruhn, W. (1993), 'Is Lowell Mason's "Manual" based on Pestalozzian Principles?', *Bulletin of Historical Research in Music Education* 14 (2): 92–101.

Gruhn, W. (2003), *Geschichte der Musikerziehung. Eine Kultur- und Sozialgeschichte vom Gesangunterricht der Aufklärungspädagogik zu ästhetisch-kultureller Bildung*, Hofheim: Wolke.

Gruhn, W. (2004), 'Leo Kestenberg', *International Journal of Music Education* 22 (2): 103–29.

Gruhn, W. (ed.) (2009), *Leo Kestenberg. Gesammelte Schriften vol. 1, Die Hauptschriften*, Freiburg: Rombach.

Gruhn, W. (2015), *'Wir müssen lernen, in Fesseln zu tanzen.' Leo Kestenberg's Leben zwischen Kunst und Kulturpolitik*, Hofheim: Wolke.

Gruhn, W. and F. Rauscher (eds) (2008), *Neurosciences in Music Pedagogy*, New York: Nova Sciences.

Günther, U. (1967), *Die Schulmusikerziehung von der Kestenberg-Reform bis zum Ende des Dritten Reiches*, Neuwied: Luchterhand.

Hegel, G. F. W. (1835/1967), *Einleitung in die Ästhetik*, Munich: Fink.

Hientzsch, J. G. (1829/30), 'Der Gesang-Unterricht in Schulen', *Eutonia* (1) 1829, vol. 1, 42–9, 205–22; vol. 2, 210–31; *Eutonia* (2) 1830, vol. 3, 229–43.

Hohmann, C. H. (1838), *Praktischer Lehrgang für den Gesang-Unterricht in Volksschulen*, Nördlingen: Becksche Buchhandlung.

Humboldt, W. von (1960–4), *Werke in 5 Bänden*, Darmstadt: Wissenschaftliche Buchgesellschaft.

Kestenberg, L. (1921), *Musikerziehung und Musikpflege*, Leipzig: Quelle & Meyer.

Key, E. (1900), *The Century of the Child (Barnets århundrade)*. Stockholm: Albert Bonniers Förlag

Kübler, G. F. (1826), *Anleitung zum Gesang-Unterrichte in Schulen nebst einem Anhange von 55 zwei- und dreistimmigen Gesängen*, Stuttgart: Metzlersche Buchhandlung.

Lemmermann, H. (1984), *Kriegserziehung im Kaiserreich*, 2 vols, Bremen: Eres.

Mason, L. (1834), *Manual of the Boston Academy of Music for Instruction in the Elements of Vocal Music on the System of Pestalozzi*, Boston, MA: Wilkins & Carter.

Natorp, B. C. L. (1813, 1820), *Anleitung zur Unterweisung im Singen für Lehrer in Volksschulen*, Essen: Bädeker.

Nolte, E. (1975), *Lehrpläne und Richtlinien für den schulischen Musikunterricht in Deutschland vom Beginn des 19. Jahrhunderts bis in die Gegenwart* (Musikpädagogik. Forschung und Lehre, vol. 3), Mainz: Schott.

Nolte, E. (1982), *Die neuen Curricula, Lehrpläne und Richtlinien für den Musikunterricht an den allgemeinbildenden Schulen in der Bundesrepublik Deutschland und West-Berlin. Einführung und Dokumentation: Teil I: Primarstufe* (Musikpädagogik. Forschung und Lehre, vol. 16), Mainz: Schott.

Nolte, E. (1991), *Die neuen Curricula, Lehrpläne und Richtlinien für den Musikunterricht an den allgemeinbildenden Schulen in der Bundesrepublik Deutschland und West-Berlin, Teil II: Sekundarstufe I,3 Bde.* (Musikpädagogik. Forschung und Lehre, vol. 17), Mainz: Schott.

Pemberton, C. A. (1985), *Lowell Mason: His Life and Work*, Ann Arbor, MI: UMI Research Press.

Pfeiffer, M. T. and Nägeli, H. G. (1810), *Gesangbildungslehre nach Pestalozzischen Grundsätzen*, Zurich: Nägeli.

Ribke, J. (2010), *Elementare Musikpädagogik*, Regensburg: ConBrio.

Rousseau, J. J. (1782), 'Essai sur l'origine des langues', *Œuvres complètes*, vol. 16, Deux-Ponts, pp. 153–231.

Schiffler, H. and R. Winkler (1991), *Tausend Jahre Schule*, Stuttgart: Belser Verlag.

Schmidt, H.-C. (ed.) (1986), *Geschichte der Musikpädagogik (Handbuch der Musikpädagogik, Bd.1)*, Kassel: Bärenreiter.

Schulz, K. (1816), *Leitfaden bei der Gesanglehre nach der Elementarmethode mit besonderer Rücksicht auf Landschulen*, Leipzig: Darnmannsche Buchhandlung.

Sowa, G. (1973), *Anfänge institutioneller Musikerziehung in Deutschland (1800–1843)* (Studien zur Musikgeschichte des 19. Jahrhunderts, Bd. 33), Regensburg: Bosse.

Stiller, B. (2008), *Erlebnisraum Konzert. Prozesse der Musikvermittlung in Konzerten für Kinder*, Regensburg: ConBrio.

Zeller, C. A. (1810), 'Elemente der Musik' in *Beiträge zur Beförderung der Preußischen Nationalerziehung 4*, Heft, Königsberg.

Chapter 4

Ireland: Curriculum development in troubled times

Marie McCarthy

This chapter traces the history of music education in primary schools in Ireland from colonial times in the nineteenth century through the decades of cultural nationalism in late nineteenth- and early twentieth-century Ireland to political independence in 1921, which was followed by a wave of educational reform. Opening with the foundations of music in the curriculum of the National School System from the 1830s to the beginning of the 1870s, the narrative goes on to describe the plight of music in an era of accountability, and cultural nationalism and political upheaval between approximately 1870 and 1920. The following section documents educational reforms introduced in the newly established Irish Free State that impacted music education, culminating in 1926 with legislation for compulsory schooling for children aged six to fourteen years. Finally, the legacy of the past is viewed as gift and burden in light of contemporary music education. The chapter ends with reflections on one nation's story of the origins and foundations of music in compulsory schooling.

Introducing music into the National School System 1831–1871

Valuing music in the National School System

Ireland had been a colony of Britain for centuries before a national education system was put in place and any consideration of the role and nature of music in the community and in education must be made within this socio-political context. Through the agency of Lord Stanley, Chief Secretary for Ireland, the National School System was established in 1831 and a board of seven Commissioners of National Education was to represent various religious denominations in the country (Coolahan 1981: 12–13). Earlier efforts to provide schooling for the Irish were seen by the native people as a strategy to prose-lytize them and make them loyal subjects of the British Crown, so when the National School System was founded on non-denominational principles, with the goal of keeping religious instruction separate from literary and moral instruction, the native Irish remained suspicious, even though the members of the Board were drawn from various religious denominations to represent the total population.

As the National School System began to develop in the 1830s, there was considerable discussion about the value of including music in the curriculum and the most efficient method for teaching it. Values assigned to music were its strong humanistic base and its power to inculcate moral, religious and social values in the young. These values were central to discussions that guided the development of music in the National School System. In the *Report from the Select Committee on Foundation Schools and Education in Ireland* (National Commissioners of Education 1837), there are many references to the social influence of music on the lower classes of an increasingly industrialized society – how music would serve to humanize and civilize the people, provide them with a source of innocent recreation, elevate their lifestyle and social manners and, particularly in the Irish context, provide a pastime for those who spent too much time in the alehouses.

The importance of music as an adjunct to religious practice was also central to the report, but, given the sensitivity to religious matters in Ireland, this value was presented with great care. While the report of the Select Committee focused mostly on social, religious and moral values of music, Catholic MP Sir Thomas Wyse looked to the aesthetic and cultural aspects of a musical education. In his speech to the House of Commons in 1835, and in his book *Education Reform* in 1836, he presented his view of the state of Irish music and culture. As he looked around the country, he saw a gloomy picture of native musical culture, was critical of the standard of music in religious worship and asked why music-making was so rare and why musical taste was inferior. Based on the impoverished musical culture he saw, Wyse advocated an aesthetic approach to music education, one that would educate the 'whole spiritual man' and nurture 'all the finer perceptions and higher sensibilities' of human nature (Wyse 1836: 195, 197). Like most educated people at the time, he viewed folk traditions as unworthy of inclusion in popular education and omitted reference to the rich instrumental, song and dance folk traditions of the country. His emphasis on developing a love of the arts through education was a noble one, but perhaps premature for people who were struggling to make a living and as yet not literate or socially mobile as they later would become. As one school inspector later commented in this regard: 'So long as the children can read, write, calculate the price of a load of hay, or a bag of flour, they [parents] are perfectly satisfied' (*Annual Report of the Commissioners of National Education* 1863: 189; hereinafter referred to as *Annual Report*).

The introduction of music to the curriculum was surrounded by political, religious, economic and cultural tensions. In the official rhetoric, music was seen to elevate cultural taste, build moral fibre, provide an innocent pastime and improve church singing. However, these arguments were hardly relevant to the majority of communities in which national schools were established. The one context in which they were accepted was the model schools, a class of school originally set up in Dublin for teacher training purposes but which later spread to towns throughout the country *de facto* to serve the children of Anglo-Irish, middle-class families. It was in these model schools that music was first developed as a curricular subject beginning in the 1840s.

Finding a method for teaching music in the National School System

In the early nineteenth century, Britain depended heavily for its cultural and musical models on the continent, regarding its own music as inferior (Rainbow 1967). This was the case when the British Committee of Council on Education set out to find a method for teaching music. Having observed and reviewed many continental schemes, the Council sanctioned the use of the French Wilhem method – published in *Manuel Musical* – in 1840. In this method, modelled on teaching language, Wilhem (1836) approached music as a science and focused on breaking down music theory into a carefully planned sequence. A British version was prepared by John Hullah and published in 1842 as *Wilhem's Method of Teaching Singing*. It was granted government approval for use in British schools. Without further investigation or modification, it was adopted by the Commissioners of National Education in Ireland. Two Irish music teachers were sent to the Battersea Training College in Britain in 1840 to learn the method and bring it back into the model schools.

In addition to the pedantic, overly scientific nature of the method, an even greater problem with the Hullah approach was the content of the songs – these were songs that were created for use in British schools and were designed to illustrate theoretical aspects of music. After Head Inspector James Keenan listened to children singing these songs, he wrote that they 'do not pretend to any national character … are foreign to all sympathy … belong to no country… [and] are sung in no home' (*Twenty-Second Annual Report* [Appendix] 1855: 74). The weakening of identity with native Irish culture was one of the aims of the National School System and the teaching of Hullah's tunes was in accord with that aim. The method never took root in Irish education. An alternative song repertoire, Thomas Moore's *Irish Melodies*, released in ten volumes between 1808 and 1834, became popular in schools, as they were seen as being inoffensive, mildly nationalist in sentiment and classical in genre.

Barriers to the development of music in the curriculum

When examining the entry of music into national schools in Ireland beginning in the 1840s from an official vantage point, it seems to have been founded on a sound, comprehensive philosophy that was carefully constructed and supported and on a foreign teaching method that was well established. In reality, however, the introduction of music into the National School System was surrounded by barriers that worked against its widespread development – barriers caused by political mistrust, social and economic inequities, and diverse cultural values, religious beliefs and educational aspirations.

The use of religious music in the school song repertoire was treated with utmost sensitivity due to the socio-political implications of such repertoire and the goal of keeping religious instruction separate from literary and moral instruction. The use of music to elevate musical taste resonated with certain middle-class communities but not with the majority of the native, lower-class Irish. Promoting the national songs of the people brought up the question of whose nation. Whereas in Britain such songs were seen as an important means for engendering the national spirit and forming an industrious, loyal working class, the use of British national songs in Irish schools may have caused the native Irish to protest. At the same time, Irish national songs would be in direct opposition to the British policy of cultural assimilation. These were songs that may incite nationalism among the young Irish and contribute to advancing a rebellious spirit. Songs in the Irish language were of the peasant, suppressed class and not appropriate for a colonial educational system. In any case, a majority of parents were eager to have their children learn English in order to be economically mobile and prepared for emigration.

Music developed first in model schools where the middle-class values of Victorian society complemented those developed in the Hullah music curriculum. In the majority of ordinary national schools, however, the Hullah songs and method were culturally and socially foreign compared with the values of the majority of people and, in the end, the method failed. As denominational education developed during the nineteenth century and the Catholic clergy had more say in the running of national schools, Moore's melodies and songs of Irish origin were taught, using methods such as rote singing and John Curwen's tonic sol-fa system of sight singing.

Music and schooling in an era of accountability and political upheaval 1872–1921

Music in the payment-by-results system

In the period leading up to compulsory schooling – the decades of the late nineteenth and early twentieth centuries – music in primary or national schools came under the influence of the economic climate, changing educational philosophy and political nationalism. In 1872 a payment-by-results system was introduced into the National School System and continued until 1899, when it was abolished. Highly structured syllabi were laid down for each subject, board inspectors evaluated student progress regularly and teachers were paid according to pupils' results. As teachers' salaries were dependent on the results of their pupils, they were forced to comply with the system and to succumb to its regulations even if they were opposed to them.

The curricular status of music improved in 1883 when it was changed from being an 'extra' and therefore non-compulsory subject to being an 'ordinary and optional subject' – a subject that was accepted for examination along with the basic subjects. Commenting on the change of status for music, School Inspector Connellan considered it as 'the first recognition of what all educationalists and all men of reflection regard as one of the most potent and subtle elements of culture' (*Fiftieth Annual Report* [Appendix] 1883: 211). Yet, there were many obstacles impeding its development in the curriculum. Due to the focus on students' results, those aspects of music that could be standardized, quantified and measured were emphasized. When teachers put forward students for examination in music, there were additional risks when compared to other subjects.

Fees paid for pupils in the lower primary classes were dependent on the musical proficiency of pupils in the upper class levels and the annual gratuity for teaching music first
made available in 1859 was now granted only to teachers employed in model schools,
or teachers in ordinary national schools who taught music outside normal school hours
(*Thirty-Ninth Annual Report* 1872: 25).

The 'rote-note' controversy – singing by ear, as opposed to singing from staff notation
– was widely debated during this period of payment by results. Singing by rote was not
recognized as legitimate for examination purposes. Many teachers and inspectors criticized
this policy on the basis that in Britain, from 1882 onward, singing by rote gained half the fees
out of the possible grant for singing by note (Sneyd-Kynnersley 1908: 287). Many inspectors
believed that singing by note was inappropriate for primary-age children and they supported
the tonic sol-fa method because it was more accessible to them (*Fiftieth Annual Report*
[Appendix] 1883: 144). An inspector's report from Limerick in 1893 illustrated how singing
taught through tonic sol-fa before school hours improved school attendance and punctuality: 'The pupils are enthusiastic about Tonic Sol-fa; they beam with delight when asked
to sing by it. This ardour has been utilized to insure punctuality in several schools' (*Sixtieth
Annual Report* 1893: 234). Whether this practice was regional or national, it does provide
evidence of the success of the tonic sol-fa system, a method of sight singing that by the
end of the nineteenth century had received strong official support. In 1884 tonic sol-fa was
granted official recognition and a programme was designed for teachers using this method
(*Fifty-First Annual Report* [Appendix] 1884: 82–83). It became an institution of Irish primary
education until the introduction of *An Curaclam Nua* (*The New Curriculum*) in 1971.

During the payment-by-results era, teachers became discouraged and irate due to
new conditions (*The Irish Teachers' Journal* 12 April 1873; *Thirty-Ninth Annual Report*
[Appendix] 1872: 295). The number of pupils presented for music examinations
decreased in the 1870s and 1880s; at the same time, the percentage pass rate
increased, making the subject exclusive and serving a minority of students. By 1896, only
14 per cent of national schools presented students for music examination, compared to
99.8 per cent of schools in Britain and 96.6 per cent of schools in Scotland in the same
year (*Commissioners of National Education* 1898: 54). It is clear that music did not thrive
in national schools during the payment-by-results era. In 1899, music inspector Peter
Goodman advocated change in the approach to music in national schools, heralding
the new educational philosophy of the twentieth century after the abolition of payment by
results in the same year: He wrote: 'Would it not be well, therefore, to seek to make Music
loved and cherished in the school for its own sake … as a means of bringing pleasure
and happiness into the lives of the little ones' (*Sixty-Sixth Annual Report* 1899: 193).

Music, schooling and changing educational philosophy

The early twentieth century brought reform within education and much thought was given
to making the system democratic and more in touch with the realities of the surrounding

culture (Selleck 1968: 102–238). Music in national schools came under the influence of this new thinking – it began to be valued as a medium for establishing self and group discipline, confronting moral issues, and linking home, school and community. Attention was focused on the needs and characteristics of the child and the provision of age-appropriate instruction. At the same time, national schooling became increasingly associated with the process of nation building and the promotion of patriotism, civic responsibility and common national ideals. When taken as a whole, the new education movement addressed the total development of the child – physical, social, intellectual, aesthetic and emotional – and set it in the larger socio-cultural context.

Reflecting this new educational philosophy, vocal music became an obligatory subject of the new *Revised Programme of Instruction in National Schools* (Commissioners of National Education 1900) and the beginning years of the century were marked by waves of reform in school music.

The elitist attitude towards music that dominated previous decades gave way to a more democratic one. An effort to disseminate music to the remotest regions of the island was evident in the increasing percentage of schools that offered music instruction, from 17 per cent in 1899 to 78 per cent in 1907 (*Annual Reports* 1899, 1907).

To assist teachers with the goal of universal music education, the Commissioners of National Education provided an intensive programme of teacher in-service training. Between 1900 and 1904, 168 teachers' classes were held, attended by about 6,400 teachers, nearly equally distributed over all parts of Ireland. Care was taken to reach teachers in remote, rural districts, based on the assumption that 'outside the towns, Music in Ireland is practically an unknown art' (*Seventy-First Annual Report* 1904: 4). Tonic sol-fa was the recommended method of sight singing and Curwen's music education charts and modulators were supplied to schools.

In addition to vocal music, this period saw development in instrumental music in the National School System. While it had been granted status as an 'extra' subject in 1859, a new regulation of 1885 elevated it to a subject that could be taught to fifth and sixth classes within school hours. The curriculum described a two-year programme for piano similar to the syllabus of the Royal Irish Academy of Music and other colleges of music of the day (*Fifty-Fourth Annual Report* 1887: 69). Instrumental music was primarily available in the schools of affluent communities and in convent schools where 'daughters of respectable well-off parents had many opportunities for practising at home' (*Fifty-Eighth Annual Report* 1891: 322). The number of schools presenting pupils for examinations in instrumental music increased from 47 schools in 1884, to 168 in 1891, to 180 in 1899 (*Annual Reports* 1884, 1891, 1899).

School music attuned to the ideals of cultural nationalism

The nationalist movement of late nineteenth- and early twentieth-century Ireland impacted the course and direction of music in schooling. Literature on Irish education in the early years of the century reflected the country-wide preoccupation with nationalism (Ní Niocaill 1909: 258). The Gaelic League, founded in 1893, sought to revive Irish culture and build national identity. Primary schooling was seen as an important site for achieving such goals. Nationalists viewed music in the schools as a primary source for stimulating nationalist ideals, and the inheritance of native music traditions was considered central to the formation of Irish cultural identity.

A circular issued by the London Board of Education to teacher training colleges in Great Britain in 1902 suggested that students in teacher training should be impressed with the importance of passing on the national songs of England and Wales, Scotland and Ireland to the next generation, thus setting 'a wholesome standard in musical taste' (*Irish School Weekly*, 6 December 1902: 10). The 'wholesome standard' envisioned here through use of national music was not the standard embraced by Irish cultural nationalists. The political agenda of the London statement represented Ireland's continued union with Britain; the nationalist agenda was diametrically opposed to this, as its goal was independence from Britain.

The teaching of Irish music in the schools received support from the teaching profession, but certain challenges needed to be overcome before implementation could be effected. First, no general consensus existed as to what constituted Irish music, and opinions on the future of Irish traditional music varied. Second, it was only in 1904 that the Irish language was introduced into the schools as part of a bilingual programme, and much native song material had Irish lyrics. Third, a repertoire of Irish music appropriate for primary school pupils was needed. From the early years of the century, those who published song materials began to balance their collections between Irish language songs and Anglo-Irish music. Examples of such collections were Peter Goodman's *The Irish Minstrel* (1907) and Father Walsh's *Fuinn na Smól* (1913) and *Songs of the Gael* (1915).

Goodman's *The Irish Minstrel* served as a symbol of official recognition of native Irish music in the curriculum of national schools. Its exclusive focus on Irish songs and airs may be interpreted as a response to the demands of cultural nationalists. Viewed from another perspective, it may be seen as part of the wider British discourse on the use and value of folksong in education that was maintained during the early years of the century. A second song collector, Father Patrick Walsh [An tAthair Pádraig Breathnach], visited the Gaeltacht (Irish-speaking) regions of the island – 'those favoured glens and mountains where anglicisation has not yet triumphed' (Ó Casaide 1915: 33). There he transcribed songs that were still part of the living tradition and published them with tonic sol-fa notation in a series of seven booklets, *Fuinn na Smól* (1913). Recognizing that a great number of teachers and students did not understand the Irish language sufficiently well to be able to sing songs in Irish, he compiled another collection of 200 Anglo-Irish songs and ballads and wedded them to traditional Irish airs in *Songs of the Gael* (1915). Goodman and Walsh's efforts to provide Irish music for the national schools represent but a fraction of the rising tide of native Irish song materials in both languages in the early decades of the twentieth century.

Collections of hymns in the Irish language were also published – *Dia Linn Lá 'Gus Oídhche* (1917) and *Raint Amhrán* (1916–17). The provision of hymns in the Irish language in these decades was aimed at wedding Catholicism and nationalism and presenting them to the next generation as essential elements of Irishness. Irish-language songs and Catholic hymns, the staple diet of singing later in independent Ireland, were already established as the canon of Irish school music when the Irish Free State was established in 1921–2. Nationalist songs were also part of the canon, evident in the autobiographical writing of Patrick Shea (1908–86). Shea described his Irish childhood in Deerpark in the midlands and recalled a singing class at Deerpark National School around 1916: 'We fairly belted out "The Minstrel Boy", "Let Erin Remember", "A Nation Once Again", and, out of respect for the Principal's native county, "The Bells of Shandon"' (Shea 1987: 24).

A climate of war dominated the years between 1914 and 1921 – the First World War and the Irish War of Independence – and affected how music was perceived in the school curriculum. It brought a utilitarian mentality back into the education system. The 1916 Congress of the Irish National Teachers' Organisation was critical of the overloaded curriculum of the revised programme issued in 1900 and demanded a return to the basic subjects (*The Irish School Weekly*, 6 and 13 May 1916: 453). Music was once again relegated to the periphery as an additional subject, its availability dependent upon the staffing of the school and local needs and resources (*The Irish School Weekly*, 3 March 1917: 122).

On the positive side, the climate of war highlighted the power of school music to unite people for a common cause and to instil patriotic sentiments for the homeland. During the First World War, for example, many school concerts were organized 'on behalf of local distress caused through the war' (*The Irish School Weekly*, 3 October 1914: 714). In the early twentieth century, there is ample evidence to show the rise in popularity of the school concert, so that by 1907 Goodman wrote that it had become 'a fixed institution' in many places (*Seventy-Third Annual Report* 1906–7: 165). The school concert provided opportunities for the performance of instrumental music. Although class instruction in instrumental music was not organized officially in primary schools, it did occur haphazardly, its development dependent on individual teachers, school traditions or local musical traditions. While the first two decades of the twentieth century witnessed major developments in group instrumental teaching both in Europe and in the United States, political and economic conditions in Ireland did not support the development of instrumental music in formal education, and this absence marks a major difference between music education in Ireland and other Western countries to this day.

Educational reform in a new nation 1922–6

After the Irish gained independence from Britain and a provisional government was set up in the Irish Free State in late 1921 and early 1922, one of the first tasks was to reform the educational system and align it to nationalist goals. In January 1922 Pádraig

Ó Brolcháin, Chief Executive Officer of National Education, spoke to the agenda of education in the newly established state: 'It is the intention of the new Government to work with all its might for the strengthening of the national fibre, by giving the language, history, music and tradition of Ireland their natural place in the life of Irish schools' (*Commissioners of National Education* 1922: 2–3). Three aspects of this agenda influenced the course of music in primary education: the Irish language revival movement, the promotion of Catholic Church music and a national effort to improve musical culture and 'the national fibre'.

The language revival movement exerted the single most dominant influence in the early years of compulsory schooling in independent Ireland. Father Thomas Corcoran of University College Dublin, a zealot for language revival and an active educational policymaker (Corcoran 1923, 1933), acted as a consultant in the preparation of a new curriculum issued in 1922 – the National Programme of Primary Instruction. He advocated that 'the union of simple Irish with Irish music, in our Irish schools to-day, would certainly be the royal high road to the restoration of the spoken language and to the development of new literature, really Irish, for the people of Ireland' (Corcoran 1923: 340). The curriculum recommended that all songs taught should be in the Irish language and taught through the medium of Irish (National Programme Conference 1922: 14). This report was adopted by the government of the Irish Free State and came into operation in national schools on 1 April 1922. The tonic sol-fa system was already linked to the publication and teaching of Irish-language songs, and this practice of teaching song continued.

Catholicism, a second marker of Irish identity, also affected the direction of music in Irish culture and education in the Free State, in particular through the singing of hymns and the Plain Chant movement (Rooney 1952: 19–21). In 1926, Father John Burke, Dean of University College Dublin, founded a summer school of plain song. Liturgical festivals were developed in many provincial centres such as Tuam, Ennis, Limerick and Kilkenny – festivals that were characterized by the 'massed singing of the Ordinary of the Mass by thousands of children' (Rooney 1952: 219).

A third influential factor in national education was the effort to change the musical image of Ireland. At the 1926 Annual Congress of the Irish National Teachers' Organisation, Cork school teacher Denis Breen (Donnchadh Ó Braoin) focused on the 'national indifference to and contempt for music' and argued that the state of music in education was a reflection of its state in national life, each institution being 'a little microcosm of the people with all their faults and virtues displayed' (Breen 1926a: 558). From the beginning of the National School System, blame had been placed on music in education for this state of affairs. Now the blame was shifted to the lack of national policy. School music, Breen said, would remain mere school work 'unless it is vitalized by contact with some more significant activity from outside – some trend of the national will, some settled desire of the people, some movement sufficiently powerful to keep itself from decay or destruction in the hurly-burly of life' (Breen 1926a: 558). What was needed, in his opinion, was a comprehensive national policy for music in order to defeat the 'universal indifference' toward music so obvious in Irish life – 'a result of causes historical and otherwise with which all are familiar' (Breen 1926b: 620).

In a sense, national or primary schools had indeed contributed to the development of national life in their traditions of school concerts and participation in festivals and competitions from the 1880s onwards. These traditions received a further impetus with the establishment of the Irish Free State. In 1925 the Cork School Music Committee, chaired by Breen himself, organized a school choir concert in Cork and 200 pupils were drawn from various schools in the city. In addition to the massed schools' choir, other items were featured in the programme – two convent choirs, instrumental selections, a play in Irish and Irish step-dancing. This model, one observer remarked, was 'probably the first attempt of its kind in Ireland', with implications 'whose limits are not easily defined' (*The Irish School Weekly*, 11 July 1925: 852). Such events became popular in independent Ireland.

When compulsory school attendance legislation was introduced by the Department of Education in 1926, music held a firm footing in the curriculum, less as a subject in its own right and more as a servant to the advancement of nationalist ideals of language revival, the development of a Catholic ethos in school and society and the improvement of Ireland's musical image and culture.

The gift and burden of the past, legacy for the present

From the beginning of a national state-sponsored education system in 1831, music had a place in the curriculum, albeit not as a compulsory subject. Its development was impeded by a number of political, religious and cultural factors. Among them were the use of song repertoire that reproduced colonial values not accepted by the native Irish, the use of an inappropriate method to teach music and the negative effects of the payment-by-results system on music as a school subject. As schooling became *de facto* denominational in the mid-nineteenth century and Catholic orders played a more significant role in primary education, repertoire associated with Irish native culture and heritage began to be transmitted in national schools and the use of the Curwen tonic sol-fa system proved to be accessible to teachers and students alike.

In 1900 vocal music was introduced as a compulsory subject and subsequently gained a greater presence in the national curriculum. This reflected a change in educational philosophy and coincided favourably with the rise of cultural and political nationalism. The climate of world war caused educators to turn again to a basic curriculum and the climate of the local war of independence focused the music curriculum on songs that advanced nationalist ideology. When compulsory education for six to fourteen year olds was introduced in 1926, music lost its compulsory status and was not regarded as a basic subject. However, its role in the curriculum was regarded as vital to the core agenda of reviving the Irish language and promoting a Catholic ethos.

Music education in every nation is shaped by its past – the gifts transmitted as well as the burdens inherited. Contemporary developments in music education are in many respects continuous with the past. A national curriculum is issued by the Department of Education. The curriculum for primary education includes music as a key area of arts education. The music curriculum for primary schools functions separately from that of secondary schools. The current music curriculum at the primary level was introduced as part of the Primary School Curriculum issued in 1999. At the secondary level, the current Junior Cycle syllabus was implemented in 1989 and the Senior Cycle syllabus in 1996 (National Council for Curriculum and Assessment). Music in primary education has received considerable attention in the research literature, from concerns about gener-alists teaching music (Buckley 2005) to the implementation of the 1999 music curriculum (Buckley 2005; O'Kelly 2002), the contribution of sol-fa to music education (Shaughnessy 2012) and the role of the community in advancing music education (Finnerty 2008). At the secondary level, topics such as the role of the religious in secondary school music (Feehan 2003), learning Irish traditional music (Johnston 2013) and government policy and syllabi development (Lane 2005) have been investigated.

Issues surrounding cultural nationalism, language and religion were ongoing concerns in colonial and early independent Ireland and they now provide a foundation for rich historical research topics in music education (Magner 1998). In a post-colonial, post-nationalist Ireland, topics such as Irish language songs and Catholic hymns no longer dominate the curriculum. However, with an influx of immigrants early in the twenty-first century, different kinds of issues regarding cultural and musical diversity surfaced, including the recognition of multiple nationalities in the school curriculum (More 2005; Doyle 2012). Connections between school and community have deep roots, particularly in the context of national schools and their close connections to the Catholic parish in which they were located. Such connections are now less focused on the parochial context. Other networks such as Arts Councils and community groups feature in the overall advancement of music education. One project that has gained much attention is Music Generation (Music Network 2015), a five-year programme (2010–15) initiated by Music Network and co-funded by the pop music group U2 and The Ireland Funds together with the Department of Education and Skills and local Music Education Partnerships (MEP). Within this national network, the programme helps children and youth to access music education in their own locality (Music Network). The local community is at the heart of Irish social life and the model of the MEP aligns well with promoting music education at that level. This initiative begins to address the underdeveloped system of instrumental music instruction in primary and secondary education.

Reflections on one nation's story

The historical case study of music and compulsory schooling in Ireland illustrates that music is a curricular subject that is deeply implicated with political ideologies, economic realities and socio-cultural values. When it enters the public space of schooling, its use continues to be grounded in those values. In the troubled times of nineteenth-century Ireland, the native Irish opposed any attempt on the part of Britain to advance an educational agenda that was perceived as increasing colonial control. The development of music was impeded on many fronts and not until the hidden curriculum rooted in colonial political ideology was no longer in place and Ireland gained political independence from Britain did compulsory education become legislated. And in that new brave world, the music curriculum was dominated by a political agenda aligned with the values of a new independent nation state.

Evidence from this narrative also points to the complicated and vulnerable nature of music as a school subject and the contradictions that inhere in its status as a school subject. Music education rides the waves with the values that dominate schooling and society. When a colonial agenda was associated with the goals of music education, teachers focused on non-controversial and 'safe' aspects of the subject matter; when an era of accountability set in and teachers were paid based on student examination results, music was treated as an examination subject but with several conditions not applied to other subjects. As the curriculum broadened to be more child-centred, vocal music became obligatory, but after an exploratory phase the reins were pulled in and music again lost its core status. When a nationalist agenda dictated educational values in independent Ireland and compulsory schooling was introduced, music regained its status quickly as it served a new political agenda. In post-nationalist Ireland, the political burdens associated with past practice such as native language and religion no longer dominate the selection of curriculum content.

The troubled times of nineteenth- and early twentieth-century Ireland complicated the introduction of compulsory schooling, yet music found its way into various types of national schools. The narrative of music in Irish schooling reflects a far more complicated set of values than those that were inherent in one legislative act to make school attendance compulsory.

Reflective questions

1 How was music advocated for inclusion in the curriculum of the National School System in the 1830s? In what ways were the underlying values similar to and different from those used to advocate music in the first national education system in your country or in other countries described in this book? Compare the values of music education at that time with those present in contemporary music education.

2 The development of music in education in the nineteenth century
   was surrounded by barriers, such as the mistrust of some native
   Irish in a colonial education system, the clash of musical cultures
   between home and school, and the sensitivity around teaching
   songs that were perceived as indoctrinatory. Such barriers bring
   into the foreground the power of music learning to inculcate values.
   In the narrative of music education in your nation, identify a time
   when music education served to indoctrinate particular political,
   social, cultural or religious values. Evaluate the impact of that effort
   and identify traces that may continue to be relevant today.
3 Each nation or country has its own history of music education
   with a legacy that music educators inherit. What aspect of the
   music education legacy from this historical narrative resonates
   with your nation's music education history? What do you consider
   to be a unique aspect of Ireland's story? What insights can music
   educators in other countries gain from it?
4 One of the distinctive and consistent features of music education
   in Ireland is that generalist teachers are responsible for teaching
   music in primary schools. What challenges did generalist teachers
   face in different historical eras? What does the Irish case study
   contribute to the generalist–specialist debate about music
   teaching at the primary level?

References

Breen, D. (1926a), 'School-music: Its Place in the National Life', *The Irish School Weekly* 77
    (1 May): 558.
Breen, D. (1926b), 'School-music: Its Place in the National Life', *The Irish School Weekly* 77
    (15 May): 620.
Buckley, M. (2005), 'Music education in an Irish context: perspectives on musical and
    pedagogical implications of the 1999 curriculum for primary teachers' (unpublished MA thesis,
    Mary Immaculate College, University of Limerick).
Commissioners of National Education (1834–1921), *Annual Reports,* Dublin: Office of National
    Education.
Commissioners of National Education (1898), *Final Report of Royal Commission on Manual and
    Practical Instruction in Primary Schools*, Dublin: Office of National Education.
Commissioners of National Education (1900), 'Revised programme of instruction in national
    schools', in *Annual Reports 1900–1901 (Appendix)*, Dublin: Office of National Education.
Commissioners of National Education (1922), *Minutes of the Proceedings of the Commissioners
    of National Education at their Special Meeting on Tuesday, the 31st January, 1922*, Dublin:
    Office of National Education.
Coolahan, J. (1981), *Irish Education: History and Structure*, Dublin: Institute of Public
    Administration.

Corcoran, T. (1923), 'Music and Language in Irish Schools', *The Irish Monthly* 51 (July): 338–40.

Corcoran, T. (1933), 'National Literature Through National Music', *The Irish Monthly* 61 (July): 410–12.

Crosbie, P. (1981), *Your Dinner's Poured Out*, Dublin: O'Brien Press.

Dia Linn Lá 'Gus Óidhche's Pádraig Aspal Éireann (1917), Baile Átha Cliath: Brún agus Ó Nualláin Teor.

Doyle, C. (2012), 'Primary teachers' experiences of and attitudes to multicultural music education: a case study of urban and rural contexts' (unpublished MA thesis, Mary Immaculate College, University of Limerick).

Feehan, U. (2003), 'The correlation between the decline of the religious orders and the decline of music in secondary schools' (unpublished MA thesis, Mary Immaculate College, University of Limerick).

Finnerty, M. (2008), 'Connecting community and curriculum: the role of music in primary level education in Ireland' (unpublished MPhil thesis, University College, Cork).

Goodman, P. (1907), *The Irish Minstrel: A Collection of Songs for Use in Irish Schools*, sel. and arr. by P. Goodman, Dublin: M. H. Gill.

Hullah, J. (1842/1983), *Wilhem's Method of Teaching Singing*, intro. B. Rainbow, Kilkenny: Boethius Press.

Irish School Weekly, The (1902), 'Circular to training colleges – music', 6 December, 10.

Irish School Weekly, The (1914), 'A new song', 3 October, 714.

Irish School Weekly, The (1916), 'Irish National Teachers' Organisation Congress: an influential gathering', 6 and 13 May, 453.

Irish School Weekly, The (1917), 'Memorandum on suggested changes in present school programmes', 3 March, 122.

Irish School Weekly, The (1925), 'Cuirm ceoil: Successful schools' concert in Cork', 11 July, 852.

Irish Teachers' Journal, The (1873), 'Drawing and singing of national schools', 12 April, 101.

Johnston, T. (2013), 'The bloom of youth: Conceptualising a theory of educative experience for Irish traditional music in post-primary music education in Ireland' (unpublished PhD dissertation, University of Limerick).

Journal of the Ivernian Society (1909), 'Notes', 2 (October), 124.

Lane, S. (2005), 'Government policy on Irish music education at second-level since 1921' (unpublished MA thesis, Cork School of Music, Cork Institute of Technology).

Magner, E. (1998), 'The Irish language in primary education: pedagogical aspects of the application of songs in the teaching of Irish' (unpublished MA thesis, Mary Immaculate College, University of Limerick).

Moore, T. (1834), *Irish Melodies*, London: Power & Longman, Rees, Orme, Brown & Green.

More, G. (2005), 'Exploring the relevance of multicultural music education to contemporary Irish society with particular reference to the experiences and attitudes of second level music teachers' (unpublished MA thesis, Mary Immaculate College, University of Limerick).

Music Network (2015), 'Music generation: making music education happen', http://www.musicgeneration.ie (accessed 29 April 2015).

National Commissioners of Education (1837), *Report from the Select Committee (of the House of Commons) on Foundation Schools and Education in Ireland. House of Commons* (H. C. 701).

National Council for Curriculum and Assessment, *Curriculum Online*. Dublin: NCCA http://www.curriculumonline.ie (accessed 6 April 2015).

National Programme Conference (1922), *National Programme of Primary Instruction*, Dublin: Browne & Nolan.

Ní Niocaill, E. (1909), 'Nationality in Irish Education', *Irisleabhar na Gaedhilge* 19 (19 Meitheamh): 258.

Ó Casaide, S. (1915), 'Father Walsh's Irish Song Books', *Irish Book Lover* 7 (September): 33.

O'Kelly, U. M. (2002), 'Listening and responding to music in the revised primary school curriculum (1999): a case study in music development' (unpublished MEd thesis, St Patrick's College, Dublin City University).

Rainbow, B. (1967), *The Land without Music: Musical Education in England 1800–1860 and its Continental Antecedents*, London: Novello.

Rooney, H. (1952), 'The Plainchant Movement' in A. Fleischmann (ed.), *Music in Ireland*, Cork: Cork University Press, pp. 218–21.

Selleck, R. J. W. (1968), *The New Education 1870–1914*, London and Melbourne: Pitman & Sons Ltd.

Shaughnessy, N. (2012), 'Sing it in solfa: the contribution of solfa teaching on primary school children's music literacy development' (unpublished MA thesis, Mary Immaculate College, University of Limerick).

Shea, P. (1987), 'Sounds of Thunder, from Voices and the Sound of Drums' in A. N. Jeffares and A. Kamm (eds), *An Irish Childhood*, London: Collins Sons & Co. Ltd, pp. 272–6.

Sneyd-Kynnersley, E. M. (1908*), H. M. I.: Some Passages in the Life of One of H. M. Inspectors of Schools*, London: Macmillan & Co. Ltd.

Walsh, P. [An tAthair Pádraig Breathnach] (1913), *Fuinn na Smól*, Dublin: Browne & Nolan.

Walsh, P. [An tAthair Pádraig Breathnach] (1915), *Songs of the Gael*, Dublin: Browne & Nolan.

Walsh, P. [An tAthair Pádraig Breathnach] (1916–17), *Raint Amhráin*, Cuid a I-IV, Dublin: Irish Education Co. [Comhlucht Oideachais ha hÉireann].

Wilhem, G. B. (1836), *Manuel de Lecture Musicale et de Chant Élémentaire á 'Usage des Collèges, des Institutions, des Écoles et des Cours de Chant (...)*, Paris: Perrotin.

Wyse, T. (1836), *Education Reform*, London: Longman.

Chapter 5

Kosovo: A struggle for freedom and national identity

Besa Luzha

This chapter examines the effects of historical and political changes on the development of compulsory school music education in Kosovo. The central argument is that music education in Kosovo was mainly used as a tool for constructing specific forms of the collective identity of Kosovo Albanians, depending on the different regimes that ruled over Kosovo in the twentieth century and the early years of the present century.

Kosovo: The socio-political and historical context

Kosovo is a small, land-locked country situated in south-east Europe and the Balkan Peninsula (Bjelic and Savic 2002), identified as a crossroads between West and East, geographically, politically and culturally. As a result of its geographical position and because it was ruled by several very different regimes, Kosovo remained for a long time largely rural and underdeveloped, with a mainly illiterate population (Judah 2008; Malcolm 1998). Its majority population today is ethnic Albanians (90 per cent), part of the 'Albanian nation', described by Noel Malcolm as 'one of the oldest established populations in Europe ... to have inhabited the territory of Kosovo since antiquity' (Malcolm 1998: ii). The other 10 per cent of the population includes such minorities as Serbs, Bosnians, Turks, Gorani and Roma. In the last two centuries Kosovo was driven by disputes mainly between ethnic Albanians and ethnic Serbs over autochthony and the right to rule the territory, thus shaping all aspects of Kosovan society, including education (Glenny 2001; Pettifer 2001).

Kosovo was excluded from the formally recognised borders of Albania in 1912, when the Albanian state was finally recognised and approved by the Conference of Ambassadors held in London, and afterwards in Berlin in 1912–13 (Judah 2002, 2008; Misha 2002), ending the Ottoman rule over Albania. Kosovo was left as part of Serbia, later known as the Kingdom of Serbs, Croats and Slovenes (Old Yugoslavia). At the end of the Second World War (1945), Kosovo became part of the Yugoslav Socialist Federation, as a province of the Republic of Serbia (Bacevic 2014; Schmitt 2012). When Yugoslavia finally dissolved in 1990, Kosovo remained as part of the Republic of Serbia and Montenegro, a union of two of the former six republics of the former Yugoslav Federation (see Troebst 1999).

Kosovo Albanians faced systematic oppression by the former Old Serb, Yugoslav and Serb regimes, including the spheres of education and culture (Malcolm 1998; Kostovicova 2002, 2005). This oppression increased in the last decade of the twentieth century (1989–99), culminating with an 'ethnic cleansing' campaign launched by the Serb regime, as a culmination of the 'repression, resistance, rebellion and eventually open conflict [that had] engulfed the population of Kosovo for at least a decade before' (Sommers and Buckland 2004: 24).

The ethnic cleansing campaign was brought to an end by the timely intervention of the NATO (North Atlantic Treaty Organization) peace-keeping force authorized in 1999 by the United Nations (UN) Security Council Resolution 1244. Kosovo was finally liberated on 10 June 1999, but continued to be administered by the UN in attempts to restore the peace and to build a democratic system. In 2008, after eight years of international protectorate rule, Kosovo finally achieved statehood by declaring its independence and being recognized by more than 108 countries worldwide. It is still striving for greater international recognition and aiming to become a full member of the UN and of the EU. The 'battle' between Kosovo and Serbia over the right to rule the territory and its people goes on today through the political dialogue between the two countries moderated by the EU (Bassuener and Weber 2013).

Preserving Albanian national identity (1807–1945)

Archival documents show that the curriculum of the first officially established Albanian school in 1807 (Myzyri 1978, 2004) included music instruction in the Albanian language. The subject was named *këngë* (song) and focused entirely on patriotic and secular folk songs as tools for cherishing and preserving Albanian national identity, language and culture.

Between the First World War and the end of the Second World War, the territory of Kosovo was temporarily ruled by a number of countries including Austro-Hungary, Bulgaria, Italy and Germany (Blumi 2002; Rexhepagic 1970). With agreement of these authorities, any schooling in Albanian that was operating in Kosovo was carried out under the auspices of the Albanian government. There were 173 primary schools in Kosovo, providing education in the Albanian language with the help of the Albanian government, which sent teachers, textbooks and teaching materials. The first books with Albanian songs for primary schools (*Këngëtore*) were published in 1923 and 1925 (Ministria e Arsimit 1925), followed in 1935 by the first book in Albanian on music teaching for secondary schools (Filaj 1935).

During the years between 1941 and 1944 primary schools provided education for pupils in Grades 1–5. The diary of a local teacher, Selami Hallaqi, detailed the titles of songs planned to be taught in the first grade in 1944, including such partizan songs as

'Malet me blerim mbuluar' ('Mountains covered with green') and 'Partizani i vogel ne lufte po shkonte' ('A young partisan is going to war') (Luzha 2005). Another source describes a moment when pupils 'marched beautifully in harmony with the rhythm of Albanian songs' (Veseli 2003: 31).

As far as the training of music teachers was concerned, the Law on Secondary School Reform in Albania (1938), which also affected Kosovo schools, provided for music education at the gymnasium level. The Normal Albanian School, 'Sami Frasheri', in Prishtina (1941–4) (Rexhepi 2014) was the only institution eligible to prepare teachers for elementary school and pre-school levels. The subject was called *Elementet e muzikës dhe këngë* (Music Elements and Song) for the lower grades and *Muzika dhe Kënga* (Music and Song) for the higher grades (ibid.). *Muzika instrumentale* (Instrumental Music) was added in the new Normal Schools in Kosovo in the following years (Rexhepagic et al. 1997; Veseli 2003).

One of the foremost music teachers at this time was Lorenc Antoni (1909–91), a composer, ethnomusicologist and choir leader who laid the cornerstone of music education in Kosovo. He taught music in primary schools in various Kosovo cities and also at the Normal School of Prishtina, 'Sami Frasheri', (Koci 2011; Rexhepagic et al. 1997). Many professional development courses were offered for teachers at the time that also included some music sessions. Teachers were taught to play instruments such as the guitar, violin or mandolin in order to accompany singing as well as learning music notation (Qosja et al. 2007; Vokrri 2004).

Music education under the Socialist Yugoslav Federation (1945–90)

Acculturation and assimilation (1945–68)

With the ending of the Second World War in 1945, Kosovo officially became part of the Socialist Yugoslav Federation (1945–90), and a new Kosovo education system was established. The Yugoslav regime specifically targeted Albanian ethnicity in Yugoslavia for the purposes of acculturation and assimilation (Kostovicova 2002, 2005; Spahiu 2012). Albanians in Kosovo were forced to suppress their national identity in favour of the Yugoslav and internationalist (Communist) identity that was being indoctrinated through schools and education policies, very often through music and songs.

Many of the songs Albanian school children in Kosovo were required to sing celebrated brotherhood between Albanians, Serbs and other Yugoslavian nationalities (Luzha 2008; Spahiu 2012). These included such songs as 'Hej Slaveni' ('Hej Slavs'), which was the national anthem of Yugoslavia, and other similar songs that celebrated the victory of Communism. Choral singing was one of the key school activities in these years.

The first specialist music school was opened in Prizren in 1948, under the direction of Lorenc Antoni, and another one year later in Prishtina (Berisha 2004). These were the first institutions in which specialized music instruction was offered.

Many school teachers played an active role in amateur music groups. For example, Lorenc Antoni led the mixed choir 'Agimi' in Prizren city, and at the same time arranged Albanian folk songs for it. In 1953 he also translated the book *Bazat e teorisë muzikore* (*The Basis of Music Theory*) by the Serb author Marko Tajçeviq, which is considered as a most important contribution to the development of music education in Kosovo (Spahiu 2012). Despite all the difficulties in these years, music enjoyed an important position in schools, since the Communist ideology regarded music as an effective means of indoctrinating young people in its ideals and in the development of brotherhood among Albanians and other communities in Yugoslavia.

In 1948 the Albanian curriculum that had been implemented in schools in Kosovo was finally discontinued as a result of political developments of the time: while Albania adopted the Stalinist approach to Communism, Yugoslavia resisted it. This initiated full physical and spiritual separation and non-cooperation between Albania and Yugoslavia, therefore Kosovo Albanians were not allowed any physical or cultural contacts (including a ban on textbooks and other education materials) with their co-patriots in Albania.

In 1959, the new curriculum in Serbia (which was also transferred to Kosovo) advanced the structure and scope of music education, changing the name of the subject from *Këngë* (Song) to *Edukatë muzikore* (Music Education), in which the main components were singing, playing instruments, music listening and musical creativity. A further curriculum revision in 1965 placed an emphasis upon aesthetic education through the arts, and it was requested that such subjects should be taught by specialists. However, there was a gap in all this between curriculum statements and classroom practice. The generally difficult situation in the schools in Kosovo, with a lack of qualified teachers, made it hard to implement what was a generally progressive but ideologically influenced curriculum.

A degree of liberalism (1969–80)

The general frustration and anger among Kosovo Albanians towards the Serb–Yugoslav regime, which treated them as second-class citizens and did not allow them to express their Albanian national and ethnic identity explicitly, resulted in a massive demonstration organized by the Albanian population in Kosovo in 1968 (Schmitt 2012).

The demonstrators protested about their oppression by singing Albanian patriotic songs, and required the right to have higher education in their native Albanian language. This unrest resulted in the granting of certain political and cultural rights, which were regarded as an important advancement of Kosovo's political status undertaken by the Yugoslav government, led by Communist leader President Tito.

The new political status brought a variety of positive changes for the life of Kosovo Albanians, including the opening of the University of Prishtina in 1970, the first and only higher education institution in Kosovo that offered instruction in both official languages (Albanian and Serb). Further changes to the Yugoslav constitution in 1974 lead to a

USHTARËT E VEGJËL

Sod ne përpara në hap marshojmë,
nëpër fusha dhe kodrina
kangë të re këndojmë.

Tra ta ta, tra ta ta, tra ta,
k'shtu ndigjohet tash burija,
n'sulme shkon ushtrija.

Topat kërcasin, shokët thërrasin:
„Tash anmikun ne ta sulmojm'
luftën ta fitojm'."

Figure 5.1 'Ushtarët e Vegjël' ('Little Soldiers'), a song in the Albanian language in the first music textbook for schools in Kosovo (Grades III and IV). It is based on a march rhythm and calls little soldiers to unite and fight the enemy. As indicated, it was a song written by a Yugoslav composer, but the text was adapted by authors of the textbook. (Source: Kaçinari, M. and V. Gjini (1968), *Libër i Edukatës Muzikore Për klasën III dhe IV të Shkollës Fillore* (*Music Education Textbook for Grades III and IV for Primary Schools*), Prishtina: Enti i Teksteve dhe i Mjeteve Mësimore i KSA të Kosovës [The Institute for Textbooks and Teaching Resources of KSA Kosovo], p. 58; reproduced with permission.)

degree of liberalism in education and communications, which ensured a flourishing development of education and culture in Kosovo. The local authorities used these new political circumstances to develop education, science and culture under the newly decentralized, local, self-governing regime granted to Kosovo as a unit of the Yugoslavia Federation (Bacevic 2014).

The role of music education in this period changed accordingly so as to emphasize the philosophies of the time, such as the promotion of the aesthetic and cognitive functions of music, and the ways in which, as a school subject, music could contribute to students' all-round education (Luzha 2005; Spahiu 2012). Music teachers were trained initially in the Department for Music Pedagogy within High Pedagogical Schools. Later, music teachers received their training in the Music Department within the University of Prishtina, at the Academy of Arts, established in 1975 (Vokrri 2004; Luzha 2015).

During this period, music education attracted considerable attention as a compulsory subject in Yugoslav schools, and therefore also in Kosovo. It became more multidimensional so as to include several components, such as understanding and applying elements of music theory, basic skills of reading and writing of music, and singing and playing instruments (Orff instruments and national folk instruments in particular), as well as creative listening and the appreciation of the music of the Yugoslav nations and nationalities (Luzha 2005). However, because of music's 'uncanny potential to attract, catch, and collect symbolic meanings' (Keller 2007: 93), the 'Yugoslav education experiments' (Cowen 2000) still employed music education as an ideological influence in school.

In 1977, for the first time, Kosovo authorites were free to develop their own curriculum, although the main content was developed by Serb experts. Local communities, however, were allowed to choose the music content that they thought would be appropriate for their pupils (Spahiu 2012). The content of songs related to the overall aims of Communism, but Albanian folk and composed songs were also included. The overall aim of music education was to reinforce Yugoslav patriotism through exposure to the different musics of the Yugoslav nations (see Figure 5.1, a song about 'little soldiers' uniting to fight the enemy).

Choral singing competitions, music ensembles and folk music ensembles were regular 'free activities' in schools, and there was not so much censorship over musical content and expression as there had been previously. Music literature used in schools included secular music but also the master works of European vocal church music, especially those appropriate to be sung by school choirs. Furthermore, the number of Albanian pupils enrolling in professional music schools grew considerably (Luzha 2005; Spahiu 2012). The music teaching methods employed in public schools were a replication of those used in schools in Serbia, Croatia, Slovenia and other Yugoslav republics. They included both the 'movable doh' methods of tonika-do and tonic sol-fa, and the 'fixed-doh' method of *solfège*. There was also an original method of intonation through 'song models' initially developed from Miodrag Vaslijevic in Croatia, then replicated in Kosovo, but using Albanian didactic songs created by Mark Kaçinari and Lorenc Antoni (see Figure 5.2). The method was based on Guido d'Arezzo's principle of association with the starting tone of short songs, learned by heart, and repeated until learned thoroughly, after which the tones using *solfège* syllables (do, re, mi, fa sol, la, si) were sung with great accuracy (Spahiu 2012).

The first comprehensive textbook on music teaching methods for compulsory schooling was written in the Albanian language by Seniha Spahiu (1976), who became the first teacher educator in the Music Department of the Arts Academy, University of

SOLFEXHO ORË GËZIMI...

Solfexho orë gëzimi asht.
Orë taktimi e këndimi,
Eni pra shokë, n'shkollë fill të
                              shkojmë
Se kjo orë tash na mbërrini.

Figure 5.2 'Solfexho otë gëzimi'. The words of the model song for the note 'sol' refer to 'Solfexho' (ear training class) as being 'an hour of joy for students'. (Source: Kaçinari, M. and V. Gjini (1968), *Libër i Edukatës Muzikore Për klasën III dhe IV të Shkollës Fillore* [*Music Education Textbook for Grades III and IV for Primary Schools*], Prishtina: Enti i Teksteve dhe i Mjeteve Mësimore i KSA të Kosovës (The Institute for Textbooks and Teaching Resources of KSA Kosovo), p. 115; reproduced with permission.)

Prishtina. She had introduced practical work with student teachers in schools during the training course on music teaching methods, and was also the author of the music curriculum developed in this period in Kosovo. In 1980, she and her colleague, *solfeggio* specialist Sevime Gjinali, published the first song and games book to be used for pre-school children (Spahiu and Gjinali 1980). Spahiu is also the author of music textbooks for Grades 7, 8 and 9, which are still in use in Kosovo schools.

Music education as struggle (1981–9)

Because of this 'liberal' period in education and culture, Kosovo Albanians slowly began to have more autonomy when organizing their education system, and they enjoyed increased living standards, decreased illiteracy, and raised awareness and political thinking (Schmitt 2012). However, Yugoslavian Serbs were afraid of these improvements, which they understood to be a sign of Kosovo Albanians' nationalist reawakening. The political discrimination that followed in this period affected the basic educational rights of Kosovo Albanians and led to a strong censorship of school music in Kosovo, which stemmed from the nationalist tone of much Albanian traditional folk and art music. The censorship was not focused so much upon the suppression of Western values, as was the case within inland Albania, but rather the censorship aimed to diminish the identity of individual ethnic groups in the name of a common Yugoslav identity (Spahiu 2012; Shema 2000).

This fear of Albanian nationalism articulated through music was also reflected in changes to the music curriculum in the context of the educational reforms of the 1980s called the 'joint nucleus' curriculum (Toci 1999; Spahiu 2012). These reforms aimed to revive the 'weakened' Yugoslav identity by imposing a much greater percentage of Yugoslav music, and a correspondingly much smaller percentage of Albanian music, on the curriculum for each grade. The changes were designed to resist ethnic minorities gaining sufficient autonomy to run their own territories and education systems. The restrictive approach used in all those subjects that could relate particularly strongly to national identity, such as the arts, literature, music, history and geography, meant that they became battlegrounds that reflect the lines of conflict inside and outside the classroom (Murray 2008). The dispute polarized Kosovo Albanians and Serb curriculum experts, principally around the issue of incorporating national values embedded in art, history, music and literature in the school curriculum and in textbooks. Moreover, the approach of Serb music experts called for the censorship of Albanian national music and composers from the school curriculum.

This dispute continued for ten years among various professionals. Serb experts argued that the Albanian component of identity, culture, arts and history belonged to another state, while Kosovo Albanian experts argued that national identity, culture and values transcend artificially created boundaries (Kraja 2011). Spahiu (2012) reveals how central political authorities called the experts once in the middle of the night, with attempts to convince them to go through with the 'harmonization' of the 'joint nucleus' programmes: they were threatened that if they would not vote in favour there would be consequences. Spahiu also explains how the Kosovo authorities insisted that the music of their nation could not be treated in isolation, as it encompassed all the music created across the borders that divided Albanians.

Music educators became embroiled in the ideological attempt imposed by the central regime to deny any link between Albanians in Kosovo and those in Albania, and other territories where Albanians lived (Macedonia, Montenegro etc.), thereby denying Kosovo

Albanians the right to express and appreciate any symbol of common Albanian national identity through music or by any other means (Kostovicova 2002; Spahiu 2012).

The Serb oppression of Albanians in public life during this period (1981–9) started with gradual attempts to create a segregated educational system in the following ways: initially, physically separating the Albanian from the Serb pupils in primary schools; attempting to create a curriculum that provided secondary education only in the Serb language; and pressurizing higher education institutions to organize studies only in the Serb language (Kostovicova 2005; Bieber and Daskalovski 2003). This came into force after the Serb government forcibly abolished the Kosovo Constitution in 1989. Kosovo's autonomous status of 1974 was abrogated, and the territory was made into a province of Serbia with no rights to organize the state affairs of its citizens. These provisions were massively rejected by Kosovo Albanians, educational authorities, teachers and pupils in what was referred to as 'civil resistance' (Clark 2000). Serbia expelled all educational staff from secondary and university levels and brought their own professionals into every administrative sector, including education. This action was proposed to be a 'nationalist remedy to the perceived "Albanisation"' – that is, 'Albanian cultural and numerical dominance of the educational system in Kosovo' (Kostovicova 2002: 166).

Music education as survival (1990–9)

Educational developments in Kosovo during this period were heavily influenced by repression and the attempted assimilation of ethnic Albanians (Kostovicova 2002; Schmitt 2012). Education in the Albanian language for Albanians was systematically targeted by the Serb regime until it was finally abolished in 1991. This resulted in the establishment of an underground education system run by Kosovo Albanians, who had continued to be persecuted by the Serb regime (Clark 2000; Leutloff and Pichl 1999).

While this underground system was 'rudimentary', it nonetheless worked (Judah 2008: 73), although it inevitably slowed down Kosovan pupils' educational development. Immense difficulties were experienced with teachers and pupils being arrested and killed. Music and music education were reduced to singing solely to keep the spirit alive by nourishing the Albanian identity and supporting the fight for freedom and resistance. In Kosovo, the songs in schools and in the community were concerned mainly with valorizing Kosovan freedom fighters, expressing hatred against the Serb military regime and hoping for the unification of all Albanians in one state. The Albanian identity in this parallel educational system could now be freely cultivated through music, and, in 1995, the Ministry of Education of Albania and the Ministry of Education in Kosovo (the parallel government that was not accepted by the Serb regime) decided to harmonize the national curriculum. All the previous limitations with regard to the works of composers from all Albanian territories were removed, and teachers could now select freely which composers to listen to and sing Albanian songs, including patriotic ones.

However, the difficult conditions in which schools were operating in this period (in private houses, mosques and churches, shops and any place where one could turn a space into an improvized classroom) meant that music lessons were restricted to singing. All that was possible were the songs dedicated to the new heroes (La Cava et al. 2000; Sommers and Buckland 2004).

Restoration and the new music curriculum (2000–present)

The international administration over Kosovo's institutions, which was authorized in 1999 by the United Nations Security Council Resolution 1244, required Kosovo Albanians to reconcile with their former enemies and share a commitment to create a common future in the spirit of post-war educational reforms (Murray 2008; Qirez 2016; Wenderoth and Sang 2004).

In 2000 the newly formed institutions initiated general educational reforms independently from former Communist and Serbian constraints. The New Kosovo Curriculum Framework (NKCF), which was dedicated to pre-university education, followed the European model in the hope that all Kosovan children would benefit from those free and democratic education policies (Gundara and Peffers 2005). This resulted also in changing the aims, content and methodology of music education, which had now become part of the core curriculum. This reform focused particularly on addressing the challenges that had arisen as a result of the 'underground' education system (Bartlet et al. 2004; Peffers et al. 2005). Framed within progressive, democratic and liberal aims, it aimed to free music education from the ideological and oppressive restrictions of the previous Serbian regime in the context of the internationally imposed, multi-ethnic identity of Kosovan society (Goddard 2008; Weinstein, Freedman and Hughson 2007).

This new context contrasted with the Albanian unification and nationalist tone that had prevailed in educational content and curricula just a year before. Accordingly, the limitations of the past, when the curriculum was thought to be too 'nationalistic', were resolved by the idea of multiple or 'nested' identities (Spinner-Halev 2003), as explained by the NKCF:

> The construction of identity starts in the family and in the local community and continues through a lifelong process. All new experiences are linked to previous ones. Education should enable students to know about and value the traditions of their family and their community, as well as to make them able to be open to the history and culture of other communities, and of other countries and people. (MEST 2001: 14)

The new music curriculum introduced in post-war Kosovo kept much from previous good practices, particularly keeping music as a compulsory subject within the core curriculum throughout compulsory education levels Grades K–10, and in some cases up to Grade 12, and focusing on ensuring qualified and effective music teaching throughout the school system. This involved revising music teaching content, learning outcomes, assessment methods, textbooks and other teaching materials, but it maintained the following four key aims:

- enable all pupils to appreciate music;
- develop the listening and performing skills of pupils in order to cultivate 'an educated audience';
- increase the interest of all pupils in musical activities in their daily lives;
- for the talented pupils, enable them to consider music as a future career. (MEST 2005)

The fundamental change was to move away from a general focus on theory taught in a very 'talk-and-chalk' approach and to include more Albanian songs and music, both folk and traditional, as well as Western classical music.

Despite the fact that the new music curriculum aimed to promote the new multi-ethnic society of Kosovo, it arguably did not reflect this. Each ethnic community could choose, if it wanted, to include songs or music of other ethnicities living in Kosovo in their curriculum and textbooks. In the case of Albanians, they included only Western classical music, Albanian music and a few examples of popular music, omitting any music of other ethnic communities living in Kosovo.

Across the period 2007–10 the revision of the music curriculum for all grades was completed, as were new textbooks, accompanied by a CD of examples of the various music genres that were to be taught at different grades. The revised curriculum only suggested broad orientations towards content and the way in which the three strands (singing, listening and creating) should be combined in lesson units, without offering prescribed working schemes as, for example, in the United Kingdom. Thus teachers were given the freedom to develop their own yearly, monthly and weekly lesson plans.

As far as the training of teachers is concerned, music at primary level (Grades 1–5, student ages 6–10), as in many other countries, continues to be taught mainly by generalist classroom teachers prepared within the University of Prishtina's Department of Education. Specialists teach lower secondary grades (6–9, student ages 11–15) and upper secondary grades (10–12, student ages 15–18). Specialist teachers are also in special circumstances teaching music in pre-school education institutions (children aged 3–5). It is worth noting that in 2000 around 70 per cent of teachers who taught music at Kosovo primary and secondary schools did not hold a degree in music education (Pupovci et al. 2001; Pupovci 2002).

The Kosovo Educational Ministry (MEST) with the support of UNICEF and the European Commission launched, at the end of 2011, an overall revision of the New Kosovan Curriculum Framework of 2001, resulting in the Curriculum Framework for Pre-University Education in the Republic of Kosovo, adopted at the end of 2012 (MEST 2011; Waller 2011). This most recent framework focuses on the attainment of 'key competencies for lifelong learning' (Crick 2008) and the four main capacities of the Scottish National Curriculum for Excellence: to enable each child or young person to be a successful learner, a confident individual, a responsible citizen and an effective contributor (Education Scotland 2015). The pilot schools for this framework were selected in early February 2013.

All teachers in Kosovo are currently still required to implement the provisions of the older Curriculum Framework of 2001 and the respective subject curricula developed for all Grades 1–12 as a transitional process towards a competency-based education envisaged by the new current educational reform. According to the existing curriculum, the main task of music teachers is to ensure an effective music education for all Kosovo pupils, focusing mainly on developing pupils' practical musical skills in performing, listening and creating music in various styles and genres.

However, unqualified teachers, lack of space, poor conditions and the shortage of musical instruments in schools continue to characterize music education in Kosovo schools, despite initiated reforms (Luzha 2015). The process has been defined generally by Fullan (1993: 19) as 'failed implementation … with … superficial changes of terminology and structures, but not the teaching practice itself'. It could well apply to the Kosovan context.

This chapter has described the development of music education in Kosovo in different and difficult historical periods. Music in these circumstances was mainly used to develop and maintain the collective identity of Kosovo Albanians, which was frequently under attack by several regimes that ruled Kosovo.

In practice, music teachers face many challenges ahead. They feel caught between traditional Albanian music cherished in family contexts, the European classical music canon offered in teacher training and evident in school music textbooks and materials, and pupils' musical interests mainly within popular music styles and genres cherished outside the school. However, music teacher training remains a part of university study, and hope must be placed in the young student music teachers who are the inheritors of the struggle for a strong and vibrant music education that can meet the musical and cultural aspirations of the people of Kosovo.

Reflective questions

1 In what ways can music education influence the construction and maintenance of national identities? What are the pros and cons of developing a nationalist and/or a patriotic music curriculum?

2 To what extent does music 'attract, catch, and collect symbolic meanings'? Refer to your own experience, relating to some music you enjoy.

3 In this chapter the author points to a gap between the official curriculum and what goes on in everyday music classes. Do you find that this is also the case in other national settings that you know of?

References

Bacevic, J. (2014), *From Class to Identity: The Politics of Education Reforms in Former Yugoslavia*, Budapest: Central European University Press.

Bartlett, B., D. Power and P. Blatch (2004), 'Education in a Recovering Nation: Renewing Special Education in Kosovo', *Exceptional Children* 70 (4): 485–95.

Bassuener, K. and B. Weber (2013), 'Not Yet a Done Deal: Kosovo and the Prishtina–Belgrade Agreement', *Democratization Policy Council Policy Paper*, November, http://ceas-serbia. org/root/images/The_New_Century_No05-Kurt_Bassuener-Bodo_Weber.pdf (accessed 8 September 2015).

Berisha, E. (2004), *Studime dhe vështrime për muzikën* (*Studies and Analysis of Music*), Prishtinë: ASHAK.

Bieber, F. and Ž. Daskalovski (2003), *Understanding the war in Kosovo*, London: Psychology Press.

Bjelic, D. I. and O. Savic (eds) (2002), *Balkan as Metaphor: Between Globalisation and Fragmentation*, Cambridge, MA: Massachusetts Institute of Technology.

Blumi, I. (2002), 'The Role of Education in the Formation of Albanian Identity and its Myths' in S. Schwander-Sievers and B. J. Fischer (eds), *Albanian Identities: Myth and History*, Bloomington: Indiana University Press, pp. 49–60.

Clark, H. (2000), *Civil Resistance in Kosovo*, London: Pluto Press.

Cowen, R. (2000), 'Comparing Futures or Comparing Pasts?', *Comparative Education* 36 (3): 333–42.

Crick, R. D. (2008), 'Key Competencies for Education in a European Context: Narratives of Accountability or Care', *European Educational Research Journal* 7(3), 311–18.

Education Scotland (2015), 'The purpose of curriculum', http://www.educationscotland.gov.uk/ learningandteaching/thecurriculum/whatiscurriculumforexcellence/thepurposeofthecurriculum/ index.asp (accessed 16 September 2015).

Filaj, L. (1935), *Mësimi i muzikës për shkolla të mesme. Pjesa e pare* (*Teaching Music in Secondary School*), Tiranë: Shkodra.

Fullan, M. G. (1993), 'Why teachers must become Change Agents', *The Professional Teacher* 50 (6): 12–17.

Glenny, M. (2001), *The Balkans: Nationalism, War and The Great Powers (1804–1999)*, New York: Penguin.

Goddard, T. (2008), 'Educational Leadership Development in Kosovo' in M. Brundrett and M. Crawford (eds), *Developing School Leaders: An International Perspective*, London and New York: Taylor & Francis, pp. 69–90.

Gundara, J. and J. Peffers (2005), *Quality Education for All in Kosovo*, Prishtina: UNICEF.

Judah, T. (2002), *Kosovo: War and Revenge*, New Haven, CT: Yale University Press.

Judah, T. (2008), *Kosovo: What Everyone Needs to Know*, New York: Oxford University Press.

Keller, S. M. (2007), 'Why is Music so Ideological, and why do Totalitarian States take it so Seriously?: A Personal View from History and the Social Sciences', *Journal of Musicological Research* 26 (2–3): 91–122.

Koci, A. M. (2011), *Lorenc Antoni – Jeta dhe Vepra: Njëqind vjetori i lindjes së kompozitorit Lorenc Antoni* (*Lorenc Antoni, composer – His Life and Works: One Hundred Years from the Birth of Composer Lorenc Antoni*), Prishtinë: Shoqata e Muzikologëve të Kosovës.

Kostovicova, D. (2002), 'Shkolla Shqipe and Nationhood: Albanians in Pursuit of Education in the Native Language in Interwar (1918–41) and Post Autonomy (1989–98) Kosovo' in S. Schwandner-Sievers and B. J. Fisher (eds), *Albanian Identities: Myth and History*, London: Hurst & Company, pp. 157–72.

Kostovicova, D. (2005), *Kosovo: The Politics of Identity and Space*, London: Routledge.

Kraja, M. (2011), *Identiteti Kosovar* (*Kosovar Identity*), Prishtinë: Pen Qendra e Kosoves.

La Cava, G., R. Nanetti, S. Schwandner-Sievers, A. Gjonca, T. Nezam, B. Balaj, A. Salihu, F. DelRe and D. Davis (2000), *Conflict and Change in Kosovo: Impact on Institutions and Society*, Report for the World Bank, Environmental and Socially Sustainable Development ECSSD, Washington: World Bank.

Leutloff, C. and E. Pichl (1999), 'The State of Education in Kosovo after the Ceasefire in June 1999' in *How to Construct Civil Societies? Education and Media in Southeast Europe: Country Report*, Graz: Center for Study of Balkan Societies and Cultures reports, pp. 183–94.

Luzha, B. (2005), 'Edukimi Muzikor ne Kosove me Veshtrim te Vecante ne Reformen Aktuale' ['Music Education in Kosovo focusing on actual educational reform'] (unpublished master's dissertation, University of Prishtina).

Luzha, B. (2008) 'Music, politics, identities: comparing the role of music in Albania and Kosovo under the Communist regime', unpublished paper presented at the 28th ISME World Conference, Bologna, Italy.

Luzha, B. (2015), 'Music education in post-war Kosovo: generalist and specialist teachers' identities, beliefs and practices' (unpublished doctoral dissertation, University College London, Institute of Education).

Malcolm, N. (1998), *Kosovo: A Short History*, London: Macmillan.

MEST (2001), *The New Kosovo Curriculum Framework*, http://www.abstract.lib-ebook.com/a1-economy/1765193-1-the-new-kosovo-curriculum-framework-preschool-primary-and-secondary.php (accessed 10 June 2015).

MEST (2005), *Programi mesimor per klasen e V. Edukata muzikore* (*Learning programme for grade V. Music Education*), Prishtinë: Libri Shkollor.

MEST (2011), *Curriculum Framework for Pre-University Education in the Republic of Kosovo*, Prishtinë, http://www.ibe.unesco.org/curricula/kosovo/kv_alfw_2011_eng.pdf (accessed 10 June 2015).

Ministria e Arsimit (1925), *Libër kangësh për shkollat popullore të Shqipnis/mbledhun e rreshtuem prej Hil Mosit,Ble I. Kangë nji, dy e tre zanësh* (*Singing book for national schools of Albania/collected and edited from Hil Mosi. Book I. Songs in one, two and three voices*), Tiranë: Vlora.

Misha, P. (2002), 'Invention of a Nationalism: Myth and Amnesia' in S. Schwander-Sievers and B. J. Fischer (eds), *Albanian Identities: Myth and History*, Bloomington: Indiana University Press, pp. 33–49.

Murray, H. (2008), 'Curriculum Wars: National Identity in Education', *London Review of Education* 6 (1): 39–45.

Myzyri, H. (1978), *Shkollat e para kombetare shqipe (1887–1908)* (*First National Albanian Schools [1887–1908]*), Tirana: 8 Nëntori.

Myzyri, H. (2004), *Shkolla Normale e Elbasanit (1909–1912)* (*Normal School of Elbasan [1909–1912]*), Tirana: AlbPaper.

Peffers, J., E. Reid, F. Stylianidou, P. Walsh and M. Young (2005), *The National Curriculum in Kosova: A Review of its First Steps*, London: Institute of Education, University of London.

Pettifer, J. (2001), *Blue Guide to Albania and Kosova*, London: A&C Black.

Pupovci, D. (2002), Teacher education system in Kosovo, http://www.see-educoop.net/portal/id_kosovo.htm (accessed 16 August 2004).

Pupovci, D., H. Hyseni and J. Salihaj (2001), *Education in Kosova 2000/2001*, Prishtina: Kosova Education Center.

Qirezi, B. (2016), 'Integrating identities across contexts: Kosovo postgraduate students' transformative study abroad experiences in the UK' (unpublished MS, National University of Ireland, Galway).

Qosja, R., Q. Gashi, S. Gashi, R. Zogaj, Z. Celaj, J. Shushka and A. Vokrri (2007), *Shkolla*

Normale e Prishtinës 1954–1974. (*Normal School of Prishtina 1954–1974*), Prishtinë: Libri Shkollor.

Rexhepagiq, J. (1970), *Zhvillimi i arsimit dhe i sistemit shkollor të kombësisë shqiptare në territorin e Jugosllavisë së sotme deri në vitin 1918* (*Development of Education and the School System for the Albanian Nationality in Jugoslavia until 1918*), Prishtinë: Enti i Teksteve dhe Mjeteve Mesimore te KSA I Kosoves.

Rexhepagiq, J., A. Vokrri and A. Veseli (1997), *Shkolla Normale 'Sami Frashëri' e Prishtinës: Zhvillimi, karakteri dhe rëndësia e saj 1941–1944.* (*Normal School 'Sami Frasheri' of Prishtina: Development, Characteristics and its Importance 1941–1944*), Prishtinë Prishtina. Libri Shkollor.

Rexhepi, Z. (2014), *Shkolla normale e Prishtinës gjenerata e viteve 1954–1959* (*Normal School of Prishtina: Generation 1941–1944*), Prishtinë: Valton.

Schmitt, O. J. (2012), *Kosova: Nje Histori e Shkurter e Nje Treve Qendrore Ballkanike* (*Kosovo: A Short History of the Central Balkan Territory*), Prishtinë: KOHA.

Shema, I. (2000), *Çështje të Arsimit Kombëtar Shqiptar* (*Issues of National Albanian Education*), Prishtinë: Libri Shkollor.

Sommers, M. and P. Buckland (2004), *Parallel Worlds: Rebuilding the Education System in Kosovo*, Paris: International Institute for Educational Planning.

Spahiu, S. (1976), *Edukatë muzikore: doracak metodik për arsimtarë të edukatës muzikore të shkollës fillore prej klasës I–VIII* (*Music Education: Useful Methods for Music Teachers at Primary Schools I–VIII*), Prishtinë: Enti i Teksteve dhe Mjeteve Mësimore të Kosovës.

Spahiu, S. (2012), *Muzika dhe Edukimi: Studime, analiza, persiatje (1966–2012)* (*Music and Education: Studies, Analyses, Issues [1966–2012]*), Prishtinë: Libri Shkollor.

Spahiu, S. and S. Gjinali (1980), *Gëzimi ynë: këngë, valle, ligjërime e dëgjime* (*Our Joy: Songs, Dances, Rhythms and Music Listening*), Prishtinë: Enti I Mjeteve dhe Teksteve Mësimore të Kosovës.

Spinner-Halev, J. (2003), 'Education, Reconciliation and Nested Identities', *Theory and Research in Education* 1 (1): 51–72.

Toci, F. (ed.) (1999), *Kosova: Nje vështrim enciklopedik* (*Kosovo: An Encyclopedic Review*), Tiranë: Toena.

Troebst, S. (1999), 'The Kosovo Conflict', *SIPRI Yearbook*, Stockholm: Stockholm International Research Institute (SIPRI), pp. 47–62.

Veseli, A. (2003), *Shkollat dhe arsimi shqip në Prefekturën e Prishtinës (1941–1944)* (*Schools and Education in Albanian in the Prefecture of Prishtina [1941–1944]*), Gjilan.

Vokrri, A. (2004), *Shkolla Normale e Prishtinës (1953–1974)* (*Normal School of Prishtina [1953–1974]*), Prishtinë: Libri Shkollor.

Waller, C. (2011), Report of short term expert component 2: EU Education SWAP project, http://www.eu.eduswap-ks.org (accessed 18 September 2015).

Weinstein, H. M., S. W. Freedman and H. Hughson (2007), 'School Voices Challenges Facing Education Systems after Identity-based Conflicts', *Education, Citizenship and Social Justice* 2 (1): 41–71.

Wenderoth, A. and B. M. Sang (2004), *Situation Analysis of Education in Kosovo*, Prishtina: UNICEF.

Chapter 6

Lithuania: The continuous assertion of national identity

Rūta Girdzijauskien and Emilija Sakadolskis

The origins of Lithuanian music education

Deciding on a date from which to begin a discussion of music education in Lithuanian schooling is an interesting problem in itself. Lithuanians celebrate the year 1397 – the date of earliest documentation of the Vilnius Cathedral School – as the beginning of a formal, institutional and financially supported European-style education system in Lithuania. Schools were thought to have operated on the model of the *schola cantorum* of Western Europe, with Latin being the language of instruction. Here, in addition to lessons in rhetoric, dialectics, mathematics and the reading of classic texts, boys learned ecclesiastical chant and received suitable musical training to sing in church choirs and become music teachers (Jareckaitė 2006).

By the beginning of the fifteenth century there was a network of parish and convent or monastery schools throughout Lithuania. A limited number of parish schools for the lower classes offered basic reading and writing, singing of sacred music, as well as Latin for those considering entering the clergy. By the sixteenth century the number of parish schools had increased and there were about 150 schools in the Vilnius bishopric alone (Karčiauskienė *et al.* 1983).

The fifteenth and sixteenth centuries were a time of war with neighbours of the Grand Duchy of Lithuania, which increasingly relied on treaties and dynastic ties with Poland to fend off invaders. This resulted in religious, political and cultural influences among the Lithuanian nobility, who increasingly preferred to speak Polish, considered the language of the gentry. This was also a time when Lithuania was moving towards a feudal system of landed nobility that included serfdom and even instances of slavery. In 1569 the two competing nation-states – the Grand Duchy of Lithuania and the Kingdom of Poland – formed the federated Polish–Lithuanian Commonwealth. This was the time of the Reformation and the Counter-Reformation and both factions of Christianity realized that schooling was essential in the spread of ideas. The year the Commonwealth was established is also the year when the Jesuit Order was invited to Lithuania to counter the Reformation as well as to establish schools and teacher training institutions. A Jesuit professor of rhetoric, Žygimantas Liauksminas (Sigismundus Lauxmin), wrote the first music textbook published (in Latin) in Lithuania.

During the sixteenth and seventeenth centuries, foremost attention was given to establishing primary schools. More than two hundred Catholic parish schools existed in the Lithuanian-speaking portion of the Commonwealth. In a letter to the Vatican in 1646, the head of one bishopric reported that 'almost every church has a school taught by rectors and bachelors who teach catechism, the ten commandments, all the obligations of Christian devotion, grammar, music and other sciences, which develop children's talents, and receive regular remuneration from their parishes' (Karčiauskienė et al. 1983: 27). Despite the widespread establishment of primary schools, it should be noted that there was no mention of secondary schooling for non-clerical students until the 1540s (Jurginis and Lukšaitė 1981). Protestant emphasis on developing the inner man and literacy in the vernacular encouraged Lutheran and Reformed activists to establish schools that included the seven liberal arts, including music theory (Jareckaitė 2010).

The Age of Enlightenment brought new ideas to Lithuanian education that spread through the school systems by the end of the eighteenth century. In 1773 the Commission for National Education of the Kingdom of Poland and the Grand Duchy of Lithuania was established. The new education system reflected the ideas of Rousseau, Locke and the physiocrats,[1] and stressed accessibility to education at all levels in the vernacular language without social limitations (Račkauskas 1968). The Commission is considered to be the first Ministry of Education in Europe and all schools, including private schools, those run by parishes (there were about 450 operating between 1773 and 1794) and monastery schools were under its purview (Budzinauskienė 2008). As literacy levels rose, Polonization[2] accelerated, which in turn invigorated the formation of a Lithuanian intelligentsia whose members wrote textbooks and increasingly linked ethnic identity to the Lithuanian language.

Although music was not included in the official curriculum, it is known that all children were taught to sing by rote, particularly during catechism classes. An instruction published in 1790 specified that hymns were to be sung at the beginning and end of each lesson and that Lithuanian texts were to be used (Karčiauskienė et al. 1983: 91). A school for training primary teachers was established by the Commission in 1775 and included two to four hours of music instruction per day so that teachers could also perform the functions of a church organist. Other teacher seminaries taught solfeggio, music theory, choral conducting, church hymnody and clavichord performance. Providing organists and catering to the needs of pastors was considered a form of compensation, since pastors were expected to maintain the parish primary schools and there were no schools that specifically trained church organists (Karčiauskienė et al. 1983: 102; Minginas 2007: 79; Budzinauskienė 2008).

Under Tsarist Russia

There is very little extant information about music education in nineteenth-century Lithuania. The Polish–Lithuanian Commonwealth lasted until 1795, when it was divided among Tsarist Russia, the Kingdom of Prussia and Habsburg Austria. Yet the Commission for Education continued to function, albeit in a reduced capacity. The number of Lithuanian schools decreased dramatically and after a series of uprisings, the Tsarist authorities instituted intensive Russification. The singing of Catholic hymns in Lithuanian was to be replaced by Russian Orthodox chants. Several sources describe seminars for primary school teachers that included singing, sacred and secular music history, and the popularization of Russian folk songs (Jareckaitė 2006: 173).

In 1864 Russian authorities instituted a press ban prohibiting Lithuanian books and periodicals printed in the Latin alphabet and closed Lithuanian schools. Many refused to send their children to Russian-language schools, prompting civic and church leaders to encourage the foundation of mobile secret schools. Education scholar Lukšienė (2014: 71–2) describes the situation:

> A secret network of Lithuanian schools that functioned for forty years is a unique phenomenon in educational and cultural development. Can it formally be considered a form of institutional education? It might instead be argued to have functioned as an inter-mediary form between home-education and what was normally considered schooling.

At the end of the nineteenth century more than fifty per cent of the population could read Lithuanian while only six per cent attended official schools. At the underground schools children were taught reading, writing, counting and the singing of Catholic hymns as well as Lithuanian folk songs. Song collections were provided by book smugglers, and church organists taught basic music literacy and organized choruses. Records of searches by Russian authorities reveal that folk song collections, music notebooks, music manuscripts and hymnals were among the confiscated materials found at the secret school sites.

Schooling in Lithuania Minor

In discussing the cultural history of Lithuania, it is important to mention an area called Lithuania Minor (Prussia; *Kleinlittaw* in German) that includes parts of present-day Poland, the Kaliningrad exclave of Russia and south-western Lithuania. Although the Old Prussian language was extinct by the eighteenth century and most inhabitants were assimilated by Germans, the area remained an important bastion of Lithuanian culture until the twentieth century. Of 1,700 parish schools in operation during the eighteenth century, only 400 were German; instruction was carried out in Lithuanian or Polish in the remaining schools (Karčiauskienė et al. 1983: 168). Compulsory Lutheran schooling was introduced in Prussia in 1736 and gained a foothold by the end of the eighteenth century. The curricula always included singing instruction.

In 1746 three hours of singing per week were required throughout the Kingdom of Prussia (Jareckaitė and Rimkutė-Jankuvienė 2010). In 1809 Wilhelm von Humboldt, the Prussian Minister of Culture, set forth his reform ideas in a plan for the schools of Prussia and Lithuania (*Königsberger und Litauischer Schulplan*) that helped bring the ideas of Johann Heinrich Pestalozzi to Lithuania.[3] A teacher education seminary operated in Lithuania Minor from 1811 to 1826. Every future teacher was taught to sing and play the violin. Students were also given instruction in organ, piano and music theory. Protestant activists who were maligned in Lithuania Major often relocated to Lithuania Minor, where principles of music education were strongly influenced by Martin Luther and Jan Amos Komenský (Comenius). The first book in the Lithuanian language – Martynas Mažvydas' Protestant *Catechism* – was published here in 1547 (Ford 1971), and the time-honoured Lithuanian tradition of collecting folk songs had its roots here. The first known documentation of a Lithuanian folk song was in 1634 and Liudvikas Rėza published the first collection of Lithuanian folk songs in 1825, providing a model for other collectors who often did so for reasons of national identity (Ramoškaitė 2000). The Duchy of Prussia's capital of Karaliaučius or Königsberg (now Kaliningrad) became a centre of learning and printing. During the Lithuanian press ban Lithuanian books including song collections and hymnals in the Latin alphabet were published in Lithuania Minor and smuggled to Lithuania proper for use in the secret schools.

A new education system for a newly independent state: 1918–40

Lithuanians lived under the rule of the Russian Empire until 1918. In 1904 the press ban was repealed, Lithuanian schools started to open and an intense period of national revival paved the way for the re-establishment of an independent Lithuanian state in 1918. The task of creating an educational system based on national culture was taken on immediately. The four-year primary school curriculum comprised eleven subjects, including singing, which was allocated two lessons per week. The programme included what was probably the first attempt to formulate the aim of music education: to like and to feel music, to listen consciously and understand it (Petrauskaitė 2009). Folk music was the basis of instruction through which children learned to sing with good intonation, to read notation in a one octave range and to independently write down a single-voiced melody. Upon completing the primary programme children were to 'clearly understand what they have learned; forever retain the songs learned in school in memory, and to be able to continue learning the science of music in the next tier of schooling' (quoted in Petrauskaitė 2009: 272).

Composer and musicologist Juozas Žilevičius (1891–1985) became the head of the Department of the Arts at the Ministry of Education in 1920, and today is acknowledged as the father of Lithuanian music education. Having surveyed the state of affairs in schools, he stated in 1920: 'Generally speaking, you cannot say that singing and the science of music does not exist in schools, but on the other hand, you cannot say that it does. So what have we here? None other than happenstance teaching' (quoted in Petrauskaitė 2009: 272–3). Having studied German, Czech, French, English and

Belgian practices, Žilevičius proposed a mandatory music programme for all levels that included everything a sophisticated person should know: music theory, including harmony and counterpoint, musical forms and musical genres. The Ministry of Education was sceptical, but Žilevičius convinced his critics that music requirements in other countries were even greater, and the programme was approved in 1923. According to the composer, to offset materialism in this world, the goal is to educate the soul through national pride, beauty, history, song and familiarity with one's country through geography. Žilevičius wrote the first music textbook in Lithuanian, *The Young Singer*. He strongly discouraged the use of foreign melodies before children had developed what he called a Lithuanian worldview. Žilevičius stated in 1923 that 'Song has preserved the untainted Lithuanian language, song is the mirror of the Lithuanian soul, song is the bioscope[4] of the Lithuanian character, and song is everything to a Lithuanian' (cited in Petrauskaitė 2009: 273). Among his other impressive accomplishments was the organization of the first Lithuanian song festival in 1924 that included 3,000 members of eighty choirs. The Baltic tradition of grand song and dance festivals has survived to this day and has been included in the UNESCO Representative List of the Intangible Cultural Heritage of Humanity since 2003. Undoubtedly this event has contributed greatly to the Lithuanian choral tradition in both formal and informal music education.

Eventually, the Žilevičius programme was deemed to be too demanding. Later versions of the curriculum were more tolerant of foreign music materials, but Lithuanian folk music remained at the heart of the curriculum. Eventually, instrumental music was introduced with use of the recorder and various Lithuanian folk instruments, such as the *kanklės* (psaltery) and *skudučiai* (panpipes). The music literature programme was expanded to include a survey of Lithuanian music. Despite revisions of the programme, less-qualified music teachers continued to complain about its complexity. Even so, a professional organization of music educators stood by the challenging requirements of the original version during the conference of the Association of Lithuanian Musicians in 1938. The resolution presented to the Ministry of Education proposed that:

> 1) the subject of music and singing be renamed music, 2) there should be an examination at each grade level (except grade one), 3) all music teachers should be required to use the gramophone in addition to the piano and the harmonium, 4) written assignments should be introduced and registered, 5) students should receive separate grades for music and chorus on their report cards and exit diplomas, 6) music terminology should be used uniformly in all schools, 7) conditions should be created for pupils to participate in choruses, and 8) a collection of choral music should be published. (quoted in Petrauskaitė 2009: 276)

Many consider this conference to have been ground-breaking for music education, since the Ministry implemented many of the recommendations. In addition to two weekly music lessons, four to eight additional compulsory hours per week were allocated to choral singing and instrumental music-making. Large numbers of music instruments were purchased, *skudučiai* and *kanklės* were used in primary grades and choral studies became mandatory in the upper grades. Schools compiled collections of recordings, and class teaching was supplemented by radio concerts. Textbooks for middle-school students were published between 1938 and 1940.

The reformed programme yielded widely varying results. Schools that had qualified music teachers did not find implementation difficult. However, the didactic and musical skills of many teachers were inadequate. The shortage of good music teachers was probably the main roadblock to implementing a curriculum that was not limited to the singing of simple songs. Ninety per cent of school music teachers were church organists, and 1923–4 data shows that one-third of Lithuanian schools did not have music teachers (Petrauskaitė 2009). As late as 1938 there was a shortage of 150 music teachers in Lithuania.

The situation was particularly critical in the primary grades where music was taught by classroom generalists. In many cases, music was ignored; pupils could not read music or even sing folk songs. During the 1920s teacher education programmes did not require the demonstration of any musical skills on entry, and the teacher education curriculum provided only one singing lesson and two lessons in music per week during the one-year course required to become a primary-level teacher upon completion of the eleventh grade. In later years the duration of primary-level teacher education was extended to three or four years (Tamulaitienė 1999).

Eventually the Klaipėda music school became an important institution for educating music teachers for the upper grades. Žilevičius again devoted himself to alleviating problems of teacher competence by teaching in Klaipėda, writing articles and books on teaching methods, and by organizing summer in-service courses for music teachers. After considerable discussion, it was decided that the Kaunas Conservatory – the premier school for training musicians in the country – should begin preparing music teachers in order for the overall standard of the teaching profession to improve. Unfortunately, the Second World War disrupted these plans.

Under the Soviet system: 1940–90

Education in context

During the Second World War, Lithuania was occupied in turn by Germans and the Soviets. As a consequence of the Molotov–Ribbentrop Pact between Nazi Germany and the Soviet Union, Lithuania, together with several other countries, was relegated to the Soviets by a secret protocol of the Pact. The annexation terminated Lithuania's statehood, and with the entrance of Soviet troops to the country a systematic deconstruction of all areas of life commenced. The Sovietization of education, as well as political, social, economic, cultural and spiritual life, was rapid and about 300,000 Lithuanians (from a national population of three million) were deported to Siberian labour camps and gulags as they were perceived to be antagonistic to the new Communist

AŠ SPALIUKAS

Aš labai džiaugiuosi,
Kad esu spaliukas,
Kad esu mažytis
Lenino anūkas,

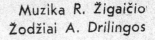
Muzika R. Žigaičio
Žodžiai A. Drilingos

Kad rausva žvaigždelė
Kaip liepsna plevena,
Prisegta tvirčiausiai
Ant krūtinės mano.

Virš plačios Tėvynės,
Virš laukų ir sodų
Panaši žvaigždelė
Šviečia, kelią rodo.

Su tokiom žvaigždelėm,
Karo audrai ūžiant,
Ėjo komjaunuoliai
Kažkada į mūšį.

Panaši žvaigždelė
Ir ant Kremliaus bokštų, —
Visos žemės žmonės
Pamatyt ją trokšta.

Ir užtai džiaugiuosi,
Kad esu spaliukas,
Kad esu mažytis
Lenino anūkas.

Figure 6.1 Soviet-era school song 'Aš Spaliukas' ('I'm a Little Octobrist'), music by Rimvydas Žigaitis, words by Antanas Drilinga. An excerpt from a first-grade textbook, *Muzika 1* © Zenonas Marcinkevičius (1974), *Muzika I*, Kaunas: Šviesa, p. 19; reproduced with permission of the publisher, Šviesa. The 'Little Octobrist' organization for children aged 7–9 was the first step to becoming a 'Pioneer', then a member of the 'Komsomol', which was the usual prerequisite for membership of the Communist Party. A summary of the text: 'I'm so happy to be a Little Octobrist, to be a little grandson of Lenin. The red star is firmly fastened to my chest. In times of war the Komsomol went to battle with such stars. All of mankind yearns to see a similar star that sits atop the Kremlin towers.'

system. The educational system of independent Lithuania was considered a relic of the bourgeoisie and immediate steps were taken to introduce the Soviet model of education. In 1940 all educational institutions were nationalized, leaving no private schools to promote innovative educational ideas. Lithuania was incorporated into an authoritarian, centralized system of Soviet education managed from Moscow.

The first decade of ideological indoctrination was particularly brutal. Antanas Venclova, the first education minister of the occupying government, required teachers to

> inculcate pupils with the idea that the homeland is the multinational land of workers, the Soviet Union, which has been illuminated by the Constitutional sun provided by Stalin, the leader of the world's workers, and which is constructing a magnificent and vibrant existence of a magnitude that has heretofore not been seen in this world. (Stašaitis 2009: 40)

Teachers who did not please the new government were dismissed and many were later exiled.

Cultural Sovietization and music education

It must be acknowledged that the Soviet government understood that what could not be attained by reasoning and regulation could be instilled by artistic activity. Impelling and emotionally-charged musical performances and the optimistic propaganda portrayed during Soviet holidays might not have been convincing, but it did have a positive effect on audiences. Composers created ostentatious works praising Communism, and schools staged competitions for the best performances. What has been termed 'a culture of facades' (Genzelis 2009) became commonplace and music was an integral part of such events. The arts and education were important tools in the anchoring of Soviet ideology.

Artists who wanted to be heard needed to adhere to government rules and to conform to its ideology. The first decades of the Soviet period were particularly direct in their adulation of social realism, while displays of modernity were interpreted as hostile intrusions. The numerous oratorios, cantatas and songs of this era extolled the 'bright tomorrows' of Communism and the Soviet state ('Love the Party, my child / The way you love your mother / It protects you like a tender bud / In this land of Lenin' – by Kostas Kubilinskas) and were a mandatory component of concert programmes and music textbooks. Musical repertoire that contained even the slightest references to religion and performance of sacred music by Western composers was forbidden in the school curriculum. (See Figure 6.1 – an example of a Soviet-era school song.)

Many musicians tried to encode hidden meanings that evoked national and historic memory. An 'Aesop's language' emerged that spoke of forbidden topics in coded symbols, allusions and concealments. These 'games' with Soviet censors extended to all aspects of Soviet life. Teachers presented one or two songs about the Soviet homeland, especially when inspectors were expected, and most then proceeded to Lithuanian repertoire that supported national consciousness. Audiences reportedly became accus-tomed to 'blocking out' the first few songs in a concert (Balčytis 2012).

The 'Khrushchev thaw'

The political thaw in the early 1960s brought pronounced changes. An attempt to generate a Soviet 'folk culture' allowed for the recognition of unique folk music cultures from the republics that made up the Soviet Union. However, authentic versions of folklore were viewed sceptically and not encouraged. Instead, folk music was to be performed as a stage art in often ostentatiously harmonized and elaborately arranged renditions with 'augmented' folk instrument orchestras that were never a part of the folk tradition. Song and dance ensembles were created to perform these works that often made the folk music of Lithuania sound much like the music of other Soviet republics. Yet throughout the Soviet period Lithuanian ethnic ensembles that fostered authentic performance of folklore held their own – both within and outside of school settings – despite instances of both indirect and outright harassment by the authorities.

In a formal sense, the conditions for music education during the Soviet period were satisfactory. Immediately following the Second World War, after-school music schools were established in every district centre of Lithuania. In the mid-1980s there were more than seventy such schools in Lithuania with a total enrolment of about 10,000 students. Music instruction was mandatory in every grade of compulsory schooling, music textbooks were published and teachers were being prepared in institutes of higher education. Choirs, orchestras and other ensembles that operated in schools and informal educational settings received ample funding. After-school musical activities thrived, especially choral ensembles. Song festivals for both adults and school-age children included tens of thousands of performers from across the country, continuing the tradition that was begun in 1924. Yet these were only the external characteristics. The main feature of the Soviet system continued to be an ideological curriculum content to prepare politically mindful builders of Communist society (Stašaitis 2009).

Change and innovation came slowly to music education. Textbooks that were written in the 1950s were used in the secondary grades until 1974. The main focus was on Lithuanian folksongs, and exercises were based on the melodic and rhythmic materials of folk literature. Concern was expressed that the main emphasis of music education was on theory and music literacy at the expense of aesthetic experience, appreciation, and aural and oral development. The curriculum was so crowded that conscientious teachers were forced into broad, generalized treatments of the subject matter. Comprehensive musicianship was a foreign concept. Music listening and instrumental performance in the general music class were minor activities (Gaidamavičienė and Marcinkevičius 1968).

Changes in the 1970s

The structure of schools was changed in 1966 throughout the Soviet Union and music education was reformed as well. New textbooks were published for the upper grades, in addition to teacher manuals and other instructional materials. Music education was supported by the national recording studio and Lithuanian television, which aired programmes on music teaching methods as well as complete music lessons. Teachers became actively involved in nationwide seminars, and working groups of music teachers met in cities and district centres. The tradition of conducting demonstration lessons for colleagues was initiated. The first music 'magnet schools' (specialist schools), where music classes took place four or five times per week, were also established at this time.

The music teaching systems of Émile Jaques-Dalcroze, Zoltán Kodály and Carl Orff began to make inroads. Dalcrozian ideas were used for teaching notation, while Kodály's views of music education based on singing and folk music were analogous to Lithuanian traditions. Unfortunately, the Kodály system of relative solmization did not take hold. At one time, pupils were expected to learn three different systems. Letter names were used for instrumental performance since metallophones and *skudučiai* were labelled in letter names. The absolute fixed-doh system used in pre-war music instruction and comparable to practices in nineteenth century and early twentieth century France, Germany and Russia continued to be used in schools. For some time a third system used throughout the Soviet Union, called the 'jo-le' relative system, was taught in Grades 1 to 4 (Daugirdas 1978; Visockienė 1983). Eventually, pressure came from instrumental music school teachers and those in higher education to abandon the relative system and to this day very few schools or choruses teach relative solmization.

The Orff system of active music-making, acting, movement and literary connections received the most attention in relation to other international methods. Although travel from the Soviet Union was severely restricted and study abroad was almost non-existent, Lithuanian educators resourcefully picked up elements of the system from foreign colleagues who supplied publications, and from short foreign visits. Methods books that encouraged 'musicing' and musical creativity were very popular among teachers. Krakauskaitė's (1965, 1967) textbooks in the 1970s and 1980s for the primary grades included rhythmics, instrumental music, chanting and creative activities. In the late 1970s amateur craftsmen produced metallophones for use in the primary grades, but their quality was substandard and a far cry from the Orff instrumentarium. Nevertheless, they served their purpose in promoting active music-making in the classroom. Despite the fact that Lithuanian music teachers could not form a deeper and more meaningful understanding of international music education methods because of a lack of information and the censure of Western ideas, even fragmentary applications did much to revive Lithuanian music education.

The creation of a Lithuanian music education system

The political 'thaw' of the 1960s and 1970s allowed for the introduction of a Lithuanian music education curriculum that differed from the other Soviet republics. The new general music curriculum stressed comprehensive musicianship through singing, listening, solfège, rhythmic exercises and performance on classroom instruments (especially on Lithuanian panpipes, *skudučiai*). The author of the new curriculum, Eduardas Balčytis, describes the goal of general music education:

to provide pupils a level of musicianship necessary for everyday life, to teach all students rudimentary, but tasteful singing, to listen with meaning, and to perceive music aesthetically; to encourage musicing, to cultivate artistic taste and the need for folk and professional music of high quality, and to educate a person of superior aesthetic and spiritual culture. (Balčytis 2008: 21)

Balčytis piloted the programme in five Lithuanian schools. Additionally, teachers throughout Lithuania provided data about their own work, student opinions and system efficacy. To this day, this series of music textbooks is the only one that has a research basis. The results of the four-year trial (1973–7) of the Grades 5 to 8 comprehensive curriculum were described by the author:

Upon completion of the eighth grade these students had learned almost everything that had been planned from the beginning: they sang in one, two and three parts, the class chorus demonstrated attractive timbre, the class could sing the solfège syllables of simple folk songs in two or three voices, and chordal patterns. They learned to listen to music relatively well, they absorbed many compositions, they listened attentively, commenting and writing about them in interesting ways; they easily sight-read various rhythms, they did not avoid playing on rhythm instruments, metallophones or pipes and had a basic understanding of the keyboard that enabled them to play simple melodies on the piano. (Balčytis 2008: 24)

The music curriculum was not met with enthusiasm by ideologues of the time. Balčytis describes a meeting in 1977 with the Minister of Education Antanas Rimkus, who had evaluated the textbook series manuscript:

The Minister rejected my textbook without mercy … I supposedly chose an historical approach so that I could promote the West. He himself had determined there was a devilish amount of music and 80 percent of the text devoted to foreign music. Soviet music was summarily discounted and there was not a single photograph of a Soviet composer … He would not grant approval for the publication, [saying] 'one of the greatest problems was that music is presented from an objectivist position as a shared human phenomenon, whereas we must present it from a position of class-consciousness' [and] 'music is also a form of class warfare'. (Balčytis 2012: 288)

After considerable effort, the textbooks were eventually approved and published in 1980. Balčytis and joint authors prepared and revised music textbooks, wrote teachers' manuals, compiled audio collections and other teaching materials. Textbooks for Grades 5 to 10 authored by Balčytis and his colleagues went through several printings of thousands of copies. The repertoire was carefully chosen and the material coherently structured and thematically organized to include all musical activities – a concept that was considered revolutionary. From today's perspective, the programme was overloaded with information, too focused on the theoretical cognition of music and disembodied from sociocultural context. Musical creativity and the active involvement of pupils were given scant attention, yet the system was in glowing contrast to the music lessons of theory and singing that existed up to that time.

An alternative to the ideas of Western educators was intensively promoted by the Russian composer and educator Dimitri Kabalevsky (Dimentman 1983; Becker, Goldin and Leibman 1993; Kabalevsky 1993). The main components of the Kabalevsky system were listening to masterpieces of music and discussions, since the aim was to prepare a music listener, not a performer. It was suggested that only more talented students should be encouraged toward performance (Kievišas 1980), and proponents of the Kabalevsky system criticized the Orff and Kodály methods for limiting the curriculum to music that students were able perform (Marcinkevičius 1979). Pupils in the first grade were introduced to the lyric song, the dance and the march, which Kabalevsky considered the basis of all musical forms. He called these forms the three whales of music, referring to an ancient Russian legend that says the earth rests on the backs of three whales (a metaphor that would be repeatedly lampooned by critics).

Most respected musicians in Lithuania actively opposed the Kabalevsky system, and due to their hard-fought efforts the system never gained a foothold in Lithuania. Balčytis (1984) continued to defend his system of comprehensive musicianship and opposed lesson material being subjugated to the understanding of world classics at the expense of other elements and areas of music, especially folk songs. Among the leading musical figures who joined in rejecting the Kabalevsky system were the director of the famed Ąžuoliukas boys' choir, Vytautas Miškinis, and the musicologist Vytautas Landsbergis (1980), who later became the first leader of independent Lithuania in 1990.

The restoration of independence – music education 1990–2015

Lithuania restored its sovereignty with the Act of the Re-Establishment of the State of Lithuania on 11 March 1990. The reform of the education system was begun in the pre-dawn of independence when Dr Meilė Lukšienė brought together a broad circle of educators, intellectuals, artists and scientists to create the Concept of National Education (1988) and other important documents during the early days of *glasnost*. Their work has encoded the principles of Lithuanian education that continue from one strategic document to the next until the present day: a caring respect for the unconditional worth of the individual, democratic values, commitment to Lithuanian culture and nationhood (see sample song in Figure 6.2), and an openness to change (Lukšienė 2014: 21).

First and foremost, the reformers foresaw that changes were needed in the entrenched mind-sets of the education community. Schools became less centralized, different types of schools were allowed to exist and teachers faced greater expectations. The amount of required material was reduced to allow teachers space to work creatively with students and to provide opportunities for self-directed learning and practical application of

AŠ PASĖJAU ĄŽUOLĄ

Aš pasėjau ąžuolą,
Žalioj girioj ąžuolą.
Tegyvuoja, tegyvuoja Lietuva
Kaip tas žalias ąžuolas.] 2 k.

Ir išdygo ąžuolas,
Žalioj girioj ąžuolas.
Tegyvuoja, tegyvuoja Lietuva
Kaip tas žalias ąžuolas.] 2 k.

Ir užaugo ąžuolas...

Sulapojo ąžuolas...

Pilnas gilių ąžuolas...

Dangų remia ąžuolas...

Šventas medis ąžuolas...

Figure 6.2 Lithuanian folk song 'Aš pasėjau ąžuolą' ('I planted an oak tree'), an excerpt from a second grade textbook, *Muzika 2*: © Eirimas Velička (1995), *Muzika 2*, Kaunas: Šviesa, p. 3; reproduced with permission of the publisher, Šviesa. Traditional culture is again used to foster national identity. A summary of the text: 'I planted a sacred oak tree in the green forest. May Lithuania thrive like that green oak. The oak tree grew, it yielded acorns, it shored up the heavens. The oak is a sacred tree.'

knowledge. More attention was paid to individual differences and school became an institution to prepare students for life, not for examinations.

Reform of the entire system stimulated the renewal of music education. First to go was the obligatory Soviet repertoire, replacing it with the music that had been excluded. The national aspects of the curriculum were enhanced. There is now a choice of several textbooks for each grade (four for primary grades and three for middle school), which was unthinkable in the Soviet era. All are grounded in comprehensive musicianship, yet each presents its own ideas and conceptions. Some focus on Lithuanian culture, others on creativity and active music-making, while others respond to contemporary sociocultural contexts.

This new freedom in planning content demands a different set of skills from educators. During the Soviet era music teachers were required to strictly follow the text and 'cover' all of the material. Teachers throughout Lithuania became accustomed to not thinking for themselves, but to go through the provided tasks and assignments diligently. The conferral of such freedoms on music teachers and encouragements to be creative architects of their own curricula created considerable angst. Many doubted whether teachers were capable of taking on the responsibility of ensuring quality and making use of the autonomy. More than a decade passed before doubts started to diminish.

Today, many music teachers employ original methods, use ideas from several textbooks or create their own teaching materials. Some implement a programme of comprehensive musicianship, while others stress one area of music over others (usually vocal performance). On the other hand, there are those who have not changed over the last twenty-five years. We still encounter lessons during which teachers dictate the biographies of composers for recall on a quiz, students fill worksheets to learn music notation and identify a few major themes while listening to a piece of music – all without moving from their seats.

The preparation of music teachers

In 1957 the Vilnius Institute of Pedagogy was the first school in the Soviet Union to prepare music teachers for the comprehensive general school. Until then music was taught by those who had degrees in performance, composition or choral conducting. The solitary programme meant there was only one model of teacher education. Requirements for music teachers have increased during the past decade. Competence in music is no longer sufficient, and pedagogical skills must be wedded to the general goals of education. Universities and academies have begun following new European guidelines on course loads, credit hours and exit requirements. Gone are the required courses in combat preparedness, Marxism–Leninism, wartime medical practicum, Soviet law, planning of communal economies and history of the USSR. There are now six universities and academies that educate general music teachers. This has made way for a more diverse set of practices, although the fostering of new ideas and the research potential are scattered and fragmented due to geography and the competition for students.

A view to the future

Assessing the last decades of general music in Lithuanian schools is not easy because changes have been swift and intense. The first years of independence saw researchers, university instructors and teachers focus on the re-anchoring of national values through music. When Lithuania joined the European Union (EU) in 2004, music education felt the inflow of EU educational priorities: the teaching of general competences, pupils more directly and actively involved with music-making and child-centred methods of teaching and learning that discouraged theoretical methods. EU structural funds for modernization opened up borders, enabled international exchanges and the flow of new experiences in music education. Students and teachers participate in conferences, Lithuanian researchers publish in foreign journals and many sources are translated into Lithuanian. Today's classrooms contain computer workstations, media systems, smartboards and reliable internet connections that change the nature of instruction. Yet pupils are often more savvy than their teachers in the workings of these new additions and have a better command of foreign languages. Inertia, resistance to change, inadequate financing, insufficiently rigorous teacher education, generalist primary teachers teaching music and broad devaluation of the arts in market-driven education could all be named as roadblocks, but when you look back the progress is so pronounced that a sense of optimism remains.

And if we look back even further to the first pages of this chapter, there is a recurring theme. Like her forerunners, Lukšienė was most concerned for the survival of the Lithuanian nation: 'The most essential concern is to create such an order in which we remain who we are and can independently participate in a polylogue[5] with other states and other cultures' (Lukšienė 2014: 15). Each era represented a new attempt at asserting national identity, the preservation of native language and the heritage of song. Consistent efforts 'to remain' in the face of Latin, Polish, German, Russian and now global culture have also coloured the history of Lithuanian music education. The challenge is to educate in such a way that personal, national and 'other' cultural identities and musics might coexist in a context of openness and diversity.

Reflective questions

1 Compare Protestant and Catholic doctrines that influenced music education in Lithuania and trace their sources.

2 What common events and conditions prompted the music educators of many countries, including Lithuania, to increasingly focus on their folk music heritage during the nineteenth and twentieth centuries?

3 Why were the music education systems of Émile Jaques-Dalcroze, Zoltán Kodály and Carl Orff not adopted as enthusiastically as in other European countries in mid-twentieth-century Lithuania?

4 What are some philosophical and practical consequences for education when a Marxist–Leninist ideology is enforced in an educational system at large? What are the consequences for music education?

Notes

1. The physiocrats were a group of eighteenth-century French economists who believed that agricultural production was the source of all wealth.
2. Polonization in this context means conformity to Polish culture and in particular the acquisition or imposition of the Polish language in territories controlled or influenced by Poland.
3. See Gruhn, Chapter 4 in this volume.
4. A bioscope was an early form of cinemagraphic projector.
5. A polylogue is a speech delivered by several people.

References

Balčytis, E. (1984), 'Ar liksime dainų kraštas?' ['Will we remain a land of song?'], *Kultūros barai* 230: 28–30.

Balčytis, E. (2008), 'Apie muzikinio ugdymo reikšmę, tikslus, uždavinius ir galimybes mokykloje' ['Regarding the meaning, goals, objectives and possibilities of music education in schools'], *Kūrybos erdvės* 9: 15–25.

Balčytis, E. (2012), *Muzikinio ugdymo labirintais* ['The Labyrinths of Music Education'], Šiauliai: Šiaulių universiteto leidykla.

Becker, J., M. Goldin and L. Leibman (1993), 'From Tsars to Whales: Dmitry Kabalevsky and Russian Music Education', *The Quarterly Journal of Music Teaching and Learning* 4 (3): 40–58.

Budzinauskienė, L. (2008), 'Muzikinis ugdymas Lietuvoje XVIII a. pabaigoje – XIX amžiuje. Bažnyčių mokyklos' ['Music education in Lithuania from the end of the 18th century through the 19th-century. Church schools'], *Menotyra* 15 (1): 13–24.

Daugirdas, R. (1978), 'Ar prisimeni muzikos mokytojo pavardę?' ['Do you remember the name of the music teacher?'], *Kultūros barai* 158, 10–11.

Dimentman, B. (1983), 'Kabalevsky: Music Educator. *International Journal of Music Education* 1: 35–38.

Ford, G. B. (ed. and transl.) (1971), *The Old Lithuanian Catechism of Martynas Mažvydas (1547)*, Assen: Van Gorcum.

Gaidamavičienė, R. and Marcinkevičius, Z. (1968), 'Muzikinis paruošimas' ['Musical training'], *Tarybinis mokytojas* 77.

Genzelis, B. (2009), 'Apie dvejopus standartus' ['About double standards'], *Bernardinai.lt*, 10 January 2010, http://www.bernardinai.lt/straipsnis/2009-01-10-bronislavas-genzelis-apie-dvejopus-standartus/26778 (accessed 17 December 2015).

Jareckaitė, S. (2006), *Muzikinis ugdymas Vakarų Europoje ir Lietuvoje: teorija ir praktika nuo Antikos laikų iki XX a. pradžios* [*Music Education in Western Europe and Lithuania: Theory and Practice from Antiquity Until the Beginning of the 20th Century*], Klaipėda: Klaipėdos universiteto leidykla.

Jareckaitė, S. and S. Rimkutė-Jankuvienė (2010), Šiuolaikinio muzikinio ugdymo sistemos [*Contemporary Systems of Music Education*], Klaipėda: Klaipėdos universiteto leidykla.

Jurginis, J. and I. Lukšaitė (1981), *Lietuvos kultūros istorijos bruožai* [*Features of Lithuanian Cultural History*], Vilnius: Mokslas.

Kabalevsky, D. (1993), 'The Basic Principles and Methods of a New Music Syllabus for General Education Schools', *The Quarterly Journal of Music Teaching and Learning* 4 (3), 10–22.

Karčiauskienė, M., M. Lukšienė, K. Žukauskas, A. Gučas, J. Laužikas, M. Ročka, A. Šidlauskas, I. Lukšaitė, J. Jurginis, A. Endzinas, E. Gudavičius, V. Nausėdas and R. Kulikauskienė (1983), *Lietuvos mokyklos ir pedagoginės minties istorijos bruožai* [*Historical Features of Lithuania's Schools and Educational Thought*], Vilnius: Mokslas.

Kievišas, J. (1980), 'Kokia bus Sistema?' ['What will the system be like?'], *Literatūra ir menas*, 15 March 1980.

Krakauskaitė, V. (1965), *Kai kurie muzikinio auklėjimo klausimai: metodinė medžiaga* [*Selected Issues in Music Education: Methodology*], Vilnius: Lithuanian SSR Council of Ministers.

Krakauskaitė, V. (1967), *Kaip mokyti muzikos pradinėse klasėse* [*How to Teach Music in the Primary Grades*], Kaunas: Šviesa.

Landsbergis, V. (1980), 'Apie du banginius ir keturiasdešimt riestainių' ['Of two whales and forty bagels'], *Literatūra ir menas*, 12 July 1980.

Lukšienė, M. (2014), *Educating for Freedom*, Vilnius: Alma littera.

Marcinkevičius, Z. (1979), 'Muzikos klausymo ir atlikimo vienovė' ['The unity of music listening and performance'], *Tarybinė mokykla* 3.

Minginas, J. (2007), *Edukacinė komisija ir Lietuvos pradžios mokykla* [*The Education Commission and the Lithuanian Primary School*], Vilnius: Vilniaus pedagoginio universiteto leidykla.

Petrauskaitė, D. (2009), 'Muzikinio švietimo padėtis bendrojo lavinimo mokyklose' ['The state of music education in general education schools'] in A. Ambrazas (ed.), *Lietuvos muzikos istorija: Vol. 2. Nepriklausomybės metai 1918–1940*, Vilnius: Lietuvos muzikos ir teatro akademija, pp. 272–85.

Račkauskas, J. (1968), 'The First National System of Education in Europe: The Commission for National Education of the Kingdom of Poland and the Grand Duchy of Lithuania (1773–1794)', *Lituanus* 14 (4): http://www.lituanus.org/1968/68_4_01Rackauskas.html (accessed 17 December 2015).

Ramoškaitė, Ž. (2000), 'Liudviko Rėzos "Dainos Oder Litthauische Volkslieder": muzikinis kontekstas ir reikšmė' ['Liudvikas Rėza's "Dainos Oder Litthauische Volkslieder": musical context and siginificance'], *Tautosakos darbai* 13, 116–26.

Stašaitis, S. (2009), 'Istorija Lietuvos mokykloje 1940–1941 metais: tautiškumo naikinimas ir sovietinės ideologijos diegimas' ['History teaching in Lithuania's schools in 1940–1941: The destruction of national identity and the implementation of Soviet ideology'], *Istorija* 70: 39–52.

Tamulaitienė, A. (1999), *Pradinės mokyklos mokytojų rengimas* [*The Preparation of Primary School Teachers*], Vilnius: Vilniaus pedagoginio universiteto leidykla.

Visockienė, A. (1983), 'Muzikinės kultūros labui' ['For the benefit of musical culture'], *Tarybinis mokytojas*, 11 November 1983.

Chapter 7

Norway: Educational progress or stasis on the outskirts of Europe?

Fred Ola Bjørnstad and Magne Espeland

When looking back at ideas and developments in music education, we sometimes wonder about the quality of ideas appearing at a moment so different from our own time. Sometimes our reflection might seem to be of a different kind, focusing on why events and ideas taking place in neighbouring countries never seemed to have surfaced in our own country. When preparing this chapter, the authors have frequently found themselves asking one another questions such as: How could this particular person write so powerfully about singing at this early stage? Why did Norwegian music education in schools seem to be so minimally influenced by ideas from other countries in Europe at certain times in history? As we dig deeper for possible explanations into our primary and secondary sources, we realize how the balance between the contextual and the personal also makes itself felt in our particular sector: how the general Norwegian political and historical situation may explain what happens in a particular singing lesson in a Norwegian classroom and how the engagement and enthusiasm of individual music educators may account for systemic changes in the teaching of music far beyond the particular singing or music lesson.

In this chapter, a short overview of Norwegian music education history will be given, bearing in mind such questions. The emphasis will be on the development of singing and music as a curriculum subject from its introduction to school programmes until 1960 when 'music' became a fully mandated subject within the curriculum of Norwegian public primary and secondary schools.

This narrative does not claim to represent the absolute truth, as there is reliance on both our own and others' interpretations of original documents, research studies and published books. The situation is further complicated when it is borne in mind that not all data are in documentary form. Accordingly any examination of the past is inevitably speculative.[1]

After a short introduction to the political history of Norway, we will focus on the following four periods in Norwegian music education history: from medieval times until the eighteenth century; from the nineteenth century until 1939; from the outbreak of war until 1960; from 1960 to the present. Our narrative will be more analytic than descriptive as there will be an attempt to provide answers to questions about the relationship between 'music' as a mandatory curriculum subject in Norway and similar developments in other countries. In an attempt to describe the evolutionary nature of this process, events will be treated holistically with a view to contextualizing information as well as analysing and commenting on developments both in school education and in teacher education.

General historical and political context

A single chapter on the history of school singing and music in Norway does not allow for a comprehensive account of Norwegian political history. However, a short synopsis should provide sufficient background to enable a better understanding of the development of music education.

Norwegian political history is closely linked to that of Sweden and Denmark. After periods as independent viking and monarchist entities during the early centuries of the first millennium, the three countries were united through the Kalmar Union – under a single monarch – from 1397. In 1523 this union was replaced by a provincial arrangement: Sweden and Denmark became independent and separate kingdoms, whereas Norway became a province of Denmark. This arrangement, referred to as the '400-year night', came to an end in 1814 when an awakening nationalism inspired by the French Revolution resulted in a limited, although separate, Norwegian constitution, representative assembly and government. Even though the political situation resulted in Norway being conceded to Sweden as a result of Denmark's role in the Napoleonic Wars, the declaration of the Eidsvoll Constitution on 17 May 1814 became the basis for a growing Norwegian nationalism and political awareness. This led to the establishment of a parliament-based Norwegian government in 1884 and Norway's separation from Sweden, heralding the rebirth of Norway as an independent state in 1905. In the first decades of the twentieth century Norway became increasingly more industrialized. This industrialization, although interrupted by German occupation during the Second World War, has been maintained firstly through a thriving oil industry established during the early 1970s and secondly through the present focus on 'high-tech' industries.

Music education from medieval times until the eighteenth century

The early history of music, or rather singing and music, in Norwegian schools is closely related to the history of the church. From the twelfth century, monasteries and cathedrals established schools where pupils (boys) were taught music as one of the '*artes liberales*'. The main aim of education was to ensure the supply of clergy to perform the ecclesiastical offices that were supported in the service by the singing of the choir.

The curriculum consisted of song repertoire and music theory. This was maintained until just after the Reformation, when the first school regulations under the union of

Denmark and Norway appeared in 1539. According to extant documents and manuals from the period, the major focus of the music curriculum was on theoretical aspects. It was expected that the standard of singing by pupils at services should be at such a level that the congregation was not required to participate musically, except for joining in some responses and in the 'amen'. Curriculum requirements at this time dictated that one hour should be allocated to singing each day. Pupils in the lower classes were required to practise Gregorian chant, whereas those in the upper classes focused on 'figure song or descant' (Bergheim 1974: 8).

However, it was not until 1739 that a new decree established singing as a mandatory subject of the school curriculum. The 1739 decree of King Christian VI – 'by God's mercy, king of Denmark and Norway' – included not only a directive that schooling should be compulsory for all children, but detailed descriptions, instructions and overall executive responsibility for the *klokker*,[2] a church official responsible for the singing as part of the liturgy. The *klokkerne* were called on not only to become schoolmasters but also teacher trainers in that they had to appoint 'substitutes' who could, after passing examinations, become schoolteachers in their own right.[3] In addition, the 1739 decree set out a specific rationale for including singing in the school curriculum:

> In the same way as the morning starts with Reading, so too should there be Singing, Prayer, and the reading of the Holy Scripture. The evening should end in this way: there needs to be sung a Spiritual Psalm, after which all children must kneel while reading the Evening Prayer; afterwards a chapter of the Holy Scripture is read, and finally the day ends with the singing of an Evening Psalm. However, be aware that in case of bad and foul weather during the winter, only a couple of verses need to be sung, so that the children can arrive home before darkness, and not be hurt or lost in snowstorms and darkness. (Tønnessen 1966: 36 [authors' translation])

It is interesting to note that, in the detailed instructions given to school teachers, there were directives regarding the welfare of their pupils and the need to take account of the harsh climatic context in which schooling took place. Not surprisingly, however, the detailed directives included in the 1739 decree became very unpopular in the rural areas and some of the regulations were consequently not carried through. Even when laws enacted in 1809 saw the separation of education from the church, the singing of psalms was retained as the main focus of musical content in the school curriculum. For this reason, schools and the church appear to have been more or less inseparable during this first period in the history of Norwegian music education.

From the nineteenth century to 1939

It is not until 1834 that what might be called 'music education methods' reflecting influ- ences from central Europe are mentioned in the national decrees (or ordinances) affecting education. The decree that appeared in 1834 was described as a 'Plan, in accordance with which the Teaching and Disciplines in the Public Schools in the Country should be adapted, and Instruction for teachers in the Public Schools'. It continued the link between singing and the psalms, but there is also reference to an instrument called the *psalmodikon* and a system of numeral notation. Section 8 of the decree says: 'In the teaching of singing, for the moment, Bohr's psalm melodies with numeral signs should be used with [the] psalmodikon' (Norsk Skolemuseums Venner 1960: 679 [authors' translation]). The system obviously drew on the ideas of the French philosopher Jean-Jacques Rousseau, who numbered the notes of the major scale from 1 to 7.[4]

The *psalmodikon* is a bowed monochord with frets, developed by the Swedish priest J. Dillner in the 1820s (Stålmarck 1962: 225, in Hole 1999). It is a one-stringed wooden instrument designed to be played from *ziffer* (numeral) notation with the use of a bow. Different fret boards could be used for different types of scale. The best-known pioneer of this instrument in Norway was Lars Roverud, a music teacher who, having been commissioned by the Ministry of Education, travelled extensively in Norway between 1835 and 1847 to promote its use (Bergheim 1974: 12). Roverud used the *psalmodikon* to teach congregations as well as school teachers and their pupils to sing psalm melodies in tune and accurately according to notation.

But Roverud was highly critical of organists and musical life in Norway in general, suggesting that little musical knowledge was apparent. 'Organists', he complained, 'have in general little education, some play wildly, i.e. not knowing notes, or accompanying psalms in their own peculiar ways; the more hocus-pocus, ornaments and scales introduced at every beginning of a musical phrase, the better' (quoted in Bjørnstad 2001: 33 [authors' translation]).

Roverud also criticized the teaching of singing by church officials (the *klokkeren*) as being incompetent and doing great damage to the overall standard of singing in churches. He argued:

> In most churches there is no organ. The singing is led by so-called *klokkere*, among whom one out of fifty hardly knows a single note, or has any music education whatsoever; and from where should they have got such a thing? Most of them sing the psalms according to their own rules, i.e. including all kinds of ornaments, and the higher and stronger they are able to scream, the better … Also, in almost every community there is one amongst the public, who competes with the *klokkeren* in screaming and shouting and such a stentor[5] has a high standing for his ability to take the tune away, i.e. overcome the *klokkeren*. (Ibid.: 33)

However, the reform of the singing practices long entrenched in Norwegian churches did not happen without conflict. A local report from the time describes this discord in the following way:

> But now there was a conflict in most congregations in that most of them wanted the old traditional tunes, whereas the teachers and their pupils tried to lead the singing in accordance with the new authorized melodies. There was conflict over the melodies, and

this conflict escalated to such an extent that, in the end, churches were emptied of the congregation during singing. The congregation came in when the priest entered the pulpit, and left when he descended. This situation lasted nearly half a century until the congregations little by little became used to the authorized melodies. (ibid.: 34 [authors' translation])

There is little doubt that, as a dedicated and enlightened pioneer, Lars Roverud affected more general reforms to music education well beyond the particular singing or music lesson. Roverud strongly believed that the improvement of music education, in particular singing, was dependent on well-established teaching methods and on a curriculum designed to promote knowledge of musical notation and theory. In assessing his contribution, however, it is important to recognize that Roverud's zeal and endeavour may very well have resulted in the loss of some traditional singing practices and repertoire of the so-called 'common people', traditions that are highly valued in modern Norwegian society.

Teacher training and resource books for schools

The new practices introduced to congregational singing soon found their way into the new teacher training 'seminaries', as they were called. Several of these 'seminaries' were established in the late 1830s across Norway in rural districts as well as in cities, one of them being Stord Seminarium, south of Bergen, to which the authors of this chapter are attached.

The 1837 national curriculum for teacher training colleges largely adopted the approach promoted by Roverud and recommended, among other things, the use of the *ziffer* notational method. The requirements were set out as follows:

The students should, when we talk about psalmody, be introduced to the theory of this popular music and by the use and help of *ziffers* in singing as well as in playing the *psalmodikon* with skills, be able to play the most common psalm melodies, and, as far as possible, one of the associated descants or bass lines. Also they should learn how to play the harmonium, and as far as possible, learn specific folk songs. In order for the students to be prepared as church singers, they should regularly attend services in the nearest church and, in cooperation with the singing master, lead the singing. (Quoted in Bergheim 1974: 11 [authors' translation])

This excerpt from the requirements for teacher education also points to two other major elements of music education at this time – namely, a focus on the harmonium as an accompanying instrument and a growing awareness of singing as a vehicle for rebuilding a national identity. One of the ideas behind the introduction of the harmonium was its capacity to lead group singing in a way that could cope with the then-unwanted ornamentation of notes that was common in the folk style of singing (Storækre 1965: 925). The immediate context of the focus on folksongs was the nationalistic movement, increasing after 1814, when Norway freed herself from 400 years of Danish rule and re-established her own constitution and parliament.

The emphasis on singing as a compulsory subject in early teacher education seemed to have naturally complemented the role of singing in public schooling. However, in 1869, the official title of the subject in teacher education courses was changed to *musik* (music), and it might seem strange that this change did not take place in public primary and secondary education until 1960, when music became fully mandated in Norwegian schools.

The promotion of teaching music through staff notation in addition to *ziffer* notation was not apparent in the official Ministry of Education documents until 1877 when the reading of the C major and C minor scales from staff notation was specified as one of the aims for singing lessons. This change seems to have been influenced by teacher courses taught by the composer J. D. Behrens in the years 1866–73. In the foreword to one of his books on singing methodology, he wrote:

> If singing in schools is to be useful in building a life of good quality, the methods for teaching normally accompanying this skill, and which consist of plain and mechanical rote learning, must be changed … In addition to this comes the fact that the teacher proceeds without a plan … [Therefore] it is very understandable that the majority of the pupils at the end of schooling stop singing completely. A good result of song teaching can only be gained through the use of methods, where the theoretical and the practical walk hand in hand from the very start of teaching. (Behrens 1868: preface [authors' translation])

Behrens' ideas appear to have dominated the methods of teaching singing in schools towards the end of the nineteenth century and at the beginning of the twentieth century. There seems to have been very little influence from corresponding debates in other European countries reflecting a focus on other important issues in music education – for example, the opposing methodologies of fixed-doh and tonic sol-fa, which, by this time, were well established respectively in France and in England. There was also nothing to indicate a mirroring of the debate over music appreciation that was beginning to surface in America and England or the so-called 'rhythmic movement practice' ('eurhythmics') pioneered by Émile Jaques-Dalcroze in Switzerland in the 1890s.

In 1917 the curriculum for singing in primary schools still emphasized the ability of pupils to sing simple melodies and to understand music theory in the tradition of Behrens. Additionally, the curriculum required that pupils from the third grade should learn to use *solfège*. In the secondary school curriculum, it was prescribed that the pupils should be trained according to the so-called 'formula method', a melody-reading approach with strong links to similar movements in England and France. Based on the use of *solfège*, the pupils were taught small melodic formulas that were supposed to help them in their sight reading from staff notation and also to perform simple musical phrasing. In the same period a music teacher named Ole Koppang developed an alternative to this methodology called the 'sound method' (*klangmetode*), which had its basis in *harmonic* formulas. Other early music educators advocated new methods for enhancing the vocal style of *skjønn sang* (beautiful singing) that emulated the Italian classic 'bel canto' song tradition and was proposed by Hans Georg Nägeli as early as 1810 in his comprehensive 300-page *Gesangbildungslehre nach Pestalozzischen Grundsätzen*. Lars Søraas, another Norwegian pioneer and teacher educator of the first part of the twentieth century, supported this approach. He advocated the ideal of 'beautiful singing' not only for music education, but for reading and speech as well. This influence can be clearly identified as German in origin in this quotation from Søraas:

> A good resonance – as well as a good pronunciation – is particularly well achieved by using Professor Edvard Engels' methodology for singing. Through the formation of the tone the resonance is developed, and by positioning the tongue towards the lower teeth and curling it, the tip of the tongue will be trained, the articulation becomes easy and clear, the tone carries more easily, and the back of the throat opens up. In Germany this method-ology has spread widely in primary as well as secondary schools. It is widely used for class teaching in schools (in conjunction with the sound method in reading) and has gained praise from teachers as well as doctors for the advantages it brings in relation to hygiene as well as the excellent sound of language in reading, speech and singing … Professor Engels' method is being used in the courses for singing teachers provided by the Ministry. (Quoted in Espeland 1974: 17 [authors' translation])

In the curriculum plans of 1922 (KUD 1922), there are further indications of the wider aims for singing lessons than just learning songs and notation. A statement such as 'the children should [be] help[ed] to develop their voice and ear. They should learn to sing the most well-known songs and psalms correctly, nicely and in pitch' is an early example of a focus on child development issues in and through music. However, there were still no real outward signs of music appreciation or other progressive educational approaches in compulsory schooling in Norway.

From the outbreak of war until 1960

It was not until a curriculum reform in 1939 (KUD 1939) that new and progressive pedagogical ideas developed at the beginning of the century by John Dewey and William H. Kilpatrick were adopted by the Norwegian school system. However, in contrast to other aesthetic subjects – for example, visual art – there was almost no sign of creative elements or even an orientation towards a broader view of the role of music in compulsory schooling in this document. In an article from 1966, Finn Benestad and Ingmar Fottland, two post-war reformers of Norwegian music education, summarized the development of music in schools until 1945 thus:

> If we examine books, regulations and methodologies in Norway before 1945, very little new was added as compared to the latter part of the 19th century. This seems to have been the case in other Nordic countries as well. New songs are added, the voice is focused, some emphasize music theory, others drills and aural training etc. (Benestad and Fottland 1966: 800)

In the same article, these two authors speculate about the reasons for this lack of development with the suggestion that many contemporary music educators had a background in the singing movements and that subject content could not deviate from centrally prescribed curriculum guidelines. This could well be part of the explanation, but can it fully explain why, during the first half of the twentieth century – a time of rich educational debate internationally as well as in Norway – there was so little influence from these developmental perspectives on music education in compulsory schooling? It could reasonably be thought that authors of textbooks and designers of school curricula would be among the educational elite and that they would therefore have been able to influence music education in schools to a large degree.

A different way of explaining this phenomenon could be to focus on the many extra-curricular aspects of singing as a school subject. Throughout the nineteenth century and well into the twentieth century, education authorities regarded singing as 'scaffolding' for other subjects, such as language and religious education. Certainly, the close relationship between the school and the church was weakened in the twentieth century, but it was nevertheless still a strong one. In school textbooks, psalms occupied an equal position with other songs, and this was also set out in the 1939 ministerial guidelines (KUD 1939). These guidelines also stressed the importance of teaching songs about the Norwegian homeland and countryside. As part of the emergence of Norway as an independent nation in 1905, there was a need to establish its national identity and accordingly songs of nationalistic character constituted a great part of the school song repertoire. Consequently, one of the main aims of compulsory schooling during this period was to initiate young children into the Norwegian nation and its state religion (Espeland 1974: 20).

It seems reasonable to conclude that as long as the focus on singing as a school subject was dictated by religious and nationalistic aims, there would be little room left for focusing on more eclectic forms of music and aesthetic education. Jørgensen (1982: 10) explains the lack of international influence on singing and music teaching in this period by referring to the fact that innovative ideas take time to travel and develop and that a broader perspective on the role of music in education based on progressive education principles did not suit the Norwegian emphasis on singing.

However, explanations other than those advocated by Jørgensen might be more important and carry greater weight. The Norwegian political situation, with the rebirth of the nation in 1905 and the whole nationalistic movement leading up to it, meant that singing had a much wider and more significant role than merely to support the church liturgy. Singing was central to the building of a new nation as well as in the celebration of national values and historical events. Around the turn of the century this coincided with similar movements in continental Europe – for example, the *Jugendbewegung*[6] in which Fritz Jöde soon became a leading figure (Varkøy 1993: 62ff.). Add to this the fact that music and singing outside the public schools played an important part during the Second World War in sustaining resistance and national feelings.

The explanations outlined in this chapter for the lack of progressive educational thinking can be characterized as a kind of educational stasis, especially in the case of music. By 1939 the ideas underpinning progressive education seem to have been accepted at a general level and for all other subjects (Årva 1987: 229), but, in the case of music, there was little evidence of such progress. Even as late as 1955 prominent educators fighting to establish 'music' as a new subject in schools complained that:

> Most of our textbooks for school subjects have undergone radical changes for a long time. But with regard to 'song' there has been a standstill for a long time. Equipment, melodies, and texts are for the most part unchanged. But there must be an end to how long we can nurture our youth on nationality and chauvinism. (Benum 1955: 22)

Ivar Benum became an important post-war figure in the movement to improve the standing of music in schools. His forthright criticism of the lack of any progressive educational reform of singing and music was one of several attempts at creating a new expanded role for music in education. Benum was deeply influenced by American as well as British educational thinking (Mork 2008: 162). Together with Egil Nordsjø, another prominent advocate for music as an aesthetic subject in Norwegian public schools, Benum led the fight to establish music as a mandatory aesthetic subject in the public school curriculum in the 1950s. Nordsjø was not an educator, but a professional singer, who wrote his first article in favour of a new subject called 'music' as early as in 1935; however, his attempts at reform and those of others were not taken seriously and failed to generate any real debate (Årva 1987: 232).

Nevertheless, Nordsjø continued with his advocacy for music after the Second World War, and this time his ideas gained ground. In an article in *Norsk Skuleblad*[7] in 1947 he sketched a broad platform for a new subject, which could provide for a comprehensive aesthetic education – including music – for all (Årva 1987: 241). In the late 1940s and the 1950s Nordsjø and Benum emerged as the informal leaders of a number of teacher educators, internationally and nationally, who introduced contemporary ideas about music education from Sweden, Denmark, Germany, England and the USA. Some of these influences can easily be linked to the Orff movement, the Kodály system and the Music Appreciation Movement. This activity laid the ground for the creation of a new mandated curriculum subject called 'music' in 1959 and its inclusion in the new 1960 school curriculum.

The main elements of 'music' can be described as a combination of the 'old' singing content and new ideas, including listening and instrumental activities. Although the new activities were strongly conceived, they did not reflect creative and multi-genre approaches to music education that had been central in the Orff movement and in some experimental music practices in Nordic countries, for example in Denmark. According to Jørgensen, the new curriculum was influenced more by a scientifically based musico-logical thinking than by progressive educational thinking. Even so, in comparing the newly conceived subject to the 200-year-old 'singing' tradition, he characterized the change as a 'revolution' (Jørgensen 1982: 29).

However, there was a considerable gap between the new music curriculum as a written document and its implementation. Norway was still a predominantly rural society with a large number of small schools in small communities. The existence of music as a newly mandated subject influenced both the structure and content of teacher training courses. Three initiatives played a particularly important role and deserve mention. First, the formation of a national organization for music in schools in 1956 – *Landslaget Musikk i skolen* – which published a music education journal; second, the institutionalizing of a three-year teacher education programme with an integrated music specialization – *Musikklinja* – in Bergen 1958; and third, the formation of a special body to provide in-service courses in music funded by the Ministry of Education – *Statens lærerkurs*. Between them, these initiatives shaped the implementation of the new subject by giving teachers and prospective teachers the competence required to implement the ideas and philosophy of the national curriculum.

From 1960 until the present

Although singing in the 1960 curriculum was still important, the new focus was on music listening and instrumental activities. However, through the 1960s, the new subject progressed so that by the following decade Norwegian music education was further influenced by other international developments such as an emphasis on classroom composition and 'creative music' – based on the work of Murray Schafer and John Paynter – as well as developing its own system for instrumental teaching through a comprehensive system of 'music schools' outside the school system, something that is now a vital part of the overall music education endeavour in Norway.

Today, school music is well established in every stage of primary and secondary public schooling as a mandatory subject for pupils between the ages of six and fifteen. The curriculum consists of performing, listening and composing, with dance and drama as integrated elements. The national curriculum reforms of 1974, 1987, 1997 and 2006 have allowed music as a subject to have developed considerably from its early foundations as 'singing' and its reformation during the 1960s to become a creative, reflective and educationally progressive subject. In recent years, there is no doubt that music has changed its emphasis on classical music to a wider array of musical genres, i.e. contemporary popular music (see Jørgensen 2001). Even so, music as an aesthetic subject for all students – together with a number of related practical and aesthetic subjects – is presently under pressure from the PISA-driven[8] accountability and back-to-basics movement, but that is outside the present focus of this chapter. However, it is hoped that the recent focus on creativity and the importance of arts and culture in society – as demonstrated by the designation of 2009 as the European Year of Creativity and Innovation – will better promote music as a school subject than has hitherto been the case.

Recently published and widely used songbooks for schools (Amsrud and Bjørnstad 2008; Weisser 2010) suggest to us that singing still is intended to be a central activity in Norwegian classrooms. An investigation of their contents give us a clear impression of the several educational dilemmas formed as results of the media pressure from popular music, internationalization and the gradual transformation of Norway into a multicultural society (Bjørnstad et al. 2014). These dilemmas are also visible in current national curricula for schools as well as in ongoing discussions about the future of music in Norwegian schooling.[9] These developments can be viewed as a threat to music and singing as we are used to thinking about them in education, but they can also be viewed as challenges and opportunities, for example, along with a growing understanding for the place of social relations and emotions in learning and understanding of all kinds.

Conclusion

This chapter opened with a question that addressed the reasons why music in the public school system seemed to have developed more slowly in Norway up to 1960 than in other comparable countries. Although it may seem unjust to characterize music education in Norway as having been in stasis, explanations can be found in the more gradual emergence of Norway as an independent nation than in some other European countries, the foreign occupation of Norway during the Second World War, which accounts for the lack of development of music education during this period, and the prevailing notion of music and singing as scaffolding activities for the building of identity and the support of religious education rather than as an intrinsically valuable subject in its own right.

Reflective questions

1 It is evident in reading this chapter that there was a close relationship between music education and the church in Norway. Does this close relationship between music education and religion parallel your own experience in your national context? What are the advantages/disadvantages of this relationship?

2 What is meant in this chapter about regarding singing as 'scaffolding' for other subjects? Is it a useful argument to use in justifying the place of singing in the curriculum today?

3 What might be some of the reasons that Norway took until 1960 to change the name of the subject from 'singing' to 'music'? How significant is this change?

4 It is pointed out that today music education in Norway has to deal with several dilemmas, including media pressure from popular music, as well as internationalization and the gradual transformation of Norway into a multi-cultural society. To what extent are these dilemmas threats or opportunities for music educators?

Notes

1. The research approach we apply can be described as 'hermeneutic content analysis' (Kjeldstadli 2000). Our work here is part of *Ideoskosa*, an acronym for a Nordic cross-institutional research project about ideology in songbooks for primary schools in Norwegian history.
2. The etymological meaning of *klokker*, plural *klokkerne*, is associated with the Norwegian word *klokke* and the German *glocke* (bell). In addition to assisting with the singing, the *klokker* was also responsible for calling the people to service by sounding the church bells.
3. The second paragraph of King Christian's 1739 decree also contains detailed regulations as to the removal of *klokkere* in case of educational incompetence or leading an ungodly life with 'drinking and swearing'.
4. The numeral notation in Norway might be based on a later revision in 1817 of Rousseau's system known as the Galin–Paris–Chevé method. In Norway, the numeral system is called *ziffer* notation (from the German).
5. From the Greek '*stenein*', to groan, make noise – i.e. a Greek herald of the Trojan War who, according to Homer, had a voice as loud as that of fifty men (*Webster's New Twentieth Century Dictionary*, 1979).
6. *Jugendbewegung* was a movement for children and youth established by the music pedagogue Fritz Jöde in Germany after the First World War. He wanted a singing society and based his work on ideas from the philosophers J. J. Rousseau and F. Fröbel.
7. *Norsk skuleblad* was and still is a major magazine for primary and secondary teachers in Norway.
8. PISA is the acronym for Programme for International Student Assessment, an OECD initiative that has been very influential on school policies globally as well as in specific countries. The influence PISA has in many countries led to a focus on the so-called 'basics', namely reading, writing and science.
9. The ongoing discussions are based in the work of a governmental expert group called Ludvigsen-utvalget. This group has invited educators to respond to their suggestions of introducing a greater awareness of in-depth learning and social and emotional competencies as key elements in the future of Norwegian national and compulsory schooling. See Summary of NOU 2014: 7: 'Pupil learning in the School for the Future'.

References

Amsrud, A. and T. Bjørnstad (2008), *Sang i Norge* (*Singing in Norway*), Oslo: Sang i Norge-Musikk I skolen.

Årva, Ø. (1987), *Musikkfaget i Norsk Lærerutdannelse 1815–1965*, Oslo: Novus forlag.

Behrens, J. (1868), *Sanglære for Skoler*, Kristiania: privately published.

Benestad, F. and I. Fottland (1966), 'Musikk i 9-årig skole, fra sangtime til musikkfag' in R. Ness (ed.), *Skolens årbok*, Oslo: Johan Grundt Tanum forlag, pp. 791–810.

Benum, I. (1955), *Musikk som personlighetsdannende fag i skolen*, Hamar: Norsk skoletidendes boktrykkeri.

Bergheim, I. (1974), 'Lærebøker i musikk for barneskolen' (unpublished dissertation, University of Oslo).

Bjørnstad, F. O. (2001), *Frå Munn og Flatfele*, Kristiansund: KOM.

Bjørnstad, F. O., Olsen, E. and Rong, M. (2014), *Med sang! Perspektiver på skolesangbøker etter 1814*, Oslo: Novus.

Espeland, M. (1974), 'Lærebøker i musikk for barneskolen. Ein analyse' (unpublished dissertation, Norges Lærerhøyskole).

Hole, B. (1999), 'The birth of the Psalmodikon: North American Psalmodikonfor-bundet', www.psalmodikon.com/history/birth_of_the_psalmodikon.htm (accessed 20 June 2008).

Jørgensen, H. (1982), *Sang og Musikk*, Oslo: H. Aschehoug & Co.

Jørgensen, H. (2001), 'Sang og musikk i grunnskole og lærerutdanning 1945–2000', *Studia Musicologica Norvegica* 27, 103–31.

Kirke-og undervisningsdepartementet (KUD) (1922), *Normalplan for Landsfolkeskolen, Kirke-og Undervisningsdepartementet*, Kristiania: J. M. Stenersens forlag.

Kirke-og undervisningsdepartementet (KUD) (1939), *Normalplan for Byfolkeskolen. Utarbeidd ved Normalplankomiteen Oppnevnt av Kirke-og Undervisningsdepartementet*, Oslo: Aschehoug & Co.

Kjeldstadli, K. (2000), *Fortida er ikke hva den engang var. (En innføring i historiefaget)* [*The Past is Not What it Used to Be: An Introduction to History*], 2 vols (2nd edn), Oslo: Universitetsforlaget.

Ludvigsen, S. et al. (2014), Summary of NOU 2014: 7: Pupils' Learning in the School for the Future, http://blogg.regjeringen.no/fremtidensskole/mandate-in-english/ (accessed 13 April 2015).

Mork, N. (2008), 'The fate of innovation: a social history of creativity and curriculum control' (unpublished PhD dissertation, University of Brighton).

Norsk Skolemuseums Venner (1960), *Skolehistoriske Aktstykker nr. 9*, Oslo: Norsk Skolemuseums Venner.

Nägeli, H. G. and M. T. Pfeiffer (1810), *Gesangbildungslehre nach Pestalozzischen Grundsätzen: erste Hauptabtheilung der vollständigen und ausführlichen Gesangschule mit drey Beylagen ein-, zwey-und dreystimmiger Gesänge*, Zurich: Nägeli.

Stålmarck, T. (ed.) (1962), *Natur og Kulturs Musikhandbok*, Stockholm: Natur och Kultur.

Storækre, J. T. (1965), *Kristen Sang og Musikk*, Oslo: Runa forlag.

Tønnessen, H. O. (1966), *Tekster og aktstykker til den norske skoles historie*, Oslo: Fabritius og sønner forlag.

Varkøy, Ø. (1993), *Hvorfor musikk?*, Oslo: Ad Notam Gyldendal.

Weisser, H. (2010), *Følgesvenner. Sanger om små og store fortellinger* (*Followers: Songs About Small and Big Narratives*), Oslo: Olifant.

Chapter 8

Spain: A journey from a nominal towards a universally implemented curriculum

Gabriel Rusinek and Susana Sarfson[1]

Historical background

A serious attempt to codify the educational system in Spain took place in 1857 with the promulgation of the *Law of Public Instruction* (Ministerio de Fomento 1857). In order to solve the then major problem of illiteracy among the rural population, compulsory schooling was introduced for children aged 6 to 9, and was free for those whose families 'could not afford it'.[2] Music was not initially stipulated, but two decades later a subject called 'music and singing' was incorporated into the curriculum of the Madrid teachers' colleges (Ministerio de Fomento 1878), and in most teachers' colleges elsewhere some time later, so that by the end of the nineteenth century classroom teachers were expected to teach singing to the children in their classes. Singing was mentioned for the first time in an educational regulation in 1884 when it was included within the 'essential knowledge' to be acquired by children aged three to seven (Ministerio de Fomento 1884). Although there is little evidence of this regulation being applied during this early period, two examples serve to indicate at least some teaching of music in schools. First, singing was taught from 1844 to 1911 in a school in the Canary Islands, a Spanish province off the northwest coast of Africa (Marrero Henning 1997). The second example of music teaching was in the model secondary school established by the Free Institution of Teaching (*Institución Libre de Enseñanza*) in Madrid, a highly influential educational and intellectual institution founded in 1876 that criticized contemporary restrictions to academic thought in official institutions. Singing at this school was considered to be an important means of transmitting moral values (Sánchez de Andrés 2005) and from 1882 the song repertoire comprised songs from the classical and folk traditions. Interestingly, the folksongs were collected and compiled by teachers and students during their field trips to rural areas.

Singing was formally introduced as a subject in public primary schools in 1901 with the liberal reforms to the education system, which also extended compulsory education to the age of twelve and assigned the responsibility for teachers' salaries to the state (Ministerio de Instrucción Pública y Bellas Artes 1901). There is evidence that music was being taught in school to a far greater extent by the beginning of the twentieth century including the following instances:

- some private and public schools in Girona from 1902 and 1908 respectively (Brugués i Agustí 2008);

- the public schools in Barcelona that were established after 1914 and influenced by the ideas of many progressive educators and *renovation* movements;

- the 'graded schools'[3] in Madrid, where singing was taught for up to one hour per week in the 1910s and 1920s (Pozo Andrés 1996);

- the Home and Professional School for Women in Madrid, a secondary school for the vocational training of girls from the age of 12, where music was included as a two-year general subject (Ministerio de Instrucción Pública y Bellas Artes 1911).

The teaching of music in schools was recognized as being important from the very beginning of the Second Republic (1931–9), even though the main educational challenge was eradicating illiteracy – an ever-present problem. Music was included in an ultimately unsuccessful proposal for primary and secondary teaching (Molero Pintado 1991) that was presented to parliament in 1932 by Fernando de los Ríos (Delgado Criado 1994). This was a time of all sorts of progressive educational ideas, including 'pedagogical missions' organized from 1931, when teachers who were sent to remote villages, principally to improve literacy, also took phonographs and recordings of classical music with them for educational purposes. Such innovations were inspired by the work of the *Institución Libre de Enseñanza* and the advocates of the 'new school' – such as Luzuriaga (1927) – and by the ideas of music educators such as Manuel Borguñó (1933, 1938). Among the few reports about school music activities at the time were details of a teacher at a 'graded school' in the province of Soria who demonstrated how the ideas of the 'active school' were being carried out (Gómez Lozano 1933). The school had a choir of 100 children who rehearsed twice each week. The teacher provided a three-part arrangement of a lullaby as an example of the choir's repertoire and he was keen for his pupils to be recorded so that the discs could then be taken into schools by these 'pedagogical missions'. During the Second Republic the government undertook a series of ambitious reforms of the education system despite severe economic restrictions and violent political conflicts, one of which was a result of their decision to ban religious orders from teaching.

Although exiled to Valencia because of the Civil War (1936–9), the republican government created a Central Music Council (Ministerio de Instrucción Pública y Sanidad 1937b), among whose responsibilities was the organization of music teaching in primary and secondary schools. The Ministry of Public Instruction sanctioned a primary curriculum that included 'singing and rhythmics'[4] (Ministerio de Instrucción Pública y

Sanidad 1937a). But these efforts were doomed because of the ongoing Civil War and were eventually dismantled by the regime of General Franco, which remained in power until Franco's death in 1975.

In 1945 the *Law of Primary Education* (Jefatura del Estado 1945) established a Catholic fundamentalist and gender-segregated educational system whose Fascist principles were thoroughly exposed in its preface. This law made primary schooling compulsory for children aged 6 to 12 – free only for those who 'could not afford it', as a century before – in a country that was suffering extreme poverty. 'Music and singing' were included in the curriculum as part of a 'complementary knowledge group'. A contemporary report by a German teacher (Rude 1952) records that singing was taking place in schools, although the songs were mainly of a religious and patriotic nature. Singing was also evident in religious schools run by Jesuits and at lay private schools. Manuel Borguñó (1946) organized a school choir festival in Tenerife and María Dolors Bonal – who in 1967 would establish the Catalan Children's Choirs Movement – was working from 1951 at two private schools in Barcelona, teaching Catalan songs at a time when the Catalan language was being repressed (Roche 2000).

The nominal music curricula

Spain's political isolation ended with its incorporation into the United Nations in 1955 and with the transfer of the national administration to a Catholic liberal élite, which started to displace the Fascist organizations that had predominated during and immediately after the Civil War. A comprehensive music curriculum was formulated for the first time[5] that sequenced the musical content into three stages and provided an officially approved song repertoire – again, a mix of folk, religious and Fascist songs (Dirección General de Enseñanza Primaria 1953).

By the end of the 1950s, the economy was slowly beginning to develop, and this favoured the extension of compulsory education to the age of 14 in 1964. Some teachers gained scholarships to study in Salzburg at the Orff Institute and were afterwards hired as specialists by private schools that incorporated music as a distinctive element of their curriculum (López-Ibor 2003; Oriol 2008; Roche 2007). One of these teachers, Monserrat Sanuy, co-edited an adaptation of the Orff Schulwerk incorporating Spanish folklore (Sanuy and González Sarmiento 1969a, 1969b) that became very influential in terms of popularizing music education. But in spite of a music curriculum and the tireless efforts of such music educators as Manuel Borguñó (1946, 1948, 1959, 1966), music was not widely taught, but remained a privilege of urban élites in a profoundly class-conscious society.

During the final period of the Franco era, 'music and singing' were included within an area of the curriculum termed 'aesthetic education' in the General Law of Education (Ministerio de Educación y Ciencia 1970), a law which also prescribed compulsory and free primary schooling for all children aged 6 to 14. Soon afterwards a detailed music curriculum was published that listed performing and individual and group creativity, clearly influenced by the Orff Schulwerk (Ministerio de Educación y Ciencia 1971).

After Franco's death in 1975 and the coronation of King Juan Carlos de Borbón, a transition process began that resulted in the enactment of the 1978 constitution and in the first democratic elections after the dictatorship. Changes in the educational system slowly began to be introduced that reflected the country's political and social progress.[6] A 'renewed' curriculum for primary schools was passed that also included music, but this time within an area termed 'artistic expression'. Written by experienced music educators, the guidelines for sixth to eighth grades (Angulo et al. 1981) and for third to fifth grades (Ministerio de Educación y Ciencia 1982) included recommendations about vocal and instrumental performance, ear training and movement, and sample Orff-style activities. However, neither the 1971 music curriculum nor the 1981–2 curriculum was widely implemented because generalist teachers were not adequately prepared to teach them (Oriol 1999) and perhaps also because there was no system of music inspection to enforce music teaching.[7] It seems that, as in the previous decades, music was still only being taught by a few highly motivated primary school teachers with some musical background and by music specialists employed in some private schools.

From 1970 to 1989 secondary education remained non-compulsory and comprised a three-year stage that started at the age of fourteen, followed by a one-year 'pre-university course'. In 1975 a one-year course called 'music' was introduced as a mandatory subject (Ministerio de Educación y Ciencia 1975). However, this was initially taught by teachers of other subjects largely to fill their teaching time allocations. A bachelor's degree was required for a teacher to teach in secondary schools and conservatoire-based qualifications held by musicians were not considered equivalent to university degrees.[8] Conservatoire graduates applied pressure until they managed to attain an official matching of the degrees (Peiteado Rodríguez 1983) and in 1984 competitive examinations for employment as music teachers for public schools began. This proved to be crucially important in raising the status of music as a subject because its teachers achieved parity with the civil servant status of other specialist teachers – this step resulted in the irreversible incorporation of music into the secondary curriculum. However, as the initial teaching of the subject had been undertaken by non-musicians and the fact that the curriculum content was heavily historical, with an emphasis on declarative knowledge, this resulted in a negative image of the subject that persisted for many years.

The 1990 reform

After the 1982 elections a series of gradual but determined changes in key social issues – including education – began. A long period of public debate and experimentation was promoted by the Ministry of Education (Ministerio de Educación y Ciencia 1984) that led to a white paper on educational reform (Ministerio de Educación y Ciencia 1987) and eventually to the enactment of the General Organic Law of the Educational System

(LOGSE) (Ministerio de Educación y Ciencia 1990). This law completely restructured the educational system and extended compulsory schooling to the age of 16, reducing primary to six years and extending secondary to six. Most importantly, it established that the first four years of secondary education would at last be compulsory and could be followed by two years of post-compulsory secondary schooling or by vocational training.

Besides extending compulsory schooling, the 1990 reform aimed at transforming the previous technical model into a constructivist model, informed by contemporary psychological research and publications (e.g. Coll 1988; Palacios et al. 1984, 1985). There was also a belief that access to a basic arts education should be available to all children, backed by increasing social demands in a country that was rapidly developing and had just been incorporated into the European Union.

With the restoration of democracy in 1978, after decades of uncertainty, Spanish music educators had begun to experience an optimistic time.[9] Many conferences were held during the 1980s to support the universality of music education – in Cáceres in 1981 (AAVV 1981) and 1982, in Madrid in 1984 (Oriol 1984), in El Escorial in 1986, in Valladolid in 1988 and in Alicante in 1989. Eventually, the concerns of music educators were being seriously considered. Most significantly, the ensuing reforms made the teaching of music in primary schools by specialists mandatory, which was also extended in secondary schools.

The primary music curriculum (Ministerio de Educación y Ciencia 1991a) advocated that children's musical activity in the classrooms should be undertaken through singing and playing instruments, through improvising and composing and through participating in active listening activities. To that end, music rooms started to be designated in all primary schools and musical instruments were allotted. All public schools were provided with pitched and non-pitched percussion instruments, electronic or acoustic pianos and hi-fi audio equipment.

Eventually, competitive examinations to fill music education posts in public primary schools were instituted[10] and music teachers were also hired in private schools. This led to an effective and universal implementation of a primary music curriculum for the first time. The key factor in this implementation was not the *enactment* of another official curriculum but, as with secondary music in the previous decade, the new 'civil servant' status of music teachers. Music education in primary schools was now firmly established.

The 1990 reform also extended the teaching of music in secondary schools to three years as a mandatory academic subject and as an optional subject in succeeding years. The secondary curriculum (Ministerio de Educación y Ciencia 1992) advocated active engagement with music-making as a continuation of the experience in primary schools.[11] The content was organized in six blocks: singing, playing, movement and dance, music theory, music history and music in mass media (Ministerio de Educación y Ciencia 1991a), each being divided into concepts, procedures and attitudes.[12] The attainment targets included not only aural recognition of musical elements or a contextual understanding of classical music (as was previously expected for secondary music) but also skills such as group singing, group instrumental performance, group dance, melodic improvisation, reading of staff notation and basic accompaniment of songs with tonic, dominant and subdominant chords.

Training of teachers

Teachers' colleges (*escuelas normales*),[13] modelled on the French 'école normal' model, were established from 1838 in different Spanish cities. Forty years later, in 1878, the subject of 'music and singing' (Ministerio de Fomento 1878) appeared for the first time in the teachers' colleges in Madrid. The subject was taken over two years and focused on music theory and sight singing. Different approaches to musical training emerged at the beginning of the twentieth century. Juan Vancell Roca (1902), a music lecturer at Barcelona Teachers' College, promoted an active methodology that connected theory with musical practice through ear training and the singing of Spanish folksongs (Sarfson 2007). Miguel Arnaudas and Manuel Soler (1911), music lecturers at Zaragoza and Madrid respectively, employed a more conservative approach and relied solely on teaching sight singing without pedagogical adaptations.[14] Tomás Sobrequés, music lecturer at the teachers' colleges of Girona from 1914 to 1945, published an article advocating the addition of two courses on choral singing, a music entrance examination at the teachers' colleges and even a music examination within the competitive examinations to hire primary teachers (Sobrequés 1917). Although he subsequently met with the Minister of Public Instruction, his requests were not acceded to (Brugués i Agustí 2008).

A major effort was made during the Second Republic to improve the training of teachers (Sarfson 2010), but most of the colleges were eventually closed during the Civil War. Following their reopening in 1942, a purge took place to eliminate any progressive ideas, and coeducation was suppressed. The Catholic Church and the Falange – the Fascist organization that predominated during the Civil War and the first years of the dictatorship – assumed a dominant role in educational matters. Musical training was kept to a minimum at teachers' colleges, but the Falange soon realized the possibilities for singing as an indoctrinating medium. To this end, after the war its 'women's section' undertook the musical preparation of the female instructors who would teach the so-called 'home skills' to girls in schools (Lizarazu de Mesa 1996). During the 1960s this preparation became a two-year course for 'music instructors' (Alonso Medina 2002; Luengo Sojo 1998), which was implemented in Madrid and many other cities, providing intensive music education training, including the Orff method, by invited foreign instructors and later by Spanish educators who had studied at the Orff Institute in Salzburg.

There was much discussion at the end of the 1980s about who should teach music in primary schools, which culminated in a conference held in Alicante in 1989. Various viewpoints were expressed about whether it should be taught by conservatoire music education graduates, by conservatoire music graduates with an additional training in education or by primary teachers with an extra training in music and music education

(Oriol 1988). Following these discussions, music education workshops started to flourish nationwide. Universities and government agencies in several Spanish regions also offered non-academic in-service training programmes of 500 to 800 hours' duration to provide primary teachers with training in music education. For instance, in 1986 the programme 'Música a l'escola' (Pastor i Gordero et al. 1990) started in Valencia to train infant and primary teachers and in 1989 two-year training programmes were offered in Madrid by the Royal Conservatoire of Music, coordinated by Elisa Roche, and by the Complutense University, coordinated by Nicolás Oriol. Under likely pressure from trade unions, the Ministry of Education eventually decided that only those holding a 'maestro' [primary teacher] three-year degree[15] would be entitled to teach in primary schools.[16] It also established teaching specialties, but specialist teachers were also to train as generalists and teach in that capacity if required (Ministerio de Educación y Ciencia 1991b). Music education was included among the teaching specialties and, accordingly, since 1992, most universities have offered three-year academic programmes for students wanting to become primary music teachers (*maestro, especialidad: educación musical*). In addition to a third of the training being assigned to music education, students undertook 320 hours of supervised teaching practices in schools (see Sustaeta and Oriol 1996).

The training of secondary teachers was rather different. Secondary teachers were required to hold only a bachelor's degree and, after 1971, a 'certificate of pedagogical aptitude' as well. Pre-service training for the 'certificate of pedagogical aptitude' was organized nationally through a series of short courses – in some universities even as distance learning evaluated with multiple-choice exams – and non-supervised teaching practices. The system was clearly inadequate as a preparation for teachers to cope with the inclusion of seventh and eighth graders in secondary schools after the 1990 reform; it could not prepare them to understand early adolescence. Neither did it help them to cope with the presence of numerous disaffected learners, who would have been excluded from schooling in previous educational systems and with the increasingly conflicting classroom interactions that occurred due to social changes (Defensor del Pueblo 2006; Hernández and Sancho 2004).

Relating the past to the present

Thus far, this chapter has outlined how music was integrated into compulsory schooling in Spain. Despite a musical tradition that can be traced back to the Middle Ages, it was a long journey, highly polarized by political stances and determined by historical conflicts and socio-cultural changes. Following the introduction of music to the training of classroom teachers at the end of the nineteenth century, singing seems to have only sporadically taken root in a relatively small number of Spanish schools. There was an increasing interest in music education at the beginning of the twentieth century and even specific proposals during the Second Republic, but all progressive endeavours were dismantled after the Civil War. Education suffered a significant regression during Franco's regime and music was deliberately used as an ideological medium. Music curricula were introduced in 1953, 1971 and 1981, but essentially they existed in name only because they were implemented in so few primary schools. The 1975 secondary music curriculum was the first to be effectively taught, eventually by music specialists, but secondary education was still not compulsory. Only in 1990 did the universal teaching of music become a reality, after the first democratic educational reform. Only with the mandatory appointment of specialist teachers in primary school was the primary music curriculum properly and universally implemented. The 1990 reform extended compulsory schooling to secondary schools and also extended the teaching of music as a mandatory subject taught by specialists.

In retrospect, the 1990 reform achieved success, but within limits. Despite considerable enthusiasm and hard work, many changes were limited by bureaucratic processes. The extended application of its child-centred pedagogical principles was hindered by insufficient funding for a generalized in-service training of teachers[17] and by the reluctance of a great number of teachers to change their classic teacher- and subject-centred approaches to teaching. Nevertheless, there have been encouraging innovations, including work with individual composition (Murillo 2006), collaborative composition (Rusinek 2007), composition with computers (Alegret 2004), inclusive students' concerts (Rusinek 2008), school choirs (Sotelo 2002; Elorriaga 2011), school operas (Sarmiento 2012) and school orchestras (Murillo and Bravo 2005).

However, after the change of government with the 1996 elections, progress was somewhat hindered by limited funding for the public educational system in favour of a considerable and largely concealed subsidy for private schools. Increasingly difficult teacher–student interactions and a consistent 30 per cent school dropout rate were then attributed by teachers and public opinion to the 1990 reform rather than to short-falls in funding or to the inadequacy of teacher training. A conservative counter-reform resulted (Ministerio de Educación, Cultura y Deporte 2000, 2002), which returned classic historicist approaches to teaching (Coll 2004); then the socialist government elected in 2004 overturned this counter-reform with a new national curriculum (Ministerio de Educación y Ciencia 2006), and again the conservative government elected in 2012 changed it (Ministerio de Educación, Cultura y Deporte, 2013). Regrettably, all the latest educational reforms have been driven by the pressures of political parties, religious groups, trade unions and lobbies rather than being informed by pupils' needs, by teachers' demands or by educational research. Perhaps even more detrimental were the regulations for the reform of higher education studies (Ministerio de Educación y Ciencia 2007). Due to the Bologna Declaration, designed to make the higher education systems in Europe converge towards a more transparent system by 2010, eighteen subject specialisms within pre-service primary teacher training courses have been removed, thereby opening the possibility of a situation similar to the 1970s and 1980s when the primary school music curriculum reverts to effectively becoming nominal once more. In this self-destructive game played by Spanish political parties, which is not different from the game they play in other political areas, ideology counts for more than a pragmatic evaluation of reality.

In summary, the position of school music in Spain has been under threat for a considerable time, and this is still the case. If the 2006 curriculum had reduced the presence of music in secondary schools, the 2013 reform is changing its status in primary and secondary schools from a compulsory subject to that of a subject that can be taught or not, according to decisions to be taken by the different regional educational authorities and by the schools, thus opening the doors to the situation of unequal educational opportunities previous to 1990. Nevertheless, countless Spanish children and adolescents in the last twenty-five years have experienced music as a living force in their school education, independently of their families' social status or of their economic circumstances. Spanish school music continues to be resilient.

Reflective questions

1 We have seen that, while music curriculum reforms were introduced in Spain in 1953, 1971 and 1981, essentially these existed in name only. Can you identify periods in your own country when rhetoric outstripped reality in the development and implementation of the music curriculum?

2 The 1980s and the 1990s were years of optimism among Spanish music educators when their concerns were being seriously considered by government authorities. Would you say that there had been a similar period in your own national context? What, if any, developments in your own country have paralleled the Spanish experience?

3 There was much discussion in Spain in the 1980s about what comprised the necessary musical training for primary school teachers. What is your own view on the essential content of teacher education programmes for primary schools teachers? To what extent generally has the musical preparation of primary school teachers responded to changing musical styles and educational priorities both historically and today?

Notes

1.   We are indebted to Nicolás Oriol, to Lluís Brugués, to the late María Martorell and to the late Elisa Roche for sharing their first-hand knowledge. We are also thankful to José Luis Aróstegui, to the late Steve Dillon and to the late Julio Hurtado for their suggestions and careful reading of the manuscript.
2.   Note that this and the subsequent reforms applied only to public schools that had a charitable mission and that they educated only a fraction of the children attending schools, who were

themselves only a small fraction of all Spanish children. Most private schools were religious, but early in the nineteenth century lay private schools had also been founded.

3. The *escuelas graduadas* were public primary schools in which, since 1898, teaching was organized according to age grades and where subjects had a detailed timetable.

4. Dalcroze's eurhythmics had been promoted in Barcelona by Joan Llongueras since 1911 (for a further development, see Llongueras 1942). Llongueras was awarded a scholarship by the Council for Scholarships and Scientific Investigations (*Junta para la Ampliación de Estudios e Investigaciones Científicas*) to study in Geneva (López Casanova 2002).

5. These curricula, called 'questionnaires', were the first attempt to regulate officially teachers' instructional activities. However, they were 'compulsory for public and advisory for private [schools]'.

6. This was one of the few music education dissertations at the time and showed, from a positivist perspective, the contemporary preoccupation with the underdevelopment of Spanish music education. Dionisio del Río (1982) administered a Spanish version of Seashore's test (Seashore et al. 1977) to a wide sample of school children to confirm the hypothesis that the underdevelopment was not caused by the Spanish population's musical aptitudes being below standard, but rather by the country's general underdevelopment.

7. There were not – and there are still not – specialist inspectors and specifically there is no inspection of school music. Moreover, the evaluation of the quality of the teaching in schools was not – and is not – included among Spanish education inspectors' duties.

8. In 1970 the Ministry of Education and Science began a process of incorporating existing schools of arts into university colleges. The music conservatoires boycotted the process and stayed outside the higher education system, thus giving rise to institutional problems that still persist today.

9. The Spanish section of ISME was founded by Rosa María Kucharsky in that year.

10. For a report about teachers' perspectives of the hiring system and of the professional profile it fosters, see Rusinek (2004). For a biographical study of primary music teachers' careers, see Ocaña (2006).

11. Note that Spanish secondary schools do not provide teaching of orchestral instruments or the possibility of participating in a wind band. Such experiences are provided by private or community-based 'schools of music' for amateurs or by elementary/intermediate conserva-toires for those aspiring to become professionals. Thus, Spanish secondary music is equivalent to 'general music' in the USA.

12. Inspired by contemporary notions about a 'hidden curriculum' (Torres Santomé 1991), the reform provided a curriculum frame that opposed previous technical conceptions of education as non-value-laden transmission of information.

13. Men and women studied in separated colleges until coeducation was established in 1931 during the Second Republic. Throughout Franco's regime teacher training was again gender segregated until coeducation was re-established with the new democracy. Teachers' colleges became university colleges after 1970.

14. Both manuals used the fixed-doh method for sight singing.

15. The Spanish university system included, until the changes due to the Bologna Treatise, three-year degrees (*diplomatura*) and five-year degrees (*licenciatura*) equivalent to bachelor's degrees. There were no academic master's degrees and the 'third cycle' of higher education studies were doctoral degrees. Primary teachers were required to hold three-year degrees (*diplomatura*) in order to be employed, and were paid less than secondary teachers, who were required to possess five-year degrees. There was, first, an intention to reduce costs and, second, to have all-purpose specialist teachers who could complete their timetables as generalists.

16. It has to be noted that within the Spanish system people with higher degrees – even with postgraduate degrees – are not allowed to teach in primary schools if they do not hold the

'*maestro*' degree. Contrariwise, those holding a '*maestro*' degree are not allowed to teach in secondary if they do not hold a bachelor's degree (*licenciatura*).

17. A major part of the funding was devoted to building more secondary schools and to extend existing buildings. This was necessary because of the massive influx of students with the incorporation of seventh and eighth graders into secondary schools and because 15- and 16-year-olds were previously excluded from schooling.

References

AAVV (1981), *La formación humana a través de la música: II Congreso Nacional de Pedagogia Musical*, Cáceres: Institución Cultural 'El Brocense'.

Alegret, M. (2004), 'La creación musical a través de la información: estudio de un caso en primer ciclo de secundaria' (unpublished PhD dissertation, Universidad de Barcelona, Barcelona).

Alonso Medina, J. A. (2002), 'Cursos de formación musical para instructoras de la Sección Femenina y para el profesorado en general', *El Guiniguada* 11: 11–21.

Angulo, M., C. Sanuy, M. Sanuy and E. Roche (1981), 'Programas renovados de la E. G. B. Educación Artística (I). Música. (Documento de consulta)', *Vida Escolar* 211, 1–48.

Arnaudas, M. and M. Soler (1911), *Tratado de música para las escuelas normales*, Leipzig: Breitkopf & Haertel.

Borguñó, M. (1933), *La música, el cant i l'escola*, Barcelona: Librería Bastinos.

Borguñó, M. (1938), 'Elementos para la organización de la pedagogía musical escolar', *Música* 4: 33–9.

Borguñó, M. (1946), *Educación musical escolar y popular*, Santa Cruz de Tenerife: La Tinerfeña.

Borguñó, M. (1948), *La música, los músicos y la educación*, Santa Cruz de Tenerife: Instituto Musical de Pedagogía.

Borguñó, M. (1959), *Cincuenta años de educación musical*, Santa Cruz de Tenerife: Instituto Musical de Pedagogía.

Borguñó, M. (1966), *¿Ha fracasado la educación musical?*, Santa Cruz de Tenerife: Galarza.

Brugués i Agustí, L. (2008), *La música a Girona. Historia del Conservatori Isaac Albéniz*, Girona: Diputació de Girona.

Coll, C. (1988), *Psicología y currículum: Una Aproximación Psicopedagógica a la Elaboración del Currículum Escolar*, Barcelona: Laia.

Coll, C. (2004), 'La revolución conservadora llega a la educación', *Aula de Innovación Educativa* 130: 7–10.

Defensor del Pueblo (2006), *Violencia Escolar: el maltrato entre iguales en la educación secundaria obligatoria 1999-2006 (Nuevo estudio y actualización del informe 2000)*, Madrid: Defensor del Pueblo.

del Río, D. (1982), 'Aptitudes musicales de la población escolar española' (unpublished PhD dissertation, Universidad Complutense de Madrid, Madrid).

Delgado Criado, B. (ed.) (1994), *Historia de la educación en España y América*. Vol. 3: *La educación en la España contemporánea (1789–1975)*, Madrid: Fundación Santa María – SM – Morata.

Dirección General de Enseñanza Primaria (1953), *Cuestionarios nacionales para la enseñanza primaria*, Madrid: Servicio de Publicaciones del Ministerio de Educación Nacional.

Elorriaga, A. (2011), 'The construction of male gender identity through choir singing at a Spanish secondary school', *International Journal of Music Education* 29 (4): 318–32.

Gómez Lozano, P. (1933), *Mi escuela activa*, Madrid: Compañía de Artes Gráficas.

Hernández, F. and J. M. Sancho (2004), *El clima escolar en los centros de secundaria: Más allá de los tópicos*, Madrid: Centro de Investigación y Documentación Educativa – Ministerio de Educación y Ciencia.

Jefatura del Estado (1945), *Ley de Educación Primaria*, Madrid: Boletín Oficial del Estado.

Lizarazu de Mesa, M. A. (1996), 'En torno al folklore musical y su utilización: el caso de las Misiones Pedagógicas y la Sección Femenina', *Anuario Musical: Revista de Musicología del CSIC* 51, 233–46.

Llongueras, J. (1942), *El ritmo en la educación y formación general de la infancia*, Barcelona: Labor.

López Casanova, M. B. (2002), 'La política educativo-musical en España durante la Segunda República', *Música y Educación* 50: 15–26.

López-Ibor, S. (2003), 'Entrevista con Montse Sanuy', *Orff España* 3: 10–2.

Luengo Sojo, A. (1998), 'La pedagogía musical de la Sección Femenina de F. E. T. y de las J. O. N. S. en Barcelona: Escuela de Especialidades "Roger de Lauria"' in X. Aviñoa (ed.), *Miscellània Oriol Martorell*, Barcelona: Publicacions de la Universitat de Barcelona, pp. 333–43.

Luzuriaga, L. (1927), *La educación nueva*, Madrid: Museo Pedagógico Nacional – J. Cosano.

Marrero Henning, M.d.P. (1997), *El Colegio de San Agustín en la enseñanza secundaria de Gran Canaria*, Las Palmas de Gran Canaria: Unelco.

Ministerio de Educación, Cultura y Deporte (2000), *Real Decreto 3473/2000, de 29 de diciembre, por el que se modifica el Real Decreto 1007/1991, de 14 de junio, por el que se establecen las enseñanzas mínimas correspondientes a la educación secundaria obligatoria*, Madrid: Boletín Oficial del Estado.

Ministerio de Educación, Cultura y Deporte (2002), *Ley Orgánica 10/2002, de 23 de diciembre, de Calidad de la Educación*, Madrid: Boletín Oficial del Estado.

Ministerio de Educación, Cultura y Deporte (2013), *Ley Orgánica 8/2013, de 9 de diciembre, para la mejora de la calidad educativa*, Madrid: Boletín Oficial del Estado.

Ministerio de Educación y Ciencia (1970), *Ley 14/1970, de 4 de agosto, general de educación y financiamiento dc la rcforma educativa*, Madrid: Boletín Oficial del Estado.

Ministerio de Educación y Ciencia (1971), 'Segunda etapa de la Educación General Básica. Nuevas orientaciones pedagógicas', *Vida Escolar* 128–30: 4–66.

Ministerio de Educación y Ciencia (1975), *Decreto 160/1975 de 23 de enero de Plan de Estudios de Bachillerato*, Madrid: Boletín Oficial del Estado.

Ministerio de Educación y Ciencia (1982), *Programas renovados de la Educación General Básica. Ciclo medio. 3er, 4° y 5° curso*, Madrid: Escuela Española.

Ministerio de Educación y Ciencia (1984), *Hacia la reforma: Documentos de trabajo*, Madrid: Servicio de Publicaciones del Ministerio de Educación y Ciencia.

Ministerio de Educación y Ciencia (1987), *Proyecto para la reforma de la enseñanza: Educación infantil, primaria, secundaria y profesional*, Madrid: Centro de Publicaciones del Ministerio de Educación y Ciencia.

Ministerio de Educación y Ciencia (1990), *Ley Orgánica 1/1990, de 3 de octubre, de Ordenación General del Sistema Educativo*, Madrid: Boletín Oficial del Estado.

Ministerio de Educación y Ciencia (1991a), *Real Decreto 1007/1991, de 14 de junio, por el que se establecen las enseñanzas mínimas correspondientes a la educación secundaria obligatoria*, Madrid: Boletín Oficial del Estado.

Ministerio de Educación y Ciencia (1991b), *Real Decreto 1440/1991, de 30 de agosto, por el que se establece el título universitario oficial de Maestro, en sus diversas especialidades, y las directrices generales propias de los planes de estudios conducentes a la obtención de aquel*, Madrid: Boletín Oficial del Estado.

Ministerio de Educación y Ciencia (1992), *Secundaria obligatoria. Música*, Madrid: Ministerio de Educación y Ciencia.

Ministerio de Educación y Ciencia (2006), *Ley Orgánica 2/2006, de 3 de mayo, de Educación*, Madrid: Boletín Oficial del Estado.

Ministerio de Educación y Ciencia (2007), *Orden ECI/3857/2007, de 27 de diciembre, por la que se establecen los requisitos para la verificación de los títulos universitarios oficiales que habiliten para el ejercicio de la profesión de Maestro en Educación Primaria*, Madrid: Boletín Oficial del Estado.

Ministerio de Fomento (1857), *Ley de Instrucción Pública*, Madrid: Gaceta de Madrid.

Ministerio de Fomento (1878), *Real Decreto de 24 de agosto de 1878*, Madrid: Gaceta de Madrid.

Ministerio de Fomento (1884), *Real Decreto de 4 de julio de 1884*, Madrid: Gaceta de Madrid.

Ministerio de Instrucción Pública y Bellas Artes (1901), *Real Decreto de 26 de octubre de 1901*, Madrid: Gazeta de Madrid.

Ministerio de Instrucción Pública y Bellas Artes (1911), *Real decreto disponiendo que en la Escuela del Hogar y Profesional de la mujer, se cursen las enseñanza que se indican*, Madrid: Gaceta de Madrid.

Ministerio de Instrucción Pública y Sanidad (1937a), *Decreto fijando el plan de estudios que ha de regir en la escuela primaria española*, Valencia: Gazeta de la República.

Ministerio de Instrucción Pública y Sanidad (1937b), *Orden de creación del Consejo Central de la Música*, Valencia: Gaceta de la República.

Molero Pintado, A. (ed.) (1991), *Historia de la educación en España. Vol. 4: La Educación Durante la Segunda República y la Guerra Civil*, Madrid: Ministerio de Educación y Ciencia.

Murillo, A. (2006), 'Atrapando los sonidos: Experiencias compositivas en el aula de música de secundaria', Eufonía. *Didáctica de la Música*, 37: 112–18.

Murillo, A. and V. Bravo (2005), 'Com sona L'ESO: un encuentro musical en la ESO', *Eufonía. Didáctica de la Música* 34, 106–11.

Ocaña, A. (2006), 'Desarrollo profesional de las maestras de educación musical desde una perspectiva biográfico-narrativa', Revista *Electrónica Complutense de Investigación en Educación Musical* 3 (3): 1–14.

Oriol, N. (ed.) (1984), *I Simposio Nacional de Didáctica de la Música: Escuela Universitaria de Formación del Profesorado María Díaz Jiménez de Madrid*, Madrid: Editorial Complutense.

Oriol, N. (1988), 'Las escuelas universitarias y la formación musical del profesorado de educación básica', *Música y Educación* 1 (1): 17–31.

Oriol, N. (1999), 'La formación del profesorado de música en la enseñanza general', *Música y Educación* XII (1), 49–68.

Oriol, N. (2008), personal communication.

Palacios, J., A. Marchesi and M. Carretero (eds) (1984), *Psicología evolutiva*, Vol. 2: *Desarrollo cognitivo y social del niño*, Madrid: Alianza.

Palacios, J., A. Marchesi and M. Carretero (eds) (1985), *Psicología evolutiva*, Vol. 3: *Adolescencia, madurez y senectud*, Madrid: Alianza.

Pastor i Gordero, P., A. Porta Navarro, Equipo de Monitores a l'Escola and M. J. Rocamora Martínez (eds.) (1990), *Música a l'escola. Formación del profesorado de educación infantil y del primer ciclo de primaria. Guía del programa*, Valencia: Consellería de Cultura, Educació i Ciéncia.

Peiteado Rodríguez, M. (1983), 'La reforma de los programas de música en la enseñanza media', *Aula Abierta* 37, 57–65.

Pozo Andrés, M.d.M. (1996), 'La escuela graduada madrileña en el primer tercio del siglo xx: ¿Un modelo pedagógico para el resto del Estado Español?', *Revista Complutense de Educación* 7 (2): 211–74.

Roche, E. (2000), 'Entrevista: María Dolors Bonal', *Orff España* 3: 3–9.

Roche, E. (2007), personal communication.

Rude, A. (1952), *La Escuela Nueva y sus procedimientos didácticos*, México: Labora.

Rusinek, G. (2004), 'The profile of the music teacher in Spanish primary schools, according to the teachers themselves', *Proceedings of the 26th International Society for Music Education World Conference, Tenerife.* CD-ROM.

Rusinek, G. (2007), 'Students' perspectives in a collaborative composition project at a Spanish secondary school', *Music Education Research* 9 (3): 323–35.

Rusinek, G. (2008), 'Disaffected learners and school musical culture: an opportunity for inclusion', *Research Studies in Music Education* 30 (1): 9–23.

Sánchez de Andrés, L. (2005), 'La música en la actividad educativa institucionista', *Boletín de la Institución Libre de Enseñanza* 57: 7–18.

Sanuy, M. and L. González Sarmiento (1969a), *Orff Schulwerk: Música para Niños*, Vol. 1, Madrid: Unión Musical Española.

Sanuy, M. and L. González Sarmiento (1969b), *Orff Schulwerk: Música para niños. Introducción*, Madrid: Unión Musical Española.

Sarfson, S. (2007), 'Juan Vancell y Roca. Teoría y práctica musical en la formación de maestros', *Música y Educación* 70, 37–46.

Sarfson, S. (2010), 'Educación musical en Aragón (1900–1950)', *Legislación, publicaciones y escuela,* Zaragoza: Prensas Universitarias.

Sarmiento, P. (2012), 'La ópera, un vehículo de aprendizaje (LÓVA)', *Eufonía. Didáctica de la Música* 55, 40–47.

Seashore, C. E., Lewis, D. and Saeveit, J. G. (1977), *Tests de aptitudes musicales de Seashore*, Madrid: TEA.

Sobrequés, T. (1917), 'Deficiències del pla de l'enseñança de la música a les escoles normals', *Scherzando: Revista Catalana Musical* 75: 49–50.

Sotelo, C. (2002), 'Los encuentros de corales de enseñanza secundaria de Cataluña', *Eufonía. Didáctica de la Música* 26: 115–20.

Sustaeta, I. and N. Oriol (1996), 'La especialidad de Educación Musical en la Facultad de Educación de la Universidad Complutense de Madrid', *Música y Educación* 9 (1): 45–54.

Torres Santomó, J. (1991), *El currículum oculto*, Madrid: Morata.

Vancell Roca, J. (1902), *El libro de música y canto*, Barcelona: Fidel Giró Impresor.

PART II: THE AMERICAS
A *NORTH AMERICA*

Chapter 9

Canada: Diverse developments across the decades

Nancy F. Vogan

Early education in Canada was influenced by various groups of immigrants – particularly those from Britain and France – and usually reflected the beliefs and heritage (including the musical heritage) of these settlers, as well as those of missionaries, members of the clergy and military personnel.

The fact that the British North America Act, which created the Dominion of Canada in 1867, made education a provincial responsibility has had a profound influence. This delegating of responsibility to the provinces has resulted in a lack of uniformity of standards for all subject areas, including music. In 1867 there were just four provinces (Ontario, Quebec, New Brunswick and Nova Scotia) but by 1873 three more had joined – Manitoba (1870), British Columbia (1871) and Prince Edward Island (1873). Saskatchewan and Alberta did not become provinces until 1905 and the most easterly province, Newfoundland and Labrador, remained a separate British colony until 1949. There are also three northern territories that are part of Canada – Yukon, Northwest Territories and Nunavut. Canada today covers a large geographic area, but has a relatively small population that is primarily spread out along the southern border from coast to coast.

During the early years of European settlement music instruction was included in several of the private and religious schools in the various regions that are now part of Canada. Private instrumental instruction and choral training for religious services were offered to both young men and women by various Roman Catholic orders. Hymns, simple songs and 'national airs' were prevalent in those parts of Canada settled by Protestants – English, Scottish and Irish immigrants and the United Empire Loyalists from the United

States following the Revolutionary War. For several of the Protestant denominations, singing schools similar to those in the American colonies and parts of Britain provided an early form of music instruction during the late eighteenth and nineteenth centuries. With the emergence of more formal systems of public education in various regions of the country during the second half of the nineteenth century, music was included more frequently, but this was still sporadic in many places. It was usually little more than casual singing, often taught by individuals outside the school system – private music teachers, church choir directors and bandmasters. This instruction was primarily available in the larger urban centres (see Kallmann 1960; Keillor 2006).

As school enrolments increased and support for music instruction grew, many of these special instructors became music supervisors who were responsible for music instruction in all the schools of a certain district. This meant that the elementary school teachers were expected to provide most of the music instruction for their own classes but frequently they had had little or no training in music themselves. Early instructional programmes in music usually consisted of rote singing and a study of the rudiments of music. Support for music instruction in the schools was often obtained by mounting massed children's choirs for special occasions such as royal visits or Empire Day celebrations. The introduction of music in rural schools followed later in a pattern somewhat similar to that of the urban centres, but standards were rarely as high. Music's importance as a subject in the school curriculum was slight in many regions until at least the 1920s and 1930s; major advances were made in the period following the Second World War.

Establishment of free public education

Free public schools were established in Ontario in 1846; they were established in most other regions of Canada during the second half of the nineteenth century. Most of these schools were non-sectarian. However, the education situations in Quebec and Newfoundland differed from those in the rest of Canada. In addition to the private religious schools in Quebec, public schooling was also divided along religious lines until the mid-twentieth century. This resulted in Catholic schools for most of the French-speaking children and Protestant schools for most of the English-speaking. Consequently, developments in education, including those in music, evolved along entirely different paths. Similarly, in Newfoundland, schools were organized along religious lines with separate schools and school boards for the Roman Catholic and the various Protestant denominations until the late twentieth century. The three Maritime provinces on Canada's east coast – New Brunswick, Nova Scotia and Prince Edward Island – although small in both area and population, have always had separate governments, including their own departments of education.

In Ontario, vocal music was listed in the first programme of studies for schools and music instruction for classroom teachers was begun at the provincial Normal School by

1848. This reflected the influence of Egerton Ryerson, Chief Superintendent of Education for Upper Canada or Canada West (Ontario) from 1844 until 1876. Ryerson was very supportive of music instruction, partly because of his interest in the education theories of Pestalozzi, which had spread throughout parts of Europe, Britain and the United States. He had visited many schools whose practice was based on these theories during his travels to more than twenty countries in the British Empire and Europe while he was developing his plans for a public school system for Ontario. Ryerson subsequently brought Henry Francis Sefton from Britain to teach the Wilhem–Hullah music method in the schools and at the Normal School. This method was based on the fixed doh. Sefton worked in Toronto from 1858 to 1882 and created the earliest music books in Ontario intended specifically for school use; some of these materials were later used in other provinces as well, including his *Three-Part Songs* (1869) and *A Manual of Vocal Music* (1871) (see Trowsdale 1962, 1970).

Music appeared in the programme of studies in other provinces at various times – Nova Scotia in 1855, Quebec in 1871, New Brunswick in 1872 and Prince Edward Island in the late 1870s (see Green and Vogan 1991; Vogan 1979, 1986, 1988). In British Columbia, the first superintendent of education was appointed in 1872. He had arrived from England via Ontario where he had worked with Ryerson, whom he admired greatly, so the educational policies established in British Columbia bore a close resemblance to those advocated by Ryerson in Ontario with a strong emphasis on music in the schools. In the schools of Winnipeg (Manitoba), music was taught before 1900, but the first detailed music curriculum for the province of Manitoba did not appear until 1928.

Much of the land that formed the provinces of Saskatchewan and Alberta in 1905 consisted of pioneer settlements, many with new immigrants. There were formal musical activities in some regions but generally not in rural areas. There was limited support for music instruction in the early days of establishing schools. However, inspectors encouraged the singing of patriotic songs in areas where students were of European ancestry in order to develop English-language skills and patriotism for their new country.

Music has played an important role in the life of Newfoundland both in the folk tradition and in music instruction. The major influences on education in Newfoundland have been English and Irish, in music as in general education. Several members of the English-speaking Roman Catholic orders (many of them from Ireland) played an important role in music instruction, as did teachers from the various Protestant denominations. The differences between private and public school music teaching were not as clear in Newfoundland as in other provinces because the two types of music instruction already co-existed at denominational institutions: 'Though some private teachers maintained studios in their homes, a large number of them worked in institutional settings with church affiliations. The music departments in these schools functioned almost as small conservatories' (Green and Vogan 1991: 298; see also Woodford 1988).

Lobbying for instruction came from different sectors, sometimes from an official within the education system, sometimes from a music teacher or organist in the area and sometimes from the parents. School instrumental ensembles were scarce and the majority were extra-curricular. In most of the early schools in Canada, the aims of music were justified in terms of its extrinsic values. To Ryerson, music was a powerful agent of moral culture. Church music encouraged religious participation. Tomkins (1986: 90) sums up the situation:

> Singing 'national airs' promoted patriotism. Fireside melodies, including 'moral songs' had leisure value in displacing questionable social amusements such as drinking. For some educators, music reinforced classroom discipline and had positive physiological effects that assisted all teaching. Music gained its strongest acceptances as a mental discipline; where it was promoted for 'relaxation' it was accepted merely as an 'auxiliary' subject.

Influence of the tonic sol-fa movement

From the 1860s to the 1890s John Curwen's tonic sol-fa methodology for developing music reading skills that had become so popular in Britain was introduced in various regions of Canada. The influence of this method based on the moveable doh was felt from St John's, Newfoundland, in the east, to Victoria, British Columbia, in the west, as well as in several other regions of the country. Tonic sol-fa teaching in each of these regions often developed quite independently with little or no influence from activities in other areas.

Most of the early teachers of this approach were from Britain; prior to the First World War, English-speaking Canadian schools relied heavily on British music teachers, many of whom had received tonic sol-fa training prior to migrating to Canada. The introduction of this system had a lasting effect on music instruction in several parts of the country. In some places it was very well received, while in others there was great controversy regarding its use. The use of staff notation was especially preferred by those who taught instruments. The French-speaking programmes continued to use the fixed doh.

During the 1870s, the Chief Inspector of Schools for Toronto, George Hughes, was looking for a way to improve music instruction in his schools. He expressed dissatisfaction with the situation and wanted classroom teachers to teach music for fifteen minutes every day. Through his influence, the first detailed course of study in vocal music for Toronto schools appeared in 1876. Subsequently a new provincial course of study was issued and a new music teacher, S. H. Preston, was appointed to the Toronto Normal School. Preston was familiar with American materials and was particularly interested in the work of Hosea Holt, a leading educator from the USA and a strong advocate of note reading using traditional notation. Preston produced his own adaptation of Tufts and Holt's *Normal Music Course* (1883) for schools in Canada in 1885.

Meanwhile, Hughes had been enquiring about the tonic sol-fa system being used in Britain as it had already been introduced in parts of Ontario including Hamilton and London. In 1886 Hughes appointed a fellow Scot, Alexander T. Cringan, as music supervisor for the Toronto schools. Cringan, a strong supporter of tonic sol-fa, taught music in Toronto in a variety of capacities for the next forty-four years.

Cringan became involved in a methods controversy in his very first year in Toronto and this continued for quite some time. In 1887 a special music summer school for teachers was held in Toronto. Preston arranged that Hosea Holt from the USA be invited to teach his method of music reading. At the conclusion of the course, it was recommended by the teachers in attendance that Holt's method (and Preston's adaptation of the textbook) be sanctioned for Ontario schools. The following year, Cringan taught the summer school, using the tonic sol-fa approach, and the teachers were so impressed that they recommended the use of this method in the schools. Subsequently, a controversy arose over the virtues of staff versus tonic sol-fa notation and Preston and Cringan emerged as the main protagonists in an issue that attracted much public attention. The provincial department of education did not give exclusive authorization to either of these methodologies but, as a result of Cringan's leadership, the tonic sol-fa movement was firmly established by the turn of the century. In 1895 the Ontario Department of Education issued a music syllabus for public schools that outlined two separate courses, one using tonic sol-fa and the other using staff notation. Until the 1920s the emphasis in school music in Ontario continued to be on singing and the development of reading skills. Cringan published instructional materials, including *The Canadian Music Course* (1888). In 1901 he became music master at the Toronto Normal School and in 1919 he was appointed Inspector of the Teaching of Music for Ontario schools.

In 1886 the Montreal Protestant School Board hired a Mr Dawson to give a course of thirty lessons in tonic sol-fa for their teachers; they also issued an edict requiring classroom teachers to teach singing to their own classes. The following year a new course in this method was introduced in schools and children's concerts. Cringan's 1888 publication was introduced as the textbook and all teachers were required to provide instruction in music using the tonic sol-fa method or have $10 deducted from their salaries. This ruling was kept on the books until at least 1920, by which time the penalty had increased to $40.

Tonic sol-fa was also introduced in other parts of the country. In the Maritimes, a Presbyterian minister from Scotland, Reverend James Anderson, played an important role in the introduction of tonic sol-fa instruction throughout the region. In 1884 he took a charge in Musquodoboit Harbour outside Halifax, Nova Scotia, and was soon involved in giving lessons in this method for teachers in the Halifax area. His involvement in music increased so much that in a few years he gave up his work as a minister in order to devote his entire time to music teaching. He travelled to all three Maritime provinces, working with teachers both during the year and at summer workshops. He used some of Cringan's publications in his teaching but he also published a series of articles on tonic sol-fa in *The Educational Review*, a Maritime periodical for teachers. Anderson later moved to Ontario where he lived in several small communities before retiring to California. Two of his pupils continued his work in the Maritimes and published materials for the schools. In western Canada, tonic sol-fa became popular in British Columbia, particularly in Victoria.

Expansion of music programmes after the First World War

Following the First World War there was a gradual change in music programmes in most parts of Canada (for example, see Vogan 1993). Vocal music eventually became an integral part of elementary school education in most regions, but music in the high schools was generally offered on an extra-curricular basis, if at all. Even after music was introduced as a subject in Grade 9, extra-curricular music activities (both choral and instrumental) were undertaken to supplement the often insufficient time scheduled during school hours. It was a long time before music gained the status of an accredited subject at the secondary school level.

Various aspects of education in Canada were influenced by the child development movement in the USA where school administrators and teachers had adopted principles of progressive education advocating a student-centred approach focusing on motivation and individual growth. This influence led to the adoption of the song method with less emphasis on music literacy and more emphasis on music for enjoyment:

> This meant that songs were introduced by rote and the quality of the repertoire became increasingly important as a means of placing a higher priority on appreciation. Canadian music educators were attracted to song series published in the USA; a number of US companies produced Canadian editions which often contained (with the exception of two or three Canadian patriotic songs) the same material found in the US version. (Kallmann and Potvin 1992: 1190c)

Most school music programmes began to expand with the impact of technology. The introduction of the gramophone and radio contributed to improved methods and materials for music education. Phonograph companies prepared music appreciation units consisting of recordings, teacher guides and student workbooks. Radio broadcasts were skilfully devised as supplements to classroom work, offering imaginative presentations that were as beneficial to teachers as they were to their students. Although some of the first radio programmes used in Canadian schools were those directed by Walter Damrosch in New York City, by 1943 the Canadian Broadcasting Corporation was producing programmes that served the special needs of Canadian education. Orchestras in several large cities also contributed to the development of music appreciation by presenting live concerts designed specifically for student audiences. The annual competitive music festival (based on the British model) became an important venue for displaying the achievements of music students in many areas of the country. Although undue emphasis on competition has been a controversial issue, many teachers and supervisors have continued to regard festival participation as a vital outlet for their performing groups. By the late 1930s most provinces had replaced the terms 'vocal music' or 'singing' with 'music' in their programmes of study for the elementary grades.

Another influence from education in the United States was a change in the structure of the school system in some provinces. The introduction of the junior high school was a major innovation in Canadian education, musically leading to a growing interest in participation in group music-making. Green and Vogan (1991: 162) highlight the significance of the junior high school development:

> The junior high school was the product of an attempt to liberalize the rigid curriculum that existed before the First World War. The movement reflected a growing recognition that schools should address themselves to the motivation of students – through activities and projects which appealed to students themselves – rather than to their mastery of prescribed subjects ... To realize these objectives, teachers possessing specialized expertise were selected to develop more fully the potential of students at this level. The western provinces experimented with junior high schools long before they were introduced elsewhere ... The patterns and traditions associated with music education in the west are significantly different from those in other parts of the country. To a certain extent these differences can be attributed to the three-level structure which had its conception in the junior high movement.

Developments in music education after the Second World War

Music instruction in secondary schools expanded in the post-Second World War period, especially in the field of instrumental music, and music courses for credit were offered at the secondary level in most provinces by the 1950s or 1960s. Universities and teacher training institutions had not anticipated the need for specialized training, so many provinces had to import music teachers or certify ex-service bandsmen and other musicians in order to meet the demand for instrumental specialists. Instrumental music programmes were aided by an expansion of the competitive music festival movement. Kiwanis and other service clubs not only established new competitions but also rejuvenated a number of older ones.

Most teachers in elementary schools continued to use some form or version of the song method. The curriculum, therefore, was determined to a large extent by the textbooks (or song series) approved by the various provincial governments. In the 1960s and 1970s several new approaches such as those of Orff and Kodály were introduced into the elementary music curriculum in many areas. An interest in multiculturalism led to an expansion of repertoire to include music of other cultures as well as music of native peoples. There was also an interest in promoting creativity and music composition in the classroom as well as performance of works by Canadian composers, an initiative encouraged by the John Adaskin Project for Canadian Music (see Shand 1986). In this connection, the late George Proctor observed: 'the most original contribution that Canada has made in music education has been through the work of R. Murray Schafer, whose approach emphasizes original creative work in developing music sensitivity and the use of all types of sound, including environmental ones, as material for musical organization' (Proctor 1980: 35).

Changes in instructional content or methodology were often initiated by those who taught music at teacher training institutions (both teachers' colleges and university departments of education and/or music) or by music supervisors in the employ of large urban school boards. Several provinces appointed directors of music to deal with the complex demands of the post-war period that included finding solutions for increasing enrolments and teacher shortages. Summer schools and in-service training sessions became popular as well as increased emphasis on pre-service training in music teaching. This pre-service training was gradually transferred to universities from the teachers' colleges or normal schools and specific programmes in music education became more common in institutions offering a bachelor's degree in music. Opportunities to obtain graduate degrees in music, including degrees in music education, were also expanded (see Davey 1977; Green 1974).

When the International Society for Music Education (ISME) was formed in 1953, Arnold Walter, director of the Faculty of Music at the University of Toronto, was elected its first president. At this time there was still no national organization of music educators in Canada; the Canadian Federation of Music Teachers' Associations had been formed in 1935, but it was primarily for those who taught music privately. A few provinces had provincial music education associations and the largest of these was the Ontario Music Educators' Association (OMEA), which had its beginnings in 1919 as a group within the Ontario Education Association (see Brault 1977). There had been talk for many years about the need for a national body of music educators in the country. Finally, in the spring of 1959, over 100 music educators from various parts of Canada gathered in Toronto at the spring meeting of OMEA to form the Canadian Music Educators' Association (CMEA). This organization has played an important role in the development of music education in Canada. Subsequent formation of provincial music educators' associations was promoted by CMEA in provinces where they did not already exist.

At the time of formation of CMEA only five provinces had individuals in the government who were responsible for music, but this situation improved over the next few years. However, a few decades later, several ministries of education eliminated their provincial music supervisors and reduced the number of music consultants. Whereas ministry officials generated most of the curriculum documents in the past, more recently there has been a tendency to use curriculum committees comprising of teachers. In many provinces, the burden of writing course outlines has been shifted to local boards.

In their publication on provincial music curriculum documents, Shand and Bartel (1993) noted that, for those interested in studying music education in Canada, published curriculum documents are rich sources of information. 'While not all teachers actually follow the guideline set forth by provincial ministries or departments of education, the published documents do reveal the orientation of provincial officials and leading music educators of a given time' (ibid.: ix). They also pointed out that the amount of leadership assumed by provincial authorities varies considerably from province to province:

> In Newfoundland, for example, the Department of Education provides very detailed guidance for local teachers, and even publishes collections of songs for use at specific grade levels. In Ontario, on the other hand, the Ministry of Education provides guidelines and some sample approaches, but more responsibility for curriculum development is given to local boards of education, many of which produce their own curriculum documents. (ibid.)

Some of the large city boards have now discontinued their director of music positions and have dismantled their centralized music departments. In some cases, music supervisors have been replaced by arts coordinators or curriculum resource personnel. Typically, such changes have been implemented as part of administrative restructuring in times of financial restraint. This has led to increased lobbying for music education. In 1992 a Coalition for Music Education in Canada was founded (Coalition for Music Education 2015a). Members represent a wide range of national music education-based associations as well as organizations from almost every province in the country and include educators, industry representatives, artists and performers, parents and music lovers across the country. This organization continues to lobby for music instruction through a number of initiatives, including Music Monday.

> Launched in 2005 by The Coalition for Music Education, [Music Monday] is the world's largest single event dedicated to raising awareness for music education. Each year, hundreds of thousands of students, educators, and music makers participate in a simultaneous nationwide concert performance of an original song written by a Canadian artist. (Coalition for Music Education 2015b)

Teachers and administrators are still interested in sharing ideas about music teaching and continue to look for opportunities to meet. CMEA national conventions played an important role in this sharing for over three decades, beginning in 1960. For budget reasons, these large conferences were discontinued, but they have recently been reinstated. The organization publishes a quarterly journal, the *Canadian Music Educator*, which assists in keeping teachers in touch with one another. The organization also produces a series of books containing articles on music education research and the biennial series *Research to Practice*[1] as well as sponsoring music education essay contests and national performance awards. Other specialized groups (Orff, Kodály, band and various choral organizations, etc.) hold national meetings and some Canadian music educators take part in American music education conferences as well as international meetings, including those of ISME.

In 2005 a pan-Canadian music education think tank meeting entitled *Music Education in Canada: What is the State of the Art?* was organized at the University of Western Ontario.

The idea for this gathering had been discussed by Canadians attending ISME meetings in previous years who missed the opportunity to get together for national conferences as they had in the past. Music educators from across the country were invited to attend and address the question posed in the title of the gathering. Discussions involved a number of issues facing music education in Canada including curricular concerns as well as a 'cross-Canada' panel of reports of the current state of music programmes in the various provinces. Subsequent gatherings have been organized (St John's, NL, in 2007 and Victoria, BC, in 2009). *From Sea to Sea: Perspectives on Music Education in Canada* (Veblen and Beynon 2007), published as an e-book, brings together several reports and articles that were presented at the first symposium. *Critical Perspectives in Canadian Music Education* (2012), a more recent publication edited by Beynon and Veblen, brings together a number of articles by leading researchers in music education across the country. In a review of this collection, Marie McCarthy comments: 'this insightful collection represents a landmark contribution that challenges the status quo and bridges the past, present, and future of Canadian music education' (see Beynon and Veblen 2012, reviewers' comments).

Today, some type of music instruction is included in the programme of studies for Grades K–6 in most Canadian schools but who undertakes the teaching – classroom teachers or music specialists – varies from region to region. The study of music is usually optional for other grade levels, but some regions have mandated music classes up to Grades 8 or 9. Although classroom singing, choirs, band and orchestral ensembles still form the basis of many school music programmes, the offerings in some areas have greatly expanded to include musical theatre, keyboard, guitar and ukulele classes, electronics, jazz, rock and popular music groups, as well as instruments and music of other cultures, Some programmes are coordinated with community groups as well. Recently instrumental initiatives based on the Venezuelan *El Sistema* youth orchestra programme have been introduced in several communities across the country.

Many differences in music teaching continue to exist among schools in the ten provinces and three territories, particularly in budgeting, curricula, scheduling and the training and certification of teachers, as well as the kinds of activities and the quality of musical experience available to students. Certain music educators mention the negative aspects of this diversity of approach, others believe that it allows teachers to develop programmes that better suit their particular jurisdictions.

Commenting on situations in countries in which teachers have little say in the development of curriculum for their nation, Paul Woodford (2005: 65) notes that Canadian music teachers are fortunate 'in part because education remains a provincial and not a federal jurisdiction … Provincial ministries of education sometimes collaborate on curriculum reform, but Canada does not have a government sanctioned national music curriculum set of standards, or standardized assessment regime for music education.' After discussing both the English National Music Curriculum and the National Standards for Music Education in the United States, Woodford clarifies the distinctiveness of the

Canadian approach: 'Although subject to many of the same reforms as their American and British counterparts, including at the provincial level an increased reliance on standardized (and other conservative) curricula coupled with a corresponding emphasis on accountability, most Canadian music teachers remain wary of the idea of a national music curriculum or set of standards' (ibid.). Given the variety of school music policies and practice in Canada – from both a historical and a contemporary perspective – diversity may well be one of the distinctive aspects that has characterized music education and will continue to do so.[2]

Reflective questions

1 Discuss the implications of music education as a provincial responsibility (British North America Act) across Canada, rather than the imposition of a national music curriculum.
2 What vocal music methodologies became popular in parts of Canada? Discuss these influences and why you think they were adopted.
3 Compare and contrast the major changes that came about in music education after the First World War and the Second World War.

Notes

1. For more detailed information, see Canadian Music Educators' Association website, http://www.cmea.ca.
2. For a more detailed discussion of the development of school music in each province and a more in-depth reference list, the reader is encouraged to consult Green and Vogan's (1991) study in which the 'evolution of school music [in Canada] is portrayed within a cultural milieu which comprises many aspects of musical activity in an emerging network of national and provincial institutions, community programmes, and agencies of government support' (Green and Vogan 1991: Prologue). For more recent developments and a wider variety of topics related to the history of music education, see Beynon and Veblen's (2012) collection of essays.

References

Beynon, C. and K. Veblen (eds) (2012), *Critical Perspectives in Canadian Music Education*, Waterloo: Willfrid Laurier University Press
Brault, D. (1977), 'A history of the Ontario Music Educators' Association (1919–1974)' (unpublished PhD dissertation, University of Rochester).
Canadian Music Educators' Association (2015), 'Canadian Music Educators' Association / Association canadieene des musiciens éducateurs [website]', http://www.cmea.ca (accessed 24 June 2015).
Coalition for Music Education in Canada (2015a), 'About Music Monday', http://www.musicmonday.ca/coalition/ (accessed 27 July 2015).

Coalition for Music Education in Canada (2015b), 'Music Monday', http://www.musicmonday.ca/coalition/ (accessed 27 July 2015).

Cringan, A. T. (1888), *The Canadian Music Course*, Toronto: Canadian Publishing Co.

Davey, E. (1977), 'The development of undergraduate music curricula at the University of Toronto, 1918–68' (unpublished PhD dissertation, University of Toronto).

Green, J. P. (1974), 'A proposed doctoral program in music for Canadian universities with specific recommendations for specialization in music education' (unpublished PhD dissertation, University of Rochester).

Green, J. P. and N. F. Vogan (1991), *Music Education in Canada: A Historical Account*, Toronto: University of Toronto Press.

Kallmann, H. (1960), *A History of Music in Canada, 1534–1914*, Toronto: University of Toronto Press.

Kallmann, H. and G. Potvin (eds) (1992), *Encyclopedia of Music in Canada* (2nd edn), Toronto: University of Toronto Press.

Keillor, E. (2006), *Music in Canada: Capturing Landscape and Diversity*, Montreal and Kingston: McGill-Queen's University Press.

Proctor, G. (1980), 'Canada' in S. Sadie (ed.), *New Grove Dictionary of Music and Musicians*, London: Macmillan, pp. 35–6.

Sefton, H. F. (1869), *Three-Part Songs for the Use of Pupils of the Public Schools of Canada*, Toronto: James Campbell & Sons.

Sefton, H. F. (1871), *A Manual of Vocal Music*, Toronto: Hunter Rose.

Shand, P. (1986), 'The John Adaskin Project (Canadian Music for Schools)', *The Canadian Music Educator* 27 (3): 33–39.

Shand, P. M. and L. R. Bartel (1993), *A Guide to Provincial Music Curriculum Documents Since 1980*, Toronto: Canadian Music Education Research Centre, University of Toronto.

Tomkins, G. S. (1986), *A Common Countenance: Stability and Change in the Canadian Curriculum*, Scarborough, ON: Prentice-Hall Canada.

Trowsdale, G. C. (1962), 'A history of public school music in Ontario' (unpublished DEd dissertation, University of Toronto).

Trowsdale, G. C. (1970), 'Vocal Music in the Common Schools of Upper Canada: 1846–76', *Journal of Research in Music Education* 18 (4), 340–54.

Tufts, J. W. and H. E. Holt (1883), *The Normal Music Course*, Boston, MA: D. Alperton & Co.

Veblen, K. and C. Benyon (eds) (2007*)*, *From Sea to Sea: Perspectives on Music Education in Canada*, London, ON: University of Western Ontario e-book.

Vogan, N. F. (1979), 'A history of public school music in the province of New Brunswick 1872–1939' (unpublished PhD dissertation, University of Rochester).

Vogan, N. F. (1986), 'Music Education in Nineteenth and Early Twentieth Century New Brunswick' in M. Fancy (ed.), *Art and Music in New Brunswick Symposium Proceedings*, Sackville, NB: Centre for Canadian Studies, Mt Allison University, pp. 19–33.

Vogan, N. F. (1988), 'Music Instruction in Nova Scotia before 1914' in J. Beckwith and A. Hall (eds), *Musical Canada: Words and Music Honouring Helmut Kallmann*, Toronto: University of Toronto Press, pp. 71–8.

Vogan, N. (1993), 'Music Education in the Maritimes between the Wars: A Period of transition' in G. Davies (ed.), *Myth and Milieu: Atlantic Literature and Culture, 1918– 1939*, Fredericton, NB: Acadiensis Press, pp. 77–86.

Woodford, P. G. (1988), *We Love the Place, O Lord: A History of the Written Musical Tradition of Newfoundland and Labrador to 1949*, St John's, NL: Creative Publishers.

Woodford, P. G. (2005), *Democracy and Music Education: Liberalism, Ethics, and the Politics of Practice*, Bloomington, IN: Indiana University Press.

Chapter 10

The United States of America: Reflections on the development and effectiveness of compulsory music education

Jere T. Humphreys

This chapter consists of an overview of the history of music in compulsory schooling in the United States of America. There are sections on the colonial period, the common school movement, compulsory schooling and the modern era, followed by conclusions.

A few points should be kept in mind. First, the configuration of the British colonies in North America shifted several times before they became states after the Revolutionary War with Great Britain (1775–83). Second, after nationhood was achieved, jurisdiction over education transferred from the colonies to the states, not to the federal government. Specifically, the 10th Amendment to the Constitution of the United States reads: 'The powers not delegated to the United States by the Constitution, nor prohibited by it to the States, are reserved to the States respectively, or to the people' (The Constitution, 1787/1791). Third, individual colonies and states were influenced by each other's laws and practices. Finally, in most instances, the term compulsory schooling is employed in this chapter rather than compulsory education, because the latter refers to educational outcomes and the former to physical attendance.

Colonial America

The roots of modern compulsory schooling can be traced to sixteenth-century Protestant reforms in Europe. The English 'poor laws', enacted soon thereafter (1563 and 1601), became the basis for early education legislation in the British colonies of North America (see Kotin and Aikman 1980; Melton 1988; Rothbard 1974).

The colony at Massachusetts Bay (now Boston), settled by English Calvinists (Puritans) beginning in 1630, enacted the first education law in the New World in 1642. This law compelled education for children of all social and economic strata in both academic and vocational subjects. It placed the burden of education on parents and the masters of indentured servant children and thus compelled education but not schooling.

However, subsequent laws and amendments enacted in 1647 and 1648 required the provision of education and schooling, respectively, and thereby affirmed the right of the state (colony) to determine the content and scope of education and to expend public funds for those purposes (Jernegan 1918; Kotin and Aikman 1980). The laws of the colony at Boston soon prevailed throughout Massachusetts.

All the (largely Calvinist) New England colonies, except for religiously heterogeneous Rhode Island, adopted compulsory and other education and school laws within thirty years of the enactment of the 1642 law. These early New England colonial laws differed from the earlier Protestant reform and English poor laws in their provision for the education and training of all children, not just the indigent. More generally, scholars believe that the statutes and acts regarding schooling from early Reformation Germany to the Puritans in New England 'were the work of religious oligarchies' (Jernegan 1919a: 24).

Scholars could have mentioned that the first permanent British colony in North America, at Plymouth, Massachusetts (1620), was slow to enact school laws perhaps because its inhabitants were lightly educated religious separatists who had lived for a decade in Leiden, Holland (1609–20), a city then known throughout Europe for its religious tolerance. At the other end of the continuum, the larger colony at Boston was characterized by religious homogeneity and relatively high levels of education and it became the New World's early leader in universal education and compulsory schooling. More generally, Cremin (1970: 92) maintained that 'schooling' in the British colonies of North America 'was viewed as a device for promoting uniformity'.

The North American colonies outside of New England followed suit to varying degrees, including the Quaker-influenced colonies of Pennsylvania and New Jersey and the former Dutch colony of New York. Maryland and (Anglican) Virginia and colonies further south passed compulsory education legislation early on, but they neither expanded the English poor laws model to cover all children nor established public schools (Kotin and Aikman 1980).

After what had been a strong beginning for education in New England, and to a lesser extent in the middle and southern colonies (Jernegan 1919b, 1920), compulsory school laws were weakened after the protracted Indian Wars broke out in New England in 1675, and because of frontier conditions resulting from the expanding geographical perimeters of settlement and increasing religious and cultural heterogeneity. Only Connecticut retained relatively strong compulsory school laws throughout the colonial era, while the other colonies generally maintained them only for indigent children (Kotin and Aikman 1980).

Music education in colonial America

European-style music instruction in what is now the United States was begun by Spanish Catholic priests following Hernando Coronado's expedition to the present state of New

Mexico in 1540. Thereafter the Spaniards taught music to Spanish and Native American children in dozens of missions in the (present) southwestern United States (Britton 1958). From that point onward, most if not all groups that settled in North America provided organized music instruction. These countless influences notwithstanding, the early British Calvinist colonists of New England played a major role in the widespread establishment of what proved to be long-standing practices in music and education.

The most common form of group musical activity in colonial New England was congregational singing in the Calvinist churches. John Calvin had directed that music play a prominent role in the church service and that the musical aspects of the service be simple enough to allow participation by ordinary churchgoers. Toward those ends, he had eschewed the use of professional musicians and musical instruments in the church service.

Calvin had also commissioned the first 'psalter', a musical setting of the biblical Psalms of David for use in church by lay choirs and congregations. After its publication in Geneva in 1562, the (popularly called) French Psalter was translated into several languages. The Dutch Psalter by Ainsworth, brought to the New World by the first settlers at Plymouth, and the English Psalter by Sternhold and Hopkins, brought by the settlers at Boston, were musically inferior to the original. The English Psalter was further simplified and diminished in quality when it was published in Boston in 1640, only ten years after the first settlers arrived there – the first book published in British North America. Popularly called The Bay Psalm Book (after Massachusetts Bay), it contained no musical notation until the ninth edition (1698). The New England Calvinists' simple, egalitarian musical practices and frontier conditions that prevented mass instruction in music and the technological means of printing musical notation led to an alarming deterioration in the quality of congregational singing from the arrival of the first permanent settlers in 1620 throughout the remainder of that century (Birge 1966; Britton 1958, 1961, 1966).

Early in the eighteenth century the singing school arose to address the poor quality of congregational singing and to provide social outlets for the colonists. These schools were commercial classes led by amateur, largely self-taught, mostly itinerant singing masters, many of whom produced instructional materials in the form of tunebooks. The first two tunebooks appeared in 1721, both compiled by New England Calvinist ministers. These and hundreds of later tunebooks contained theoretical introductions describing aspects of notation and singing techniques, followed by 'tunes' compiled from various sources (Birge 1966; Britton 1958, 1966).

Some tunebook compilers wrote some of their own music, including the most famous composer and singing school master of the revolutionary period, William Billings (1746–1800) of Boston. One of Billings' six published tunebooks, The New England Psalm Singer, contained all original music composed by Billings, including his patriotic tune 'Chester'. Billings called King George of England a tyrant in the preface of the book, which was published on the eve of the revolution in 1770. Except during the revolutionary period, when there was heightened patriotism and significantly reduced immigration from Europe, most music used in the singing schools was based on simplified European folk and art music. Many other tunes used during the singing schools era were religious in nature, reflecting the original purpose of the singing schools and tunebooks: the improvement of congregational singing (Birge 1966).

The singing schools, which began in New England and eventually spread south and west, provided the basis for public school music in the first half of the nineteenth century, after which they declined in popularity. Although they were supported by participant fees, not public funds, singing schools were open to the public. The teaching methods appear to have been eclectic. One notable original teaching innovation was shape note notation, where each degree of the scale was represented by a different shaped note head. This system appeared in Boston at the end of the eighteenth century, after the revolution but well before music entered public schools, and came into widespread use before giving way to traditional notation (Britton 1966).

The New England settlers also played instruments and sang outside the church (Britton 1966) and we cannot rule out the possibility that musically inclined teachers led school children in singing during the colonial and early federal periods. Whatever the case, substantial evidence about the poor quality of congregational singing throughout the seventeenth and eighteenth centuries suggests that any music instruction that occurred in schools, homes and churches was insufficient to maintain acceptable standards in congregational singing.

The common school movement

The number of public and private schools appears to have increased faster than the population from the late seventeenth century through the revolution in the late eighteenth century (Cremin 1970), but the number and prevalence of laws requiring schools or school attendance declined during that period. Soon after the revolution, Massachusetts passed the first state-wide law requiring the establishment of schools (Rothbard 1974). After that, the struggle continued within what had become the traditional dual system: public schools for the poor versus (mostly church-related) private schools.

The period 1830–65 saw the evolution of universally available public schools (Binder 1974), when most New England states established free tax-supported schools, the middle and 'western' (e.g. Ohio) states followed New England, and the southern states, except North Carolina, retained the dual system (Butts and Cremin 1953). During that general period other democracy-oriented shifts occurred, such as the extension of voting rights to men who were not land owners, and the election of Andrew Jackson, the seventh president and the first from a non-aristocratic background (Humphreys 2015).

Free public elementary schools became the norm by the middle of the nineteenth century, due in part to the public's optimistic belief that schools and other social agencies could improve conditions and help pave the way toward a brighter future for citizens of many types. Paralleling this optimism were fears over social problems resulting from immigration, industrialization and urbanization. Industrialization provided jobs for millions of new immigrants, huge numbers of whom had arrived not from the traditional origination countries of England, Scotland, Germany and Holland, but from Eastern and Southern Europe. These new immigrants tended not only to be poor and uneducated, but they looked and acted differently too (Everhart 1977). Other immigrants were viewed with suspicion due to their Roman Catholic religion (Greenbaum 1974), including the large numbers who emigrated from Ireland during the famine years in that country (1846–51).

Ultimately 'it took alliances of educators, Protestant ministers, social reformers, businessmen, politicians, and even concerned parents to take this strange mixture of hopes, fears, contradictions, and paradoxes, and meld it into legislative action resulting in the evolution of state-supported school systems' (Everhart 1977: 510). Advocates, led by Horace Mann, overcame huge obstacles in their quest to promote the development of universal schooling (see Binder 1974).

Music in the common schools

Beginning in the 1820s, when the common school movement was gaining momentum, various individuals, some of whom had observed successful music teaching in Europe by followers of the Swiss pedagogue Heinrich Pestalozzi, began to advocate adding music to the common school curriculum. By then experiments in school music teaching were occurring in a number of cities and states (Humphreys 2013, 2015). However, some of the strongest and most visible promotion efforts occurred in Boston, led by school reformer William Woodbridge, musician/educator Lowell Mason and the Boston Academy of Music and its president, Samuel Elliot, who became mayor of Boston (Birge 1966).

Lowell Mason began teaching music on a formal basis in an upper elementary school in Boston on 30 August 1838, an event celebrated today as the beginning of permanent public school music instruction in the United States. Among the many justifications for adding music to the curriculum, religious motives appear to have predominated (Miller 1989). Thereafter, music spread gradually until it became a required subject in many American cities by the end of the Civil War (1865) and in most American elementary schools (Grades 1–8) by the end of the century. Regular classroom teachers provided most of the music instruction, but increasingly in larger cities this instruction was overseen by trained music supervisors. The acquisition of sight singing skills was the primary objective because many music supervisors were former singing school teachers and because little live music was available to the still largely rural populace before the invention of electronic reproduction devices. The focus on sight singing notwithstanding, nineteenth-century school music education was what today would be called general music because it was for general students (Birge 1966; Humphreys 1995).

The first music instruction book intended for public school use was co-authored by Lowell Mason and published in 1831 in anticipation of regular public school music instruction. Progressively graded music textbook series began to appear in the second half of the nineteenth century. The most prominent series were dedicated to one side or the other of the 'note-versus-rote' controversy, which had begun in Calvinist churches in the seventeenth century and contributed to the emergence of singing schools and tunebooks (Birge 1966).

Many of the first school music supervisors continued the singing masters' practice of teaching simplified European-style folk and art music. Also like the singing masters, early school music supervisors were self-taught or trained in singing schools, and some had attended summer 'musical conventions' such as those offered by Lowell Mason at the Boston Academy of Music. Although Mason and other early leading music educators advocated Pestalozzian methods, like their singing master predecessors they generally eschewed European methods such as tonic sol-fa in favour of eclecticism. Most classroom teachers were trained in normal schools, first private and then public, in which music was a required and often popular subject. The first state-supported normal school was founded in Lexington, Massachusetts, in 1839 (Heller and Humphreys 1991).

The common school movement provided universally available schools, some of which offered music instruction, but many children did not attend school or enrolled for only short periods of time. Music instruction in schools was preceded and then paralleled by other types of musical experiences, such as vocal and instrumental lessons and classes in conservatories, music academies, colleges and private homes and studios as well as through community choirs, choral societies, orchestras and brass bands (Humphreys 1995).

Compulsory schooling

Colonial and common school legislation had provided for some forms of education, but neither had stipulated specific attendance requirements nor sufficient freedom from labour to permit regular attendance (Kotin and Aikman 1980). By the mid-nineteenth century, however, laws and agencies aimed toward social control were emerging as a result of immigration, industrialization and urbanization. These phenomena contributed to growing social problems such as crime, poverty and general social chaos, which many immigrants had sought to leave behind them, and to the enactment of truancy (i.e. anti-vagrancy) laws in many states, which established a legal basis for compulsory school laws (Everhart 1977; Kotin and Aikman 1980). All these factors contributed to the 'increasing centralization and bureaucratization of school systems, particularly ... in large urban areas' (Everhart 1977: 511). The centralization of school systems was probably the biggest single impetus for new compulsory school laws (see also Katz 1971; Tyack 1966).

At first the common non-compulsory and then compulsory schools were 'viewed as a means of shaping the right character and implanting the right morals for the responsible exercise of freedom – in other words, to produce citizens for the state' (Spring 1974:

140; see also Friedenberg 1965). Also important were a 'majoritarian mood' (Burgess 1976: 202) and the popular concept of a 'melting pot' nation that would 'Americanize' immigrants with 'compulsory school attendance laws' intended as 'means to standardize American behavior' (Richardson 1980: 155). Compulsory schools fulfilled what some today call 'custodial' functions (e.g. Cremin 1980; Ensign 1969; Jorgensen 1997; Kotin and Aikman 1980). Other institutions and legislation aimed toward social control began to appear as well, including child labour laws, which went hand in hand with compulsory school laws. Thus, fears over rapidly increasing immigration, industrialization and urbanization resulted in shifts in the motivations behind compulsory schools and other agencies: from religious to those of social control.

For all these reasons, states began to enact new compulsory schooling statutes in 1852, with Massachusetts once again leading the way. All persons responsible for children aged between eight and fourteen were required to send them to school for at least twelve weeks each year (at least six of them consecutive) (Cook 1912). These statutes were one manifestation of the public's growing confidence in the power of education to ensure the continuation of democracy and reduce social problems, confidence that lasted from the mid-nineteenth century until well into the twentieth (Everhart 1977; Kotin and Aikman 1980). All states and territories outside the South and Alaska passed compulsory school legislation between 1852 and the end of the nineteenth century and all southern states did so by 1918 (Department of Education 2004).

Despite their rapid spread, the new compulsory school laws were conspicuously ineffective in most instances (Everhart 1977). For example, before the Civil War, African Americans generally had not been permitted to attend school in the south (see Bindor 1974; Bullock 1967). Other formal exceptions to the laws were common, particularly when a child's family pleaded poverty, but more often the laws were simply ignored (Ensign 1969). In 1890, by which time the majority of states and territories had passed compulsory legislation, Connecticut became the first to enact a full-time compulsory school attendance law with enforcement provisions; by 1900, thirty states had enacted laws that required attendance for specified periods of time for certain age groups. The southern states did likewise between 1900 and 1918, although some of those statutes included local 'opt-out' provisions for towns and counties (Kotin and Aikman 1980). Also beginning in the second half of the nineteenth century, in situations where federal laws prevailed, the federal government required school attendance for Native Americans (Handel and Humphreys 2005).

At no time in the history of the colonies or states was compulsory schooling supported enthusiastically by all segments of the population, but over time the public's faith in education had gradually shifted to the school as an institution (Everhart 1977). John Dewey's (1916) belief that universal schooling was crucial to democracy was shared by many, and the surprisingly low levels of literacy among conscripted soldiers in the First World War led to increased enforcement of compulsory school laws (Everhart 1977; Kotin and Aikman 1980).

Music in compulsory schools

Music instruction during the common school era (1830–65) was compulsory in the minority of schools where it was part of the curriculum, at least for the small percentage of children who attended school regularly. As compulsory school attendance laws and their enforcement became more prevalent and as music instruction spread to most of the nation's schools, music became a *de facto* compulsory subject, albeit unevenly in different states and localities.

School music changed significantly around the beginning of the twentieth century for two major reasons. First, general music changed as a result of new technology: initially the player piano, next the phonograph, then the radio. These inventions made feasible the teaching of 'music appreciation' through music-listening activities and they provided ready access to music for people who lacked access to live music. From about 1910 the phonograph played a particularly important role in general music's shift from a nearly exclusive focus on sight singing to a mixed approach that included listening and performing, vocally and with newly available toy instruments (Humphreys 1995).

The second factor was the powerful progressive education movement, which evolved in Europe and North America in response to the industrial revolution. Progressives sought to make the schools 'levers of social reform' and to prepare students for what they foresaw as an adult life with copious amounts of leisure time. The movement led to expanded ideas about the purposes of schooling and thus to an expanded curriculum, in part to serve the increasing numbers of students attending high schools (Humphreys, 1988; see also Lee 2014), schools that doubled in number during the twenty-five years between 1890 and 1915 (Rugg 1926; see also Humphreys 2015).

Music education benefited from this public confidence and belief in the public schools during the progressive era, a period when 'devotion to education was strong' (Everhart 1977: 521). Specifically, during this period general music took on its modern forms; performing ensembles (primarily choirs, orchestras and bands) entered the schools and flourished; both general music and ensembles developed stronger roles in school and community life. These changes occurred during a period of major educational reform, much like general music instruction was added to the curriculum during the common school movement (Humphreys 1995).

While classroom teachers continued to receive musical training in normal schools, during the late nineteenth century some music supervisors began to receive specialized training in summer institutes sponsored by music textbook publishers. Normal schools and some church-related colleges more readily embraced both music and teacher education than did state-supported universities. A specialized normal school for music educators was founded by Julia E. Crane at Potsdam, New York, in 1882. However, by the early decades of the twentieth century, when states were partially enforcing their compulsory schooling laws, 'public school music' departments were cropping up in many teachers' colleges and some universities. These departments supplanted textbook publishers' institutes in the production of general music teachers by the end of the First

World War. The earliest orchestra and band directors in the schools were vocal music teachers, teachers of other subjects, professional performers, and students. However, the college- and university-based music departments began to turn out trained instrumental teachers during the 1920s (Humphreys 1989, 1995).

The modern era

Direct federal initiatives in education began during the late 1950s after the launching of the Soviet space satellite Sputnik. Federal initiatives in the arts, including arts education, began in 1962 under the Kennedy administration (see Gauthier 2003). Most of the responsibility and resources continued to derive from the states, but federal legislation and judicial rulings helped bring about changes in specific aspects of education. Among the most significant changes were the US Supreme Court's decision outlawing racially segregated schools (1954) and Congressional legislation that provided for students with special needs (1975). Other influences, such as accrediting agencies and subject matter organizations (e.g. the Music Educators National Conference, now the National Association for Music Education), contribute to the enterprise in many ways and the states continue to influence each other.

Music education in the modern era

Educational reform efforts have been continuous since the late 1950s, and presently reform movements continue in all fifty states. Federal legislation called 'No Child Left Behind', through which funds can be awarded or withheld based on various criteria imposed at the state level, continues into the second decade of the twenty-first century under the guise of newer federal 'Race to the Top' statutes. Both federal programmes emphasize standardized testing and are generally seen as detrimental to school music programmes, although school music education has largely been bypassed by the standardized testing movement. To date, most states have aligned most of their respective education systems with federal guidelines. However, some states and teacher and parent groups are beginning to rebel against the latest initiative, national 'common core' standards, in part because they rely heavily on 'high-stakes' standardized testing. Music education organizations developed national standards for music education and some are attempting to align those standards with the new common core standards, but to date the common core standards include only English language arts and mathematics.

All fifty states compel school attendance, typically until age sixteen. All states also require music instruction for at least a portion of the time in Grades K–6, but for an average of less than one hour per week, with some also requiring it for portions of Grades 7–8. Most secondary schools offer ensembles – sometimes orchestras, usually choirs and almost always bands, and, in some cases, other types of group as well – but ensemble participation is virtually never required. Approximately 25 per cent of secondary students participate in elective ensembles. Thus, most general music classes are compulsory, but ensemble participation is not.

Most public school music teachers hold university degrees and state-issued certificates aimed toward the teaching of music. Some 84 per cent of American elementary schools are served by credentialed music teachers, by far the largest percentage in history, and nearly all public high schools employ one or more credentialed ensemble directors. General music series books, and to lesser extent band method books, include music from wider, more diverse geographical, ethnic and cultural sources than ever before. School and university music ensembles also perform a wider array of music of higher quality, much of it written by competent and in some cases even prominent composers (Humphreys 1995; Wang and Humphreys 2009).

Surveys show that the American public overwhelmingly supports music in schools, but consistently ranks it at or near the bottom in importance among school subjects. This means that the public wants music in the schools, but not too much of it, much like the often quoted dictum paraphrased from Aristotle's writings: 'All gentlemen play the flute, but no gentleman plays it well' (for related writing by Aristotle, see *Politica*, Book VIII in Mark 1982: 36–44). There is also evidence that students, especially boys, are more favourable toward their general music classes in the lower elementary grades than in the higher grades.

Conclusions

Today, the vast majority of American elementary schools offer general music; a majority of secondary schools offer elective ensembles and a few offer other specialized secondary music courses; and many middle schools offer both general music and ensembles, sometimes required and sometimes not. Therefore, it could be said that music is compulsory only in the lower grades, for an average exposure of slightly less than one hour per week, whereas music is not compulsory in the upper grades despite the fact that young people are compelled to attend school until age 16 in most states. Thus, music is offered in compulsory schools, but in the upper grades it is not a compulsory subject.

Questions remain, however, about the effects of compulsory education and music education. For example, there is evidence that compulsory attendance legislation may not have increased school attendance in the nineteenth century, at least not before the laws were enforced (Landes and Solmon 1972). More troubling are questions about the results of compulsory schooling aside from actual school attendance. Early critics worried about the loss of privacy and individualism inherent in universal, compulsory schooling (see Cremin 1961), and since the 1940s sociologists have seen the schools as perpetuators of existing social classes (Spring 1972). Indeed, studies in political socialization have shown that children learn in elementary school to equate good citizenship with obeying the law – that is, with passivity and obedience as opposed to active citizenship (Hess 1968; Spring 1974; Tyack 1966). Studies also show that local school boards tend to be dominated by the upper classes, again often in the interests of the status quo (Counts 1969; see also Spring 1972).

In addition to problems that can result from people being compelled to do things against their will, most schools still utilize an industrial-era paradigm. Because the nation has long since moved beyond industrialism and into the information age, this outdated paradigm might be working against student achievement in and of itself. In music, one could argue that the ensemble format itself is a conservative paradigm taken from military (band), church (choir) and élite cultural (orchestra) traditions (Britton 1958; Humphreys 1995, 1999).

There is little solid evidence about the outcomes of the approximately ten years of compulsory schooling on American students, or on society as a whole, except that it is probably fair to credit schools with the nation's very high rate of reading and writing literacy. However, tests of knowledge of subjects other than reading and writing show increasingly dismal results. Whereas public schools were once seen as equalizers for less fortunate elements of society, later commentators began to see them as part of the problem. Some see education as being not about what children need, but instead about the perceived needs of society – that the current system of schooling has been helpful to some children, but 'its long-range effect has been to restrict the options by which most children can be educated' (Everhart 1977: 526). For example, Small (1977) believes that the university music major curriculum limits students' musical options.

Surviving evidence does not permit comparisons in musical achievement among children or the general populace before and after the advent of music in compulsory schooling. We cannot determine how many people learned music or much about what they learned or how they learned it beyond the contents of the singing school tunebooks (Britton 1966). However, much like many children learned to read and write and a few to 'cipher' before the passage of compulsory attendance laws, some children and adults learned to sing and play instruments without the benefit of formal schooling. Judging from the increasing instrument and sheet music sales, number of magazines devoted to musical topics (Campana 2013), and other indicators, including the plethora of singing schools, choral societies, bands, orchestras and widespread parlour piano and organ playing and singing and other musical activities, we can conclude that music learning outside the schools was ubiquitous during the eighteenth and especially the nineteenth centuries (Birge 1966; Humphreys 1995).

In the modern era, results from the three nationwide assessments of achievement in general music are extremely discouraging (National Assessment of Educational Progress 1974, 1981; Persky, Sandene and Askew 1998). Documented contributing factors include too little class time and, in the case of classroom teachers teaching music, inadequate teacher qualifications. What has not been discussed as a possible factor in these dismal results is compulsory schooling itself (including most general music), with its emphasis on middle- and lower-achieving students and therefore minimal standards of achievement (Humphreys 2006).

Perhaps not surprisingly, the elective ensembles are a different story. On the negative side, the ensembles serve only a minority of students, deal with limited types of music and focus primarily on performance skills, not composition, arranging, conducting, listening or other musical activities. Furthermore, school music experiences do not seem to extend into adulthood for most participants (Humphreys, May and Nelson 1992). On the positive side, ensembles offer one of the relatively few truly challenging experiences in schools for students with high levels of ability and motivation (Humphreys 2006), and there is ample evidence that the performance quality of school performing ensembles has improved markedly over the century of their existence. Many teachers and some scholars also attribute significant extra-musical benefits to ensemble participation (Humphreys, May and Nelson 1992). The performing ensembles remain, on balance, a distinctive and positive feature of American music education.

As for repertoire, it was the colonial singing school masters who began the non-working practice of trying to 'reform' the musical tastes of the American public (Britton 1958). Unfortunately, recalcitrant music teacher education institutions have continued the practice as evidenced by their failure to train pre-service teachers in popular and non-Western music (Humphreys 2002, 2004; Wang and Humphreys 2009). Despite these failures, however, persistent attempts by individual teachers, professional organizations and the profession at large to improve the musical repertoire in schools have met with some success.

The American public has lost confidence in the nation's public schools and a few alternatives to the current system of schooling and education are being promoted, such as charter (public but semi-autonomous) schools and home schooling. However, no serious attempts to discontinue compulsory education or schooling loom on the horizon today. On the contrary, the national standards and various forms of related federal legislation and incentive programmes, including common core standards and standardized testing, are attempts to impose even more stringent 'top-down' control over the education enterprise than existed in the past (Humphreys 2002), a phenomenon that continues as of this writing.

It is probably fair to say that compulsory general music exhibits many of the same failings of compulsory education as a whole, including minimal standards of expectations and achievement and lack of student motivation, problems that become worse at successively higher grade levels. Secondary school music ensembles, by way of contrast, are not compulsory even in compulsory schools. Due at least partially to their voluntary, non-compulsory nature, the ensembles appear to be more successful in fulfilling their purposes.

Given the distributed power structure in American education, with authority and influence coming from numerous sources, it is likely that, as in the past, any significant changes to the existing programmes will be driven by economic and social structural shifts, coupled with popular demand and support from the general public.

Reflective questions

1 Which entities have the power to include music in public schools of the United States? Which forces influence those entities? Also refer to any personal knowledge you may have of the public school systems in your own country in this regard.

2 To what extent is music instruction compulsory for students in the public schools of the United States?

3 What evidence do we have of the success, or lack thereof, of music instruction in American schools – today and in the past?

4 What are some ways in which compulsory music education might be extended to a larger proportion of American school students? What about voluntary music education?

References

Binder, F. M. (1974), *The Age of the Common School, 1830–1865*, New York: John Wiley & Sons.

Birge, E. B. (1966), *History of Public School Music in the United States*, Reston, VA: Music Educators National Conference [first published in 1928, revised in 1937].

Britton, A. P. (1958), 'Music in Early American Public Education: A Historical Critique' in N. B. Henry (ed.), *Basic Concepts in Music Education: Fifty-Seventh Yearbook of the National Society for the Study of Education, Part I*, Chicago: University of Chicago Press, pp. 195–207.

Britton, A. P. (1961), 'Music Education: An American Specialty' in P. H. Lang (ed.), *One Hundred Years of Music in America*, New York: Grosset & Dunlap, pp. 211–29.

Britton, A. P. (1966), 'The Singing School Movement in the United States' in *International Musicological Society, Report of the 8th Congress, vol. I*, Kassel: Bärenreiter, pp. 89–99.

Bullock, H. A. (1967), *A History of Negro Education in the South: From 1619 to the Present*, Cambridge, MA: Harvard University Press.

Burgess, C. (1976), 'The Goddess, the School Book, and Compulsion', *Harvard Educational Review* 46: 199–216.

Butts, R. F. and L. A. Cremin (1953), *A History of Education in American Culture*, New York: Henry Holt & Co.

Campana, D. (2013), 'Periodicals' in C. H. Garrett (ed.), *The New Grove Dictionary of American Music*, 2nd edn, vol. 6, New York: Oxford University Press, pp. 404–37.

Constitution of the United States (adopted 17 September 1787), Bill of Rights, Amendment 10 – Powers of the States and People (ratified 15 December 1791).

Cook, W. A. (1912), 'A Brief Survey of the Development of Compulsory Education in the United States', *The Elementary School Teacher* 12: 331–35.

Counts, G. S. (1969), *The Social Composition of Boards of Education*, New York: Arno Press [reprint from original, Chicago: University of Chicago Press, 1927].

Cremin, L. A. (1961), *The Transformation of the School: Progressivism in American Education, 1876–1957*, New York: Alfred A. Knopf.

Cremin, L. A. (1970), *American Education: The Colonial Experience, 1607–1783*, New York: Harper & Row.

Cremin, L. A. (1980), *American Education: The National Experience, 1783–1876*, New York: Harper & Row.

Department of Education, National Center for Educational Statistics (2004), *Digest of Education Statistics*, Washington, DC: US Department of Education.

Dewey, J. (1916), *Democracy and Education*, New York: Macmillan.

Ensign, F. C. (1969 [1929]), *Compulsory School Attendance and Child Labor*, New York: Arno Press & *The New York Times*.

Everhart, R. B. (1977), 'From Universalism to Usurpation: An Essay on the Antecedents to Compulsory School Attendance Legislation', *Review of Educational Research* 47: 499–530.

Friedenberg, E. Z. (1965), *Coming of Age in America: Growth and Acquiescence*, New York: Random House.

Gauthier, D. R. (2003), 'The Arts and the Government: The Camelot Years, 1959–1968', *Journal of Historical Research in Music Education* 24: 143–63.

Greenbaum, W. (1974), 'America in Search of a New Ideal: An Essay on the Rise of Pluralism', *Harvard Educational Review* 44: 411–40.

Handel, G. A. and J. T. Humphreys (2005), 'The Phoenix Indian School Band, 1894–1930', *Journal of Historical Research in Music Education* 27, 144–61.

Heller, G. N. and J. T. Humphreys (1991), 'Music Teacher Education in America (1753–1840): A Look at One of its Three Sources', *College Music Symposium* 31: 49–58.

Hess, R. D. (1968), 'Political Socialization in the Schools', *Harvard Educational Review* 38, 528–36.

Humphreys, J. T. (1988), 'Applications of Science: The Age of Standardization and Efficiency in Music Education', *Bulletin of Historical Research in Music Education* 9: 1–21.

Humphreys, J. T. (1989), 'An Overview of American Public School Bands and Orchestras before World War II', *Bulletin of the Council for Research in Music Education* 101: 50–60.

Humphreys, J. T. (1995), 'Instrumental Music in American Education: In Service of Many Masters', *Journal of Band Research* 30: 39–70.

Humphreys, J. T. (1999), 'On teaching pigs to sing', http://www.maydaygroup.org/colloquium/can-music-teachers-influence-a-cultures-musical-life/on-teaching-pigs-to-sing/ (accessed 22 April 2015).

Humphreys, J. T. (2002), 'Some Notions, Stories, and Tales about Music and Education in Society: The Coin's other Side', *Journal of Historical Research in Music Education* 23: 137–57.

Humphreys, J. T. (2004), 'Popular Music in the American Schools: What the Past Tells Us About the Present and the Future' in C. X. Rodriguez (ed.), *Bridging the Gap: Popular Music and Music Education*, Reston, VA: MENC, The National Association for Music Education, pp. 91–105.

Humphreys, J. T. (2006), '2006 Senior Researcher Award Acceptance Address: "Observations About Music Education Research in MENC's First and Second Centuries"', *Journal of Research in Music Education* 54: 183–202.

Humphreys, J. T. (2013), 'Change in Music Education: The Paradigmatic and the Praxial', *The Journal of the Desert Skies Symposium on Research in Music Education 2013 Proceedings*, http://repository.asu.edu/items/18958 (accessed 14 September 2015).

Humphreys, J. T. (2015), 'Energizing the "Birge Story" of Public School Music in the United States: Some Ideas on How to Amp it Up', *Journal of Historical Research in Music Education* 36, 91–109.

Humphreys, J. T., W. V. May and D. J. Nelson (1992), 'Music Ensembles' in R. Colwell (ed.), *Handbook of Music Teaching and Learning*, New York: Schirmer, pp. 651–68.

Jernegan, M. W. (1918), 'Compulsory Education in the American Colonies: I', *The School Review* 26, 731–49.

Jernegan, M. W. (1919a), 'Compulsory Education in the American Colonies: I (continued)', *The School Review* 27: 24–43.

Jernegan, M. W. (1919b), 'Compulsory Education in the Southern Colonies', *The School Review* 27: 405–25.

Jernegan, M. W. (1920), 'Compulsory Education in the Southern Colonies: II', *The School Review* 28: 127–42.

Jorgensen, E. R. (1997), *In Search of Music Education*, Urbana, IL: University of Illinois Press.

Katz, M. B. (1971), *Class, Bureaucracy, and Schools*, New York: Praeger.

Kotin, L. and W. F. Aikman (1980), *Legal Foundations of Compulsory School Attendance*, Port Washington, NY and London: National University Publications, Kennikat Press.

Landes, W. M. and L. C. Solmon (1972), 'Compulsory Schooling Legislation: An Economic Analysis of the Law and Social Change in the Nineteenth Century', *Journal of Economic History* 32: 54–91.

Lee, W. R. (2014), 'Why Bands Stuck: A Historic Look at Bands and Progressive Reform', paper presented at History Special Research Interest Group session, National Association for Music Education Convention, St Louis, MO.

Mark, M. L. (ed.), *Source Readings in Music Education History*, New York: Schirmer.

Melton, J. V. H. (1988), *Absolutism and the Eighteenth-Century Origins of Compulsory Schooling in Prussia and Austria*, Cambridge: Cambridge University Press.

Miller, D. M. (1989), 'The Beginnings of Music in the Boston Public Schools: Decisions of the Boston School Committee in 1837 and 1845 in Light of Religious and Moral Concerns of the Time' (unpublished PhD dissertation, University of North Texas).

National Assessment of Educational Progress (1974), *The First Music Assessment: An Overview*, Denver, CO: Educational Commission of the States.

National Assessment of Educational Progress (1981), *Music 1971–79: Results from the Second National Music Assessment*, Denver, CO: Educational Commission of the States.

Persky, H., B. Sandene and J. Askew (1998), *The NAEP 1997 Arts Report Card (NCES 1999–486)*, Washington, DC: US Department of Education.

Richardson, J. G. (1980), 'Variation in Date of Enactment of Compulsory School Attendance Laws: An Empirical Inquiry', *Sociology of Education* 53: 153–63.

Rothbard, M. N. (1974), 'Historical Origins' in B. A. Rogge (ed.), *The Twelve-Year Sentence*, LaSalle, IL: Open Court Publishing Company, pp. 11–32.

Rugg, H. O. (ed.) (1969), *Curriculum-Making: Past and Present*, New York: Arno Press & *The New York Times* (reprinted from Bloomington, IL: Public School Publishing Company, 1926).

Small, C. (1977), *Music, Society, Education: An Examination of the Function of Music in Western, Eastern and African Cultures with its Impact on Society and its Use in Education*, New York: Schirmer.

Spring, J. H. (1972), *Education and the Rise of the Corporate State*, Boston, MA: Beacon Press.

Spring, J. H. (1974), 'Sociological and Political Ruminations' in J. F. Rickenbacker (ed.), *The Twelve-Year Sentence*, LaSalle, IL: Open Court Publishing Company, pp. 139–59.

Tyack, D. (1966), 'Forming the National Character: Paradox in the Educational Thought of the Revolutionary Generation', *Harvard Educational Review* 36: 29–41.

Wang, J. C. and J. T. Humphreys (2009), 'Multicultural and Popular Music Content in an American Music Teacher Education Program', *International Journal of Music Education* 27: 19–36.

PART II: THE AMERICAS
B *LATIN AMERICA*

Chapter 11

Argentina: From 'Música Vocal' to 'Educación Artística: Música'

Ana Lucía Frega with Alicia Cristina de Couve and Claudia Dal Pino

Introduction

From colonial times music education in Latin American territories was associated principally with the Roman Catholic Church, for which music played an important liturgical role. Jesuit and Franciscan priests in the missions and chapel masters in the cities, together with independent music educators, employed music as a means of reinforcing religious and cultural concepts (de Couve, Dal Pino and Frega 1997, 2004; de Couve and Dal Pino 1999).

During the nineteenth century, Spanish colonies in the Americas – from Mexico in the north to those in Central and South America – underwent political revolution, which led to their independence. In Argentina the revolutionary process began in 1810 and culminated with the promulgation of successive national constitutions in 1853 and 1860. Thus a representative, republican and federal system of government was established. Although the role of education was emphasized, by 1869 only 20.2 per cent of children attended school, and 77.9 per cent of the population was illiterate.

Music accompanied the revolutionary process and soon after the first patriotic government took charge on 25 May 1810 several songs were composed in order to promote patriotic feelings. Although music was not conceived as a school subject, students sang this repertoire at public celebrations. For example: 'the "Patriotic Song" by López and Parera (the National Anthem) was intoned for the first time in public, the 25th of May 1813 at the Victory Square, near the Pyramid of May, by the pupils of Don Rufino Sanchez' school' (Gesualdo 1961: 133).

In 1822 Antonio Picassarri (1769–1843) and Juan Pedro Esnaola (1808–78) founded the first music teaching institution in Buenos Aires, the Escuela de Música y Canto. Local authorities supported this private enterprise and provided a public building for teaching to take place.

During the nineteenth century, intellectual figures encouraged music education and pointed out its values. For example, in 1832 Juan Bautista Alberdi (1810–84), lawyer, politician and composer, published *Ensayo de un método nuevo para aprender a tocar el piano con mayor facilidad* (*Essay on a new method of learning to play the piano easily*) and the *Espíritu de la música a la capacidad de todo el mundo* (*The spirit of music within the reach of everybody*), both of which promoted the value of musical knowledge. Domingo F. Sarmiento (1811–88), teacher, politician, journalist, writer and Argentine President, affirmed that:

> Music teaching at school instils discipline. Without music, that is if they do not sing during the marches, there is lack of order. It is important to teach children at an early stage how to memorize sounds, to listen to the intervals and to sing accurately. In order to achieve these aims all pupils must begin each music lesson with the following exercises: the scale, the scale with notes accompanied by manual signs, vocalizing the scales, singing the scale in quavers, and learning the songs that are associated with marching. (Sarmiento 1848: 196, quoted in Sarmiento 1938: 43–4)

Music was taught in several schools around this time. For example, the *Colegio de Pensionadas de Santa Rosa* was opened at San Juan City in 1839 and its programme stated that there were daily music lessons devoted to learning musical notation, playing the piano, applying the methods designed by Muzio Clementi and Juan Bautista Alberdi. Pupils of the *Colegio Filantrópico Bonaerense*, founded in 1843, presented a concert in 1848 playing arrangements of pieces by Carulli, Bellini and Rossini for piano, guitar, violin and flute. There were similar performances by the students of the *Colegio de Niñas de Montserrat* in Buenos Aires in 1848 and of the *Colegio de la Independencia* in Salta City in 1849 (Gesualdo 1961: 323–5).

Compulsory education

Despite Argentina having been conceived as a federation of provinces, a centralized system of government administration emerged in which the politicians looked to European and North American models to consolidate and modernize the country. The government increasingly recruited European immigrants to work in the fields, but many of them decided to settle in the cities. In under fifty years between 1870 and 1915, the population quintupled, with considerable diversity of linguistic and cultural backgrounds.

In this context, the First National Pedagogical Congress was organized in 1882 with 250 delegates, including the most prominent political and intellectual figures of the time. They debated the ideas and principles that should inform public education. Religious issues generated political conflict; some members of the Congress wanted to include Catholic education in public schools, while others maintained the principle of secular schooling.

As a result of the Congress, legislation approved in 1884 provided compulsory, free and graded primary education for all children between the ages of 6 and 14 (Ley No.1420, www.bnm.me.gov.ar/giga1/normas/5421.pdf). Singing was included as a mandatory subject: '[D]aily lessons at public schools will alternate with breaks, physical training and singing' (Art. 14). Religious education, by way of contrast, could only be provided 'before or after the hours of class' (Art. 8). It was also stipulated that a teacher's diploma would be granted by national or provincial normal schools. Foreign teachers had to revalidate their credentials and had to be competent in Spanish if they wanted to teach in primary public schools (Art. 25). The first normal school had been founded in 1870 in Paraná, the capital city of Entre Ríos province, under the direction of the American educator George A. Stearns. The training generally lasted for four years, and 'song' or 'music' was included in the curriculum.

Introduction of music into compulsory schooling 1884–1920s

Vocal music and its repertoire

Although the official syllabi and training programmes did not include specific objectives for music education at the primary level, it appears from other documentary sources that music was conceived as a means of promoting national identity: 'School singing helped to revive patriotic feeling … some patriotic songs that had been sung by the people and the Argentine armies in the struggles for freedom arose from their memories' (Consejo Nacional de Educación [CNE] 1913: 10). But this intention was not always achieved in practice:

> Music, that so important factor for the education of the feelings, was also neglected in primary education. In some schools they sang pieces of operas, in others foreign songs, generally badly translated, and in the rest, worthless songs that each professor adopted according to his own criterion. As I have personally checked, there were many of these teachers who did not know the National Anthem. (CNE 1913: 10)

In addition to promoting patriotism, music education was highly valued because of its beneficial influence on child development and because it strengthened Spanish as the national language. José María Torres, a well-known educator of the time, pointed out that:

> The song is offered in the schools as a way to vary and to animate the occupations of the children, and exerts a healthful influence on the lungs and the chest. Giving fullness, clarity and extension to the voice, it helps to perfect the choral expression; it prepares the vocal organs to later produce the sounds and the inflections of the foreign languages; and, forming the habit of free and prolonged breathing … it facilitates elocution, and it tends to

correct the defects of the pronunciation. A musical ear, that is the faculty to distinguish and to imitate musical notes, can be cultivated in almost all children ... If vocal music spreads like a branch of obligatory teaching in all the schools of primary education, it would modify with time the unpleasantness of the provincial accent, it would contribute to the homogeneity of the intonation in the national pronunciation, and it would give more melody to our language. (Torres 1887: 23–4)

As far as vocal repertoire was concerned, the National Anthem was the cornerstone. This had been approved by the General Assembly in 1813 but, by the end of the nineteenth century, it had become somewhat problematic. The original manuscript of 1812 by Blas Parera (1778?–1838?) had been lost and so there were several versions of it. But, as José André pointed out in 1927, 'Combined public performances became impossible because the schools under the jurisdiction of the National Council of Education and the Normal Schools of the Ministry of Justice and Public Instruction sang different versions' (*La Nación*, 26 June 1927, in Mondolo 2005). These problems notwithstanding, the practice of singing the National Anthem became compulsory in all schools, especially in the celebration of the patriotic anniversaries: 'All the schools of the Capital should sing the National Anthem on the morning of May 25th (anniversary of the assumption of the first patriotic government) at 9 a.m. in the squares or avenues in the jurisdiction of each district' (CNE 1913: 36). Moreover: '[I]t was set down that the headmasters should give lectures to the children on diverse topics related to May Week, including ... the origin and adoption of the National Anthem: its poet and its composer' (CNE 1913: 35).

Furthermore, in 1909 the National Council of Education specified that in order to pass Grade 3 of primary school the pupils should know the National Anthem by heart (Circular No. 31 in Mondolo 2005). It was not until 1944 that the score by Juan Pedro Esnaola (1808–78), originally published in 1860, was approved as the official version of the Argentine National Anthem.

The National Council of Education approved a number of textbooks and music scores as a syllabus and published the corresponding listing in the periodic government report *El Monitor de la Educación Común* (*The Monitor of Common Education*). Several musicians composed school songs with particular attention to the range of children's voices. The lyrics were based on moral, national or poetic precepts. For example: '[T]he credited professor of music of some of the public schools, Mr. Orestes Panizza, has sent us a book containing several school songs ... Those that we have now received are titled 'A la noche' [To the night], 'El canto del Cisne' [The swan song] and 'Vals' [Waltz]' (CNE, *El Monitor de la Educación Común* 1891/92: 271). An example of a female contributor was Manuela Cornejo de Sánchez (1854–1902), who composed and taught 'El sol de Julio' ('The sun of July') – a reference to Argentine Independence Day – at Normal School No. 1 of Salta City in the north of the country in 1900 (Frega 1994). Other composers, such as Gabriel Diez, also made adaptations and arrangements for voice and piano of works by composers such as Donizetti, Handel, Haydn, Verdi and Weber.

These vocal practices in schools appear to have generally achieved satisfactory results, as was stated in this official report: 'In all the schools pupils sing in one or more parts … this was evidence of the good quality of teaching which resulted in the pupils' public performances' (CNE 1938: 57).

As far as musical accompaniments for singing in schools were concerned, it was debated in the National Council of Education in 1893 whether the piano or the harmonium was more appropriate. The opinions of music educators and composers were sought, including Alberto Williams (1862–1952) and Julián Aguirre (1868–1924). They stated that:

> Considering the numerous advantages that the harmonium has over the piano for elementary music teaching, such as the greater prolongation of the sound, the most exact and durable tuning, the reduced cost and size, and, finally, its adoption in the schools of the more advanced countries in Europe, we do not hesitate in indicating to you, as beneficial, the substitution of the pianos of the common schools by the harmonium. We must also add that the execution is easier and less subject to inaccuracies in unskillful hands. (CNE, *El Monitor de la Educación Común* 1893: 143–4)

Although music had not previously been a compulsory subject for adult and rural schools, it was included in their programmes from 1905 to 1911. They provide an interesting listing of vocal activities and repertoire:

> 1) The students will daily sing suitable songs learnt by ear, during such a time so as not to interfere with the instructional subjects. The practice of the National Anthem is compulsory.
> 2) The National Anthem and the songs 'Saludo a la Bandera' ['Greeting to the flag'], 'Viva la Patria' ['Long live our country'], 'El Viejo Hogar Argentino' ['Old Argentine home'], 'La Canción Nacional' ['The national song'], 'Himno a Sarmiento' ['Hymn to Sarmiento'], 'Himno al Árbol' ['Hymn to the tree'], 'Himno al Trabajo' ['Hymn to labour'] and every other song approved by the National Council of Education are obligatory. (*Consejo Nacional de Educación* 1938: 119)

Finally, it is remarkable that no evidence has been found of school repertoire based on Argentine folk music or of the use of the guitar in the classroom during the first decades of compulsory music education.

Textbooks and methods

The music curriculum at the turn of the twentieth century, while emphasizing singing, also included musical theory. The approved textbooks utilized the fixed-doh system of sol-fa, following the tradition of the Italian and French conservatories. The following texts, approved by the National Council of Education in 1889, give some indication of the method: *Abecedario musical* (J. G. Panizza), *Tratado de música* (Saturnino Berón), *Método de solfeo* (Hilarión Eslava), *Método de solfa* (J. G. Guido), *Carteles y método de solfeo* (Gabriel Diez) (CNE, El Monitor de la Educación Común Año XI No. 151 1888/89: 522).

The *Nuevo Método Teórico Práctico de Lectura Musical y de Solfeo* (*New Theoretical and Practical Method for Music Reading and Sol-fa*) (1877) by Juan Grazioso Panizza (1851–1898) was not only approved by the National Council of Education but also by the Conservatoire of Milan and was used in the choral classes at the Metropolitan Cathedral of Milan as well as in normal and common schools in Buenos City and in the Province of Buenos Aires. In the preface, the author pointed out that 'the lack of a theoretical and practical treatise on Musical Division and Solfa both easy and suitable to be adopted in the classes of the Normal and Common schools of the Province has induced me to publish this Method' (Panizza 1877: n.p.). He based his work on those by Hilarión Eslava,[1] Fétis[2] and Panseron[3] and stated:

> In this book I attempt to put science within the reach of infants' intelligence, simplifying the study and trying to make it pleasant to the student, to simultaneously follow theory and its application, to induce the pupil to proceed progressively from the first rudiments of music to the theoretical principles of harmony, to be clear and concise. (Panizza 1877: n.p.)

Its contents included the staff, tonalities, enharmonic scales, the *seticlavio* or table of the seven keys, major, minor, perfect, diminished and augmented intervals and their inversions. Panizza maintained that sol-fa should comprise the basis of all branches of musical art (Panizza 1877: 21).

In a later publication by Panizza, *Método de Lectura Musical y Solfeo* (*Music Reading Method and Sol-fa*) (1885), he suggested singing in unison applying dynamics (piano, crescendo and forte) with piano accompaniment in unison or at the octave in order not to tire children's ears. Sol-fa practice should take fifteen or twenty minutes every day and the remaining time should be spent on singing songs. The study of musical theory should begin at the third grade:

> Each pupil will have a slate with a [musical] staff. The teacher will first write on the black-board what his pupils have to write on their slates. Music reading will begin by reading from the blackboard, then copying on the slates writing the names of the notes up to the moment they may read them easily and with confidence. Pupils should learn every rule by heart. (Panizza 1877: n.p.)

The *Gramática Musical arreglada especialmente para el uso de los colegios donde se enseña canto sin previo estudio de un instrumento* (*Musical Grammar Especially Arranged For Use in Those Schools Where Singing Teaching Does Not Follow the Previous Study of an Instrument*) (1882) was written by Josefina B. de Farnesi, Professor of Song at the Normal School of Paraná. She advocated attention to musical dictation:

> My work does not include useless details nor sol-fa as other books do … In my opinion the quickest way to teach musical theory is to make the pupil write, analyse and read the combinations of signs and parts of the dictated musical pieces. This method has another advantage: all pupils no matter their number may be simultaneously engaged in the task. (Farnesi 1882: n.p.)

The book contains no exercises or melodies for singing.

The most unusual pedagogical method was proposed by Pablo Menchaca (1855–1924), a stenographer by profession, who created a notational system that facilitated both reading and writing music. It consisted of a chromatic musical alphabet in which each sound was called by an invariable syllabic name: la, se, si, do, du, re, ro, mi, fa, fe, sol, nu. A petal-like symbol represented each note by its angle and position on a single line staff. There was much else besides.

Menchaca promoted his system internationally. He presented a lecture on his system at the Sorbonne in Paris in 1889 where it was positively received and subsequently made promotional tours to Belgium, Britain, Germany, Italy and the United States. In 1903 he carried out a pilot test, applying his system at the Boys' School No. 1 in La Plata City with the approval of the local school council and a year later published his proposal as *Nuevo sistema teórico gráfico de la Música* (*New System of Musical Notation*) (see Menchaca 1912). By 1907 his system was being used at the normal schools of Buenos Aires and La Plata cities. Between 1911 and 1913 he continued to promote his system in the hope that it would be applied in general education. He estimated that his system was being followed by 5,000 students throughout the country (ibid.). However, the Inspector for Music, Rosendo Bavío, rejected Menchaca's petition, arguing that it was not a universally accepted code (Fernández Calvo 2001a, 2001b).

Teacher training

In the early years of music being introduced in compulsory schooling it was expected that classroom teachers would teach the subject as there was no provision for specialist teachers. Graduates from the normal schools were expected to have taken at least two subjects in music education. The following comprised the syllabus:

> *First Grade*. 1. Music. Sound. Musical characters. 2. Staff. Notes. Treble clef. Additional lines. 3. Notes, their values. Rests, their values. 4. Metre. C (Common) or 4/4 time. Bar lines. 5. Dot and double dot. 6. Even and odd metres. Simple and compound metres. 7. Tie and syncopation. 8. Triplet and sextuplet. 9. Accidentals: sharp, flat, natural, double sharp and double flat. 10. Whole step and half step. Diatonic and chromatic half step. 11. Bass clef. The position of notes in this clef. 12. Conventional symbols and marks. 13. Diatonic and chromatic scales. 14. Major scales with sharps: key signatures. 15. Major scales with flats: key signatures. 16. Differences between major and minor scales. How to find the relative minor of a major scale. 17. Major scales with sharps and their relative minor scales. 18. Major scales with flats and their relative minor scales. 19. Reading and division in treble and bass clefs.

> *Second Grade*. 1. Conventional symbols. Ornaments. 2. Diatonic major scales. Diatonic minor scales. 3. Intervals. Intervals in the major and minor diatonic scales. 4. Mode. Key signatures. Major tonalities and their relative minor tonalities. 5. Musical metres. (CNE, *El Monitor de la Educación Común* 1883: 80–81, 94)

School inspectors, having detected unequal musical achievements in classrooms, gradually promoted the appointment of specialist music educators: 'At first elementary schoolteachers conducted children's singing practices, but in a short time the authorities appealed to specialized teachers, resulting in a standardization and intensification of teaching' (CNE 1938: 56).

In the 1870s and 1880s music educators had usually studied abroad or had taken private lessons with local professors as there had been very few and often short-lived institutions at which to study music. Such as there were included the *Escuela de Música y Declamación de la Provincia de Buenos Aires* founded in 1874 and presided over by Juan Pedro Esnaola, and the Conservatoire of Music, opened in 1880 by Juan Gutiérrez (1840?–1906?).

Alberto Williams (1862–1952), who had won a grant to study in the Paris Conservatoire, founded the *Conservatorio de Música de Buenos Aires* in 1893, where the most distinguished musicians of the time taught sol-fa, piano, violin, violoncello, flute and singing. By the 1900s the institution had almost fifty professors and more than 1,000 students. Intent on spreading music education, Williams established branches all over the country (Roldán 1999: 86). This private enterprise obtained state subsidies and its qualifications received official recognition. These privileges were lost when the state opened its own conservatories.

In 1919 the Buenos Aires Town Hall Band conductor, Galvani, promoted the foundation of several town hall music schools that by 1927 had become a unified organization – the *Conservatorio Municipal de Música Manuel de Falla*. A parallel development was the establishment in 1924 by the National Ministry of Public Instruction of the *Conservatorio Nacional de Música*, which took the Paris Conservatoire as its model. Both institutions offered degrees in several instruments and singing and were the main training ground for school music educators in Buenos Aires city. In the same year the Departments and Superior Schools of Music of the National Universities of La Plata, Córdoba, Tucumán, Mendoza, San Juan and Santa Fe were established. These developments notwithstanding, there were never enough music specialists to teach in the primary schools, and non-graduate, often amateur musicians took on the teaching positions.

Conclusion

The twentieth century saw compulsory music education in primary schools being influenced by international and local pedagogical developments. During the 1940s Émile Jaques-Dalcroze's ideas gained the approval of the Music Inspector Athos Palma, during the 1950s Guillermo Graetzer promoted Carl Orff's method, and during the 1960s Edgar Willems lectured in Argentina and Maurice Martenot's method was translated into Spanish. During the following decades, several books by John Paynter, R. Murray Schafer, Brian Dennis and François Delalande were published in Argentina. Local music educators such as Susana Espinosa, Ana Lucía Frega, María Inés Ferrero, Silvia Furnó, Violeta

Hemsy de Gainza, Silvia Malbrán and Juan José Valero became prominent through their pedagogical ideas and trained new generations of music teachers. This process resulted in an increasing number of musical activities in the classroom, such as playing musical instruments (mainly recorder, guitar and Orff instruments) and improvising.

Public and private conservatoires and universities provided courses in preparation for traditional performing careers and added subjects in composition, choral conducting, orchestral conducting, ethnomusicology, early music, popular music, electroacoustics and so on to their programmes.

Following contemporary trends, the subject *Música* (Music) became *Educación Musical* (Music Education) in primary schools in 1972. In 1993 a new law, No. 24.195, established ten years of compulsory education from kindergarten to the age of fifteen and confirmed a system of administrative and pedagogical decentralization. In 1995 the Federal Council of Culture and Education approved a basic common curriculum that each province and Buenos Aires City had to take into consideration when designing their own curricula. Although *Educación Artística* (Artistic Education) remained as a mandatory area of study, *Música* was no longer a compulsory subject, but just one of the artistic options that each jurisdiction could include in its own curriculum. Although many provinces maintained primary school music education, some did not include it in all grades of basic education.

In 2006 a new law (No. 26.206) prescribed that in thirteen years of compulsory education 'every pupil should have the opportunity to develop his sensibility and creative capacity in at least two artistic disciplines' (Art. 41) and that the training of music teachers was to

Table 11.1 History of school music education in Argentina

Date	Subject description	National documentary sources
1884	Música vocal (Singing [literal: vocal music])	Law of Common Education N° 1420.
1887	Canto y Música (Singing and Music)	Plan de Estudios (Curriculum/Syllabuses for Primary School). Consejo Nacional de Educación.
1903	Música (Music)	Plan de Estudios para las Escuelas Normales de la Nación (Curriculum/Syllabuses for Normal Schools). Ministerio de Justicia e Instrucción Pública
1972	Educación musical (Music education)	Lineamientos Curriculares de 1° a 7° grados (Curriculum/Syllabuses for First to Seventh Grades). Ministerio de Cultura y Educación de la Nación
1995	Educación artística: música (Artistic education: music)]	Contenidos Básicos Comunes (Basic Common Curriculum Contents). Consejo Federal de Cultura y Educación.
2006	Educación artística: música (Artistic education: music)	National Law of Education N° 26.206

be supported at high-level institutes (Art. 39). Nowadays both the Ministry of Education and the Federal Council have to approve the new basic common curriculum and each jurisdictional educational authority has to reform its own curricular documents accordingly.

To conclude, the historical progression of school music education in Argentina can be summarized as shown in Table 11.1.

It will become apparent that the history of music education in Argentina has incorporated some highly distinctive features, including the influence of the Roman Catholic Church, nineteenth-century political revolution and the development of a network of music conservatoires. Only by acknowledging such influences can we come to appreciate something of the complexity that underpins the achievement of music educators in providing a musical education for the majority of children in the schools of Argentina today.

Reflective questions

1 National anthems have been traditionally a cornerstone of the vocal repertoire in schools, as exemplified in this chapter. To what extent is this the case in your own country? What values do such anthems instil in pupils?

2 In Argentina, music conservatoires, the Roman Catholic Church and political revolution have been key factors in influencing the teaching of music. How does this compare with other systems?

3 In common with some other countries, music education in Argentina has moved from *Música* to 'Artistic Education' (*Educación Artística*). How significant is this move?

4 A feature of music education in Argentina has been the prevalence of the fixed-doh method. What the advantages/disadvantages of this approach?

Notes

1. Miguel Hilarión Eslava y Elizondo (1807–78) was a Spanish priest, musician and composer who wrote a *Método de Solfeo* (*Method of Sol-fa*) (1846).
2. François Joseph Fétis (1784–1871) was a Belgian musicologist, composer, critic and teacher who wrote *Biographie universelle des musiciens* (1966).
3. Auguste Matheu Panseron (1796–1859) was a French composer and singing teacher who wrote a *Méthode complète de vocalisation* (*Complete Vocalization Method*) (1855) and *ABC Musical ou Solfège* (*Sol-fa Musical Rudiments*) (n.d.).

References

Alberdi, J. B. (1832a), *El espíritu de la música a la capacidad de todo el mundo*, Buenos Aires.

Alberdi, J. B. (1832b), *Ensayo sobre un método nuevo para aprender a tocar el piano con la mayor facilidad*, Buenos Aires.

Consejo Nacional de Educación (1883), *El Monitor de la Educación Común* 2: 21–40.

Consejo Nacional de Educación (1888–1889), *El Monitor de la Educación Común* 9: 141–60.

Consejo Nacional de Educación (1891–1892), *El Monitor de la Educación Común* 12: 201–20.

Consejo Nacional de Educación (1893–1894), *El Monitor de la Educación Común*, 13: 221–40.

Consejo Nacional de Educación (1913), *La Educación Común en la República Argentina. Años 1909–1910, presidencia del doctor don José María Ramos*, Buenos Aires: Penitenciaría Nacional.

Consejo Nacional de Educación (1938), *Cincuentenario de la Ley 1420. Tomo II. Memoria sobre el desarrollo de las escuelas primarias desde 1884 a 1934*, Buenos Aires: Consejo Nacional de Educación.

Couve, A. de, and C. Dal Pino (1999), 'Historical Panorama of Music Education in Latin America: Music Training Institutions', *International Journal of Music Education* 34: 30–46.

Couve, A. de, C. Dal Pino and A. L. Frega (1997), 'An Approach to the History of Music Education in Latin America', *Bulletin of Historical Research in Music Education* XIX (1): 10–39.

Couve, A. de, C. Dal Pino and A. L. Frega (2004), 'An Approach to the History of Music Education in Latin America. Part 2: Music Education from the Sixteenth to Eighteenth Centuries', *Journal of Historical Research in Music Education* XXV (2): 79–95.

Eslava y Elizondo, M. G. (1846), *Método de Solfeo (Method of Sol-fa)*, Madrid.

Farnesi, J. B. de (1882), *Gramática Musical arreglada especialmente para el uso de los colegios donde se enseña canto sin previo estudio de un instrumento*, Buenos Aires: Imprenta Porvenir.

Fernández Calvo, D. (2001a), 'Reformas a la notación tradicional. Una propuesta argentina: Ángel Menchaca', *Boletín de Investigación Educativo Musical* 8 (24): 23–8.

Fernández Calvo, D. (2001b), 'Una reforma de la notación musical en la Argentina: Ángel Menchaca y su entorno', *Revista del Instituto de Investigación Musicológica 'Carlos Vega'* XVII (17), 61–130.

Fétis, F. J. (1866), *Biographie universelle des musiciens* (12th edn), Paris: Librairie de Fermin Didot Frères, Fils et Cie.

Frega, A. L. (1994), *Mujeres de la Música*, Buenos Aires: Planeta. New updated and expanded edition (2012): Editorial sb.

Gesualdo, V. (1961), *Historia de la Música en la Argentina. III. La Época de Rosas. 1830–1851*, Buenos Aires: Libros de Hispanoamérica.

Ley de Educación Nacional No. 26.206 (Law of National Education No. 26.206) (2006), Buenos Aires: Ministerio de Cultura y Educación.

Ley Federal de Educación No. 24.195 (Federal Law of Education No. 24.195) (1993), Buenos Aires: Ministerio de Cultura y Educación.

Ley No. 1420 de Educación Común (Law of Common Education No. 1420) (1884), www.bnm.me.gov.ar/giga1/normas/5421.pdf (accessed 16 September 2015).

Menchaca, A. (1912), 'New music notational system' in *Report of the Fourth Congress of the International Musical Society*, London: Novello, pp. 267–78.

Mondolo, A. M. (2005), 'Siglo XX: leyes, decretos, resoluciones y fallos judiciales' in C. Vega, *El Himno Nacional Argentino*, Buenos Aires: EDUCA, Apéndice Quinto, pp. 1–19.

Panizza, J. G. (1877), *Nuevo Método Teórico Práctico de Lectura Musical y de Solfeo*, Buenos Aires: Hartmann.

Panizza, J. G. (1885), *Método de Lectura Musical y Solfeo*. Manuscript.

Panseron, A. M. (1855), *Méthode complète de vocalisation (Complete vocalization method)*, Paris: Brandus, Dufour et Cie.

Panseron, A. M. (n.d.), *Abc Musical ou Solfège (Sol-fa musical rudiments)*, Paris.

Roldán, W. A. (1999), *Diccionario de Música y Músicos*, Buenos Aires: El Ateneo.

Sarmiento, D. F. (1938), *Ideas Pedagógicas*, Buenos Aires: Consejo Nacional de Educación.

Torres, J. M. (1887), *Primeros Elementos de Educación*, Buenos Aires: Imprenta de M. Biedma.

Chapter 12

Brazil: Towards the consolidation of music as a mandatory curriculum subject

Jusamara Souza

Introduction

The chapter illustrates the struggles and negotiations that have characterized the relationship between music education and government policies in Brazil. Five distinct historical eras provide the focus for this narrative: the period prior to the 1930s, which encompasses the colonial and early republican eras; the 1930s, dominated by Villa-Lobos and massed choral singing; the 1970s, with music integrated with the other arts under 'Artistic Education'; the 1990s, when music was recognized as a discrete subject within 'Art Education'; and, since the new millennium, the consolidation of music as a unique art form in the school curriculum.

Music in schools before 1930

The history of Brazil presents a great cultural diversity, which reflects the country's mix of artistic and cultural values of Portuguese colonization as well as those of the native population. From 1559 to 1759, some rudiments of a public education system began to take shape. During the seventeenth and eighteenth centuries, Jesuit missionaries formed choirs and small orchestras with indigenous Indians and *mestizos* (people of mixed race, particularly Spanish and South American Indian), whom they introduced to the European musical culture. Harder and Zorzal (2007: 149) report that the Indians made music using their own instruments, and black musicians and those of mulatto (people of mixed white and black ancestry) background participated in procession bands.

During the nineteenth century, Brazil experienced a growth in urbanization, industrialization and the bourgeoisie. In this environment, there was intense debate on popular education, including the role that the school should play as an agent or instrument of modernization, progress and social change. In order for the school to be responsive to the demands of urbanization and industrialization, new forms of school organization, new teaching methods and textbooks, new approaches to teacher education and a broadening of the curriculum to include disciplines such as science, drawing and physical education became important in the formal education of young people for a new society. With Brazil's independence from colonial rule in 1822, education reform began to be discussed, part of which resulted in music becoming part of the standard curriculum. Music in schools was viewed as having an aesthetic function associated with the development of a citizen's moral and civic character.

In 1824, the so-called 'Empire Constitution' formally established schooling for Brazilian citizens. In 1847, the first music conservatory was founded by Francisco Manoel da Silva in Rio de Janeiro, which was the earliest attempt to establish music as a profession that could encompass the teaching of music as well as its performance (Oliveira 2007). To promote the practice of music in schools, numerous decrees, laws and official acts were created, such as that of 4 February 1881, which stipulated the inclusion of music and singing in the normal school curriculum as a mandatory part of teacher education (Del Ben and Hentschke 2007). At the end of the nineteenth century and during the early twentieth century, new ways of conceptualizing and representing the educational process in public education challenged the continued delivery and implementation of school music programmes.

During the early twentieth century, Brazil was under intense pressure to engage in nation-wide development following the First World War. Among the challenges confronting Brazil were high rates of illiteracy, the responsibility for and the nationalization of school education, and the financial investment required for implementing secondary and higher education. The changes and reforms in education were implemented during the 1920s. By the 1930s Brazilian education had undergone a further transformation, prompted by the end of the 'Old' or 'First' Republic (1889–1930), the revolutions of 1930 and 1932, the beginning of the period known as the Vargas Era (1930–45) and the promulgation of the new 1934 Constitution.

Villa-Lobos and music in schools during the 1930s

To understand how music has taken root in school education, it is important to consider the new legal frameworks that emerged with the revolution of 1930 as a historical moment in education. The large number of specialized publications, laws, decrees and ordinances in the 1930s and 1940s confirmed the great advances in music as a school discipline and in the provision of specialist teachers to meet the demands of schools. National legislation and the implementation of these reforms in the various Brazilian state jurisdictions were setting the scene for future music education development and contributing to the emergence of a national social order (Souza 1993).

From the early 1930s, the educational policy of President Getúlio Vargas' government (1930–45) and his promotion of 'national awareness' and 'cultural renewal' directly affected music education in schools by introducing a compulsory music programme at all levels of schooling (Law 19.890 of 18 April 1931, Article 3). Prior to this, music had been a mandated subject only at primary grade levels (Law 3281 of 23 January 1928, and Law 2940 of 22 November 1928). In Articles 55 and 57 of the 1931 legislation, provision was made for the appointment of inspectors grouped by related disciplines and specific areas including music. The responsibilities of the inspectors included reporting to the appropriate ministry on the quality of the programmes developed and implemented by teachers, and their reception by students. Interestingly, no specific skills other than a knowledge of general pedagogy, school hygiene and physical education were required for the appointment of the inspectors responsible for music (Article 60). Article 75 clearly revealed the lack of qualified music teachers in secondary schools and the need to employ more teachers. Unlike other disciplines, the provision of class time for music was not specified. Nevertheless it was expected that music should be an important part of the school curriculum, and should be included whenever possible. This official government measure was received positively by music educators. In his book *O Ensino Popular da Música no Brasil* (*The Teaching of Brazilian Popular Music*), published in 1937, the composer Heitor Villa-Lobos (1887–1959) noted that the 1931 law followed the example of such great nations as France, England and Germany. The reform not only included the standardization of music programmes and methodological guidelines, but took music teaching in schools far beyond its previous aesthetic and pedagogical functions.

In 1930, the composer Lorenzo Fernandez (1897–1948) had also written along similar lines: namely, that music, in particular, should be used to eliminate social differences and this process should be controlled by the government. He highlighted the role of choral singing as a way to generate 'national feeling' (Lorenzo Fernandez 1930: 115).

After music became mandatory at all school levels, music education in Brazil underwent a decisive transformation. This educational reform led to a proposal for the introduction of new models of music teaching practice. In the course of researching written sources from these decades, I was able to identify innumerable proposals and documents from different committees and associations including the *Bases para a Organização da Rádio-cultura no Brasil* (*Principles for Developing a Radio Culture in Brazil*) organized by Luciano Gallet (1930), the Brazilian Music Association (April 1930), the Brazilian Association of Artists (June 1930) and the Central Commission of Brazilian Music (November, 1930) (see Souza 1993: 50–5). Although these proposals represented a variety of opinions, it was Villa-Lobos' own submission that gained the support of the Secretary of Education of Rio de Janeiro, Anísio Teixeira, who saw in 'this great musical genius' the possibility of the 'integration of art in popular education' (Souza 1993: 57). The document written by Villa-Lobos on 12 February 1932 was entitled *Apelo ao Chefe do Governo Provisório da República Brasileira* (*Appeal to the Provisional Head of Government for the Brazilian Republic*). It was sent to President Getúlio Vargas and highlighted the need to 'find a practical and quick way to save the artists in Brazil who were living in poor conditions', and pointed to the musical education reform as 'the solution' to the educational problems (Souza, 1993: 55).

Villa-Lobos proposed that a music programme should be implemented through the Superintendence of Artistic and Musical Education (SEMA) in São Paulo from 1931 and in Rio de Janeiro from 1932. It was intended that it would cover all school levels nationwide. He recognized the need for a popular education programme based mostly on choral singing as a means of promoting an aesthetic, social and artistic education as a part of the 'cultural renewal' or modernization initiated by the Getúlio Vargas administration. For this reason, Villa-Lobos emphasized that music instruction should be available to all the Brazilian population as an educational right aimed at promoting social life through music so as to form a 'singing group ideal' and promote 'popular collective action'. This was similar to the German notion of society as a *Volksgemeinschaft*, prevalent during the 1930s (Villa-Lobos 1940: 50). The key position that choral singing occupied was, according to Villa-Lobos, justified by its focus on patriotism and discipline. At the same time, it provided a means of mass music education through the medium of massed choral singing. For Contier (1988: 33), Villa-Lobos was obsessed with discipline that aimed to transform 'the noisy mass' into a population that accorded with the principles of a 'progressive and civilized society', such as in France and Germany.

With a concentration on discipline and patriotism, the aesthetic function of choral singing was overlooked in favour of instrumental outcomes. In other words, even though Villa-Lobos recognized that in choral singing 'all fundamental elements for a real musical formation, such as the rhythmic education, auditory perception, chord formation and knowledge of the repertoire' were included, its most important characteristic should be 'the support it gave to promote a civic attitude and habits among Brazilian children' (Villa-Lobos 1940: 9–10). Villa-Lobos considered that musical education was not just a matter of improving musical understanding. It also had the purpose to 'elevate Brazilian culture' (Villa-Lobos 1937: 22). It was his intention that 'art music' (also known as 'formal music') should permeate all layers of society. In line with Vargas' cultural policy, Villa-Lobos aimed to create 'a bridge between the people and music', an idea which was developed in countless passages of his writings (Souza 1993).

The design of a musical education that was based on the formation of choral groups with the purpose of instilling civic awareness required new approaches. Regarding the methodology for promoting choral singing, Villa-Lobos developed *manossolfa*, a method of solmization based on the movable doh, and utilizing hand signs as an instructional technique that was similar to Kodály´s approach (see Villa-Lobos 1946: 510). Using this teaching tool, Villa-Lobos conceived an effective way to conduct large school choirs and massed choral singing, while not necessarily teaching the skills of reading and writing music (ibid.: 544). He always stressed the pedagogical significance of using hand signs to engage children fully in music learning.

To facilitate the introduction of music education in schools, Villa-Lobos proposed a course of action not only from the methodological viewpoint (choral singing performance), but also from the institutional perspective, by creating laws, decrees and teaching material as well as promoting the teacher education courses of SEMA.

There were varied reactions concerning the music pedagogy advocated by Villa-Lobos, which, in the 1930s, represented the official policy for music education in schools. Music educators such as Lellis Cardoso (1937) and Sodré (1938) attempted to follow his ideas regarding the purposes, goals and outcomes of school music. In contrast, there were different reactions inspired by the nineteenth-century approach of pedagogical renewal – including those of educationists such as Sá Pereira, Nicolau dos Santos and Silvia Guaspari – that were more child-centred in their focus.

The discussion about the goals and objectives underpinning the implementation of the music programme during the 1930s has made it possible to situate them historically by identifying the purposes they were supposed to serve. Choral singing contributed significantly to such political goals as the formation of a national awareness and the construction of nationalism, establishing a 'social harmony' and representing the Vargas regime in a favourable light. The nationalist discourse was thus embedded in these musical–pedagogical discussions. The findings from historical research into music education in Brazilian schools during this era have demonstrated that some aspects of the educational policy that characterized the Vargas regime were decisive for the development of musical education in the following years. However this left little room for alternative approaches.

Towards the implementation of Educação Artistica (Artistic Education) in the 1970s

From the end of the *Estado Novo* (the Vargas government) in 1945 to the beginning of the 1960s, efforts were made to promote democratization with the formation of political parties and free elections and the promulgation of the Constitution in 1946. Despite fifteen years of democracy, some major problems, including the challenges of underdevelopment, widespread corruption, and the need for economic and political emancipation of the country, still remained.

During this period, high rates of inflation and unemployment resulted in popular discontent. At the end of the 1950s, Janio Quadros and João Goulart were elected as President and Vice President respectively with strong support from the mass of Brazilian society. In August 1961, Quadros resigned under severe financial pressure from monopoly interests, and Goulart succeeded him as leader of the government. However, support for the Vice President on this occasion caused alarm among the military and oligarchies, and on 31 March 1964 there was a military coup, which disrupted the democratic movement that had been in place since 1946. This was a tumultuous period. The national educational system created by the dictatorship reforms was marked by a technocratic ideology. Structural changes were implemented in basic education, which increased compulsory schooling from four to eight years and included two school levels – Elementary and Middle education. The changes proposed were committed to the principle of the 'alignment of the country to a new world order based on the development associated with … international capital, mainly American capital' (Oliveira 2002: 53).

The inclusion of music into the Brazilian school curriculum during the 1960s and 1970s can be charted by examining the Brazilian Educational Laws and Guidelines (LDB). The first of these (Law 4024) was implemented in 1961 and did not specifically include music. A decade later it was followed by the educational reform, Law 5692 of 1971 (Presidência da República Casa Civil 1971), passed during the military dictatorship (1964–85). This focused upon 'basic discipline, standardization, high performance, and pedagogical effectiveness' (Oliveira 2002: 53).

A related significant curriculum change was the recognition of the arts as a compulsory subject to be called *Educação Artística* (Artistic Education), and for it to include the plastic arts, music, drama and dance. This triggered the publication of many teaching method books with titles such as *Integrando as Artes* (*Integrating the Arts*) by Abrahão Gonçalves and Melo (1977), *Educacão Artística* (*Artistic Education*) by Aguiar (1980), *Educação Artística: Expressão Corporal, Musical e Plástica* (*Artistic Education: Corporeal, Musical and Plastic Expression*) by Cotrim (1977a) and *Educação Artística* (*Artistic Education*) by Vieira and Moura (1975) (see Souza 1997b). Although the titles of these publications certainly indicate a multi-disciplinary approach, an analysis of their pedagogical content by Subtil (2012: 140) demonstrated that 'even when it is considered an activity' music did not play an important part in the overall discipline of 'Artistic Education'. He concluded that 'the field of artistic education was predominantly represented by the plastic arts, a synonym of artistic education in school' (ibid.).

In teaching 'Artistic Education', teachers were supposed to be multi-disciplinary and able to build paths and flexible articulated learning in all artistic fields. Initially, the universities offered short two-year courses to train teachers in 'Artistic Education'. To meet the demands of the 1971 legislation, other colleges were founded, specifically to cater for the training of teachers. However, these institutions 'could not offer a more solid training for those teachers. Instead, the course would address the technical but not the conceptual bases' (Brasil 1995: 27). Moreover, the official curriculum documents, also called curricular guides, 'did not mention the fundamentals, the theoretical–methodo-logical guidelines or even the specific bibliographies' (ibid.).

Later research aimed to verify the extent to which schools were contemplating the inclusion of 'Artistic Education' in the curriculum, and how classroom teachers, specialist teachers, government education secretaries and educational administrators came to view music education in schools (Trope 1984; Vieira 1992; Tourinho 1993). There were four main findings: municipal Secretaries of Education did not fully comply with Article 7 of Law 5692/71, which stated that music should be included within all schools, particularly those further from an urban centre; there were few specialists and college-graduate teachers with a degree in 'Artistic Education' and thus they were not able to put this concept into pedagogical practice; many teachers questioned the validity of teaching 'Artistic Education' as a field of study that brought together plastic arts, music, performing arts and dance; educational administrators were not aware of how to fully meet the legal determination of law 5692/71 and how to provide the necessary conditions so that updated pedagogical practices in 'Artistic Education' delivery could be implemented in schools.

The concept of 'Artistic Education' demanded new ways of working, new functions and new curricula. Therefore, music educators had also to 'discover' other more effective means of implementing music teaching for their classes. Some key publications supporting these new ways of working included: *Música e Comunicação* (*Music and Communication*) by Abrahão (1977); *Educação Musical* (*Music Education*) by Botelho (1975); *Ouvinte consciente* (*The Conscious Listener*) by Corrêa (1975); *Música é comunicação* (*Music is Communication*) by Kocher (1976); and *TDEM2 – Trabalho Dirigido de Educação Musical* (*Guided Study in Music Education*) by Cotrim (1977b) (see Souza 1997b).

With the end of the military regime in 1985, Brazil began its transition towards democracy. The changes brought in new perspectives and possibilities for new curricula in all disciplines. There were numerous discussions on such topics as the socio-political role of education, and future directions for teaching the arts in schools. With a discrediting of Artistic Education, the focus was now on the 'musical experience', including practical music-making. In the late 1980s, some publications focused specifically on the teaching of musical instruments. Since then, and largely due perhaps to market demands, music textbooks were updated to take into account children's interests and attitudes and also the need for the overall modernization of schooling in Brazil. The new approach also included what children experience in their everyday engagement with sound and music, but without however abandoning the traditional musical repertoire.

The demise of Artistic Education in the 1990s

In 1996 'Art Education' replaced 'Artistic Education' in the Brazilian curriculum with the announcement that 'Art Education shall be mandatory at various levels of basic education so as to promote the cultural development of students' (Law 9394/96, Article 26, Paragraph 2). The term 'Art Education' allowed for different interpretations, and over the years it has had to be defined more precisely.

The Ministry of Education drew up a number of key documents as guides for the implementation of 'Art Education' and these established objectives and teaching methods for different levels. Significantly they treated the individual arts as subject-specific areas of the curriculum that had their own methodologies (Brasil 1997, 1998a, 2000). As a result, the previous curriculum documents of 1971 (Law 5692/71) were replaced, and with them went the notion of 'Artistic Education'. In addition to the publication of the *National Curriculum Standards* (*PCNs*) (Brasil 1995), debates ensued regarding the undergraduate courses that prepared music teachers, and the need to develop a professional qualification that included a more comprehensive range of music pedagogies with greater relevance to the Brazilian school context (Souza 1997a; Penna 2002).

The mandatory inclusion of music education in the 1996 legislation was based on contemporary theories that dealt with the role of the arts in the transformation of society.

Consequently this legislation emphasized the specific artistic production processes of music, the visual arts, drama and dance. The music curriculum established by the *National Curriculum Standards for Basic Education* (*PCNs*) (Brasil 1997) was based on three main components: assessment, production and reflection. These components were differentiated and aimed to foster an understanding of how a particular art form is capable of creating new realities.

During the same period the Ministry of Education drew up the *National Curricular References for Early Childhood Education* (Brasil 1998b), which represented a fairly detailed curricular and pedagogical proposal for the area of music, although this was not realistically achievable given that in the public schools it was the general classroom teachers, and not the teachers with specialist music training, who were responsible for promoting artistic expression.

In the *National Curriculum Parameters for Secondary School* (Brasil 2000) 'Art Education' was placed within the area of 'Languages, Codes and Related Technologies' and encompassed visual arts, music, drama, dance and audio-visual arts. This documentation briefly outlined some examples of content that could be used and how the subjects might be interchanged. These parameters have consolidated the transition from the curricula produced during the military dictatorship to a more democratic form of curriculum. However, these new proposals faced some difficulties regarding the implementation in the school system.

Under the provisions of Law 9394/96, many different practices of 'Art Education' were adopted. Classroom teachers with little specific training experienced difficulties in putting the proposed objectives as stated in the Ministry of Education documents into practice. This was exacerbated by a lack of subject-based resources. Despite all of the efforts involved with curriculum development and the political speeches delivered in favour of the specificity of each art form, the situation in practice was that many schools still considered the 'Art Education' area as 'Artistic Education', as spelt out in the previous Law (5692/71). Minimum weekly workloads were not guaranteed, and accordingly many schools chose to offer the four modes of Arts in an alternating series in the Basic School programme – that is, music in Grades 1, 3 and 7 for the respective age ranges of 6–7, 8–9 and 12–13, and visual arts in Grades 2, 4 and 8 for the respective ages of 7–8, 9–10 and 13–14.

The discontinuity was justified as the only way to comply with the law given the shortage of trained professionals. In order to solve this problem, the development of state competency examinations was deemed necessary so that teachers could become licensed or certified to teach 'Art Education' with an emphasis in either music, drama, dance or the visual arts. It should also be mentioned that in many examinations for 'Art Education' teachers the programmatic content did not reflect the legal requirements and focused only on one or another artistic area. Even given the legislation and curricular documents available for the teaching of 'Art Education', there were still many doubts about what the discipline dealt with, and its role in the curriculum. In the opinion of many educators, the *National Curriculum Parameters* did not resolve 'the uncertainty and the multiplicity of interpretations' because, as Penna expressed it:

> The current LDB (Law 9394/96) refers to art inaccurately, while the National Curriculum Parameters for elementary and secondary education establish a *potential space* for music in the curriculum, as part of the field of art; however, without ensuring its *effective presence* in school practice. The introduction of Music depends ultimately on the pedagogical decisions of each school. (Penna 2003: 76)

Towards music becoming a mandatory subject in the 2000s

The national movement that culminated in the adoption of Law 11769/08 was coordinated by the *Grupo de Articulação Pró-Musica* (GAP) (Development Group for Music), which included representation from informal organizations and associations of musicians, in partnership with the Brazilian Association of Music Education (ABEM) (Souza et al. 2010: 90). GAP commenced in 2004 with the intention of including music and music education on the agenda of cultural and educational policies. Coordinated by Felipe Radicetti, GAP organized the seminar *Música Brasileira em Debate* (Debating Brazilian Music) in the House of Representatives in Brasilia on 30 May 2006. Following this seminar, a public hearing was held in the Senate, 'where the inclusion of music in the Subcommittee of Cinema, Drama and Social Communication of the Senate was approved' (Sobreira 2008: 46). The 2008 legislation stated that music was to be a mandatory curriculum subject and no longer subsumed within 'Art Education'. This has opened up the possibility of providing an effective comprehensive musical education for children and adolescents.

GAP has organized a working group (Music Education Senate Hearing) to deal with music education in schools. A manifesto drawn up by this group was distributed nationwide. It was supported by 'nearly one hundred domestic and international organisations in the areas of music and education. This was followed by … its approval in the Senate and in the Federal Chamber' (Souza et al. 2010: 90). The manifesto highlighted music as a 'privileged example of socialization with its potential to develop different cognitive, motor, affective, social and cultural skills in children, youth and adults', adding that 'music is a fundamental tool for achieving the LDB proposals' (Souza et al. 2010: 90). Since 2008, specialist journals, public hearings, documents and guidelines for teachers and educational administrators have been used to support Law 11769/2008.

Music educators and other interested parties have also asked the National Council of Education to adopt a position on the inclusion of music in the school curriculum through its proceedings. In 2013, several public hearings were held in various regions of the country to garner support for the work of the Ministry Committee. The *Diretrizes Nacionais para a operacionalização do ensino de Música na Educação Básica* (*National Guidelines for the Implementation of Music Education in Basic Education*) as approved in December 2013 (Resolution CNE/CEB 12/2013) was the result of systematic and participatory processes to consolidate what is required by law. In other words, although the legal framework for the inclusion of music as a mandatory subject already exists, it is necessary to ensure that the role of music as a unique art is strengthened in practice and overcomes the historical legacy of 'Artistic Education', notably the idea that the arts could be represented as a single discipline entity.

Summary and conclusions

This chapter has aimed to describe the relationship of educational policies and the teaching of music in schools in Brazil through a focus upon five significant historical eras. Understanding this relationship enables us to clarify the process whereby music is included into the Brazilian educational context. Despite the importance of this kind of analysis, however, it is worth mentioning that it does not clarify the nature of classroom practices. Another difficulty in providing a fully comprehensive history of music education is the scarcity of historical research data relating to the period after 1971. Many studies refer more to the description of school practices rather than to the history of music education in schools.

The greatest challenge associated with the mandatory teaching of music as stipulated by the LBD lies with the training of teachers. The problems here include the need to reorganize the curriculum, to adapt the content to the students' reality and to establish a course that will enable teachers to qualify as music educators in schools. In order to implement music as a mandatory subject in the curriculum (Law 11769/2008), the training of teachers has emerged as a major problem that demands greater attention by the Ministry of Education and universities in providing new forms of training.

It is widely recognized that any intervention programme in the school curriculum requires coordinated training, curriculum and administrative action because production in isolation of curriculum documents is not enough. Moreover, it is necessary to propose forms of teacher training that prepare professionals to deliver school music education successfully. In contrast, we know that the best of intentions directed to professional training *per se* do not guarantee that institutions will provide space for music classes. Therefore, appropriate administrative policies need to be in place to ensure not only the presence of music education but its successful implementation.

Reflective questions

1 What is the significance of the work of Villa-Lobos as far as music education is concerned? What were the strengths and weaknesses of his approach?

2 An important, if unsuccessful, development in Brazil was the
   concept that the arts, including music, could be represented by a
   single discipline. How valid, generally, is this idea? Was it doomed
   to fail in practice?
3 Music education in Brazil became mandatory in 2008. Among
   the advocacy strategies was the drawing up of a manifesto
   highlighting music's potential as a curriculum subject. What would
   you include in a manifesto which would help to secure a firm place
   for music in the curriculum?

References

Abrahão, L. M. (1977), *Música e Comunicação* [*Music and Communication*], São Paulo:
    Companhia Editora Nacional.
Abrahão, L. M., Gonçalves, A. and Melo, E. (1977), *Integrando as Artes* [*Integrating the Arts*], São
    Paulo: Companhia Editora Nacional.
Aguiar, G. (1980), *Educacão Artística* [*Artistic Education*], São Paulo: Ática.
Botelho, S. (1975), *Educação Musical* [*Music Education*], São Paulo: Ática
Brasil, Ministério da Educação e Cultura (MEC) (1995), *Parâmetros Curriculares Nacionais para o
    Ensino Fundamental* [*National Curriculum Standards for Elementary Schools*], Versão preliminar
    [referred to as PCN].
Brasil, Ministério da Educação e do Desporto. Secretaria de Educação Fundamental (1997),
    Parâmetros Curriculares Nacionais. v.6: Arte (National Curriculum Guidelines. v.6: Art).
Brasil, Ministério da Educação e do Desporto. Secretaria de Educação Fundamental (1998a),
    Parâmetros Curriculares Nacionais (5ª a 8ª séries): Arte (National Curriculum Guidelines [5th to
    8th grades]: Art), Brasília.
Brasil, Ministério da Educação e do Desporto, Secretaria de Educação Fundamental (1998b).
    Referencial Curricular Nacional para a Educação Infantil (National Curriculum Guidelines for
    Early Childhood Education), Brasília.
Brasil, Ministério da Educação, Secretaria de Educação Média e Tecnológica (2000), *Parâmetros
    Curriculares Nacionais: Ensino médio, Brasília, Edição em volume único*. Incluindo Lei no.
    9.394/96 e (National Curriculum Guidelines: High School Education, Brasilia, single-volume
    edition, including Law no. 9.394/96 e), DENEM.
Contier, A. (1988), *Brasil Novo. Música, Nação e Modernidade: os anos 20 e 30* (*New Brazil:
    Music, Nation and Modernity: The 20s and 30s*), São Paulo: Tese de Livre Docência.
Corrêa, S. R. S. (1975); *Ouvinte consciente* (*The Conscious Listener*), 7nd, São Paulo: Editora da
    Brasil S/A.
Cotrim, G. V. (1977a), *Educação Artística: Expressão Corporal, Musical e Plástica* (*Artistic
    Education: Corporeal, Musical and Plastic Expression*), São Paulo: Saraiva.
Cotrim, G. V. (1977b), *TDEM -2- Trabalho Dirigido de Educação Musical* (*Guided Study in Music
    Education*), vol. 2, São Paulo: Ed. Saraiva S. A.
Del-Ben, L. and L. Hentschke (2007), 'Educação musical no Rio Grande do Sul: mapeando
    práticas, limites e possibilidades' [Music education in Rio Grande do Sul: mapping practices,
    limits and possibilities] in A. Oliveira and R. Cajazeira (eds), *Educação Musical no Brasil*
    [Music Education in Brazil], Salvador: Sonare, pp. 69–75.

Harder, R. and R. Zorzal (2007), 'Nos passos de Anchieta: caminhada pela história da educação musical no Espírito Santo' ['In the footsteps of Anchieta: a walk through the history of music education in (the state of) Espirito Santo'] in A. Oliveira and R. Cajazeira (eds), *Educação Musical no Brasil* [*Music Education in Brazil*], Salvador: Sonare, pp. 148–56.

Kocher, A. (1976), *Música é comunicação* [*Music is Communication*], vol. 2, Rio de Janeiro: Editora Distribuidora de Livros Escolares LTDA.

Lange, F. C. (1935), 'Villa-Lobos, un pedagogo creador' ['Villa-Lobas: a creative educator'], *Boletim Latino Americano de Música* 1, 189–96.

Lelis Cardoso, J. (1937), 'A psycologia da música e a sua aplicação no meio Escolar' ['Music psychology and its applications to the middle school'], *Boletim Latino Americano de Música* 3 (4): 351–64.

Lorenzo Fernandez, O. (1930), 'Bases para a organização da música no Brasil', *Illustração Musical*, Rio de Janeiro 1 (4), 115.

Oliveira, A. de J. (2007), 'Aspectos históricos da educação musical no Brasil e na América do Sul' ['Historical aspects of music education in Brazil and in South America'] in A. Oliveira and R. Cajazeira (eds), *Educação Musical no Brasil* [*Music Education in Brazil*], Salvador: Sonare, pp. 3–12.

Oliveira, M. A. T. de (2002), 'Educação Física escolar e ditadura militar no Brasil (1968–1984): história e historiografia' ['School physical education and the military dictatorship in Brazil (1968–1984): history and historiography'], *Educação e Pesquisa* 28 (1): 51–75.

Penna, M. (2002), 'Professores de música nas escolas públicas de ensino fundamental e médio: uma ausência significativa' ['Music teachers in public elementary and secondary education: a significant absence'], *Revista da Abem*, Porto Alegre 7, 7–19.

Penna, M. (2003), 'Apreendendo músicas: na vida e nas escolas' ['Seizing music: in life and in schools'], *Revista da Abem* 9, 71–80.

Presidência da República Casa Civil (1971), 'Lei de diretrizes e bases da educação nacional lei n. 5.692, de 11 de agosto de 1971. Fixa diretrizes e bases para o ensino de 1º e 2º graus, e dá outras providências' ['Law guidelines and bases of national education law n. 5692 of 11 August 1971. Guidelines and bases for teaching 1st and 2nd grades, and other measures'], http://www.educacao.salvador.ba.gov.br/site/documentos/espaco-virtual/espaco-legislacao/EDUCACIONAL/NACIONAL/ldb%20n%C2%BA%205692-1971.pdf (accessed 20 June 2015).

Sobreira, S. (2008), 'Reflexões sobre a obrigatoriedade da música nas escolas públicas' ['Thoughts on the requirements for music in public schools'], *Revista da Abem* 20: 45–52.

Sodré, J. (1938), 'Música – a grande arte educativa' [Music – the Great Educational Art], *Revista Brasileira de Música* 2: 47–50.

Souza, J. (1993), *Schulmusikerziehung in Brasilien zwischen 1930–1945* [*School Music Education in Brazil Between 1930–1945*], Frankfurt: Peter Lang.

Souza, J. (1997a), 'Da formação do profissional em Música nos cursos de Licenciatura' ('Professional training in the music degree courses') in *[Report of] a Seminar on Higher Education of Arts and Design in Brazil, 1997*, pp. 13–20.

Souza, J. (Org.) (1997b), 'Livros de música para a escola: uma bibliografia comentada' ['Music books for schools: an annotated bibliography'], Porto Alegre: Curso de Pós-Graduação em Música Mestrado e Doutorado/UFRGS.

Souza, J. (1999), 'A concepção de Villa-Lobos sobre educação musical' ['Villa-Lobos' principles of music education'] in *Revista Brasiliana*, Rio de Janeiro: ABM, pp. 18–25.

Souza, J. et al. (2010) Audiência Pública sobre políticas de implantação da Lei Federal nº 11.769/08 na Assembleia Legislativa do Rio Grande do Sul [Public hearing: implementation of policies of Federal Law no. 11769/08], *Revista da Abem* 23: 84–94.

Subtil, M. J. (2012), 'A lei n. 5.692/71 e a obrigatoriedade da educação artística nas escolas: passados quarenta anos, prestando contas ao presente' ['The law no. 5692/71 and the

requirement for artistic education in schools: the accountability of the past forty years'],
    Revista Brasileira de História da Educação, Campinas, v. 12, 3 (30): 125–51.

Tourinho, I. (1993), 'Usos e funções da música na escola pública de 1º grau' ['Uses and
    functions of music in the public schools for the 1st grade'], *Fundamentos da Educação
    Musical, Abem* 1: 91–113.

Trope, H. R. (1984), 'Educação Artística: um estudo das escolas oficiais de *5ª* a 8ª série do
    município do Rio de Janeiro' ['Artistic Education: a study of the 5th to the 8th grades in
    state schools in the municipality of Rio de Janeiro'] (unpublished master's dissertation,
    Universidade Federal do Rio de Janeiro).

Vieira, I. L. and J. A. Moura (1975), *Educação Artística*, Belo Horizonte: Livraria Lê Editora Ltda.

Vieira, L. B. (1992), 'O papel da música na educação escolar: pesquisa realizada em escolas
    de 1º e 2º Graus de Belém (Pará)' ['The role of music in education: a survey of 1st and 2nd
    Grades in the schools of Belem (Para)]' (unpublished master's dissertation, Conservatório
    Brasileiro de Música).

Villa-Lobos, H. (1937), *O ensino popular da música no Brasil* [*The Popular Teaching of Music in
    Brazil*], Rio de Janeiro: SEMA.

Villa-Lobos, H. (1940), *A música nacionalista no Governo Getúlio Vargas* [*The Nationalist Music of
    the Getulio Vargas Government*], Rio de Janeiro: DIP.

Villa-Lobos, H. (1946), 'Educação Musical' [Music education'], *Boletim Latino Americano de
    Música* 6 (4): 495–588.

Chapter 13

Cuba: Music education and revolution

Lisa M. Lorenzino

With a history marked by foreign domination, racism, centuries of long struggle for independence and the eventual attainment of self-government, the journey to implement music education in Cuban public schools has paralleled the country's battle for compulsory education and, in turn, nationhood itself.

It was only just over fifty years ago, after Fidel Castro's Revolution of 1 January 1959, that Cuba gained independence and began establishing a nationwide system of schooling (Johnston 1995). Building on existing institutions, as introduced by the Spanish and the Americans, Cuba took education-related matters into her own hands, developing a unique and highly effective system (Breidlid 2007; Carnoy 2007; Johnston 1995). Today, Cuba is recognized as having developed one of Latin America's most successful national education programmes, recognition that gives the country a great sense of national pride (Breidlid 2007; Carnoy 2007). Most notable within this system is Cuba's ability to provide free, high-quality, child-centred music education to all of its citizens from pre-school through to Grade 7. The country also operates an impressive specialized stream of music education, offering free professional music training nationwide for students aged 8–18 (Moore 2006).

Historical beginnings of music education in Cuba

Whereas informal music education in Cuba most likely took place among the Taino and Siboney tribes prior to the arrival of Columbus (Rodríguez and García 1989), it is believed that the first formal music educator in Cuba was an Iberian named Ortiz (Alvarez 1982). Shortly after the arrival of the Spanish in 1492, Ortiz opened a dance school in the Cuban city of Trinidad, where he began teaching melodies to the local inhabitants to accompany their movements. With the Spaniard's actions began a tradition of European-born and trained musicians of the highest quality being involved in music education in Cuba (ibid.).

In ensuing years, as seen in the development of public education, the Roman Catholic Church was the first institutionalized setting for music education in Cuba. In 1544 Miguel Vélazquez, the first church organist at the Cathedral of Santiago (founded in 1514), began to teach children to sing the church offices (ibid.). In 1612, when the organ was installed in Havana Cathedral, the capital city took over as the economic, ecclesiastic and musical centre of the nation. Throughout the seventeenth century, musical life was focused on these two institutions, and, each year, highly trained professionals arrived from Europe to strengthen the islanders' musical skills.

Hailed as the country's first native composer of Western European art music, Esteban Salas (1725–1803) initiated the tradition of locally trained music educators in Cuba. In the second half of the eighteenth century, Salas developed the Santiago Cathedral into a centre of high-quality music teaching, expanding classes to include strings, voice, winds and a small orchestra (Carpentier 2001). Despite his efforts, however, Havana reigned as the cultural capital of the country, a position that it maintains to this day (Alvarez 1982).

At the beginning of the eighteenth century, Cuban music education expanded beyond church walls into the realm of private business. Havana violinist Bousquet is believed to have been one of the first private studio teachers in the nation, whereas shortly afterwards, in Santiago, Juan Parés began teaching lessons at his home (ibid.). With the French influx following the Haitian slave revolt, private piano teaching flourished in the nation (Vega 2002).

Throughout the nineteenth century, studio teaching expanded, both in homes and in institutions. In 1814 Santiago became home to Cuba's first private music academy. Like the public schools of the time, the conservatory's clients were primarily Iberian – unlike the public schools, which were restricted to Spanish-born men, the conservatory catered predominantly for women, with lessons focused on singing, piano and the violin (Alvarez 1982). Within two years (in 1816), a similar institution, the *Academía Santa Cecilia*, opened in Havana. Staffed by Spanish-born teachers, this conservatory also was restricted to the Iberian population.

Expansion of music teaching institutions, both private and public, flourished throughout the nineteenth century as Spanish and Cuban musicians opened studios and schools in Camagüey, Santa Clara, Remédios, Cienfuegos and other municipalities throughout the island (ibid.). Just over a century later, Cuba boasted the highest number of private music academies per capita in Latin America (Gramatages 1982). By 1929 Havana alone was home to thirty-five conservatories and more than 160 smaller music schools. The census of that same year listed 1,850 music teachers nationwide, most of whom taught piano, violin and singing (Calero Martín 1929).

Racism and early Cuban music education

The first Africans to arrive in Cuba in 1515 began the process of radically altering the racial makeup of the nation (Delgado 2001). By 1811 over 320,000 black slaves had been transported to Cuba, accounting for 54 per cent of the nation's inhabitants (Moore 1995). Because public schools and music academies restricted their clientele to those who were Iberian born, the imported African population had to rely on other sources for music education. Ironically, the opportunities for their music education were available only through organizations designed to control and inhibit their actions.

Beginning as early as 1598 in Havana, slave owners began promoting the establishment of lodge-like organizations called *cabildos* or *cofradías*. For the *cabildos*
members, the groups served as centres for drumming, singing, dancing and the
preservation of culture and religion (Delgado 2001). Organized by place of origin, these
social outlets also served as havens of respite from the harsh daily reality of slavery and
assisted blacks with their social adjustment to life in the New World (ibid.).

The *cabildos* served a different purpose for the masters. For the Iberians, these tribally
based groups prevented blacks from gathering on a large scale, thereby restricting
revolts and uprisings. The groups also assisted in indoctrinating the Afro-Cuban
population with respect to the Spanish crown and the Catholic Church (ibid.).

Learning within the *cofradías* differed greatly from that of the Iberian music institutions. Rather than focusing on note reading and literacy skills, the Afro-Cuban institutions
were aurally based, using imitation and rote learning. Music performed was rhythmically
complex and polyphonic in texture and was taken from the traditional folk music of the
various tribes. In contrast to the individual study of piano and violin, the *cofradías* focused
on the fusion of drumming, singing and movement. Organizations were also communal
and multigenerational in nature (Moore 1995).

With the abolition of slavery in 1870, Cuban blacks were officially free to choose a
profession (Carpentier 2001). In reality, however, racism regarding which jobs blacks
could engage in was rampant, thereby limiting their range of employment. Because the
white population had access to a range of financially stable and upwardly mobile profes-
sions, the social climate encouraged blacks to become professional musicians, a job
considered financially 'unstable' at the time. As a result, instruments became 'secured in
the hands of people of colour' (ibid.: 153).

With money to pay for lessons, blacks began enrolling in music schools, becoming
skilled in counterpoint, opera, piano and symphonic instruments. No longer restricted
from becoming professors and private music teachers, blacks now became involved in
institutionalized music education (Alvarez 1982). The black maestros made an impact
on the teaching of European art music in Cuba, introducing pedagogical components
influenced by their traditions of rhythmically complex music, movement and rote learning.
Unfortunately, despite this progress in music, blacks continued to suffer from racist
attitudes in many areas of society (Moore 1995).

Cuban independence and the roots of public schooling

Because education was, by and large, aligned to the Iberian Catholic religious orders,
Cuban schools were elitist, racist and urban-based throughout the duration of Spanish
imperial rule (Johnston 1995). It is notable, however, that forward-thinking laws on the
part of the Spanish did make primary schooling compulsory as early as 1842 (Epstein
1987). However, in practice this did not happen. Further, the *conquistadores* did pass
administrative policies in an effort to nationalize education, but the 'social and economic

conditions of colonialism precluded any significant educational impact on the island' (Epstein 1987: 7). As a result, the poor, black, rural and female populations remained marginalized in Cuban schooling through to the beginning of the twentieth century (Johnston 1995).

Following the Liberation War of 1895–18, Cuba was granted independence from Spain. Due to substantial economic losses, the nation was left vulnerable and shortly thereafter became occupied by the United States Army (1906–9). Following a brief period of military control, Cuba was again declared 'independent' and self-governing (Milbrandt 2002). In reality, the nation was now privy to the 'supervision' of her North American neighbour, the United States. This supervision developed into governmental control akin to that of the Spanish *conquistadores* (Bethell 1993; Galeano 1997).

The change in the political climate of Cuba did have some benefits, however. With the American military occupation of 1906–9 came attempts to establish a national system of public education through the creation of the Cuban Ministry of Education. Unfortunately, as with the Spanish, the new Ministry did not have the resources to fulfil its mandate of nationwide public education and, as decades ensued, public schooling experienced minimal growth (Johnston 1995).

Under the new 'imperialism' of the United States, the early years of the twentieth century became a time of bloodshed, political tyranny and unrest (Moore 1995). From abroad, the nation was viewed as an island paradise, resplendent with beaches, music, dance and prosperity. In truth, however, at home, Cuban citizens were developing deeply seated anti-American sentiments as the administrations of General Machado (1925–33) and General Batista (1933–44 and 1952–9) developed into hotbeds of graft, corruption, absenteeism and tumult (Galeano 1997; Moore 1995). Unfortunately, public schools, music academies and Cuban society at large became subject to these vices (Johnston 1995).

Reacting to the violent leadership of General Batista in the 1930s, public confidence in the government reached a point of crisis. Batista aggressively quashed citizen protests by closing schools and withholding teachers' salaries (ibid.). As dissatisfaction escalated, the General lashed out by dismissing or deporting teachers and imprisoning students. A small elite private-school sector, funded by American companies and religious denominations, managed to survive the upheaval. As in previous centuries, only the smallest minority of the nation's population was able to access these facilities (ibid.).

The founding fathers of Cuban music education

At the turn of the twentieth century, a parallel struggle to the struggle for nationhood began as music teachers aligned themselves in an effort to organize free, compulsory, non-racist, non-elitist public music programmes in Cuba. Spearheaded by Havana pedagogues from both the music academies and the private studio sector, the efforts of these educators were a direct response to the failing social mores of the times. With a few notable exceptions, the music academies, like their public school equivalents, had become renowned locations of corruption (Alvarez 1982). Complaints about the selling of music diplomas and prizes and the exploitation of student artists proliferated throughout both the Machado and Batista regimes as staffing and administration became indelibly linked to local political parties. In Havana, mayoral elections alone brought about wide-sweeping faculty and administrative changes in music institutions. Again, citizens' displays of dissatisfaction with these changes, as found in the public school sector, resulted in teacher deportations, imprisonments and school closures (ibid.).

Within these tumultuous times emerged three of Cuba's most influential pioneers of music education. Working simultaneously to incorporate music into the public school curriculum as well as to expand the clientele of the nation's music conservatories, the efforts of Hubert de Blanck, Guillermo Tomás and César Pérez Sentenat laid the foundation for Cuba's current system of public school music.

Hubert de Blanck (1856–1932)

Born in Holland and educated in Europe, Hubert de Blanck quickly distinguished himself as a professional pianist, composer, conductor and pedagogue of the highest degree on his relocation to Havana in 1883 (Diez 1982). In 1885, along with violinist Anselmo López, de Blanck made his first contribution to the development of music education in Cuba by opening his *Conservatorio Nacional*. An institution providing classes for students aged twelve to twenty, the *Conservatorio* was the first Cuban music school to receive government support (ibid.). Using the somewhat limited funds provided, de Blanck was able to award eight scholarships annually to promising young black music students, a first in the nation (Alvarez 1982).

The curriculum of de Blanck's conservatory expanded on those of other institutions on the island. Setting rigorous standards, de Blanck developed an academic programme that focused on the development of *solféo* (*solfège*) skills, the study of harmony, training in composition, along with individual instruction on an instrument (ibid.). Employing the best musicians of the time, de Blanck's conservatory initially specialized in the teaching of piano, singing, violin, flute and guitar. In the passing decades, instrumental choices expanded to include most orchestral instruments.

Passionate to develop musical skills nationwide, de Blanck established music academies in the interior of the country that were incorporated with the Havana conservatory (ibid.). Curriculum offerings in these provincial institutions were similar to those found in the Havana school. With the development of these institutions, de Blanck distinguished himself as the first to attempt to nationalize music education in Cuba.

De Blanck was also a seminal figure in establishing a music publishing industry, creating the nation's first music education publication. He also authored numerous books and articles on music pedagogy, many of which are still in use today (Diez 1982). Active in many realms, his achievements have warranted his recognition as one of the most important figures in the development of culture in Cuba (ibid.).

Guillermo Tomás (1856–1933)

Guillermo Tomás' *Conservatorio Municipal de la Habana*, founded in 1903, became the nation's first fully state-sponsored music school to provide free lessons to students of any race (Alvarez 1982). Unlike existing conservatories and music academies of the time, the *Conservatorio Municipal* did not concentrate on teaching piano, violin or singing. Instead, the school was aligned with the Municipal Band of Havana, providing free lessons on wind, brass and percussion instruments for students aged 10 to 20 capable of passing the rigorous entrance examination (ibid.). Existing music academies did not perceive the *Conservatorio* as an economic threat as it catered to an entirely different clientele – poor, often black, working-class students.

Military bands had developed in several Cuban communities throughout the late 1880s, the most notable being in Havana, Remédios, Sancti Spíritu and Cienfuegos (Alvarez 1982). Along with the development of the bands were associated schools for winds and percussion that provided lessons for children and youth wishing to become instrumentalists. In addition to learning *solféo* and theory, student musicians were apprenticed to military musicians with the objective of taking over their positions in the band. Like de Blanck's *Conservatorio* that was known for its high standards, Tomás employed the best musicians associated with the Havana Municipal Band (ibid.).

For the initial years of the conservatory's existence, teachers taught on a *pro bono* basis, motivated by the inclusive nature of the school, but as the institution developed teachers received suitable remuneration for their services (ibid.). The conservatory went on to expand its classes to include courses in theory, harmony and music dictation. After a brief closure from 1930 to 1932 due to student revolts against the Batista government, the conservatory prospered under the new leadership of Almadeo Roldán, Tomás' protégé. The conservatory later went on to develop into one of the nation's most influential music schools (ibid.).

César Pérez Sentenat (1896–1973)

A contemporary of Roldán, César Pérez Sentenat was integral to the development of music education in Cuba (Ponsoda 2002). A pianist and composer who had trained with Debussy and Ravel, Sentenat was active in Cuban music education for over thirty years. One of his most notable contributions was to spearhead a movement to create a national teacher training institute in Cuba – the *Escuela Normal de Música* (ibid.).

Following the 1909 lead of Saint-Saëns, Massenet and Dubois, who were developing an institute of piano pedagogy in Paris, Sentenat approached politicians in 1910 with the intention of creating a school for music pedagogy in Cuba (Barreras 1928; Rodríguez 2004). With goals of protecting the public from corruption and graft and ensuring the development of quality music teaching in Cuba, Sentenat's request was not approved by the Machado government. In 1917 the maestro again proposed his plan to the government; however, it, too, fell idle in the hands of a government preoccupied with societal unrest (Ponsoda 2002).

In 1931 Sentenat, along with Roldán, focused his energy in a different direction. On this occasion, the government supported the proposal, the result being the restarting of the *Conservatorio Municipal de la Habana*. Cuba now had its first fully funded music school (ibid.). It was not until 1961 however that a state-funded music teacher training institution came into being in Cuba. In the interim, music professors continued to be tied to the whims of the government. So, too, did political unrest remain a factor hindering the development of publicly-funded compulsory music education (Alvarez 1982; Ponsoda 2002).

Primary music education and Cuba's first music pedagogue

De Blanck, Tomás and Sentenat, while making significant contributions to the Cuban conservatories, also had an effect on elementary music classrooms. In 1901 their efforts led to the addition of music to the primary school programme of studies. Using a curriculum designed in part by de Blanck, Tomás and colleague Emilio Agramonte (1844–1916), the programme emphasized unison and part singing. There was also a curricular emphasis on *solféo* and music theory (Ortega 2004).

Gaspar Agüero Barreras (1878–1951)

The work of de Blanck and his colleagues was carried on by Gaspar Agüero Barreras. With a career spanning over six decades of involvement, Barreras was seminal in developing compulsory music education in Cuba to the point that he was considered the nation's first music pedagogue (Rodríguez 2004). As an academic well versed in psychology, philosophy and pedagogy, Barreras worked in teacher training, and went on to impact generations of Cuban music educators.

A child prodigy of sorts, Barreras was playing the piano professionally by the age of 14, moving on to become a conductor of operettas and *zarzuelas*[1] shortly thereafter. Beginning in 1893, the pedagogue began a fifty-eight-year tenure as professor of the *Asociación de Dependientes del Comercio*. With his 1902 decision to leave conducting, Barreras began working at Hubert de Blanck's conservatory, teaching *solféo* and piano. Adding to his professional duties, the maestro later began one of his most influential roles at the *Escuela Normal de Maestros de la Habana* in 1915, holding a post there until 1946 (ibid.).

As a pedagogue, Barreras was considered to be forward thinking for his time. He was well trained in philosophy, especially the work of Leibnitz, Descartes and Herbart, and he was well informed of global movements in music pedagogy. In addition, Barreras had a profound knowledge of European and Latin American schools of thought, especially those of France, Switzerland, Germany, Argentina, Mexico and the United States (ibid.).

Specifically, he was impressed by the writings of the Argentinian Greppi (on modal systems), along with those of Chevé and Pestalozzi. Barreras' greatest influence in the area of general education was Dr Alfredo Aguayo, an important figure in the 'New School' movement in Cuba.

A philosophy reaching its period of greatest influence between 1930 and 1950, the New School movement in Cuba was based on the French post-revolutionary concepts of liberty, equality and fraternity, as well as the tenets of Darwinism and Gestalt theory (ibid.). Philosophically, the movement supported the ideals of vitalization, spontaneous activity, childhood, literacy and community, focusing on the concept of the child as a 'subject' as opposed to an 'object' of learning (ibid.). Along with Aguayo, the primary influences on the New School movement who also made an impact on Barreras included Rousseau, Froebel, Dewey and Montessori.

Basing his own philosophy on these global influences, Barreras went on to develop a music pedagogy that integrated theory with practice. The pedagogue placed great attention on the concept of the spontaneous and natural process of children's singing (Barreras 1928). Owing to his work with the *zarzuela* companies, where roles were taught by rote, Barreras also gave great importance to singing by imitation. Foremost in his philosophy, however, was the need to teach music in a manner that was instinctual to children, that related to their world of sounds and that was sensitive to their natural curiosity and inquisitiveness (Rodríguez 2004).

Barreras incorporated this child-centred philosophy of music education into his professional activities, going on to train classroom generalist teachers in the Havana Normal School, as well as some of the city's most prominent conservatory and studio music teachers (ibid.). Providing the philosophical basis for future generations, Barreras set the stage for innovative, child-centred music teaching in Cuba that is well informed by cognitive and psychological theory.

Developments in school music

Beginning in the 1920s the fledgling elementary school music programmes in Cuba added a new dimension into their classes – movement (Ortega 2004). Curricular requirements now mandated teaching music with physical education. In 1926 the link between the two subjects was strengthened by additional curricular reforms. Whereas these reforms were implemented into teacher training programmes in Havana through Sentenat and his contemporaries, progress in other provinces remained slow (ibid.). At the same time, specialist training for elementary music teachers remained virtually non-existent, with the government reporting only one music specialist or maestro for every 691 public students in Havana in 1931 (Pichardo 1973).

A decade later, in 1943, amidst severe political turmoil, the Ministry of Education organized the Department of Music Education with the goal of introducing music into the public schools nationwide (Menendez 1944). Philosophically, the department aspired to integrate theoretical work and singing in all the nation's classrooms. In 1943 the Ministry invited Margarita Menendez of New York University to present music pedagogy courses to interested school music teachers. A valid attempt to increase pedagogical training on the island, the programme was flawed – with no Spanish songbooks available, workshop participants sang and conducted American folksongs in English. Despite this lack of suitable materials – a perennial concern for Ministry officials – Menendez noted that 'Cubans are exceptionally musical and … there is much eagerness to cultivate this art and to participate in all kinds of instruction in it' (ibid.: 28).

Simultaneously, provisions were made for the training of specialist teachers and curricular materials were expanded to include hymns, songs, exercises, elementary theory, *solféo*, music appreciation and a limited number of rhythmic bands into Cuban elementary schools (Ortega 2004). The existence of quality school music programmes in this decade, however, was uneven, with urban areas possessing the most comprehensive offerings. Rural populations, suffering from governmental neglect for education, did not receive the benefits that Havana and, to a lesser degree, Santiago schools enjoyed.

Throughout the 1950s, political tensions reached their pinnacle and education, especially in rural areas in Cuba, was given little attention. Although improvements had been effected in terms of teacher education and administrative policy, even in the nation's capital, only one new school had been built during the first half of the century (MacDonald 1985). As political tensions rose, Fidel Castro used the battle cry of public education to fuel his January 1st Revolution of 1959 (Castro 1961).

The Cuban Revolution

Some argue that the Cuban Revolution was fought primarily for the right to universal education (Breidlid 2007; MacDonald 1985). In 1959 Cuba's literacy rate stood at 23.6 per cent. In addition, over 64 per cent of school-age children were not attending classes, with only 3 per cent completing the required six years of compulsory schooling (Bérubé 1984). To thank the largely agrarian population that had assisted in his triumph, Castro began, immediately after his transfer to power, a complete restructuring of the nation's public education system.

Indeed, many of the decisions made by the newly formed government in the months immediately following the Revolution were not well planned (MacDonald 1985; Moore 2006). However, what was eminently clear were Castro's specific goals for public schooling. Placing literacy and national pride at the forefront, Castro immediately began making policy changes to establish a system of national public education based on the writings of Jose Martí, Cuba's national poet, and Karl Marx (Breidlid 2007; Figueroa, Prieto and Gutiérrez 1974). Castro set out to formulate a public school system for Cuba, inclusive in nature, that:

> Integrated productive work with school work, the school community with the rural
> community, educational development with the country's economic, social and cultural

development, the formation of intellectual faculties with that of moral, social, physical and aesthetic faculties, the adolescent age group with the adult one, all this in a compre-hensive vision of the new man and of a society confident in its future. (Figueroa, Prieto and Gutiérrez 1974: iv)

Funded in part by Russia as part of its new alliance with Cuba, the first effort of the new government was to eliminate illiteracy. In 1961 Castro began training a force of over 200,000 volunteer teachers to move into the countryside to educate the largely illiterate rural population (Bérubé 1984). Within the year, education and specifically literacy became the focus of the nation, as volunteering for the Literacy Campaign became equated with furthering the cause of the Revolution (Breidlid 2007). Soon the peasants 'discovered the word, the volunteers discovered the poor, and all discovered their own patria' (Gumbert 1988: 122). By 1962 literacy had risen to 95 per cent and UNESCO declared Cuba illiteracy free (*New Internationalist*, 1998).

Castro continued to make sweeping changes to the education system in ensuing years. With the opening of hundreds of schools across the nation, the previously margin-alized portions of the population were now able to access free quality public education (Eckstein 1997). As Castro went on to open universities and technical schools, students were given greater access to high-quality post-secondary education. By 1986 Cuba boasted 268,000 university graduates, a substantial increase from its 1958 count of 19,000 (ibid.).

Castro's new system of education, rather than being based on material incentives, encouraged the development of a new morality emphasizing solidarity, self-sacrifice, honesty, nationalism and internationalism 'built in an atmosphere of commitment, collective effort and mutual support' (Breidlid 2007: 627). Students were taught to work collectively together and programmes were established to foster an environment stressing the cause of the Revolution as opposed to individualism and competition. As a result, biases on race, gender and geographic location were essentially eliminated within the school system (Breidlid 2007; Gasperini 2000; Lutjens 1996).

Into this new system of public education Castro began embedding Cuba's existing music academies. Starting with conservatories in Santiago and Havana, later adding those in Piñar del Rio, Matanzas, Santa Clara and Camagüey, Castro nationalized music schools, turning them into free music conservatories open to any student passing the audition (Moore 2006). With the 1961 opening of La ENA (the *Escuela Nacional de Artes* in Havana), the country now offered a nationalized programme for children aged 8 to 18 interested in becoming professional musicians (Moore 2006; Schwartz 1979). This professional stream programme expanded to include schools in every province, thereby allowing citizens access to free, high-quality professional music instruction (Moore 2006).

Building on the curriculum of the private conservatories existing in Cuba prior to 1959, the music schools provided advanced training in *solféo*, music theory, music history, complementary piano and individual instrument training (Alvarez 1982). As the specialized programme developed, the conservatories began to offer matriculation subjects as mandated by the Ministry of Education (ibid.). These professional music schools have gone on to produce some of the nation's finest musicians and music teachers for both the specialist and general education stream, a role that they continue to serve today (Alvarez 1982; Ortega 2004; Sublette 2004).

Post-Revolutionary public schools and compulsory music

Widespread changes also were implemented in public school music following Castro's triumph in 1959. Controlled by the Ministry of Education, the process of establishing a nationwide programme of compulsory music education was highlighted by a commitment to high standards, quality and locally produced materials, innovative teaching practices, and reforms linked to teacher education and professional development (Carnoy 2007; Gasperini 2000).

Attempts to implement a nationwide compulsory music programme began with the preparation of music appreciation teachers. Trained in a manner similar to that of the Literacy Campaign volunteers, the teachers were sent out to inform children about the history of Cuban music. Linked with the work of important Cuban musicologists, materials used were locally produced and of the highest quality (Ortega 2004).

At the end of the 1960s the country underwent another revolution – in pre-school programmes and teacher training. Based on the methodologies of Dalcroze, Kodály, Orff and Stokoe,[2] a programme was implemented that further employed indigenous materials (ibid.). With resources written by María Antonieta Henríquez, a specialist in music, and Elfrida Mahler, a specialist in dance, the nation began implementing the locally produced texts into Cuban classrooms. The materials – which featured traditional games and folklore – followed a nationally based curriculum that combined music and kinaesthetic expression together in one activity (ibid.). Shortly thereafter, pre-service teachers began to receive music instruction in their professional training to incorporate into the 80 minutes per week mandated for the arts education at the pre-school level (Gasperini 2000).

Curricular reform at the elementary school level now meant an eighty hours per year requirement for arts training in Grades 1–6 with seventy hours per year in Grade 7 (ibid.). In 1974 innovative elementary music programmes, following a reformed national curriculum, were implemented beginning with Grade 1. To expedite the implementation of the curriculum, programmes were offered through radio broadcasts, thereby reaching all areas of the nation (Ortega 2004).

Beginning in the late 1980s, innovative music education programmes were developed by the Ministry for use in upper elementary grades. Curricular content highlighted the study of the music and dance of Cuba as well as European art music via vocal, rhythmic, creative expression, corporal expression and dance (ibid.). Unfortunately, difficulties occurred in implementing the curriculum, and programmes were perceived as lacking a 'continuous and homogenous nature for the eight grades, from pre-school through to the 7th grade' (ibid.: 47). There were also incongruencies in the 'relationship between program content and methodological strategies used' (ibid.).

To overcome these deficiencies, once again in 2001, reforms in keeping with worldwide trends in music pedagogy were introduced for primary music education (Ortega 2004). This time the changes were more successful in their implementation. Curricular requirements for music now focused on perception, exploration and sound expression. The content of the revised programme consisted of songs, games, corporal expression, sound perception, listening activities and the creative process with students being encouraged to reflect, explore, listen, sing, describe, annotate, read, observe and compare. Curriculum reforms were based on the work of Orff, Dalcroze, Kodály, Villa-Lobos, Hemsy de Gainza and Frega along with Cuban pioneers such as Sentenat and de Blanck (ibid.).

Music education in contemporary Cuban schools

Today, over 500 years after Ortiz's humble start in Trinidad, Cuba operates a highly effective dual-stream system of music education. In the generalist stream, all Cuban children are taught music for 70–80 hours per year, from pre-school through to Grade 7. Embedded in a public school system that is recognized as being among the most successful in Latin America (Breidlid 2007; Gasperini 2000), generalist teachers are well trained and dedicated to high academic achievement for all social groups (Breidlid 2007; Carnoy 2007; Gasperini 2000; Moore 2006). Curriculum materials are of the highest quality, locally produced and linked to the cultural context of Cuban society. Lessons involving creativity, movement and singing are presented using pedagogical methods that are grounded in current cognitive and psychological theory (Carnoy 2007; Gasperini 2000).

In the specialist or professional stream, Cuban music schools are internationally renowned for producing some of the world's greatest musicians – a disproportionately high number for a population of eleven million (Levinson 1989; Moore 2006). Students aged 8 to 18 receive free professional music instruction of the highest quality alongside their regular matriculation subjects. Teachers, though less innovative in their methodology, are well trained, setting high standards as based on a nationally mandated curriculum (Rodríguez 2004).

Without any financial support from outside institutions – for example, UNESCO or the World Bank – Cuba offers a unique system of music education. Known for a focus on inclusion and equality of opportunity, Cuban schools appear to 'undermine the conventional wisdom that only well-functioning countries in the north can provide quality education for the majority of their pupils' (Breidlid 2007: 619). The system is one that bears additional study from a global perspective.

Thankfully, information on Cuba's education system is becoming more accessible than it has been for the past fifty-five years. President Obama's 2014 loosening of sanctions with the United States combined with the Cuban government's removal of travel restrictions has already allowed musicians, educators and academics to exchange ideas and information more freely. In terms of technology however, the Cuban population's access to the internet is still severely limited due to government restrictions and prohibitive costs for online connections. Despite this, it is nonetheless inevitable that, over time, increased interaction and the sharing of expertise and knowledge between the Cuban population and the rest of the world will positively impact the field of music education.

Reflective questions

1 Compare and contrast the roots of compulsory music education in Cuba to that of other Latin American nations.
2 Consider some of the ways racism has affected music education in Cuba. Relate this to the development of music education in your own country.
3 Throughout its history, what role has politics played in the development of music education and cultural identity in Cuba? How does this compare with the cultural setting in which you work?
4 Using material presented in this chapter, postulate future directions for music education in Cuba given the current climate associated with this nation.

Notes

1. A *zarzuela* is a Spanish lyric–dramatic genre that alternates between spoken and sung scenes, the latter incorporating operatic and popular song, as well as dance.
2. Patricia Stokoe (1929–96) was an Argentinian dancer and pedagogue, known for her work and writings related to corporal expression.

References

Alvarez, M. (1982), 'La enseñanza de la música en Cuba' (diploma dissertation, Faculdad de Música, Instituto Superior de Artes, Havana, Cuba).

Barreras, G. (1928), 'La enseñanza de la música', *Pro Arte Musical*, reprinted in *Educación* 111 (enero–abril, 2004): 52–3.

Bérubé, M. (1984), *Education and Poverty: Effective Schooling in the United States and Cuba*, Westport, CT: Greenwood.

Bethell, L. (ed.) (1993), *Cuba: A Short History*, New York: Cambridge University Press.

Breidlid, A. (2007), 'Education in Cuba – an Alternative Educational Discourse: Lessons to be Learned', *Compare: A Journal of Comparative and International Education* 37 (5): 617–34.

Calero Martín, J. (ed.) (1929), *Cuba Musical: Album-resumen Ilustrado de la Historia y de la Actual Situación del Arte en Cuba*, Havana: Imprenta Molina y Cía.

Carnoy, M. (2007), *Cuba's Academic Advantage: Why Students in Cuba Do Better in School*, Stanford, CA: Stanford University Press.

Carpentier, A. (2001), *Music in Cuba*, Minneapolis, MN: University of Minnesota Press.

Castro, F. (1961), *History Will Absolve Me*, New York: Lyle Stuart.

Delgado, K. (2001), 'Iyesá: Afro-Cuban Music and Culture in Contemporary Cuba', *Dissertation Abstracts International* 62 (09): 292 (UMI No. 3026270).

Diez, A. (1982), 'Hubert de Blanck: Baluarte de la pedagogí a musical en Cuba (1856–1932)' (diploma dissertation, Faculdad de Música, Instituto Superior de Artes, Havana, Cuba).

Eckstein, S. (1997), 'The Coming Crisis in Cuban Education', *Assessment in Education* 1: 1–12.

Epstein, E. (1987), 'The Peril of Paternalism: Imposition of Education on Cuba by the United States', *American Journal of Education* 96: 1–23.

Figueroa, M., A. Prieto and R. Gutiérrez (1974), *The Basic Secondary School in the Country: An Educational Innovation in Cuba*, Paris: UNESCO.

Galeano, E. (1997), *Open Veins of Latin America*, New York: Monthly Review.

Gasperini, L. (2000), 'The Cuban Education System: Lessons and Dilemmas', *Country Studies, Education Reform and Management Publication Series*, The World Bank, 1 (5): 1–36.

Gramatages, H. (1982), 'La música culta' in Ministerio de Cultura (ed.), *La Cultura en Cuba Socialista*, Havana: Editorial Letras Cubanas, pp. 124–50.

Gumbert, E. (ed.) (1988), *Making the Future: Politics and Educational Reform in the United States, England, the Soviet Union, China, and Cuba*, Atlanta, GA: Georgia State University Press.

Johnston, L. (1995), 'Education in Cuba libre, 1989–1958', *History Today* 45 (8): 26–32.

Levinson, S. (1989), 'Talking about Cuban Culture: A Reporter's Notebook' in P. Bressner, W. LeoGrande, D. Rich and D. Siegle (eds), *The Cuba Reader*, New York: Grove, pp. 487–97.

Lutjens, S. (1996), *The State, Bureaucracy, and the Cuban Schools*, Boulder, CO: Westview.

MacDonald, T. (1985), *Making a New People: Education in Revolutionary Cuba*, Vancouver, BC: New Star.

Menendez, M. (1944), 'Public School Music in Cuba', *Music Educators Journal* 30 (3): 27–8.

Milbrandt, R. (2002), *History Absolves Him: Reading Package, History 291*, Camrose, AB: Augustana University College Press.

Moore, R. (1995), 'Nationalising Blackness: Afro-Cubanismo and Artistic Revolution in Havana, 1920–1935', *Dissertation Abstracts International* 56 (06), 2376 (UMI No. 9534899).

Moore, R. (2006), *Music and Revolution: Cultural Change in Socialist Cuba*, Berkeley: University of California Press.

New Internationalist (1998), 'Jewels in the crown', 301, 27–8.

Ortega, P. (2004), 'Tendencias pedagógica-musicales del siglo XX y su influencia en Cuba', *Educación* 111 (enero–abril), 43–7.

Pichardo, H. (1973), *Documentos Para la Historia de Cuba III*, Havana: Editorial de Ciencias Sociales.

Ponsoda, A. (2002), 'César Pérez Sentenat y la pedagogí a musical cubana', *Clave* 4 (2): 49–52.

Rodríguez, D. (2004), 'Gaspar Agüera Barreras: primer pedagogo musical cubano', *Educación* 111 (enero–abril): 48–51.

Rodríguez, V. and Z. García (1989), *Haciendo Música Cubana*, La Habana, Cuba: Pueblo y Educación.

Schwartz, C. (ed.) (1979), *Impressions of the Republic of Cuba*, Washington, DC: American Association of State Colleges and Universities.

Sublette, N. (2004), *The Missing Cuban Musicians*, Albuquerque, NM: Cuba Research and Analysis Group.

Vega, A. (2002), 'Breve historia de la mú sica Cubana', www.contactomagazine.com/delavega2.htm (accessed 7 September 2002).

PART III: THE MIDDLE EAST

Chapter 14

Israel: From visions of nationhood to realization through music

Lia Laor

The story of music education in Israel goes hand in hand with the story of the formation of Israel as a nation. It began in the 1880s, with the first waves of immigration of European Jews to Palestine, after centuries of dispersion. Drawing on ancient traditions and cultures of various diaspora and local Arab influences, a new culture developed in Palestine. The Jewish community of Palestine, referred to as the *Yishuv* ('Settlement'), was culturally autonomous, both under Ottoman rule (until 1918) and under the British mandate that lasted until the State of Israel's establishment in 1948. Society in the *Yishuv* and then in Israel has always been dominated by the ideological call of mainstream Zionism to return to the nation's eastern biblical roots and to create a homogenizing melting-pot for blending the variety of formerly dispersed Jewish cultures together into a single Israeli identity. As seen below, however, this call has contrasted with more recent internal pressures to preserve the unique heritages of Israel's diverse Jewish ethnic groups that emerged over centuries in the diaspora.

During Israel's nation building, music played a role in this homogenizing agenda by bringing people together, whether as concert audiences or as active participants in choirs, bands, or folk singing (often accompanied by a growing repertoire of folk dances choreographed to the music). The deliberate revival of Hebrew as a modern language of communication was the most powerful unifying tool, and vocal music was encouraged as a potent device for disseminating the use and the correct pronunciation of the language among immigrants (Hirshberg et al. 2015).

Yet this 'melting-pot' ideology has been seriously challenged in later years. Increasingly loud voices have focused on the fragmentation existing within contemporary Israeli society, pinpointing heterogeneous communities with distinct identities that pose a challenge to the ideal of a uniform Israeli identity. Approximately one-quarter of the Israeli population is not Jewish – whether Muslim, Christian, Druze or Bedouin – and each group holds a very different and sometimes opposing identity (Sagi and Nachtomy 2009). The Jewish majority itself is fragmented into different identities with regard to religion (ultra-orthodox, orthodox, traditional, secular) and based on immigration from various countries of origin, broadly divided into Sephardic or Mizrachi Jews (whose families immigrated from Spain, the Middle East or North Africa) and Ashkenazi Jews (from Eastern Europe and English-speaking countries).

In effect, many of these diverse groups consciously struggle to maintain an Israeli identity of their own. They uphold different ways of life, goals and aspirations and may even choose to live in separate geographical spaces (Sagi and Nachtomy 2009). One of the main differences between traditional and modern societies is the demarcation between the desire for cohesiveness and the encouragement of individualism and tolerance for diversity (Eisenstadt 1996). In this sense, the very notion of what constitutes an Israeli identity has undergone a radical change, from a homogenizing melting-pot – implemented mainly through shared institutions of education, a common Hebrew language, a collective ethos and obligatory military service – to a collection of hetero-geneous groups that constitute a new map of identities undergoing a tacit or explicit struggle for recognition. As part of their struggle, these multiple groups within Israel seek cultural symbols and activities to represent their uniqueness.

The story of Israeli music education echoes these processes, events and ideologies that have guided the evolution of Israel as a nation and the development of its education system. In what follows, I will trace important crossroads in the journey of Israeli music education, from music's role in guiding the founding fathers' melting-pot vision up until the later years of multiculturalism. This chapter will discuss three major curricular reforms representing significant milestones in this journey, as well as three main advocacy and policy initiatives affecting the domain of music education. My hope is that the illumination of past visions, curricula and their implementation in this brief historical review will invite a fresh and critical look at current theories, decision-making processes and practices, thereby enabling a continuous, unfragmented perspective of music education in Israel from its inception.

Music education in search of new directions

With the State of Israel's establishment in 1948, the ideological policy of integrating and unifying the Jewish population, which manifested itself practically in all areas of cultural life and cultural expression, consequently led to attempts to unify the domains of musical expression and musical education (Hofmann 1985). The need to mould 'the new Israeli' was voiced by many, including the first prime minister of the new nation, David Ben-Gurion, as in this excerpt from one of his speeches (cited in Davidovitch 2012: 32):

> We must take the immigrant, who is a depleted, neglected, alienated, and estranged organ ... and we shall quickly teach him the language, if he does not know Hebrew, and impart to him ... knowledge of the land, and adapt him to a national setting, in an educating environment, and teach him to till the land ... and thus we shall construct a people united in their language, consciousness, strength of spirit, true to their land and their independence.
> (5 September 1949)

Indeed, concerted social, cultural and educational efforts were invested in the creation of a new nation, a new people, and a strong new Israeli – the *tzabar* ('native-born Israeli') – who would differ from the persecuted Jewish refugee. In the field of music education, it was Leo Kestenberg who was among the first to recruit music education for this national mission. Kestenberg immigrated to Israel in 1938 from Germany, where he had already led major music education reforms (the 'Kestenberg Reform'). In Israel in 1945, together with Imanuel Amiran, he founded the first college for music teacher education in Tel Aviv. Kestenberg was to become the first president of the International Society for Music Education (ISME) in 1953 (Gruhn 2004).

Kestenberg claimed that in Israel, educational issues are connected with great responsibility, both toward past traditions as well as toward the role of Israelis as creators of a new future. He stressed that Israeli music education should not be moulded on existing models. Instead, he viewed the mission of music education as developing new directions that would lead to original creations to fit the unique characteristics of the newly evolved 'Israeli' (Kestenberg 1952). The characteristics that Kestenberg identified as 'Israeli' went back to biblical times, where the shared roots for all the Jewish ethnic groups could be traced. In particular, Kestenberg observed strong ties between the Hebrew language and the conception of music as encompassing more than mere musical sounds. He pinpointed the Hebrew language as the nation's spiritual centre and unifying force, which could integrate what had previously been diverse cultures into one original culture (Kestenberg 1951).

Music as a medium for nation-building

Between 1948 and 1953, the population of Israel doubled. People from many cultures speaking different languages found themselves living as next-door neighbours, and together they faced the major task of nation-building. The country turned to music as one means of solving the problem of assimilation. A programme for bringing music to immigrant settlements was started by the Ministry of Education and Culture in 1950. The project involved an interchange of songs brought to Israel by immigrant groups (Greenberg 1965: 124). Its goals were clear: 'It brings people together spiritually and emotionally. We are using it as a tool to shape a harmonious nation' (Schisgall 1961: 240).

A decade after Kestenberg expressed his vision for Israel's music education, in which he assigned music educators an active role in creating the new Israeli, the music educator and researcher Marvin Greenberg testified to its successful implementation:

'Music educators share in the idealistic traditions of Israel. They see in music a potent force in developing the future citizen, as well as developing a new land with high cultural and musical standards' (Greenberg 1967: 60).

Although the national mission pointed at unification in all areas of cultural life, the implementation process was not as simple as some leaders might have imagined. Leading policymakers in the Israeli government and educational institutions were mostly of Jewish Western origin and had received a Western education. As a result, in almost all domains of learning, educational trends and methodologies were essentially Western in nature (Hofmann 1985). For example, in music education, song anthologies that were used in schools and at social gatherings included mainly songs of a Western orientation. The music of Eastern immigrants, with its oriental or African flavours, did not play an equal role in the early days and did not find its place in the evolving educational canon. Its absence was explained by the fact that Eastern musical traditions were mainly oral, which led to problems in transcribing them (Lichtenshtein 1998).

Constitutive values: First state educational law (1953)

The 1953 law governing Israel's national education system explicitly outlined the basic assumptions that should guide national education in Israel. In line with the collectivist melting-pot ideology of the time, this law stipulated that Israel's education system must be grounded in the following cultural values: love of the land; commitment both to the country and its people; emphasis on science, agriculture and craftsmanship; and human-itarianism built upon freedom, tolerance, equality and mutual assistance. Notably missing from these educational values were the worth of individuals' personal development, the cultural survival of ethnic minorities, the arts in general and music in particular. As naïve and archaic as this ideology may sound to twenty-first-century ears, it continued to a great extent to serve as the foundation of music education in Israel for decades (Cohen and Laor 1997). This trend was well illustrated in 1984 by Mizrahi's (1984) study exploring the views of seventeen leading music educators concerning the goals of music education. Most of these leaders identified social and cultural goals as their primary objectives, whereas only two saw individuation as their major goal for music education.

In the year 2000, intensive effort led to an amendment to the 1953 law guiding the national education system (Kam n.d.). This amendment expressed a shift from the melting-pot ideology to a multicultural ideology with openness to and tolerance of individual and ethnic differences, thereby reflecting a move from collectivist to individu-alistic values, as will be elaborated below.

The centrality of song

The genre of Israeli song was a central element in the evolving Zionist culture, playing a vital role in the construction of Israeli identity. The genre consists of Hebrew texts set to music with a monophonic texture, usually by identifiable pre-State and Israeli composers during the 1882–1948 period (Hirshberg et al. 2015). Some of the new songs in the earliest settlements were written to East European melodies and others to local tunes, mainly of oriental origin. From 1918 onward, songs were composed to biblical and traditional Jewish texts, as well as to new lyrics reflecting events of the time. The search for an authentic Israeli song style started at that juncture (Haran et al. 1980). Shlomo Hofmann, a composer and scholar of Jewish and Eastern music, claimed that in the years 1920–50 'the elements of the Israeli song were the identity signs of a musical work as being Israeli music … Israeli song was and still is … one of the most specific expressions of the unity of Israel' (Hofmann 1985: 55). Cultural researcher Ariel Hirshfeld, too, saw in Israeli songs 'the most valid musical work of Israel's culture. As opposed to Israeli art music, which was "deaf to its environment", the Israeli songs were not isolated aesthetic objects but rather penetrated life' (Hirshfeld 2000: 131–2). According to Hirshfeld, these songs were the most 'Israeli' of all artistic phenomena, comprising the only medium in which something unique was created in the nineteenth century – distinguishing Israeli song from what was created in other cultures. It was neither a 'folk' song nor an 'art' song (in the tradition of the German *Lied*, for example), nor was it a product of Israel's cultural industry (Hirshfeld 1997).

Certainly, Kestenberg himself viewed the genre as a key player in Israeli music education: 'The starting point to music is not the symphonic work but the song. Not

Figure 14.1 An example of a nation-building song: 'Hatikvah' ('The Hope'), the Israeli National Anthem, melody based on a Romanian folk song, words by Naphtali Herz Imber (composed c. 1878). A translation of the text: 'As long as in the heart, within, The Jewish soul yearns, And onward, towards the eastern edges, onward, An eye gazes toward Zion. Our hope is not yet lost, The hope that is two-thousand years old, To be a free nation in our land, The Land of Zion, Jerusalem.' An excerpt from a school songbook, *Be'Nevel Assor* (in Hebrew), Israeli Ministry of Education, 1958, p. 2.[1]

a passive appreciation but an active action' (Kestenberg 1951: 12). Kestenberg's emphasis on the importance of such songs highlights the uniqueness of the Israeli song as a musical genre as well as the role it played in social and cultural processes (for an example of a nation-building song, see Figure 14.1).

The emerging Israeli song repertoire was deliberately designed and expected to function as an 'invented tradition', following Eric Hobsbawm's concept (Hirshberg 1995: 147). Indeed, when in later years the authenticity of this tradition was threatened by Western popular music influences, many protested, adopting a national as well as educational mission to protect it. For example, in a letter to Israeli Prime Minister Levi Eshkol (26 April 1964), after attending that year's annual Hebrew Song Festival, the General Supervisor of Music Education for the Ministry of Education, Imanuel Amiran, pleaded:

> Please, regard this letter as a missive of a citizen ... who regards original [Israeli] tunes as an important factor and a powerful asset in the formation of a cultural and folk environment, and its style must influence ... our art ... I would not dare, dear Prime Minister, to turn to you and take your precious time and bother you, if I did not regard this matter of the highest national and educational importance ... I was sorry to watch the Prime Minister and other Ministers honouring, with their presence, a festival of 'songs about nothing'.[2]
>
> These events, which were planned by the Prime Minister's office, gave credit and honour to a harmful performance that should be condemned and resisted by the state and should not be the greenhouse for decaying fruits. (Amiran 1974: 249–51)

To remedy this decay in the Israeli song genre, Amiran asked the Prime Minister to nominate a committee of leading figures in music, which he called the Vision Committee, 'to review and sort musical products and then to select the best material according to musical, stylistic, and textual value'. Amiran's national plan aimed to ensure the development of original authentic Israeli music and to protect school students from 'inferior' popular music, which reflected foreign influences (Amiran 1974: 251).

Amiran's ideas about the importance of the Israeli song were directed at Israel's Arab school students as well. He claimed that songs could serve as a bridge for understanding between Arab and Jewish Israelis and as an educational means that would influence how Arab youth could relate to the State. He initiated the preparation of a collection of educational songs for Arab students, which included Hebrew songs translated into Arabic as well as newly composed songs in Arabic, among them songs praising Israel's Independence Day. Needless to say, these songs failed to achieve their educational goal and were politically as well as musically criticized. In his analysis of the situation, leading music critic and journalist Noam Ben Zeev (2009: 27) claimed that 'the pretentious Jewish Arab song project that aimed to achieve multiculturalism and equality between the two people[s], reflected the power struggle and hegemonic relations between the cultures'.

Evolving music curricula: three major reforms

Following the establishment of the national education system in the early 1950s, there have been three main curricular reforms in the field of music education between 1960 and 2011. Each reform had a different emphasis and proposed new solutions.

The 1960 curriculum: Establishing a national narrative

The first obligatory music curriculum that was developed by the Ministry of Education for Grades 1–8 became effective in 1960. Described as a most comprehensive document about music education, it reflected the thinking of the time (Greenberg 1967). It presented five main musical activities: singing, listening and ear training, music reading and music theory, eurhythmics and instrument playing (Ministry of Education and Culture 1960). Notwithstanding this rich panorama of activities, the singing of the Israeli song was the nucleus of what were appropriately termed 'singing classes' (as opposed to 'music classes'). The core of the curriculum comprised a detailed list of songs, arranged according to content and the age range of students.

The curriculum reflected, among other aspects, the importance attributed by the founding fathers to biblical times and to the Bible itself as well as to ancient Mediterranean cultures that as the wellspring of the nation had the potential to nurture the creation of the new Israeli. Thus, the curriculum's song repertoire depicted biblical scenes in Modern Hebrew and cited biblical texts. In addition, the curriculum required seventh-grade students (nearing Bar Mitzvah) to study the cantillation of liturgical text as well as the scales, modes, maqams and tetrachords (Ministry of Education and Culture 1960).

Seven years after the implementation of the music curriculum, Greenberg (1967) published the results of his rigorous research undertaken in collaboration with the Israeli Ministry of Education, which reviewed music education in general and evaluated the extent to which music education in Grades 1–8 was influencing Israel's musical life. To the best of my knowledge, this was the first and perhaps only major attempt to conduct a thorough, comprehensive examination of Israel's music curriculum and its implementation in schools. At the outset, Greenberg described the social context in which music education was situated at the time. The almost idyllic picture of the Israeli musical scene that Greenberg depicted was of a vibrant, musically informed and active society in which music education played an important role:

> Israel is a country whose citizens are musically aware. Music penetrates all phases of human activity in Israel and has become a necessary part of the life of the Israeli. The country has a large number of musical amateurs as a direct result of music education programs. Amateur chamber groups, folk orchestras, choirs, study groups, and music circles have become commonplace. To use the words of the late conductor, Dimitri Mitropoulos, Israel has become 'a paradise for musicians'. (Greenberg 1967: 67)

Attempting to identify connections between music education and Israeli society, Greenberg observed a family resemblance between the character of the nation and that of eurhythmics: 'The improvisational character of eurhythmics has found a home in the nation's life – of constant movement, dynamicism, impulsive change, and spontaneity' (Greenberg 1967: 67). Furthermore, in his pursuit of discovering what made Israeli music education unique, Greenberg regarded Israelis' development of creativity via eurhythmics as an original Israeli application:

> Various musical activities in Israel's eurhythmics programs distinguish these activities from eurhythmics in European and American schools. In Israel special emphasis is placed on vocal improvisation, the use of the modes in improvisation, the use of folk instruments, and use of rhythm instruments for improvisation and as a stimulus for movement. There is also a decided effort to stimulate creativity in the eurhythmics lessons. (Greenberg 1967: 67)

The importance of music as a school subject that plays an active role in the creation of the new nation is depicted in Ben Zeev's (2009: 51) personal memories of music lessons in primary school:

> In those days of the early sixties nobody [had] heard of multiculturalism … The focus was on national indoctrination. The most solid routine in the school … was the morning reading of psalms by the principal … But in those days … schools were very ambitious, particularly in terms of music and they got what they asked for. These were the last moments of conceiving music in terms of fulfillment of Zionist ideology and hence as an important subject matter.

The 1977/1980 music curriculum: Music as an aesthetic experience

A new expanded music curriculum was published for kindergarten and primary schools (Ministry of Education 1977) and for middle schools (Ministry of Education 1980). The head of the curriculum committee was Professor Herzl Shmueli, a leading musicologist and scholar of Israeli song, while the composer Ben Zion Orgad served as General Supervisor of Music Education for the Ministry of Education. This curriculum was very much in line with contemporary American and British music education, for example, where, at the time, the conceptualization of music education as aesthetic education formed the backbone of music curricula (Elliott 1995).

The new curriculum contained six content domains: singing, instrument playing, eurhythmics, music literature, music theory, and music in society and school. It outlined a very detailed and analytic course of study, progressing from the identification of the smallest musical elements (intervals, melodic figures, rhythmic patterns) to global comprehension of whole structures (Ministry of Education 1977: 14). The primary school curriculum's main focus was formulated in terms of:

> helping the student move from being passive to being active and discover his/her musical skills and abilities … Music as a phenomenon of sounds, in all its aspects, and as an

aesthetic-artistic phenomenon, with all its historical content and massages, should be at the centre of this activity. (Ministry of Education 1977)

The main objective of music education in the middle school system was formulated as 'the education of an active audience, and the development of the capacity to appreciate music' (Ministry of Education 1980: 7). While listening to music, students were expected to respond through performance and movement activities as well as through affective responses. However, an overall holistic perspective – combining cognition and emotion – was still missing in this second wave of curricular reform.

The implementation of the new curriculum was accompanied by the publication of various teaching materials, including song anthologies (e.g. an anthology of Arabic and Hebrew songs), recordings of Western art music repertoire, teachers' curricular guides and more besides (Itrani 2005). In 1978, the Ministry of Education asked a group of in-service teachers to prepare curriculum guides that would exemplify possible development of the curricular objectives without specifically delineating one acceptable method (Kaplan 1984).

The early days of this curriculum's implementation were characterized by an atmosphere of enthusiasm and vibrant curiosity among music teachers, as portrayed by Barbara Kaplan, who in 1979 was a visiting professor in Israel from Auburn University: 'There is an openness to new ideas, talent for adopting ideas to particular needs, and willingness to prepare thoroughly and work diligently to reach a goal. The dream of music experience for all of Israel is already a reality' (Kaplan 1984: 60). However, the introduction of change in general and the implementation of a new curriculum in particular are always complex, intense processes. Despite the implementation efforts of the Ministry of Education, neither the 1977 primary school reform nor the 1980 middle school reform was easily incorporated into the school system.

It appears that this second wave of curricular reform failed to reach teachers in the field. Complaints were voiced regarding its academic and theoretical orientation. A few years after the curriculum's inception, Hanoch Ron, a music teacher educator and music critic, slammed these new music curricula, which he called 'a collection of meaningless thoughts about music teaching from a high brow perspective that was rejected scornfully … talking about music instead of doing music' (Ron 1984: 50). Ron claimed that the 'teacher for singing' and the 'teacher for [music] listening' – products of the first and second wave of curriculum reform – were no longer relevant (ibid.). His criticism evoked professional unrest. Angry letters were sent by prominent teacher educators to the editor of the journal where Ron published his critique, as well as to Ben Zion Orgad, the Ministry's General Supervisor for Music Education who had led the development and implementation of the music curriculum, and to others (Itrani 2005). In 1988, Orgad retired, and in later years further implementation and development of the curriculum were abandoned. Between 1988 and 2011, music education operated with no comprehensive authorized curriculum that regulated music studies in the school system or provided a guide for music teacher education.

The new music curriculum (2011): Addressing identity, diversity, and the musical experience

The third wave of curriculum development emerged in 2011, when 'the new music curriculum' for primary and secondary schools was authorized and published (Ministry of Education 2011a, 2011b).The Ministry of Education assigned a committee for music curriculum development, headed by the pianist and professor of music Tomer Lev and by the late Yael Shai, the Ministry's General Supervisor for Music Education at the time, who was responsible for its implementation within the school system. The committee members included leading musicians and music educators from major music teacher education colleges and music academies.

It was explained that the need for a new curriculum resulted from, among other factors, the many changes that had transpired in various domains since the publication of the 1977/1980 curricula. These changes included: (a) the development of music education as a newly emergent research-based discipline that takes in knowledge from other fields (e.g. psychology, sociology, philosophy, anthropology and general education); (b) the collapse of the worldview that attached high value to Western art music and low value to popular and ethnic music; (c) the shift from perceiving music solely as an isolated aesthetic object to a perception of music as rooted in culture, society and time; and (d) advanced technological means that influence the ways in which music is listened to, composed and performed.

This first mission of this most recent curriculum was to acknowledge these changes and to address them via relevant methods of study. The opening words of the curriculum document express its commitments in this regard, by delineating the following objectives:

A. To reach a balance between collective/individual diversity and the need to create a shared body of musical knowledge for Israeli students.
B. To encourage exposure to a wide spectrum of musical cultures and to offer teachers criteria for informed choice of repertoire.
C. To use technology in advanced learning environments.
D. To offer connections and interfaces between music and other disciplines.
E. To teach music as a dynamic performing art that is actively practised and experienced by students as listeners, performers, and creators.

Thus, this new curriculum depicts music education as clearly situated and operating within the contexts of the individual student and the wider circles of society and culture. It recognizes that, in the current millennium, Israel is diverse and rich in musical cultures, which presents a challenge for music educators. Both the primary and secondary school curricula now assume a conceptual framework that regards the arts in general and music in particular as an expression of cultural identity. It sets the stage for discussion of fundamental questions of identity such as 'Who am I?' and 'Who are we?' while proposing music studies as an agent for cultural pluralism. Thus, by contributing to the internalization of values such as tolerance and openness, the new curriculum emphasizes respect for Israel's twenty-first-century multicultural society.

Toward this end, the 2011 curriculum innovatively advocates a shift from a rigid, closed conception of identity to an open one, according to which each member of society can belong to various cultural circles. Utilizing this open framework, the new curriculum helps each Israeli student find his or her own place within a system of three identity circles, each presented in the curriculum by a variety of musical genres such as art music, ethnic music and popular music. These circles comprise: (1) the *civic* circle, expressing students' identity as Israeli citizens; (2) the *community* circle, addressing students' religious identity (e.g. as Jews, Arabs, secular, orthodox) as well as their ethnic identity (e.g. Ashkenazi, Mizrachi, immigrants from Russia or Ethiopia); and (3) the *universal* circle, helping students construct an identity as 'citizens of the world' by using canonic repertoire of world cultures.

Another aspect of the new curriculum is its main focus on the child's musical experience, built as a spiralling sequence of listening, performance and creativity, which are all considered inherent to this experience. These three core activities are each presented separately in the curriculum but are also presented in combination (e.g. the role of listening during singing activity). The rationale for this organization is, among others, that Western musical culture assigns distinct roles for the audience, performers and creators of music; however, in most non-Western cultures these boundaries are loose, allowing the young music student to become a creator, performer and audience concurrently.

The status of music education as a core subject

Currently the status of music within the Israeli school curriculum is that of an elective subject. In 1985, music was still mentioned as a mandatory core subject (Zmora-Cohen Report 1985), but since then it has lost this status. In the past twenty years, leading music educators have initiated persistent attempts through various advocacy efforts to influence policy makers to change this elective status, but so far unsuccessfully. It is important to note that music is offered to all children in primary school, but there are almost no music studies in middle school (with a few exceptions). In high school, music is taught only as a highly specialized subject, offered in about 120 advanced music programmes throughout the country as one of multiple alternatives available when students choose their study major for the high school years. Once a student chooses the music major, the advanced level studies are taught by specialist teachers and assessed in matriculation tests and recitals (Portowitz et al. 2010). In these programmes, musical knowledge comprises the following: music theory, harmony, ear training, history of music, music analysis, as well as vocal and instrumental performance.

The high school music curriculum includes a core unit and elective classes. The core unit's foundation in Western art music is attributed mainly to the fact that such music boasts a well-developed body of knowledge and teaching methods, which can facilitate further learning and the cultivation of musical skills. In addition, these core studies are meant to serve as common ground for all Israeli high school music students. In the elective classes, each music programme selects musical styles and genres according to its speciality (e.g. jazz, classical music, popular music).

Major crossroads for advocating policy change

Looking back at major crossroads for policy change initiatives and advocacy efforts, including those aiming to change the status of music education to that of a core subject, the next part of this chapter focuses on: (a) the evaluation of art education by the Zmora-Cohen National Committee for the Arts in 1985; (b) advocacy for music as part of the core curriculum for Israel in 2003; and (c) the advocacy efforts of the Dostrovsky Forum for Music and Dance Education in 2010.

Assessing arts education

Michal Zmora-Cohen, a leading musicologist and educator, was nominated in 1983 by the Ministry of Education to head the National Committee for the Arts – the only major national committee for arts education ever conducted in Israel. The committee's mission was to assess the state-of-the-arts in the field of education at the time, to offer policy recommendations for education in the arts, to review teacher education programmes and to offer recommendations for future developments. With regard to music education, the committee's report pinpointed its insecure status and inadequate implementation in schools. It noted that the Ministry's music curriculum was not being properly imple-mented in as much as it required one or two weekly classes for all grades. Specifically, the report warned against the drastic decline in music instruction in middle school and in the first grade (Zmora-Cohen Report 1985). However, the report's recommenda-tions were not implemented (personal interview with the late Michal Zmora-Cohen, 17 January 2013).

Advocating music as a core subject

After a 1999 appeal to the Supreme Court against the Minister of Education on the need for a comprehensive core curriculum, the Ministry's Pedagogical Secretary, Professor Jacob Katz, coordinated efforts to achieve a new core curriculum to serve the Israeli school system. This reform effort seemed to offer a window of opportunity to plead the case for music education as a core subject. In March 2003, Katz was invited to a special meeting with the Ministry of Education Music Steering Committee to discuss the status of music education in the new reform. The committee, headed by Professor Judith Cohen, a notable musicologist and music educator, stressed the importance of music in the education of every child and reported on the status of music education as a core subject in the most advanced school systems around the world. Unfortunately, music and the other arts were not accepted as core subjects in the new core curriculum, but rather received the status of 'recommended subject' (Katz 2006).

Advocacy forum for music education

The Dostrovsky Forum for Music and Dance Education was founded in 2009 by the Jerusalem Academy of Music and Dance to advance music and dance education. Over the years, this forum, chaired by Michal Zmora-Cohen, whose members are leading artists, educators, researchers and policy-makers, has submitted position papers (Van Leer Jerusalem Institute 2010). It has also met with two Ministers of Education, Gideon Saar in 2010 and Shai Piron in 2013, appealing for music to become a core subject in the Israeli school curriculum. In both cases, the ministers showed great appreciation for the importance of music in our lives and education, but no further action was taken.

Conclusion

The history of music education in Israel touches upon a wide variety of topics, but the current brief review could not cover many important issues including those of teacher education, early childhood education and music education in Arab or Jewish ultra-orthodox communities. Historical research on music education in Israel is very scarce. One reason for this paucity of research is the lack of doctoral programmes in music education in Israeli higher education, which could serve as an academic habitat for such research.

This short review traced Israeli music education's first steps, while emphasizing how its evolution echoed ideologies and processes that contributed to the new nation's formation. I outlined the three major curricular reforms that reflected the country's shift from an explicit melting-pot ideological agenda in the 1950s and 1960s to a multicultural plural-istic conceptual framework in 2011. Yet, has multicultural, postmodern Israel gone too far? Israeli president Reuben Rivlin recently voiced concern for the future of 'Israeliness' – or Israeli identity – which may become subsumed by four separate groups split along 'tribal' lines (Rivlin: 7 June 2015). Referring to four communities mostly populated, respectively, by national religious Jews, Bedouin Arabs, secular Jews and ultra-orthodox Jews, the President stated that '[Children that come from these communities] – not only do they not meet each other, but they are educated toward a totally different outlook regarding the basic values and desired character of the State of Israel' (ibid.).

Overall, several major factors may be seen as contributing to Israel's possible breakdown in the negotiation between these shifting agendas for homogenization and pluralism. These factors include, first, the powerful quest after authentic identity for individuals as well as groups within Israeli society, reinforced by contemporary globalization influences; second, the division of the Israeli school system into its three segregated tracks – state (mostly secular Jews), state-religious (orthodox Jews), and independent (either ultra-orthodox Jews or Arabs); and third, the fact that the core curriculum is not enforced for everyone (Lidar and Young 2014). These processes led to many Israelis' current sense of fragmented and conflicted national identity, rather than a feeling of cohesive identity comprising an amalgamation of different sub-identities.

Can music education again be harnessed as a vehicle for uncovering shared values and shared sounds without compromising the variety of musical traditions that nourishes it? Perhaps Israel should experience the rich texture of its society as a contrapuntal work of music, where each line intertwines with others to create a cohesive fabric, while maintaining its own beauty.

Reflective questions

1 Using the Israeli experience as a point of reference, do you think music education in your country has played an active role in the formation of national identity?

2 Are you able to trace a particular musical event or a specific musical genre (like, for example, Israeli song) that had a significant influence on the development of your society?

3 How does music education in your country address multiculturalism? Is it taught through Western lenses or as an 'authentic laboratory'?

4 Identify important curricular reforms in your country's school music education system. What were the major changes and/or trends, and what do you think should be the next reform to take place in music education and why should this occur?

Notes

1. The title of the song book, *Be'Nevel Assor*, is taken from Psalms 144 verse 9, 'On the ten-stringed lyre', referring to music playing in praise of the Lord on the occasion of King David's victory over enemies and achievement of peace. The instrument itself serves here metaphorically – to represent the tenth anniversary of the State of Israel, the occasion for which the song book was compiled.

2. The song 'Things of No Importance' (Keynan and Cohen 1964) won second prize in the 1964 festival.

References

Amiran, I. (1974), *Lights and Paths in Music Education*, Tel Aviv: The Methodic Center for Music [Hebrew].

Ben Zeev, N. (2009), *An Israeli Tune*, Tel Aviv: Hakibbutz Hameuchad [Hebrew].

Cohen, V. and L. Laor (1997), 'Struggling with Pluralism in Music Education: The Israeli Experience', *Arts Education Policy Review* 98 (3): 10–15.

Davidovitch, N. (2012), 'Educational Challenges in a Multicultural Society: The Case of Israel', *Cross-Cultural Communication* 8 (2): 29–39.

Eisenstadt, S. N. (1996), 'Comments on the Post-modern Society' in M. Lissackand and B. Knei-Paz (eds), *Israel Towards the Year 2000*, Jerusalem: Magnes Press.

Elliott, D. (1995), *Music Matters: A New Philosophy of Music Education*, New York: Oxford University Press.

Greenberg, M. (1965), 'Music Education Builds a Nation', *Music Educators Journal* 52 (1): 124–6.

Greenberg, M. (1967), 'Music in Israel's Primary Schools', *Journal of Research in Music Education* 15 (1): 60–72.

Gruhn, W. (2004), 'Leo Kestenberg 1882–1962', *International Journal of Music Education* 22 (2): 103–29.

Haran, D., E. Gerson-Kiwi, G. Aldema and W. Elias (1980), 'Israel' in S. Sadie (ed.), *The New Grove Dictionary of Music and Musicians*, London: Macmillan, pp. 356–61.

Hirshberg, J. (1995), *Music in the Jewish Community of Palestine 1880–1948: A Social History*, Oxford: Clarendon Press.

Hirshberg, J., N. Shahar, E. Seroussi and A. Shiloah (2015), 'Israel' in *Grove Music Online*, http://www.oxfordmusiconline.com.ezproxy.levinsky.ac.il/subscriber/article/grove/music/41 (accessed 1 July 2015).

Hirshfeld, A. (1997), 'On the Israeli song', *Haaretz Literary Supplement,* 19 December 1997 [Hebrew].

Hirshfeld, A. (2000), *Local Notes*, Tel Aviv: Am Oved [Hebrew].

Hofmann, S. (1985), 'Music Education in a Multicultural Society – Israel: Concepts and their Implementation', *International Journal of Music Education* 5 (1): 53–6.

Itrani, E. (2005), *Music Teachers in Tel Aviv (1961–1986)*, Tel Aviv: Levinsky College of Education Publications [Hebrew].

Kam, M. (n.d.), 'The National Education Law', Virtual Library of the Center for Educational Technology [Hebrew]. http://lib.cet.ac.il/pages/item.asp?item=3332 (accessed 1 July 2015).

Kaplan, B. (1984), 'Music Education in Israel', *Music Educators Journal* 70 (6): 57–60.

Katz, Y. (2006), 'Core curricula in Israel' in D. Inbar (ed.), *Towards an Educational Revolution?*, Jerusalem: Van Leer Institute and Hakibbutz Hameuhad, pp. 186–202 [Hebrew].

Kestenberg, L. (1951), 'On Music Listening', *Music Education* 6: 11 [Hebrew].

Kestenberg, L. (1952), 'A Conversation on Music Education in Israel', *Music Education* 7: 4–6 [Hebrew].

Keynan, C. and S. Cohen (1964), 'Things of No Importance' (Chaim Keynan – lyrics, Shimon Cohen – music), https://www.youtube.com/watch?v=WfrlGDdm1D4 (accessed 1 July 2015).

Lichtenshtein, D. (1998), 'From Historiographical Narrative to Alternative Rationale in Music Education', *Mafteach* 2, 1–19 [Hebrew].

Lidar, L. and B. Young (2014), 'Ultra-orthodox do not have to learn core curriculum', *Jerusalem Post*, http://www.jpost.com/Israel-News/High-Court-Ultra-Orthodox-do-not-have-to-learn-core-curriculum-375644 (accessed 1 July 2015).

Ministry of Education and Culture (1960), *Music Curriculum for State Primary and Religious Schools*, Jerusalem [Hebrew].

Ministry of Education (1977), *Music for Kindergarten and Primary School*, Jerusalem: The Curriculum Center [Hebrew].

Ministry of Education (1980), *Music for Middle School*, Jerusalem: The Curriculum Center [Hebrew].

Ministry of Education (2011a), *Music Curriculum for Primary School*, Jerusalem: Department for Curriculum Development [Hebrew].

Ministry of Education (2011b), *Music Curriculum for High School*, Jerusalem: Department for Curriculum Development [Hebrew].

Mizrahi, M. (1984), *The Aims of Music Education in Israeli Schools*, Tel Aviv: The Methodic Center for Music [Hebrew].

Portowitz, A., Gonzalez-Moreno, P. and Hendricks, K. (2010), 'Students' Motivation to Study Music in Israel', *Research Studies in Music Education* 32 (2): 169–84.

Rivlin, R. (2015). 'Four tribes in Israel: a new order has been created', http://www.mako.co.il/news-israel/local-q2_2015/Article-1fc80c1225ecd41004.htm (accessed 1 July 2015) [Hebrew].

Ron, H. (1984),'The Challenge of New Music Education in Israel', *HedHachinuch* 5: 48–50 [Hebrew].

Sagi, A. and O. Nachtomy (eds) (2009), *Israel: Society, Culture, and History: Multicultural Challenge in Israel*, Boston, MA: Academic Studies Press.

Schisgall, O. (1961), 'The Sound of Singing in Israel', *Reader's Digest* 78 (May 1961): 240.

Van Leer Jerusalem Institute (2010), *The Dostrovsky Forum for Music and Dance Education*, http://www.vanleer.org.il/en/research-group/dostrovsky-forum-music-and-dance-education (accessed 1 July 2015).

Zmora-Cohen, M. (1985), *Report of the Committee for Education in the Arts, headed by Michal Zmora-Cohen and submitted to the Minister of Education* [Hebrew].

Chapter 15

Turkey: Historical and political influences on music education

Dilek Göktürk Cary

Introduction

The Republic of Turkey was established on a foundation of national integrity. Mustafa Kemal Atatürk (1881–1938), who founded the Republic on 29 October 1923, made several statements about the important role he saw for education. He believed that education is a life-long process for individuals that also plays an important role in the lives of nations (Özeke 2003). According to Atatürk, 'our national system of education should be something different from the old and something that grows out of our own nation … and national genius can only be developed through our national culture' (Karal 1966, quoted in Özeke 2003: 28).

The history of music education in Turkey and its quality has become an important concern for teachers and researchers, who have responded by writing numerous studies on the subject. Based on this research, the purpose of this chapter is to examine the development and the current status of music education in the Republic of Turkey from the historical and socio-political contexts. The following issues will be considered:

1 the effects of historical and political contexts on music education;
2 the aims and content of music as a compulsory subject;
3 classroom music teaching methods;
4 the training of music teachers.

At the end of the chapter, reflections on the present state of music education in the light of past developments will be presented.

History, politics and music education in the Republic of Turkey

Pre-Republic period

Turks established their first formal state, the Göktürk Empire, under the leadership of Bumin and İstemi Khan south of the Altai mountains in Central Asia in 552 CE. We have little information about educational practices of that time, but the existence of an alphabet composed of thirty-eight letters is evidence of the existence of formal education in the Göktürk Empire. Because of a number of interrelated factors and reasons, such as the economy, climate changes and the pressures of stronger neighbours, some of the tribes moved west and came to Anatolia, the land where today's Turkey is located. After embracing Islam, they started the Turkishizing and Islamizing of Turkey. There was massive adult and religious education during this time. In 1299, based on the now matured foundations of the Selcuk Empire, the Ottoman Empire started to rise and became a world-class state, which lasted until the beginning of the twentieth century (Turan 1997). Paul Wittek (1894–1978), an Austrian historian who specialized in Ottoman history, summarizes the political rise of the Ottoman Empire as follows:

> The Ottoman Empire holds a special place on account of the vast extent of its realm and the long duration of its existence. Arising about 1300 from very modest beginnings, only a century later it was clearly inspired by the idea of universal domination, which it was after-wards to realize by occupying vast territories in the three continents of the ancient world, Europe, Asia and Africa. In this enormous area the Ottoman Empire was for centuries the unrivalled power which determined all political events, and at the same time represented for these countries a cultural epoch, the traces of which still remain visible long after the empire itself has disappeared. (Wittek 1971, quoted in Turan 1997: 6–7)

During the early years of the empire, music was included at the *Mehterhane* (military band headquarters) and the *Enderun Mektebi* (Palace School to educate state officials), the latter being a secular rather than religious insitution (Kocabaş 2010). In addition, there were two other schools that educated students for religious purposes: *Darül Kurra* (school for teaching the reading of the Quran) and *Darül Huffaz* (school for teaching students to memorize the Quran). All of these schools prepared students and future teachers in music for religious and military purposes (Kocabaş 2010). In addition the age-old military band, the monasteries of Mevlevi dervishes, *gynecium* (originally meaning the inner section of a house used as women's quarters), music traders' guilds and private homes where music was performed could also be thought of as being educational in that they enabled the transfer of music composition and performance practice of the Ottoman period from one generation to the next (Tanrıkorur 1999; Tufan 2006). Schools called *gyneciums* have special significance because they have been identified as the first forms of secular education during the Ottoman period. However, it is recognised that the education provided through these schools was not systematic (Tufan 2006). At *Enderun*

Mektebi, the Palace School where state officials were educated, traditional art music was taught by famous musicians of the time and secular music training was mandatory in these schools.

The educational legacy of the Ottoman Empire was its formal and informal institutions that were wholly and partially based on religious principles. The success of the Ottoman Empire and civilization with its differing educational system to that in Western Europe was its grounding in Islamic thought, which was seen as permeating all aspects of life during this period. With the decline of the Ottoman Empire, which started at the end of the sixteenth century, some efforts were made to reform and Westernize its educational institutions. By the beginning of the seventeenth century, notions of reform, modernization, change and the Westernization of the educational system became part of the Turkish social, political and educational ethos (Turan 1997) and had a long-term influence on the political and cultural fabric of the Ottoman Empire (O'Connell 2000).

Present-day music education has its origins in the modernist movements that arose in the first quarter of the nineteenth century. Ottoman music originated from Middle Asia (the ancient motherland of the Turks) and was then shaped by Anatolian culture and surrounding cultures. However, under the influence of Western cultures, Turkish music education took a rather different slant (Tufan, 2006). After the establishment of higher education institutions for general teacher training, the need for specific music teacher education became apparent. Music was introduced into the curriculum of the *Kız Öğretmen Okulu* (Girls' Teacher Training School) in 1875 and other teacher training schools had added music to their curricula by 1910. In 1917, the first music school, *Darülelhan* (Music School), opened in İstanbul and, although it was closed in 1926, the school later reopened as a conservatory during the Republic period in 1927 (Göktürk 2009). Although the primary purpose of these schools was to train musicians for the military, some lessons on teaching music were included in their curricula. Both the Imperial Military Music School and what was simply called the 'Music School' were important institutions for the preparation of music teachers during the Ottoman period. The need for the establishment and development of these types of schools began to be realized more during the constitutional period, which began in 1908. This realization became a major influence on the establishment of the Music Teacher Training School (1924), the first official institution for music teacher education during the Republic period (Özeke 2003; Göktürk Cary 2014).

Republic period (1923–present)

The leadership of the new Republic regarded education 'as the most important foundation' of the transformation (Kazamias 1966; Turan 1997). In order to create a modern state, it was necessary to create new values, new ideologies and new ways of looking at things (Kazamias and Massialas 1965; Turan 1997). Education was viewed as a means of disseminating such ideas and values in addition to the 'state ideology'.

For such dissemination, the leaders of the time thought that it was necessary to create a powerful mechanism that would help educational and political leaders to reject the traditional educational institutions of the Ottoman era. It was thought necessary to centralize the educational system and make only the Ministry of Education responsible for education of the people (Turan 1997).

On 3 March 1923, *Resmi Gazete* (*The Official Gazette*) published the *Tevhid-i Tedrisat Kanunu* (Law on Unification of Educational Institutions). This law required the unification of all educational institutions under the control of the Ministry of National Education. The primary reason for implementing this law was the abolition of religious instruction in all schools. This action was extremely important to the development of secularism in modern Turkey (Göktürk 2009). In their book *Educational Problems in Turkey 1920–1940* Başgöz and Wilson describe the new educational system as follows:

> After the establishment of the Turkish Republic, the new government began to search for a general system of education. Previously, the Ottoman Empire had included diverse religions and nationalities. After the collapse of the Empire, the new Turkish government began to develop a national system of education. Some of the biggest difficulties faced by the new government were an insufficient number of schools and teachers, a high illiteracy rate, and a lack of sufficient funds. (Başgöz and Wilson 1968, quoted in Göktürk 2009: 704)

Atatürk believed that Turkey should find a place in the modern world through strategic thinking and through the development of a forward-looking educational vision. In this context, he advocated that Turkish educators should embrace mutual goals and shared beliefs in the importance of particular critical issues. Likewise, educators were asked to create a safer learning environment for all students. In order for this vision to be effective, Atatürk believed that it should be (a) competitive, (b) open, (c) memorable, (d) participatory, (e) visible, (f) active, (g) guiding and (h) unified with the needs of the students. As a primary component of the big picture, music educators were encouraged to embrace a vision containing all of the qualities stated above. A law that was passed on 8 April 1929 articulated this vision (*Official Gazette* 1169, 16 April 1929, cited in Göktürk Cary 2011).

Atatürk was enthusiastic about gathering role models for the new educational system in Turkey. He invited renowned educators from several other countries to visit Turkey and offer their suggestions for educational reform. Among the notable scholars who visited Turkey were John Dewey from the United States in 1924, Alfred Kühne from Germany in 1926, Omar Buyse from Belgium in 1927, and a team led by Walter Kemmerer from the United States in 1933. When the Turkish Ministry of Education invited Dewey to observe and analyze the Turkish educational system in 1924, he visited the country from 15 July to 18 September 1924. He made recommendations for restructuring and reorganizing the existing educational system and prepared two reports in which he made specific recommendations for the formation and implementation of an educational plan, the development of schools as community centres, the reorganization of the Ministry of Public Instruction, the training and treatment of teachers, the redefinition of the school system, the improvement of health and hygiene issues in schools, the improvement of discipline and other areas of schooling. The reports constituted 'a comprehensive theory of public education' (Turan 1997).

Reforms made in music and music education were considered as a part of the new educational perspective. A fresh attempt was made to create a national style of polyphonic Turkish music based on the Turkish folk music tradition (Gökalp 1973; Tufan 2006), since it was believed that neither the music associated with the Ottomans, nor the music which developed under Arabian and Persian influence, could reflect the true music of the Turkish people. Music and music education in this period took its shape in accordance with the views of the influential thinkers of the time, namely Ziya Gökalp and Atatürk. In the light of these views, the Music Teacher Training School was established in Ankara in 1924, and for the first time music teachers were trained in accordance with the principles of educational and pedagogical sciences. Following this development, *Darülelhan* (Music School) in İstanbul was reconstructed and transformed into a conservatoire in 1926 (Tufan 2006).

An important development during 1940 was the establishment of the village institutes movement. The major purpose of the village institutes was to carry education to every possible place in Turkey. Music education and music teacher training in these institutes were two areas in which quality instruction was given. Many intellectuals today believe that the village institute model was an ideal one in Turkish education history (Özeke 2003; Göktürk Cary 2014). During the application of the modern educational system in the village institutes, the teaching of the fine arts was important. From the upper levels of government administrators to school directors, everybody supported artistic practices (art exhibitions, musical concerts and stage acting) at these institutions. These schools successfully spread an appreciation of music and the arts among citizens (Tunç 2009). The village institutes were opened with good intentions, but they did not survive because officials of the Republican Party (CHP), which was the only party of the early Republic, wanted to use these schools as centres for the dissemination of their party ideology (Turan 1997).

The next significant development occurred in the 1960s when the student demonstrations that had their origins in France also spread to Turkey. During this period, the population at large began to view all universities as breeding grounds for anarchy, and society became divided into two extremist groups: right-wing and leftist. All aspects of education in Turkey were affected by this societal division, particularly in the area of curriculum development (Göktürk 2009; Göktürk Cary 2014).

The 1970s were similar to the 1960s in terms of the political and ideological chaos. In addition, new political parties appeared on the political scene, such as the *Milli Selamet Partisi* or MSP (National Salvation Party). MSP was a religious-based political party that exerted a great deal of influence on the Ministry of Education. Textbooks were rewritten with a stronger religious emphasis and socialist teachers either lost their jobs or were transferred to other districts because of their ideological views. According to many scholars and intellects, this was a return to the pre-Atatürk period (Göktürk 2009; Göktürk Cary 2014).

The unrest that characterized the previous two decades continued unabated into the 1980s. On 12 September 1980, the military intervened to bring order to the prevailing chaos. According to the new military government, the only solution to the politicization of education was to ban teachers from becoming involved in politics. Yet this resulted in hostility and ideological divergence. In reality, little had been changed, because the *Yükseköğretim Kurulu* (YÖK/Higher Education Council) meant that all universities were placed under direct control. Moreover, new national curricula began to be implemented (Göktürk 2009; Göktürk Cary 2014).

Since the 1990s, the main social crisis has been related to the Islamists' desire for greater religious freedom. Governmental power resided in the hands of the *Adalet ve Kalkınma Partisi* or *AK Parti* (*AKP*) (Justice and Development Party or White Party), which has an Islamic democratic political perspective (Göktürk 2009; Göktürk Cary 2014). At the elections on 7 June 2015 the AK Parti lost the majority in the parliament, and the party leader Ahmet Davutoğlu has since attempted to form a coalition government. The educational policies and goals, however, have remained consistent as when the AK Parti formed them in 2002.

Aims and content of music as a compulsory subject

Since the early years of the Republic, music has taken its place as a compulsory course in the primary school curriculum. (Until August 1997, three-year middle schools and high schools were referred to as the secondary school level. After that date the government restructured the school system so that the resulting eight-year programme at elementary and middle schools was consolidated into what became known as the primary school level.) However, because of a music teacher shortage, positions were filled by non-specialist teachers. Under these circumstances music courses were often lacking the necessary artistic basis and understandings (Tufan 2006).

General music education has great significance in passing the social culture from one generation to another. The subject is compulsory in the Ministry of Education curriculum in pre-school and primary education schools and is an elective in high schools. The strategy underpinning general music education is to educate the community to use and consume music for pleasure and to approach music more consciously, sensitively and in an intellectual way. Thus, music teachers play an important role in realizing this strategy (Tufan 2006).

From the 1960s, major improvements have been made both in school music education practice and in curriculum development. The curricula for these years were designed with children and their immediate environment in mind. By 1968, a major step was taken in Turkish music education, when the primary schools' curriculum began basing music education on Turkish folk music culture (Bozkaya 2003; Tufan 2006).

The two types of music instruction in Turkish schools are, firstly, General Music Instruction, which is compulsory at the primary level and optional at the secondary level, and Instrumental/Vocal Music Instruction, which is taught at the high schools of fine arts, conservatories and university music schools. The goal of the general music programme, which is allocated one hour per week, is to provide basic information and to cultivate an appreciation of music for all students. The goal of the instrumental/vocal music programme is the preparation of professional musicians (Göktürk 2009).

Although behaviorism was the main pedagogical underpinning for the previous 1994 music curriculum, the current primary school music curriculum was developed in Ankara in 2007 with the constructivist approach as its foundational principle (Albuz and Akpınar 2009; Göktürk 2010). Based on the study conducted by Göktürk in 2009, several problems were identified in relation to this curriculum, including overloaded course work for students and teachers, overcrowded classes, the need to increase the weekly time allocation for music to two hours a week, a perceived lack of knowledge about new educational philosophies and approaches among music teachers, too little professional development for music teachers, and insufficient music materials, instruments and facilities in many primary schools (Göktürk 2010).

Music teaching methods

During the earlier years of the Republic, the transmission of musical culture was viewed as an essential element in the formulation of musical taste. Republican commentators attempted to introduce particular methods of teaching music that supported their aesthetic preferences. They tended to equate the teaching of Turkish classical music – especially as it was taught within traditional educational contexts (*meşkhaneler*) – with a larger heterodox position, which represented the symbolic capital of an unfashionable Ottoman past and which deviated significantly from the Westernizing ideals underpinning Republican musical taste. They criticized the emphasis placed upon the oral mode of musical transmission, the textual conception of musical interpretation, the repetitive method of musical instruction and the religious contexts chosen for musical training. Fundamentally, the pedagogical value of Turkish classical music was disputed. Instead there was a focus upon the theoretical principles and the aesthetic ideals of Western art music. In other words, for these republican commentators, traditional methods of musical transmission perpetuated the cultural values of the late Ottoman period (O'Connell 2000).

Since the foundation of the Republic, the music curriculum has been revised six times (1957, 1971, 1986, 1991, 1994 and 2007), with the first five being teacher-centred and behaviouristic in approach. In contrast the 2007 curriculum is based on constructivist theory and is student-centred. Also, while the first two currricula included predominantly Western music, the curricula prepared after 1986 included more Turkish music (Göktürk 1996). The main elements of these curricular areas follows:

1957 – Music Curriculum: Rote learning; Kodály hand signs; note learning

1971 – Music Curriculum: Playing recorders and mandolins as the main instruments in the class; note learning.

1986 – Music Curriculum: Playing recorders as the main instruments in the class; note learning; Dalcroze method.

1991 – Music Curriculum: Western music history; Turkish music history; playing recorders as the main instrument in the class; note learning.

1994 – Music Curriculum: Playing recorders as the main instruments in the class but also including percussion instruments; rote learning for the first two years and later note learning; teaching music through the deduction method. (Göktürk 1996)

Teaching methods including Orff, Kodály, Dalcroze and rote learning approaches were included in the first five years of the 2007 music curriculum. However, music is taught differently in the sixth to eighth grades, with irregular rhythms and notation reading being included. These tend to be technically too advanced for many students. As a result, many students become estranged from the subject (Tarman 2012).

Music teacher training

Music was included in the curricula in female primary teacher training institutions from 1869 and then in the primary male teacher training institutions and male middle schools from 1910 (Tufan 2006). During this period music took its place as a course in formal education (Uçan 1994, quoted in Tufan 2006: 2). During the late Ottoman era there was an increase in the number of schools offering music courses, but these increases were mostly in larger cities and were not widespread throughout the country. However, there was no parallel increase in the training of music teachers and as a result the interest in Western music and the newly promoted forms of Turkish music were limited to the enlightened elite (Tufan 2006).

Although the governments of some European countries and Turkic states did not attach much importance to music teacher training, specialist music education began in 1924 at *Musiki Muallim Mektebi* (Music Teacher School) in Ankara in response to Atatürk's policies (İssi, 2008). The purpose of this school was to prepare music teachers to teach in secondary schools. The institution was housed in a building designed by Austrian archtitect Ernst Arnold Egli (see Figure 15.1) and produced many graduates over several decades (see Figure 15.2 for a photograph of staff and students from the 1930s). One of the founders of the Music Teacher School was Professor Eduard Zuckmayer (1890–1972), a German composer, pianist and music educator. He was invited to organize the foundation of the institution along with the distinguished German composer Paul Hindemith (1895–1963). Although Zuckmayer stayed in Turkey to teach at the Music Teacher School in Ankara until his death in 1972, Hindemith lived in Turkey only for a total of five months between the years 1935 and 1937. In 1938, the school's name was changed to the *Gazi Terbiye/Eğitim Enstitüsü ve Müzik ubesi* (Gazi Education Institute and Music Branch) and provided music teacher training until 1978. The curriculum at this institute consisted primarily of music theory and instrumental training in violin, piano, flute and cello, and all students were required to learn to play at least one of these instruments (Göktürk 2009). Other courses were gradually added as follows:

1 Music Courses: Music Theory, Harmony, Composition, Counterpoint, Music History, Solfege, Ear Training, Choir, Instrumental Ensembles, Musical Forms, Vocal Studio, Musical Interpretation, Piano Accompaniment, and Instrument Care.

2 General Courses: Turkish Literature, History, Geography, Psychology, Chemistry, Mathematics, German, French, Art, and Rhythmic Gymnastics.

3 Education Courses: History of Education, Psychology of Education, Sociology of Education, and Teaching Methods. (Yayla 2004, quoted in Göktürk 2009)

After 1978, all music teacher training took place at *Gazi Yükseköğretmen Okulu Müzik ubesi* (Gazi Higher Teacher Education School – Music Branch), whose curriculum was similar to that of *Gazi Eğitim Fakültesi Müzik Eğitimi Bölümü* (Gazi Faculty of Education Music Department). Additional courses were added to the curriculum, such as musical analysis, Turkish classical music, traditional folk music, art history, history of Atatürk's principles, and measurement and evaluation. In 1979, the Ministry of National Education further mandated that the following electives also be added to the curriculum: philosophy of education, educational administration, history of Turkish education, comparative education, educational technology, statistics and special education (Göktürk 2009). By 1978, three other teacher training institutions in different locations had added music departments. However, one of these institutions was closed in 1980, but another university (Uludağ University in Bursa) added a music department in 1981 (Özeke 2003).

A main change in the higher education system took place in 1981 (Güven 2008), and in 1982 the Turkish constitution was changed to include new provisions for higher education. Previously, teacher education programmes had been associated with education institutions affiliated with the *Milli Eğitim Bakanlığı* (Ministry of National Education), but under the restructure they were transferred to the Higher Education Council (Özeke 2003). It is fair to say that teacher education policy in Turkey since the early 1980s moved from evolutionary to technocratic modernization as successive governments tried to make the system both more efficient and more cost effective, as well as attempting to solve such problems as pupil drop-out and the low levels of achievement associated with urban schools. However, with its priority of greater control, technocratic modernization has created new problems such as teacher demoralization and a fall in recruitment, especially in subject areas prone to teacher shortages, such as physics and technology (Güven 2008).

Since the introduction of eight years of compulsory education, teacher education departments in universities have been reorganized to meet the short- and long-term

Figure 15.1 The *Musiki Muallim Mektebi* (Music Teacher Training School) building, purpose-built accommodation designed by Austrian architect Ernst Arnold Egli. (Source: Wikipedia, https://tr.wikipedia. org/wiki/Dosya:Musiki_Muallim_Mektebi_(literally_Music_Teachers%E2%80%99_School,_later_became_ Ankara_State_Conservatory),_1930s_(16230087064).jpg)

Figure 15.2 Teachers and students at the *Musiki Muallim Mektebi* (Music Teacher Training School) during the 1930s. (Source: http://www.konser.hacettepe.edu.tr/sayfa/hakkinda/tarihce; reproduced with permission)

demands for teachers in primary and secondary schools. A new system of teacher education has been implemented since 1997 that focused on, firstly, the training of pre-primary and primary school teachers through a four-year bachelor's degree programme, and secondly the training of secondary school teachers through a bachelor's degree to teach foreign languages, music, arts, physical education, special education and computer skills (Güven 2008).

Music teacher training schools use a standardized curriculum prepared by the Higher Education Council in order to unify the teaching and musical knowledge for all future music teachers. As of mid-2015, there were approximately 1,200 students enrolled at twenty-five teacher training institutions in Turkey. Clearly, the purpose of YÖK (Higher Educational Council) is to standardize music teacher training in Turkey (Güven, 2008).

According to Özeke (2003) and Sevgi (2003), students at music teacher training institutions are trained in the same manner as performers, and often lack the pedagogical skills that they need to become effective music teachers. This emphasis on training music education students in the same manner as performers may be attributed to the fact that many string professors at the university level encourage their students to be performers rather than pedagogues (ibid.). These problems alone indicate that there is a great need for educational reform in music.

Conclusions

It may be argued that many changes to the music education system in Turkey have been made prematurely without a thorough study by the central organization. The Ministry of Education has become a rigid bureaucracy over the years, with all decisions related to educational matters, including preparation of the national curriculum and the appointment of teachers and educational leaders, being made by central authorities. In this highly centralized system it is difficult for these personnel to create a positive environment for teaching and learning as well as coping with technological and educational changes (Turan 1997).

In Ancient Greece, the disciplines of the Quadrivium had a deep and lasting influence upon society and human relationships. The art of music retains its powerful effect as much today as in the past. In the service of this distinguished art form, educators and administrators have an obligation to strive for the continual improvement of institutions that provide music education (Yener 2005). To accomplish this, Turkish pedagogues should be encouraged to follow the new developments in music education taking place in other countries and to develop their own teaching techniques to maximize educational effectiveness. Globalization provides unique opportunities for such cultural interaction in music education.

Reflective questions

1 This chapter has focused upon the effects of historical and political contexts on music education in the Republic of Turkey. How would you summarize the main effects?

2 Discuss the influence of Westernization on Turkish music education, with particular reference to Turkish musical traditions.

3 To what extent do you agree that music education generally should 'embrace the positive and beneficial effects of globalization'?

4 Are the music curricula and teaching methods being used in teacher training institutions and in primary schools in Turkey comparable with current international 'best practice'?

References

Albuz, A. and M. Akpınar (2009), 'İköğretim Müzik Dersi Öğretim Programı ve Yeni Yaklaşımlar' [Primary-School Music Curriculum and New Educational Approaches], paper presented at 8. Ulusal Müzik Eğitimi Sempozyumu [8th National Symposium in Music Education], September 23–25, 2009, Ondokuz Mayıs University, Samsun.

Bozkaya, İ. (2003), 'Müzik Öğretmenliği Lisans Programı 3. Yıl Öğrencilerinin Müzik Eğitiminin Sorunlarına Bakış Açıları' ['Perspectives of 3rd-year students at music teacher training schools on the issues of music education'], a paper presented at Cumhuriyetimizin 80. Yılında Müzik Sempozyumu, Malatya, 30–31 October 2003, www.muzikegitimcileri.net (accessed 20 June 2015).

Gökalp, Z. (1973), Turkçuluğun Esasları [Principles of Turkishness], Istanbul: Varlık Press.

Göktürk, D. (1996), 'Türkiye'deki Müzik Eğitiminin Programlar Açısından Değerlendirilmesi' ['Evaluation of music education in Turkey from a curricular angle'] (unpublished Master's thesis, Ankara, Turkey: Gazi University, Institute of Science).

Göktürk, D. (2009), 'Historical Development of Public School String Education in the United States and Connections with Turkey', Uludağ Üniversitesi Eğitim Fakültesi Dergisi 22 (2): 689–716.

Göktürk, D. (2010), 'The Role of Constructivist Approach on Creativity in Primary School Music Curriculum in the Republic of Turkey', Procedia Social and Behavioral Sciences 2 (2): 3075–9.

Göktürk Cary, D. (2011), 'Globalization of Academics and its Effects on Music Education in Turkey,' 6th International Conference on Interdisciplinarity in Education – ICIE11, Karabük Üniversitesi, Karabük, 14–16 Nisan 2011, Conference Proceedings (Greece: National Technical University of Athens School of Electrical and Computer Engineering), https://www.academia.edu/1303636/GLOBALIZATION_OF_ACADEMICS_AND_ITS_EFFECTS_ON_MUSIC_EDUCATION (10 June 2015).

Göktürk Cary, D. (2014), 'The Evolution of Music Education in Turkey', Debates Magazine 13: 13–22.

Güven, İ. (2008), 'Teacher Education Reform and International Globalization Hegemony: Issues and Challenges in Turkish Teacher Education', International Journal of Social, Behavioral, Educational, Economic and Management Engineering 2 (4): 16–25.

İssi, A. D. (2008), 'Gazi Üniversitesi Gazi Eğitim Fakültesi Güzel Sanatlar Eğitimi Bölümü Müzik Öğretmenliği Ana Bilim Dalı Öğrenci Profili' ['Student profile at Gazi University, Gazi College

of Education, Department of Fine Arts Education, Division of Music Teacher Education']
(unpublished Master's thesis, Gazi University, Ankara).

Kazamias, A. M. (1966), *Education and the Quest for Modernity in Turkey*, Chicago, IL: The
University of Chicago Press.

Kazamias, A. M. and B. G. Massialas (1965), *Tradition and Change in Education: A Comparative
Study*, Englewood Cliffs, NJ: Prentice-Hall.

Kocabaş, A. (2010), 'Müzik Eğitiminin Çoklu Zeka Alanlarına Etkisi ve Köy Enstitüleri' ['The
influence of music on multiple intelligence and village institutes'], *Yeniden İmece Dergisi* 4,
53–57.

Müzik Öğretmenliği Lisans Programı [Music Teacher Training School Curriculum], http://bys.trakya.
edu.tr/file/open/14819783 (accessed 25 June 2015).

O'Connell, J. M. (2000), 'Fine Art, Fine Music: Controlling Turkish Taste at the Fine Arts Academy
in 1926', *Yearbook for Traditional Music* 32: 117–42.

Özeke, S. (2003), 'A history of music teacher education in the Republic of Turkey: 1982–1998'
(unpublished doctoral dissertation, Arizona State University).

Sevgi, A. (2003), 'Nasıl Bir Müzik Öğretmeni?' ['What type of music teacher?'], paper presented
at Cumhuriyetimizin 80. Yılında Müzik Sempozyumu, Malatya, 30–31 October 2003, www.
muzikegitimcileri.net (accessed 20 June 2015).

Tanrıkorur, C. (1999), 'Osmanlı Musikis' [Ottoman Music], Osmanlı Medeniyeti Tarihi [The History
of Ottoman Civilization], Istanbul.

Tarman, S. (2012), 'Türk Müzik Devrimi: 1924'den 2012'ye Genel Bir Değerlendirme' ['Revolution
in Turkish music: a general evaluation from 1924 to 2012'], *Proceedings of KTÜ 1. Uluslararası
Müzik Araştırmaları Sempozyumu-Müzik ve Kültürel Doku*, 16–19 October 2012, Trabzon,
557–68, http://www.ktu.edu.tr/dosyalar/56_00_00_62f40.pdf (accessed 15 April 2015).

Tufan, E. (2006), 'The history of music education in Turkey: the role and importance of Gazi
Faculty of Education', APERA Conference, 28–30 November 2006, Hong Kong, http://edisdat.
ied.edu.hk/pubarch /b15907314/full_paper/901259428.pdf (accessed 24 June 2015).

Turıç, A. Z. (2009), 'Köy Enstltülerinde Sanat Egitimi ve Donemın Yoneticilerinin Sanata
Yaklaşımları' ['Fine arts education at village institutes and approaches of the administration
towards arts'], *Dokuz Eylül Üniversitesi Buca Eğitim Fakültesi Dergisi* 26.

Turan, S. (1997), 'John Dewey's report of 1924 and his recommendations on the Turkish
educational system revisited', paper presented at the Annual Meeting of the American
Educational Research Association, 24–28 March 1997, Chicago, Illinois, http://files.eric.ed.gov/
fulltext/ED416159.pdf (accessed 5 July 2015).

Yener, S. (2005), 'Müzik Eğitimi Kurumlarında Toplam Kalite Yönetimi Kültürü Kavramı' ['The
Concept of total quality management culture at music education institutions'], *Atatürk
University Journal of Social Sciences Institute* 5 (1): 331–42.

PART IV: AFRICA AND ASIA-PACIFIC

Chapter 16

Australia: Recurring problems and unresolved issues

Robin Stevens and Jane Southcott

As a political entity, Australia began as a set of British settlements and colonies that were established from the late eighteenth century. As with other members of the far-flung British Empire, early colonists attempted to replicate the social institutions that they had left behind in their 'home country'. By the time of federation in 1901, all colonies had established systems of state-supported schools, which, alongside the various denominational and private schools, provided elementary education for their child populations. This chapter will consider the progress in three Australian colonies (later states under a federal government) that represent the development of music as a subject within compulsory schooling in Australia.

The first colony to institute compulsory school attendance was Victoria in 1872, followed by South Australia in 1875 and New South Wales in 1880. However, as a mandatory subject of the school curriculum, the status of music varied in the respective colonies. Singing was included in the required 'standards of proficiency' in New South Wales from 1867 and was a mandated subject in the Victorian 'course of free instruction' in 1874 (Stevens 1978). In South Australia, singing – at least by ear – was expected to be taught in schools from 1890, but it was not until 1900 that music became a required subject with a prescribed syllabus (Southcott 1997). These three colonies, with their differing histories, encompass all of the significant issues associated with the introduction of music to compulsory schooling in Australia.

The chapter will discuss the implementation of music in elementary education – the provision of music in schools, the training of generalist and specialist teachers of music and the desired curriculum content and pedagogy. The rationale for including music in the curriculum will be outlined and, lastly, the nature of the school song repertoire and the experiences of the recipients of school music – the children – will be considered. Many of the current issues identified in the 2004–5 National Review of School Music Education (Pascoe et al. 2005) have their origins in the past and it is not only useful, but also, as Aldrich (1996: 3) reminds us, essential to consider the past as a means of informing present circumstances and future directions in educational policy and practice.

The education of indigenous Australian (Aboriginal) children is not considered as a separate topic for two main reasons. First, during the nineteenth and early twentieth centuries, what schooling was available for Aboriginal children was left largely in the hands of missionary organizations. Second, prior to 1967, when Australian citizenship was formally granted to Aboriginal people, an essentially assimilationist policy was in place, which meant that there was no special provision for the education of those few Aboriginal children who did attend their local state school.

Colonial background and context

European settlement of Australia began in 1788 with the arrival in Botany Bay (the site of modern-day Sydney) of the 'First Fleet' – a convoy of ships bringing government officials, convicts and marines to establish the penal colony of New South Wales. Further convoys brought more convicts and, as they earned the limited freedom of their 'tickets of leave' and as free settlers began to arrive, the colony started to grow and become increasingly self-sufficient. Between 1788 and 1850 over 162,000 convicts arrived by the time transportation ceased (Marvic n.d.). Convicts were accommodated in penal settlements principally at Port Macquarie in New South Wales, at Morton Bay (now part of Queensland), at Port Arthur in Van Diemen's Land (later Tasmania) and at Norfolk Island. Other settlements were established by free immigrants at Swan River Colony – founded in 1829 and renamed Western Australia in 1836 – and subsequently at Adelaide, where the colony of South Australia was proclaimed in late 1836. In 1851 the southern Port Phillip District separated from New South Wales to become the colony of Victoria. The founding of the colonies of Tasmania and Queensland followed in 1856 and 1859, respectively. With a growing tide of nationalism towards the close of the nineteenth century, a series of referenda and an act of the British parliament in 1900 finally resulted in the proclamation of the Commonwealth of Australia in which the six previously self-governing British colonies became a federation of states on 1 January 1901.

Provision for music in colonial schools and teacher training

As separate entities under the British Crown, each colony was responsible for the provision of elementary education. This has continued to be the case to the present day with school education remaining a state issue. During the early years of the three selected colonies, schooling for the juvenile population was provided by private tutors, church organizations and proprietors of private venture schools. The establishment of schools was often a priority with the early colonists. For example, in South Australia, within the first year of the colony's existence, three private schools were established (Smeaton 1927). Ten years later, a Board of Education was established to supervise the financial aid granted to licensed schools. Singing was included in their revised curriculum but was not mandatory (Southcott 1997). It was not until the Education Act 1875 that state-supported, compulsory and secular schooling came into being in South Australia (Miller 1986). In New South Wales, given many pressing demands on government funding, it was some years before colonial authorities turned their attention to school education. In 1848 the New South Wales colonial government appointed a Board of National Education (modelled on the Irish National System) to establish a system of non-sectarian schools, as well as a Denominational Schools Board to support the efforts of the churches in providing elementary education. Much the same happened in Victoria, with dual education boards being set up in 1851 (Stevens 1978). However, it was not until 1872, 1875 and 1880 respectively that elementary education became compulsory for children in Victoria, South Australia and New South Wales.

Singing, or 'vocal music' as it was often called, was introduced as one of the 'subjects of ordinary instruction' at the National Model Schools established by the respective National Boards of Education in Victoria and New South Wales. In the National Schools of New South Wales, it was recommended in 1851 that singing should be timetabled for half an hour each day, and that generalist classroom teachers should give singing lessons (ibid.). Unfortunately, the vast majority of national school teachers had little background or skill in music. This is hardly surprising, since most teachers at this time were inadequately trained as teachers of 'the three Rs', let alone music. Although vocal music, initially based on Hullah's method, was included in the course of study at the teacher training institutions attached to the National Model Schools in both Sydney and Melbourne, most teacher education was undertaken through a system of pupil–teacher apprenticeship. However, with supervising teachers generally lacking musical knowledge and skills themselves, this system achieved little in preparing pupil–teachers to teach singing (ibid.).

Given the general lack of musical competence among teachers in all colonies, music was soon regarded as an extra subject rather than as part of the ordinary curriculum. Despite recognizing the importance of music in education, the New South Wales School Commissioners in 1855 could nevertheless 'only lament its all but universal neglect' (Stevens 1981: 68). Accordingly, vocal music was introduced to teacher education under the National School system – for example, into pupil–teacher training undertaken in schools and to courses at Fort Street Training School – as well as being included as a subject for teacher classification examinations (the means through which teachers could gain promotion). All these measures were designed to encourage music teaching by generalist teachers, but success was limited (Stevens 1978).

About the same time, educational authorities in Victoria decided to appoint itinerant singing masters to overcome deficiencies in musical knowledge and skill among generalist teachers. The first full-time singing master, George Leavis Allan (1862–1897), was appointed by the Denominational Schools Board in 1853 to give musical instruction at several of its Melbourne schools. More appointments of itinerant singing masters followed. In 1859 a gratuity of £5 per annum was offered to generalist teachers in rural areas in an effort to encourage them to give 'systematic' instruction in vocal music (ibid.). Local unpaid singing teachers (generally amateur musicians) were also fairly common in denominational schools at this time. The Board of National Education in Victoria decided to follow the lead of its denominational counterpart and also appointed itinerant singing masters to ensure at least some provision for music teaching in its schools. However, in New South Wales, the teaching of singing was left entirely to generalist teachers to do as best they could. Given that many teachers were still largely untrained and that those who had been through training courses had generally covered little more than the musical content stipulated in the school curriculum, the extent and quality of music teaching by generalist teachers was very limited.

All this laid the foundations for three of the major issues that have bedevilled school music education in Australia ever since:

1 the provision of music teaching in government elementary schools, specifically the issue of whether generalist or specialist teachers should teach music;

2 the inclusion of music in teacher education, specifically courses of training for elementary generalist teachers who generally come to teacher education with little or no prior musical experience; and

3 the notion that music can be an optional inclusion in school curricula.

Nevertheless, singing was still highly valued by education authorities, and in New South Wales it was formally introduced to the ordinary school curriculum in 1867 by the new (consolidated) Board of Education. Under this arrangement, generalist classroom teachers were responsible for teaching singing to their pupils according to a prescribed syllabus based on the tonic sol-fa method, notation and curriculum sequence. Vocal music through tonic sol-fa was also introduced as a compulsory subject for teacher training courses as well as for the system of teacher classification examinations. With the formation of the Department of Public Instruction in 1880, music continued to be a mandatory subject of the school curriculum, and by the 1890s virtually all children in New South Wales public schools were being taught music by generalist classroom teachers, with 75 per cent to 80 per cent cent pass rates being achieved at the annual school inspectors' examinations (ibid.). The system was supported by a superintendent of music whose role it was to train teachers in music and to assist established teachers to prepare the music requirements for their classification examinations. Initially, this role was taken by James Fisher (1826–1891), the officially appointed 'Singing Master' (Stevens 2002), and then, from 1885, by his successor, Hugo Alpen (1842–1917), the first Superintendent of Music (Stevens 1993).

In contrast to the steady progress made in New South Wales, school music in Victoria regressed during the period of the Council of Education that had replaced the dual board system of National and Denominational Boards in 1862. This was due chiefly to the introduction in 1864 of a special fee of one penny per week for children attending singing lessons. The fee scheme was designed to offset the now substantial cost of maintaining a staff of specialist teachers – the itinerant singing masters – in public schools. Under these arrangements, music effectively became an optional extra in the school curriculum and, due to the extra fee involved, the number of children receiving musical instruction declined markedly (Stevens 1978).

With the coming of 'free, compulsory and secular' schooling under the Victorian Education Department in 1872, fees for singing were abolished, and the subject was included in the 'course of free instruction'. Singing was to be taught 'where practicable' in what were now termed 'state schools' either by an itinerant singing master or by a generalist classroom teacher who was licensed to teach singing and who received an annual bonus of £10 for giving musical instruction. Itinerant singing masters and licensed generalist teachers were supervised by an inspector of music. Although it was intended, over time, to replace the specialists with generalist teachers properly trained in music, the economic depression of the 1890s forced the government of the day to withdraw all paid instruction in singing from state schools, retrench professional singing masters and abolish the post of inspector of music. Therefore, despite its mandatory inclusion in the school curriculum, the teaching of singing 'by note' all but ceased in Victorian state schools and, for the remainder of the century, children were generally taught only singing 'by ear' by musically untrained generalist teachers (ibid.). The vulnerability of music as a school subject taught by specialists rather than generalists in government elementary schools continues to be a significant factor in school music education to the present day.

In South Australia prior to the Education Act 1875, which established state-supported education as compulsory and secular, there were several attempts to manage schooling in the colony more effectively. The first ten years were difficult but, in 1847, financial aid was given to schools and a supervisory Board of Education was established. The Education Act 1851 created an independent Central Board of Education. Initially, this semi-governmental body had considerable impact, but the achievements of the enthusiastic but largely untrained teachers varied considerably. It was not until 1860 that the regulations for Board Schools recommended the teaching of singing, but this was not compulsory, nor was any method suggested. However, with the active promotion of music teaching in schools by Alexander Clark (1843–1913), initially as head teacher of the demonstration model schools in Adelaide from 1876 and then more widely in the colony as a school inspector from 1884, singing – at least 'by ear' – was prescribed in the Education Regulations 1890. Clark developed a school music syllabus modelled on the contemporary English code and adapted for use in South Australia that came into force in 1900 (Southcott 1997). This course was similar to the requirements of the Elementary Certificate of the Tonic Sol-fa College and also formed the basis for the music curriculum taught to students at the Adelaide Training College, which opened in 1876.

The nature of and rationale for music in colonial schools

Clearly, the colonial educational authorities in the early days had difficulty providing even a rudimentary education in 'the three Rs', let alone including music in the school curriculum. However, from the outset, there seems to have been a desire among educational authorities, parents and the general public to include music in schooling. It is reasonable to ask what the nature of and rationale for music in schools was during the colonial and subsequent federation periods. The school curriculum *per se* and its inclusion of music were part of an inherited tradition from Great Britain – the 'home country'. The system of national schools in New South Wales and Victoria, established in the early 1850s, was closely modelled on the Irish National System[1] and colonial educational authorities simply adapted the existing Irish National School Curriculum, including vocal music, to local circumstances.

The introduction of school music had a strongly utilitarian basis founded on the belief that music could be of great value as a humanizing and civilizing influence on society in general and on children in particular. The social environment in which many colonial children found themselves during the mid-nineteenth century was often far from good. Most colonies were initially populated by convicts and then by free settlers, many of whom were redundant paupers or dissidents from Great Britain. The situation was aggravated by the influx of fortune seekers following the gold strikes of the early 1850s, many of whom were considered by respectable colonists as 'undesirables'. The situation on the goldfields in New South Wales and Victoria represented a highly unstable environment for many children. According to James Bonwick, a school inspector, children on the Victorian goldfields at this time lived in a world of 'gambling, swearing, drunkenness and licentiousness' (Stevens 1981: 67). Even without the presence of convicts or the decadence of the goldfields, South Australian government authorities perceived music in schooling as an antidote to larrikinism and roughness – vocal music could be a powerful agency for refining the individual (Southcott 2004).

Colonial education authorities were anxious to imprint whatever civilizing and reforming influences they could on rising generations. Music, in the form of class singing, was widely held to be of value in this respect. For example, the New South Wales School Commissioners in reporting the 'all but universal neglect' of music in the schools during 1855 cited its ability to soften manners, prevent intemperance and civilize. In 1857 the Victorian Denominational School Board recognized the importance of school music for children living on the goldfields by appointing itinerant singing masters. Two years later, when a shortage of educational funding threatened the dismissal of singing masters, the public response was one of indignation. A petition from the residents of Ballarat district argued that the music teacher helped the intellectual and moral progress of lower-class children (Stevens 1981). In New South Wales during the same year, Inspector William Wilkins put forward a scheme to encourage national school teachers in country districts to teach singing with much the same idea in mind, adding that it would make schools popular with parents (Stevens 1978).

By the late 1860s the recreational value of school music began to be recognized by education authorities. In advocating an extension of music teaching in New South Wales in 1867, Inspector William McIntyre maintained that school music preserved morals, offered innocent amusement and had a cheerful effect on all endeavours. A colleague, Inspector Allpass, added: '[F]ew teachers seem to understand that a burst of song acts as a safety valve to children of excitable temperament, and enlivens those who are sluggishly disposed' (quoted in Stevens 1981: 68).

In South Australia, from the 1890s, there was a vigorous campaign to improve the vocal tone of both children and teachers. In 1911 the South Australian Minister for Education gave a very clear directive to schools, stating that: 'It was felt necessary to eradicate unclear enunciation, general slovenliness of speech … [and] Australian twang and slang' (Parliament of South Australia 1911: 24). Singing was seen as a major weapon in this campaign and was also perceived as a relieving break between other subjects that could both calm and enliven children. Singing could be a 'pleasant break', relieve the 'tedium' of ordinary lessons and included at 'odd moments, never interfering with the work, but just giving the necessary stimulus to classes in danger of weariness' (Southcott 1997: 84). Singing could also be an accompaniment to mechanical activities such as sewing and, particularly, drill. At this time, almost every school had a drum and fife band, which could accompany drill and perform at school and community functions (Southcott 1997). There was also some recognition of the 'intellectual progress' attending the study of 'music by notes' (Stevens 1978) – in modern-day parlance, promoting cognitive skills through a study of music theory and development of music literacy.

Music curriculum content and implementation

In all colonies, there was an assumption – based on contemporary English and Irish curricula – that vocal music should be taught 'by note' rather than merely 'by ear'. In all three colonies, Hullah's fixed-doh method had been tried, but found wanting. In New South Wales, William Wilkins promoted tonic sol-fa as the most effective teaching method and notational system for use in schools. Tonic sol-fa teaching was undertaken by James Fisher, who was appointed as Singing Master in 1867. Although Fisher's professional conduct was later deemed unsatisfactory, the tonic sol-fa method became the basis of a 'movable-doh' staff notation method that was successfully developed and implemented by his successor, Hugo Alpen, the new Superintendent of Music. In Victoria, the 'tonic numeral' method (an application of the numbers one to seven on a movable system to staff notation), based on the principles of the English clergyman John Waite (Rainbow 1967), was adapted to local needs by the senior Singing Master George Allan during the 1850s. The method continued to be officially endorsed and supported by the Inspector of Music, Dr Joseph Summers (1839–1917), who was appointed in 1878 (Stevens 1997). During the 1880s, however, the tonic numeral method was challenged by proponents of tonic sol-fa, led by Dr Samuel McBurney (1847–1909) who later succeeded Summers as Inspector of Music (Stevens 1986). Both methods were later put on an equal footing through the publication in 1890 of a Tonic Sol-fa Programme, which supplemented the earlier 1884 Programme of Instruction in Singing for State Schools (Stevens 1978). In South Australia, after an early and unsatisfactory trial of Hullah's method, tonic sol-fa was introduced by Alexander Clark (Southcott 1995), and its promotion was continued by his successor Francis Lymer Gratton (1871–1946), himself a talented product of the South Australian public school system (Southcott 1996).

By the turn of the twentieth century, school attendance had been compulsory in Victoria since 1872, in South Australia since 1875 and in New South Wales since 1880, and music was now mandated in the elementary school curricula of all three colonies (from 1867 in New South Wales, from 1872 in Victoria and from 1900 in South Australia). However, with technological innovations (such as the gramophone) and new methods of manufacture (such as the mass production of fifes and other musical instruments), singing as a school subject now became known as 'music' to reflect a broadening of content and the intro- duction of new approaches to music education. From the 1920s school music began to include music listening and appreciation and percussion band activities. The ubiquitous school drum and fife bands that had existed in Australian schools from their inception were now acknowledged in the syllabus. Other forms of instrumental music – such as the Manby group approach to teaching violin in Victoria – were introduced to schools (Cameron 1969; Southcott 1993), and Dalcroze eurhythmics was introduced through radio broadcasts from the 1930s (Pope 2006). Few of these developments were uniquely Australian, most being modelled on overseas practices. This trend continued with the introduction of school recorder playing in the 1950s, the Orff Schulwerk and Kodály approaches in the 1960s and creative compositional approaches from the early 1970s.

The school music repertoire and the experiences of children

The songs chosen for class singing were, especially in the early years of the colonies, carefully selected to include moralistic and didactic texts. As well as inculcating religious and moral values through hymns and other such edifying songs, the singing repertoire chosen for children could also carry texts that evinced the virtues of home and family life.

Figure 16.1 Empire Day, Mount Templeton School, South Australia. (Education Department, South Australia 1915: 169)

Later, particularly with contingents of colonial soldiers being sent to the Sudan War and the South African (Boer) War, songs with patriotic and nationalistic words were popular as a means of promoting imperial citizenship. For example, one important national celebration was Empire Day, first officially celebrated in Australia in 1905. On this day children listened to stories about the Empire, sang 'God Save the Queen' and 'Advance Australia Fair', performed callisthenic and martial drill exercises, participated in patriotic tableaux and took part in march-pasts and trooping the colours. One schoolgirl memory was typical of many: 'Empire Day was a very special day. I can remember being Boadicea one year, wearing a white flowing gown and the British flag and a gold-painted helmet and three pronged fork' (quoted in Hetherington et al. 1979: 99) (see Figure 16.1). The celebration was not complete without songs, some Australian, but most British, such as 'The Sea is England's Glory' and 'Ye Mariners of England' (Southcott 2002). As the colonies moved towards federation, school singing also became an important medium for imbuing children with feelings of national identity.

Perhaps the most authoritative statements regarding the value of music in colonial education came from William Wilkins (1827–1892), chief architect of the New South Wales' education system. In 1870 he recounted the reasons for including singing in the new public school system. Wilkins cited the example of Germany, which had, by the influence of music in schools, been changed from the most drunken to the most sober nation in Europe. He reiterated his belief in 'the humanizing and civilizing influence of

Figure 16.2 Alexander Clark and the Thousand Voices Choir rehearsing for the Decoration Society Concert, 1912. (Education Department 1912: 216)

music as an instrument by which a child might be trained in those social feelings which frequent intercourse with his fellows nurtured' (quoted in Stevens 1978: 51). This was seen as being particularly important in sparsely populated regions where opportunities for social intercourse might be few and far between. Even more, music had a strong disciplinary influence, by which a song could render corporal punishment unnecessary.

Although a natural outgrowth of class singing, the development of choral singing festivals enabled children to experience music as a performing art in the same way as adults did in choral societies or church choirs. End-of-year and charity concerts, musical pageants and system-wide events appear to have been fairly common in colonial schools (Stevens 1978). In New South Wales, massed singing by school children was arranged for important public occasions, such as in 1868, when Prince Alfred, Duke of Edinburgh, visited the colony. Ten thousand children from Sydney schools, accompanied by military bands and conducted by James Fisher, sang 'God Save our Noble Queen' in apparently faultless unison and with 'glorious effect' on the lawns of Government House (ibid.: 98). A schools choir of a similar number performed choral and massed singing items – including Hugo Alpen's 'Federated Australia' – at the 1901 inauguration ceremony for the Commonwealth of Australia at Centennial Park in Sydney, again evincing the strong patriotic and nationalistic sentiments (Chaseling 2003). Later still there were annual choral festivals, such as the South Australian Decoration Society concerts that featured the 'Thousand Voices Choir' (see Figure 16.2), which, in modified form, continues to the present day as the Primary Schools Music Festival.

Other songs simply allowed children to enjoy singing about such aspects of their lives as games, toys, outdoor adventures and other childhood pleasures. For example, 'Paddling Song' described the experience of the Australian child running across the beach: 'Across the shining sand we fly, With naked feet and gowns pinned high' (Macrae

Figure 16.3 'Tale of the Bellbirds', music by Samuel McBurney, words by Andrew Barton 'Banjo' Paterson (S. McBurney, n.d. [c. 1895]: 35–6). An excerpt from a late nineteenth-century Australian children's song with both staff and tonic sol-fa notation.

and Alsop 1910: 1–3). One of the recurring themes in such recreational songs was that of nature, particularly the Australian bush. One of the earliest songs about Australian fauna was the 'Joey's Song', published in 1879. This was included at the back of a cautionary tale in verse form, entitled 'Marsupial Bill or the Bad Boy, the Good Dog and the Old Man Kangaroo' (Stevens 1879). Another example, 'Tale of the Bellbirds', composed by Samuel McBurney in Victoria (see Figure 16.3), again has a cautionary aspect to it, with words that tell of children attracted by the bellbird's call becoming lost in the bush (Stevens 2006).

From the later years of the nineteenth century it was usual for all Australian schools to have a drum and fife band of between ten and forty members (see Figure 16.4). Initially, these bands were extra-curricular, but they eventually became part of the school music programme. The bands, militaristic in their practices, often accompanied school drill. In 1894 Alexander Clark was one of the co-authors of the official South Australian Education Department's *Manual of Drill* that was modelled on the British Army Manual. As part of the school concerts, boys often performed their physical drills – carbine drill (with mock or real weapons) was visually impressive and particularly popular. There were other callisthenic drills for boys and girls, the latter often using apparatus such as hoops, wands and clubs.

Figure 16.4 Sturt Street School Band (South Australia) 1917. (Postcard in the author's possession)

The lessons of history for contemporary policy and practice

There are several major issues to have emerged from this review of music in compulsory schooling during the nineteenth and early twentieth centuries that remain relevant to the contemporary Australian situation and from which 'the lessons of history' may be drawn in terms of future policy decisions. There are three overriding 'lessons' to be learnt. The first is that there are inevitably economic constraints on the provision of elementary school music teaching through any system of specialist teachers. This has generally not been a problem in the non-government school sector – the so-called independent schools, most of which have a religious affiliation. With the exception of low-income church schools (such as some Catholic parish primary schools), music has had an assured status as an integral part of the school curriculum, and music teaching has usually been undertaken by specialists. However, the situation in government schools, particularly at the primary school level, has often been precarious, especially in times of economic recession – as occurred in Victoria in the 1890s – when specialist teachers were dismissed and responsibility for teaching music in primary schools was given to largely ill-equipped generalist teachers. Moreover, when specialist teachers were again employed as the principal means of providing music in Victoria from the 1950s, history repeated itself, although more through a change in curriculum policy than for economic reasons. In the late 1970s the Music Branch of 107 specialist music educators, most of whom taught music as itinerant teachers in primary schools, was disbanded in favour of school-based music teachers (Stevens 1978). Unfortunately, the new system failed to adequately deliver music teaching in schools due to progressively more school-based music positions being filled by specialists in other curriculum areas.

Since that time, the situation in Victoria has seen little if any improvement, with generalist primary teachers having nominal responsible for delivery of a music teaching in the absence of specialist appointments. It has been much the same in other Australian states, with the notable exceptions of Tasmania and particularly Queensland, where specialist music teachers have been appointed to primary schools. These appointments remain tenuously linked to the economic climate and political will. After several draft versions, the Australian Curriculum, Assessment and Reporting Authority (ACARA) released *The Arts [Learning Area] Scope and Sequence* in 2013 (ACARA 2013b) as part of the new Australian Curriculum for Foundation to Year 10 that has been endorsed by all state education authorities. The *Scope and Sequence* document includes curriculum objectives for music as well as the other four subjects forming The Arts Learning Area and is currently being customized by those states who have endorsed the *Australian Curriculum: The Arts* (ACARA 2013a).[2] However, the actual implementation of the music curriculum will be quite another matter, given that, in the case of state government schools in most states, responsibility for ensuring that the curriculum is taught to all children still lies essentially with generalist teachers. Despite some cutbacks in recent years, the provision of specialist music teachers for Years 7 to 10 (and beyond) in government secondary schools is generally more secure. Nevertheless, it is a matter of historical record that the place of music in schools in the past was never fully secure and with the problem of implementing the music curriculum set out in the *Australian Curriculum: The Arts* in primary schools through a workforce consisting mostly of generalist teachers being responsible for teaching the subject, there was no great cause for optimism, particularly in times of economic restraint. Aside from Queensland and Tasmania, where specialist music teachers are appointed centrally, there are many government primary schools in other states that are without a music teacher to implement a sequential and continuous music programme. Where they are appointed – for example, in some Victorian primary schools (see Heinrich 2012) – it is due to individual school decision making and to the availability of specialist teachers rather than to system-wide policy.

The second 'lesson' is that there is a need for all generalist elementary teachers to receive comprehensive training in music education through both pre-service and in-service education – as was the case in New South Wales during the last decades of the nineteenth century – to ensure their ability to implement effective music programmes in elementary schools. The historical justification for this claim is the success, using an appropriate music teaching method (tonic sol-fa), of the 'generalist approach' in New South Wales, where by the early 1890s nearly all children in New South Wales public schools were being taught music with 75 per cent to 80 per cent pass rates at the annual school inspectors' examinations (Stevens 1978).

Aside from the teacher training provided for secondary music specialists,[3] the current situation in Australian primary teacher education is somewhat more problematic. A recent survey of mandatory music discipline and music education content in pre-service primary courses identified that, on average, 41.75 hours were allocated to creative arts subjects, but only 16.99 hours were available in the surveyed teacher training programmes for training in both music discipline content and music pedagogy (Hocking 2009). The variation between institutions ranges from zero and 52 hours for music. The point was also made that the average of credit points dedicated to music within primary teacher education courses was a mere 1.51 per cent of the total course (ibid.). Therefore, if the provision for music teaching in primary schools remains the responsibility of generalist teachers, the only way of adequately ensuring the place of music in primary education will be for music education within pre-service courses to be given considerably greater emphasis and for there to be widespread and sustained professional development for already practicing teachers in order to adequately upskill their musical competency.

The third 'lesson' is that music educators must continue to advocate for the inclusion of music as a mandated school subject in its own right. As is currently the case, the *Australian Curriculum: The Arts* and several previous state and national curricula have included music as one of many arts subjects which, though the requirement that all arts subjects in an already overcrowded curriculum should be given their fair share of class time, may well result in school students not receiving a sequential, developmental and continuous music education from Foundation to Year 10.[4] To deny children such a holistic education by failing to fully accommodate such an important subject as music is reprehensible.

Like many other countries, Australia continues to suffer from several longstanding and unresolved problems in its provision of school music education in its public schools. Accordingly, the lessons of history should be considered in the formulation of future policies in school music education.

Reflective questions

1 How have the geographical locations and historical development of the Australian colonies – later federated states – impacted on the provision of music education in schools?

2 What is the heritage that has characterized the successive waves of pedagogical practice that has shaped contemporary school music education in Australia?

3 What are the factors that have, over time, influenced the generalist–specialist debate concerning who will teach music in government primary schools?

> **4** A committed, empowered and skilled advocate for music in
> schools has been an essential factor where successful music
> policies and practices have been realized during the course
> of the compulsory schooling in Australia. What have been the
> characteristics of such advocates? Have they been musicians
> first and teachers second, or have they been teachers first
> and musicians second? How have they been able to influence
> governments and education authorities in order to achieve
> successful music education outcomes?

Notes

1. For details, see McCarthy, Chapter 4 in this volume.
2. Most specialist music teachers have completed a three-year Bachelor of Music degree and a one- or two-year course of teacher education.
3. More detailed information regarding the Music Curriculum – Band Descriptions, Content Description and Achievement Standard – is at http://www.australiancurriculum.edu.au/the-arts/music/curriculum/f-10?layout=1 (accessed 6 April 2016).
4. Since the introduction of more broadly based arts curricula generally consisting of five subjects (Dance, Drama, Media, Music and Visual Arts) in government schools from the 1980s, some secondary schools have taught arts subjects on a rotational basis over four school terms or two school semesters, which, in the case of music, is not conducive to a sequential and continuous development of musical concepts and skills.

References

Aldrich, R. (1996*), Education for the Nation*, London: Cassell.

Australian Curriculum, Assessment and Reporting Authority (2013a), *Australian Curriculum: The Arts*, Canberra: ACARA, http://www.australiancurriculum.edu.au/the-arts/introduction (accessed 28 February 2015).

Australian Curriculum, Assessment and Reporting and Authority (2013b), *The Arts Scope and Sequence: Foundation to Year 10 (by band)*, Canberra: ACARA, http://www.australiancurriculum.edu.au/the-arts/content-structure (accessed 28 February 2015).

Australian Curriculum, Assessment and Reporting Authority (2013c), Music Curriculum – Band Descriptions, Content Description and Achievement Standard, http://www.australiancurriculum.edu.au/the-arts/music/curriculum/f-10?layout=1 (accessed 28 February 2015).

Cameron, A. E. (1969), 'The class teaching of music in secondary schools in Victoria, 1905–1955' (unpublished MEd thesis, University of Melbourne).

Chaseling, M. (2003), 'The Great Public School Choir' in K. Hartwig and G. Barton (eds), *Artistic Practice as Research: Proceedings of the XXVth Annual Conference of the Australian Association for Research in Music Education*, Sydney: AARME, pp. 25–43.

Education Department, South Australia (1912), *Education Gazette* XXVIII (312).

Education Department, South Australia (1915), *Children's Hour*, Classes IV and V, Grades 7 and 8, XXVII (308).

Heinrich, J. (2012), 'The provision of classroom music programs to regional Victorian primary schools: a mixed methods study' (unpublished MEd thesis, LaTrobe University).

Hetherington, H., R. Sharam and P. Rymill (1979), *Penola Primary School Centenary History*, South
    Australia: Penola Primary School Centenary Committee.
Hocking, R. (2009), *National Audit of Music Discipline and Music Education Mandatory Content
    Within Pre-Service Generalist Primary Teacher Education Courses: A Report*, Sydney: Music
    Council of Australia.
Macrae, D. F. and M. Alsop (1910), 'Paddling Song', in *Some Children's Songs*, Melbourne:
    George Robertson, pp. 1–3.
Marvic, A. (n.d.), [Australian] Historical timeline, http://home.vicnet.net.au/~pioneers/ pppg10.htm
    (accessed 30 August 2008).
McBurney, S. (n.d. [c. 1895]), *The Australian Progressive Songster No. 2 for Senior Classes*,
    Sydney: Angus & Robertson.
Miller, P. (1986), *Long Division: Schooling in South Australian Society*, Adelaide: Wakefield Press.
Parliament of South Australia (1911), Report of the Minister of Education in *South Australian
    Parliamentary Papers* 44.
Pascoe, R., S. Leong, J. MacCallum, E. Mackinlay, K. Marsh, B. Smith et al. (2005), *National
    Review of School Music Education: Augmenting the Diminished*, Canberra: Australian
    Government.
Pope, J. (2006), 'Music through Movement over the Radio: A Dilemma for Dalcroze' in
    A. Giráldez, M. J. Aramberri, F. Bautista, M. Díaz, L. Hentschke and M. Hookey (eds),
    Proceedings of the 26th World Conference of the International Society for Music Education,
    Kuala Lumpur: ISME. CD-ROM.
Rainbow, B. (1967), *The Land without Music: Musical Education in England 1800–1860 and its
    Continental Antecedents*, London: Novello & Co. Ltd.
Richards, M. (1879), 'Letter', *Tonic Sol-fa Reporter,* November, 245.
Smeaton, T. H. (1927), *Education in South Australia from 1836 to 1927*, Adelaide: Rigby.
Southcott, J. E. (1993), 'Martial Strains' in V. Weidenbach and J. Callaghan (eds) *The
    Transformation of Music Praxis – Challenges for Arts Education: Proceedings of XIVth Annual
    Conference of the Australian Association for Research in Music Education*, Sydney: AARME,
    pp. 269–86.
Southcott, J. E. (1995), 'The Establishment of the Music Curriculum in South Australia: The Role
    of Alexander Clark', *Research Studies in Music Education* 5, 1–10.
Southcott, J. E. (1996), 'Curriculum Stasis: Gratton in South Australia' in V. Weidenbach (ed.),
    *Proceedings of the 15th Annual Conference of the Australian Association for Research in Music
    Education*, Sydney: AARME, pp. 51–9.
Southcott, J. E. (1997), 'Music in state-supported schooling in South Australia to 1920'
    (unpublished PhD thesis, Deakin University).
Southcott, J. E. (2002), 'Songs for Young Australians' in J. E. Southcott and R. Smith (eds), *A
    Community of Researchers: Proceedings of the XXIInd Annual Conference of the Australian
    Association for Research in Music Education*, Melbourne: AARME, pp. 164–71.
Southcott, J. E. (2004), 'The Singing By-ways: The Origins of Class Music Education in South
    Australia', *Journal of Historical Research in Music Education* XXV (2): 116–27.
Stevens, J. B. (1879), 'Marsupial Bill: Of the Bad Boy, the Good Dog and the Old Man Kangaroo',
    reprinted from *The Queenslander*, Brisbane: Gordon & Gotch.
Stevens, R. S. (1978), 'Music in State-supported Education in New South Wales and Victoria,
    1848–1920' (unpublished PhD thesis, The University of Melbourne).
Stevens, R. S. (1981), 'Music: A Humanizing and Civilizing Influence in Education' in G.
    Featherstone (ed.), *The Colonial Child*, Melbourne: Royal Historical Society of Victoria, pp.
    63–72.
Stevens, R. S. (1986), 'Samuel McBurney – Australian Tonic Sol-fa Advocate', *Journal of Research
    in Music Education* 34 (2): 77–87.

Stevens, R. S. (1993), 'Hugo Alpen – New South Wales Superintendent of Music, 1884–1908', *Unicorn: The Journal of the Australian College of Education* 19 (3), 93–6.

Stevens, R. S. (1997), 'George Leavis Allan' in W. A. Bebbington (ed.), *The Oxford Companion to Australian Music*, Melbourne: Oxford University Press, p. 20.

Stevens, R. S. (2002), 'James Churchill Fisher: Pioneer of Tonic Sol-fa in Australia' in J. E. Southcott and R. Smith (eds), *Proceedings of the XXIInd Annual Conference of the Australian Association for Research in Music Education*, Melbourne: AARME, pp. 172–82.

Stevens, R. S. (2006), '"Forward Gaily Together" – The School Music Compositions of Samuel McBurney' in J. E. Southcott and P. de Vries (eds), *Proceedings of the XXVIth Annual Conference of the Australian Association for Research in Music Education*, Melbourne: AARME, pp. 116–25.

Chapter 17

China: A socio-political perspective on the introduction and development of school music

Wai-Chung Ho

Introduction: Socio-political contexts of traditional Chinese music education

Traditional Chinese culture was isolated from the rest of the world by geography. Bordered by mountains to the west and by the sea to the east, China has long regarded itself as the 'Middle Kingdom'. As Huang (1988) argues, Chinese culture and values have been remarkably consistent over the nation's long history, mainly due to the domination of its education system by the teachings of Confucius (or Kong Fuzi) (551–479 BCE). Chinese emperors used the Confucian value system to rationalize the hierarchical structure of Chinese society, to persuade its people to adopt more virtuous lives, to legitimize their political leadership and to promote socio-political harmony. Rites and music, defined in terms of the unity of beauty and goodness, were important to the development of social harmony and morality (Wang 2004). One of the most famous sayings of Confucius on music education is 'To educate somebody, you should start from poems, emphasise ceremonies, and finish with music' (*The Analects*, 8.8, see Legge 1971). This was the reason why Confucius gave priority to the arts as a whole, to rites, music, archery, charioteering, writing and numbers (known as the 'six arts') as the standard content of Imperial education (Chen 1986: 92; Dawson 1981: 20).

The government of Imperial China adopted the Confucian view of music education, which saw it as an instrument for the management of Chinese social and political life, and to consolidate Imperial rule. The Imperial Music Bureau, which collected and edited ancient melodies and folk songs and formalized the structure of music education in the Zhou Dynasty (1122–256 BCE), was mainly concerned with music administration, education and performance. Teaching content was based on the Classics of Poetry (*Shi Jing*), the Book of Documents (*Shu Jing*), the Record of Rites (*Li Chi*) and the Classics of Music (*Yue Jing*), which were reportedly written by Confucius. The music education system offered nine-year courses, which started at the age of thirteen for boys. During the Han Dynasty (200 BCE to 220 CE), the Music Bureau – *Yueh Fu* – was set up by Emperor Wudi. The culture of the Tang Dynasty (618–907 ce) is described as the 'golden age' of Chinese history when both Chinese and foreign music were promoted.

In the most important dynasties of Imperial China, i.e. from the Zhou Dynasty (1075–256 BCE) to the Qing Dynasty (1644–1911 CE), the government always adopted the Confucian view of music education as a means to consolidate social and political life. Confucius emphasised that 'music without good connotation[s] should be excluded from the curriculum' (Ji 2008: 129), and that beautiful music must have 'a magnificent beginning' and be 'harmonious', 'clear' and 'smoothly continuous' (Ji 2008: 130). In accordance with its close association with the stable, conservative elements of Confucian society, music was thought of more in terms of ethics than aesthetics or pleasure, and for achieving political stability in the well-governed and well-ordered 'Confucian state' (Gulik 1969: 27). The rulers of Imperial China established a standardized system for the organization of pitches in order to regulate human relationships (Falkenhausen 1993). Altogether, the role of music education was to control people within a well-ordered Confucian society.

Music education after the First Sino-British War

Beginning with the First Sino-British War of 1839, China suffered repeated military defeats at the hands of other countries – first the European powers, and then the Japanese and Russians. Christianity was brought to China by Roman Catholic priests and Protestant missionaries, who were probably the earliest teachers of Western music (Scott 1963). Matteo Ricci (1552–1610), an Italian missionary who came to China in 1583 to preach Catholicism, was not only the first to introduce the religious music of the West to China, but also the first to introduce Western opera. Ricci carried a primitive clavichord with him across China from 1583, which he was allowed to present to the Ming Emperor Wanli in 1601 (see Gong 2004; Lindorff 2004). Protestant missionaries reached China in 1805 and introduced congregational hymn singing and organ music in the nineteenth century (Yoshihara 2007: 16). Hong Xiuquan (1814–1864), who led the Taiping Revolution (1851–64) against the Qing Dynasty, became acquainted with various features of Protestant worship under the influence of a Baptist minister from Missouri. Among the hymns Hong learned was 'The Old Hundredth', which he later adopted, with a new text, as the state hymn of the Taiping Heavenly Kingdom between 1850 and 1864 (Wong 1984: 113).

Western music was introduced throughout Asia, including China, not only as a purely aesthetic phenomenon, but also to promote 'military strength, discipline, and modernity' (Yoshihara 2007: 16). Western compositional techniques were introduced on a widespread scale in the last decades of the nineteenth century, in particular tonic sol-fa, which was promoted by James Legge, a leading sinologist and a representative of the London Missionary Society in Hong Kong, in 1862 (see Gong 2006; Stevens 2007).

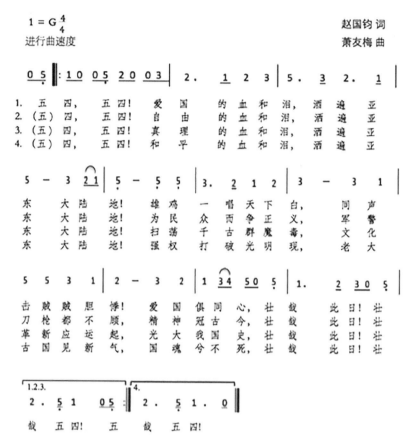

Figure 17.1 Xiao's song 'May Fourth Memorable Patriotic Song' in *jianpu* notation

In 1872 John Curwen noted that this system was employed by missionaries all over the world, and that 'Hong Kong was the third site' to establish the method (cited in Southcott and Lee 2008: 215). By 1877, sixty-three different hymn books were in circulation in China (Yoshihara 2007: 16). The Reverend Timothy Richard, a Welsh Baptist missionary who came to China in 1882, generated two different Chinese modulators and wrote a book in Chinese on the history and theory of music (see Bohr 2000; Stevens 2007).

The defeat of China by Japan in the first Sino-Japanese War (1894–5) and the threat of partition by foreign imperialism made clear to Chinese scholars the necessity to reform the government and education in order to survive. Many associations sprang up across China to call for educational reform on the Western model. A military band was established by Yuan Shikai (1859–1916, an influential Chinese general and politician in the late Qing Dynasty) in 1898, and subsequently several such Western-style bands were organized and trained in various cities (Yoshihara 2007: 11). At primary and secondary levels, Japanese school songs and others from Europe and the USA were adopted as teaching materials. Luo (1991: 11) identifies Chinese school songs as a 'new cultural phenomenon' in the early twentieth century, and a 'double cultural contact' between Western, Japanese and Chinese cultures. He characterizes the performance of Chinese school songs as the result of the 'reception of western culture through Japan' (Luo 1991: 12). This Western-style music education was introduced into China by Western-trained musicians and music educators. Early school songs in Shanghai adopted the melodies of British and American songs (Zhuang 2005). As Zhang (1991: 411) notes, 'the introduction of western music into China and the exchange between western and Chinese music represent the irresistible historical trend favourable to people which no one can change or stop'.

However, classroom learning was still traditional and rote-oriented, and teacher education received very little attention in education reforms. In 1897, the Qing Government founded the Nanyang Public School, which was regarded as the first school to provide teacher education in China, and the first to introduce the study of teaching methods in formal training. In 1898, Kang Youwei (1858–1927), a key figure in the intellectual development of modern China, and a leader of the 104-Day Reform Movement of 1898, promoted school music education, and argued that music lessons and singing should be fundamental for improving wellbeing in society (Cai 1996: 43). Subsequently, music was chosen as a school subject in 1903 at the government-financed Affiliated Elementary School of Nan Yang College in Shanghai (Shen, cited in Lin 2012: 55). Early reforms in school songs were led by Chinese music students who had studied in Japan. Shen Xingong (1869–1947), Zeng Zhimin (1879–1929) and Li Shutong (1880–1942), who all returned from music training in Japan, were the three most important school song composers. Shen wrote Chinese school songs based on Japanese ones, and taught at the aforementioned elementary school from its establishment in 1901 (Lin 2012: 55). In 1903 Zeng 'published the first serious article about school songs' and was regarded as 'the first person to introduce western music terminology to China in a systematic manner' (Melvin and Cai 2004: 87). Shen and Li, who believed that music could help to save the country, were the first 'modern' composers to synthesize European and Japanese songs with Chinese marches (Gild 1998: 111–12; also see Ho 2006: 438). The texts of their songs call for patriotism, self-discipline and the strengthening of the wills of Chinese children.

Chinese music educators suggested a major restructuring of the education system by developing new areas of learning. Music educators and musicians began to adopt a notation known as the 'jianpu system', which adapted the French Galin–Paris–Chevé way of using the Arabic numerals 1 to 7 to denote pitches. This notation was borrowed from Japan, where it had been successfully introduced by a French musician. Jianpu uses numbers to replace characters, and is a natural extension and unification of gongche notation, which was named after two of the Chinese characters used to represent musical notes. It was invented in the Tang Dynasty (618–907 CE) and became a popular form of music notation in ancient China (see Chen, Zhang and Cui 2012: 86). Toward the end of the Qing Dynasty, *jianpu* was also promoted by Chinese students who studied music in Japan, where, in the 1920s and 1930s, many Chinese students received musical training, as well as in the West. Xiao Youmei (1884–1940), Huang Zi (1904–38), Chao Yuen Ren (1892–1982) and others used Western compositional techniques to enrich school music education. In particular, Xiao Youmei, the 'father of contemporary Chinese music education', played an important role in the promotion of Western musical learning, particularly with respect to the theory of composition (see Figure 17.1).

Cai Yuanpei (1868–1940), the first Minister of Education of the Chinese Republic after 1911, Chancellor of Peking University and a leading figure in aesthetic studies and liberal education in the early twentieth century, acknowledged the integrity and uniqueness of every culture, but nonetheless suggested that Western cultures could be assimilated into China (Cai 1983, 1987; Xiu 1998; Zhang 2000). Education reform in school music became more widespread and an inseparable part of the school curriculum. Cao also argued that Western music could solve what he took to be the backwardness of Chinese music. Music as a school subject, which was based mainly on teaching and learning songs, used songs that, despite Western influences, provided a collective and shared memory among students and the general public.

The development of patriotic and revolutionary songs from the 1910s to the Cultural Revolution (1966–76)

After the establishment of the Republic of China in 1911, a commission on music education was formed to provide suitable music for schools and for civic and national gatherings (Wiant 1966). Between 1912 and 1919, the Ministry of Education (MoE) established policies on a range of issues including primary school regulations and timetabling, middle school curricula and teacher education. The MoE encouraged both primary and secondary schools to implement music lessons in their curricula, and as a consequence music textbooks underwent a period of significant development (Cao 1996: 45). The end of the First World War coincided with the advent of the 1919 May Fourth Movement that influenced the development of Chinese literature and music, and led its intellectuals to attack Confucian values. Now Chinese musicians aimed to introduce nationalism and democracy into their music through the use of Western compositional skills and methods.

The music curriculum guidelines for primary, junior and senior high schools were implemented in 1923, 1932 and 1940 respectively (Cao and He 2000: 7). In 1923, the Chinese government renamed 'lessons on national songs' as 'music lessons' for six-year primary and three-year junior high schools. In 1934, the Committee for Music Education was established to plan the production of primary and secondary teaching materials (Zhang 1990: 445). Music education was now thought to be a valuable component of the school curriculum. Music performance such as singing was promoted as the education of personal intelligence, ethical discernment and moral responsibility. Moreover, Huang

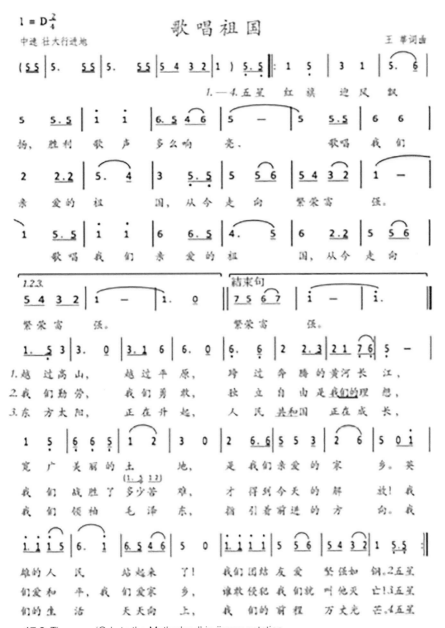

Figure 17.2 The song 'Ode to the Motherland' in *jianpu* notation

Zi and other composers were requested to edit a set of music books in June 1933, and six such sets were published in October 1939 (see Liang 1985: 138–9; Liu 1990: 439–45).

The growth of nationalism in Chinese music education was further reinforced when the country was militarily invaded during the Second Sino-Japanese War (1937–45). Consequently, the Chinese MoE promoted the singing of anti-war songs from 1937 to 1945. According to Kwok (1987), the Western diatonic tonal system influenced the production of the Chinese 'folk songs' that supplemented new teaching materials aimed at countering Japanese aggression during the 1930s and 1940s. Communist musicians in China produced 'a deluge of songs', mostly published on mimeographed sheets and in pamphlets (Hung 1996: 906). Patriotic/Communist composers such as Nie Er (1912–35) and Xian Xinghai (1905–45), who all made use of tunes in national styles, produced large numbers of songs designed to motivate the masses to resist the Japanese invasion and to articulate national liberation. Nie Er's 'March of the Volunteers', 'Docker's Song' and 'Female Singer under Cruel Oppression' were representative of the new popular style. 'The March of the Volunteers', which became 'the quintessential song of resistance against Japan', was 'sung at schools, in the army, at rallies, and on the street' in order to capture 'the hearts and minds of millions' during the War of Resistance between 1937 and 1945 (Hung 1996: 901). The MoE sent officers to observe music lessons that used both Chinese and English versions of the 'Collections of Anti-War Songs' and trained pupils to sing the 'Choral Work for Thousands of People' (Liu 1998: 246). The first such mass choral singing was organized in the spring of 1941 in Chongqing, Szechwan's largest city, with participants coming from different social sectors including middle schools, vocational schools, universities and workers' organizations. The Music Education Committee also promoted military music through a three-year programme that recruited teenagers aged fifteen to eighteen for formal vocal and instrumental training (Liu 1998: 248). Owing to the anti-foreign and anti-Japanese wars of the 1910s and 1940s, musicians and music educators became primary agents of cultural transformation, encouraging the musical expression of patriotism as a socio-political tool for disciplining society through compulsory education (see Figure 17.2).

In 1942, following the growth of the Communist movement in China, Mao Zedong (1893–1976) delivered a famous speech at the Yenan Forum on the use of literature and art to serve Communist ideology, and on the nature of art in a class-based society. In 1949 the Kuomintang (the Chinese Nationalist Party) led by the Chinese Nationalist Chiang Kai-shek (1887–1975), which claimed to rule China from the 1930s through the Second World War, retreated to Taiwan, and the People's Republic of China (PRC) was formally established on 1 October 1949 with its national capital at Beijing. The Chinese Communist Party (CCP) promoted revolutionary music while suppressing traditional and popular styles. Many of the protest and revolutionary songs supported by the party were Chinese versions of existing Soviet songs. Values education and politics were blended with traditional Chinese thought; role models, cultural heroes and politically sanctioned models were used to ensure the cohesion of Chinese culture and to create a well-ordered and cordial society (Reed 1995). For example, the song 'Without the Communist Party There Would Be No New China' was very popular with the CCP. Thus, in Communist China, music and the arts in general were governed by Marxist–Leninist–Maoist ideology, and were required to serve the interests of students, workers, peasants and soldiers, as well as to convey the messages of the government. In the mid-1950s Communist China sent groups of 'politically reliable' students and party members from diverse fields of music to study at the Moscow Conservatory of Music and to other such institutions in Eastern European countries (Mao 1991: 109).

The First National Conference on Education was organized by the MoE in December 1949. Ma Xulun, the Minister of Education, in his opening speech to the conference, defined education in the PRC as 'national, scientific, and mass-oriented' (cited in Shen 1994: 2). After the establishment of the PRC in 1949, its first regulation for primary school students declared that they should develop a new democratic ideology and an international spirit, dedicate their love for the nation, its people and its public properties, and instil national morals, strive for democracy, and thereby become brave, healthy and disciplined people (Yao 2000: 32). In 1950, the MoE focused on teaching revolutionary songs to junior elementary pupils and on how music curriculum guidelines could be positively implemented in primary and secondary school education (Yao 2000: 14–15).

In 1952, the Chinese MoE announced the reform of teacher education, which should henceforth be based on the Soviet Russian model. Education studies for trainee teachers represented 18.1 per cent of total curricular time in 1952, and 23.5 per cent in 1956 (Jin 1989: 44). There were nine compulsory music courses for student teachers: (1) an intro- duction to the arts, (2) music theory, (3) important musical works, (4) vocal and choral music, (5) instrumental learning, (6) music teaching methods, (7) leisure activities, (8) music and singing and (9) education practices (Ma 2002: 170). Weekly tutorials were scheduled for music teaching methods, and teaching practice was usually conducted for six weeks in the sixth and seventh terms. All student music teachers were required to take four subjects for their graduation examinations, including the basic ideology of Marxism–Leninism and the new democracy, general educational and music teaching methods, music theory, and instrumental and vocal performance (Ma 2002: 170–71).

The Cultural Revolution (1966–76), which was officially launched on 8 August 1966, was driven by its slogan 'grasp revolution, [and] promote production'. Its anti-intellectual policies brought chaos to the music educational establishment and, as the politics of music in the PRC increasingly came to reflect the Cultural Revolution, tensions mounted within musical circles. The anthem that typified the Cultural Revolution was 'The East is Red', an old revolutionary song. In it, Chairman Mao was 'deified' as the sun in heaven: 'The east is red, the sun has risen. China has produced Mao Zedong. He works for the people's happiness. He is the saviour of the people.' It became the movement's anthem. Such songs were regarded as 'political commodities' and were monitored to ensure that they conformed to the state's political ideology.

The Cultural Revolution took Chinese music education into a new phase of devel- opment, thereby bringing about educational disorder and loss of cultural life. Aesthetics ceased to exist as a topic of education and all research into school music education was stopped (Ma 2005: 200). Between 1966 and 1969 all music programmes in teacher education terminated (Ma 2002: 181). Though some teacher training institutions operated individual music education programmes between 1970 and 1976, they did not share teaching goals and materials, and their operational styles depended on local practical needs. Even when music activities were carried out in these educational institutions, they were mainly limited to a few revolutionary songs. Yao (1989: 25) maintained that 'singing one song' was, by implication, to have one 'political education' lesson. The only extra-curricular musical activities schools were allowed to attend were eight revolutionary musicals, including the symphonic suite *Shachiapang*, two ballets, *The Red Detachment of Women* and *The White-Haired Girl*, and five operas: *Red Lantern's Record*, *Capturing the Tiger Mountain by Strategy*, *On the Docks, Raid on the White Tiger Regiment* and *Shajiabang* (Yao 1989; Chen 2002). The themes of the eight model dramas were 'drawn from the proletarian struggles during the Civil and Sino-Japanese War' (Liang 1985: 157). This small group of officially sanctioned works (also known as 'the eight revolutionary works'), with regard to both artistic and ideological contents, limited what people in China could watch, hear, perform and appreciate in the community.

   With the fall of the 'Gang of Four' (the group of Chinese Communist Party leaders, including Jiang Qing, Zhang Chunqiao, Yao Wenyuan and Wang Hongwen, who played key roles in the Cultural Revolution), Mainland China entered a new era of rapid economic growth from 1978 onwards under the leadership of Deng Xiaoping (1904–97). This was a time of transition for mainland China from the revolutionary stage towards a more open and inclusive type of politics and an increase in economic cooperation, trade and interdependence between countries. Deng Xiaoping criticized the effects of the Cultural Revolution on the arts and asked, 'How can eight shows [i.e. the eight revolutionary musicals] satisfy an audience of eight hundred million people?' (cited in Manuel 1988: 232). Thus traditional Chinese music and Western classical music were turned to once again. The development of music and music education in China underwent considerable change, with the influence of the Eastern Bloc countries waning, and that of Western countries increasing after the 1978 declaration of the Open-Door Policy.

Changes to school curricula following the 1978 Open-Door Policy

The ten years of the Cultural Revolution brought the Chinese education system to a virtual halt, so much so that formal and structured music education was very difficult to conduct. In 1978, during the aftermath of the Revolution, Deng Xiaoping affirmed the nation's commitment to science and technology, and proclaimed four areas for modernization – agriculture, industry, science and technology, and the military – as key means for achieving China's national goals. Deng succeeded in setting the country on the road to socialist modernization. In 1979, he visited the United States to tour the Ford auto plant in Atlanta, and attended a performance by popular folksinger John Denver at the Kennedy Center in Washington.

   Openness and reform under Deng Xiaoping's leadership in the 1980s shifted the national focus away from class struggle and towards economic reconstruction and compulsory education was identified as the pathway for advancing science and technology (see Kau and Marsh 1993; Rosen 1985). With the implementation of the Open-Door Policy, an emphasis on English education emerged, and the MoE launched numerous English as a Foreign Language (EFL) teacher training projects. In June 1979 Isaac Stern (1920–2001), the world-renowned Ukrainian–American violinist, made an unprecedented tour of China and was credited with boosting Western classical music and helping foster cultural exchanges with the West. In the same month, the MoE distributed a new music syllabus for primary and secondary schools, and instruction methods for teaching secondary school education were enforced in teacher training courses in December 1979 (Cao and He 2000: 8; also see Ma 2005: 153).

From the late 1970s to 2000 China enacted several major education laws and over 200 regulation changes in order to promote good educational practice, to enhance and universalize primary and junior secondary (i.e. Grades 1–9) school education, to increase the number of schools and qualified teachers, and to reform education in order to enable China to compete in the global economy (Law 1999, 2007). After the mid-1980s, there was an expansion of teacher education programmes in order to reshape the teaching force through a system of examinations and credentials.

The Fourth Session of the Sixth National People's Congress in Beijing in 1986 adopted the Compulsory Education Law of the PRC. This stipulated that the state should provide nine years of compulsory education (i.e. Grades 1–9) for all children, and this should include music lessons in all primary and junior high schools. In the same year, the MoE established the Arts Education Institute with a membership of forty-seven professionals, scholars, teachers and researchers to positively renew arts education reform and to affirm arts education as the foundation for the balanced moral, cognitive, aesthetic and social development of children and youths (see Cai 1996: 54). In July 1994, the MoE officially announced the organization of music appreciation lessons in senior secondary schools. This was a significant advance, as these schools had not included music lessons in their curriculum for more than forty years (Guo 2006: 9).

In November 1996, the MoE called for a working committee on arts education, and promoted a national school music education. The Chinese government aimed to build a highly committed teaching profession so as to improve the quality of music teaching in schools. In August 1997, the Chinese government, for the first time since the establishment of the PRC in 1949 (Guo 2006: 9), honoured 250 excellent primary and secondary school music teachers on a national basis at the Beijing's Great Hall of the People. Then, in 1999, nine music conservatories, including the Shanghai Conservatory of Music, the Central Conservatory of China and the China Conservatory of Music, ran faculties of music education or developed faculties for teacher education (Ma 2002: 322). The provision of teacher education has helped music teachers equip themselves with the attitudes, behaviours, knowledge and skills to perform their tasks effectively within the implementation of basic education in China.

As far as the content of the music curriculum was concerned for Grades 1–6 in the 1990s, the main activities included singing, instrumental learning, music appreciation, music reading and sight singing. Basic music theory and aural training was added to the junior high school music curriculum (see Table 17.1). Music teachers for primary schools, kindergartens and special education are generally generalist graduates from junior schools who have been trained in three- or four-year programmes that include music as one of several compulsory courses. There has been a great shortage of school music teachers, particularly in rural areas (Ma 2002).

The curriculum reform launched in 2001 (Ministry of Education 2001) has brought about tremendous changes to many areas, including the philosophy of music education, instructional contents, varieties of musical styles and teaching methods. This curriculum was updated in 2011 (Ministry of Education, 2012). It highlighted the importance of developing traditional Chinese culture in schools. Students were encouraged to 'listen to Chinese folk songs, folk dances, instrumental pieces from representative regions, as well as Chinese dramas and art music as represented by the Beijing Opera to experience diverse musical styles' (Ministry of Education 2012: 16–17, translated by the author).

Music teaching materials must now be accepted by the MoE, which reviews and approves all music textbooks for primary and secondary schools in Shanghai, Beijing, Harbin and other major cities of China. The recent textbook revisions, newly published materials and recommended technological resources for teaching musical cultures are all designed to make education truly meaningful to Chinese youth, to help them to 'break free' from the limitations of traditional education, and to construct learning experiences with links, not only to society and technology, but also to students' lives (Teaching Resources Editing Group for High School Teachers 2001; Guo 2005; Song 2007). There has been a call to promote creativity as a vital component of its education system in the new global age. According to Guo's survey (2006: 13) of Beijing's elementary and

Table 17.1 Teaching content and hours of music lessons for compulsory music education as suggested by the Ministry of Education, China (as reported by Lu 1999: 65–6):

Grades	Teaching contents	Teaching hours
1–2	Singing	50
3–4	Singing	50
5–6	Singing	40
7–9	Singing	30–40
1–2	Instrumental learning	20
3–4	Instrumental learning	20
5–6	Instrumental learning	20
7–9	Instrumental learning	20
1–2	Music reading and sight singing	10
3–4	Music reading and sight singing	10
5–6	Music reading and sight singing	15
7–9	Music appreciation	20–30
7–9	Learning of basic music theory and aural training	20

secondary schools, the most important function of school music education is to facilitate students' intellectual development and their growth of creativity and imagination.

Although *jianpu* is still present in Chinese school education, teachers are advised to teach students five-line notation (Ma 2002: 200; Yao 2000: 37), which is used in most music textbooks. As instructed by the MoE, the People's Music Publisher issued standard music textbooks for primary and secondary school education in 1980, and its publications ended the long-term lack of educational music materials (Jin 2003: 4). Since then, a uniform standard for school curricula, textbooks and teacher qualifications has been established. However, provinces, autonomous regions and special municipalities retained significant autonomy, and variations were allowed.

Governmental reaction to political dissent and perceived international threats has continued to impact on music education through the 1990s until the present. In the wake of the 1989 Tiananmen Square Incident, the PRC authorities attempted to reform and strengthen patriotic education focused on the history of the 'Chinese humiliated century' through the national patriotic education campaign that began in 1991. The focus of patriotic education was on the arts, drama, music, film, stories and television, and used rich and vivid imagery to provide a powerful link between collective memory and history in the education system. In October 2004, the 'three one hundred' project was launched, including 100 films, 100 songs and 100 recommended books to encourage patriotism (Wang 2008). China continues to emphasize the ideal of nationhood to reconstruct collective national, cultural and ethnic identity in approved textbook songs such as 'Huanghe' or 'Yellow River' (considered to be the birthplace of Chinese civilization) and 'The Great Wall' (the longest wall in the world). Communist ideology still dominates the school curriculum through the inclusion of revolutionary and patriotic songs in the approved music textbooks so as to cultivate students' revolutionary spirit and their sense of belonging to the new China (Ho and Law 2012: 403). These songs include 'A Red-Starred Song' (in praise of the glorious Communist Party and the will to follow the heart of Chairman Mao), 'Praise of the Red Flag', 'If There Was No Communist Party There Would be No New China', 'Suite of Songs for the Long March', 'The Flying Flag' and 'Protect the Yellow River'.

Although China is no longer threatened by foreign countries, the domestic discourse of nationalism in music education is still influenced by PRC propaganda, school activities and curriculum content. For example, in the run-up to the eighty-third anniversary of the Mukden Incident (an incident staged by Japanese forces as a pretext to invade Manchuria on 18 September 1931) in 2014, the government launched a month-long anti-Japanese campaign to strengthen patriotic education in the daily lives of Chinese people. Students all over China were encouraged to sing the Chinese National Anthem, 'March of the Volunteers', in remembrance of the martyrs: 'Arise, all who refuse to be slaves. With our flesh and blood, let us build our new Great Wall! … Arise! Arise! Arise! Millions with but one heart, Braving the enemy's fire, march on! Braving the enemy's fire, march on! March on! March on!'

Conclusion

This chapter has examined Chinese music education from the 1840s to today's rapidly modernized society, focusing on state power and its ongoing efforts to incorporate values education into compulsory music education. Despite different extents and emphases, the government has promoted social harmony and political unity as means to consolidate political leadership through school music education. Both internal and external circumstances have contributed to the ways in which Chinese nationalism and Communism in school music education has grown in terms of culture, history and political ideologies. During periods of socio-political transformation in China, cultural roles were established for music that served political ideologies, while state power was exercised to turn the less-obviously political institution of the school into an ideal venue for music education. We have seen that school music education in China has been aligned with shifts in dominant Chinese political ideology. In particular, music education has been a medium for fostering resistance to Japanese aggression and support for nationalism in the 1930s, and to support revolution and Communism from the 1940s to the 1970s. The cultivation of correct political consciousness has sometimes involved an obsessive selection of suitable musical resources for education. China's Open-Door Policy has moved the country from isolation to engagement and has intensified external pressures on China to increase its cultural interaction with the rest of the world.

In an increasingly connected and interdependent world, China's school music education is contextual, multi-levelled and always in response to and part of both domestic and global interactions. This chapter has demonstrated that musical culture in China's school music education is in dialectical relationships with political and social factors. The relationship between music and nationalism in twenty-first-century China still opens up new avenues for discussion and research.

Acknowledgement

This research project is funded by a Faculty Research Grant from Hong Kong Baptist University [FRG1/13-14/069].

Reflective questions

1 To what extent is the Confucian idea that 'music without good connotations' should be excluded from the curriculum relevant today? What are some of the arguments for and against this idea?

2 Review the extent to which Western missionaries and Japan influenced music education after the First Sino-British War. In what ways does this demonstrate that school music education in China is in a dialectical relationship with political and social factors?

3 Assess the impact of nationalist and communist values on music education from the 1910s to the Cultural Revolution.

4 What conclusions do you draw about the role of the state, ideology and school authorities in relation to music education as a result of reading this chapter?

References

Bohr, P. R. (2000), 'Famine in China and the Mission: Timothy Richard as Relief Administrator and Advocate of National Reform 1876–1884', *International Bulletin of Missionary Research* 24: 75–80.

Cao, L. (1996), *Putong Xuexiao Yinle Jiaoyuxue* (*Education Method for Teaching General Schools*) (2nd edn), Shanghai: Shanghai Xiaoyu Chubanshe.

Cai, Y. P. (1983), *Miexue Wenxuan* (*The Selected Works on Aesthetics by Cai Yuanpei*), Beijing: Beijing Daxus Chubanshe.

Cai, Y. P. (1987), *Jiaoyu Lunji* (*A Collection of Education Treatises by Cai Yuanpei*), Hunan: Jiaoya Chubanshe.

Cai, L. (1996), *Putong Xuexiao Yinyue Jiaoyuxue* (*General Education: Pedagogy of Music Education*), Shanghai: Shanghai Educational Publisher.

Cao, L. and G. He (2000), *Yinyue Xueke Jiaoyuxue* (*The Educational Theory of Music Teaching*), Beijing: Capital Normal University.

Chen, G. F., W. J. Zhang and H. J. Cui (2012), 'Extracting Notes from Chinese Gong-che Notation Musical Score Image Using a Self-adaptive Smoothing and Connected Component Labeling Algorithm', *International Journal of Advancements in Computing Technology* 4 (1): 86–95.

Chen, L. F. (1986), *The Confucian Way: A New and Systematic Study of the 'Four Books'*, London: KPI Limited.

Chen, X. M. (2002), *Acting the Right Part: Political Theater and Popular Drama in Contemporary China*, Honolulu: University of Hawaii Press.

Dawson, R. (1981), *Confucius,* Oxford: Oxford University Press.

Falkenhausen, L. V. (1993), *Suspended Music: Chime-Bells in the Culture of Bronze Age China*, Berkeley: University of California Press.

Gild, G. (1998), 'Dreams of Renewal Inspired by Japan and the West: Early 20th Century reforms in Chinese music', *Chime* 12–13, 116–23.

Gong, H. Y. (2004), 'Western Classical Music in China from Matteo Ricci to Li Delun', *Musicology in China* 4: 138–40.

Gong, H. Y. (2006), 'Missionaries, reformers, and the beginnings of Western music in Late Imperial China (1838–1911)' (unpublished PhD dissertation, The University of Auckland).

Gulik, R. H. van (1969), *The Lore of the Chinese Lute* (2nd edn), Tokyo: Sophia University, in cooperation with Charles E. Tuttle Co.

Guo, S. J. (2005), *Yishu Jiaoyulun* (*Discussion on Arts Education*) (3rd edn), Shanghai: Shanghai Educational Publisher.

Guo, S. J. (2006), *Yinyue Jiaoyulun* (*Discussion on Music Education*), Hunan Literature and Art Publishing House.

Ho, W. C. (2006), 'Social Change and Nationalism in China's Popular Songs', *Social History* 31 (4), 435–53.

Ho, W. C. and W. W. Law (2012), 'The Cultural Politics of Introducing Popular Music into China's Music Education', *Popular Music and Society* 35 (3): 399–425.

Huang, R. (1988), *China: A Macro History*, Armonk, NY: M. E. Sharpe.

Hung, C. T. (1996), 'The Politics of Songs: Myths and Symbols in the Chinese Communist War Music, 1937–1949', *Modern Asian Studies* 30 (4): Special Issue: War in Modern China, 901–29.

Ji, Y. (2008), 'Confucius on Music Education,' *Nebula* 5 (1–2): 128–33.

Jin, Y. Q. (1989), 'Zhongdeng shifan jiaoyu zhuanye kecheng gaige jiyi' ['Urgent comments on the reform of educational studies in the normal school curriculum'], *Jiaoyu Yanjiu* 5, 44–6.

Jin, Y. W. (2003), *Chuzhong Yinyue Xin Kecheng Jiaoxuefa* (*Early Secondary School New Music Curriculum Teaching Methods*), Beijing: Higher Education Publisher.

Kau, M. Y. M. and S. H. Marsh (eds) (1993), *China in the Era of Deng Xiaoping: A Decade of Reform*, Armonk, NY: M. E. Sharpe.

Kwok, T. J. (1987), *Zheng: A Chinese Zither and its Music*, Michigan: University Microfilms International.

Law, W. W. (1999), 'New rules of the game in education in the People's Republic of China: education laws and regulations' [Guest Editor's Introduction], *Chinese Education and Society* 32 (3): 3–8.

Law, W. W. (2007), 'Legislation and Educational Changes: The Struggle for Social Justice and Quality in China's Compulsory Schooling', *Education and Law* 19 (3/4): 177–99.

Legge, J. (1971), *Confucian Analects: The Great Learning and the Doctrine of the Mean*, New York: Dover.

Liang, M. Y. (1985), *Music of the Billion: An Introduction to Chinese Musical Culture*, New York: Heinrichshofen Edition.

Lin, T. H. L. (2012), 'The development and conceptual transformation of Chinese Buddhist songs in the twentieth century' (unpublished PhD thesis, University of California, San Diego).

Lindorff, J. (2004), 'Missionaries, Keyboards and Musical Exchange in the Ming and Qing Courts', *Early Music* 32 (3): 403–14.

Liu, C. C. (ed.) (1990), *History of New Music in China 1946–1976: Collected Essays*, Hong Kong: The University of Hong Kong.

Liu, C. C. (1998), *Zhongguo Xin Yinyue Shilun* (*Historical Record of New China Music*), Vol. 1, Taipei: Yaowen Shiye Co.

Lu, M. D. (ed.) (1999), *Xiandai Zhongxiaoxue Yishu Xiaoyue Lun* (*Education in Modern Arts Education in Primary and Secondary Schools*), Nanjing: Jiangsu Educational Publisher.

Luo, C. K. (1991), 'Double Cultural Contact: Diffusion and Reformation of Japanese school songs in China' in Y. Tokumaru, M. Ohmiya, M. Kanazawa, O. Yamaguti, T. Tukitani, A. Takamatu and M. Shimosako (eds), *Tradition and its Future in Music: Report of SIMS 1990*, Osaka, Tokyo: Mita Press, pp. 11–14.

Ma, D. (2002), *Ershi Shiji Zhongguo Xueshao Yinyue Jiaoyue* (*Chinese School Music Education of the 20th Century*), Shanghai: Shanghai Educational Publisher.

Ma, D. (2005), *Yinyue Xiaoyu Kexue Yanjiu Fangfa* (*The Scientific Research Method in Music Education*), Shanghai: Shanghai Music Chubanshe.

Manuel, P. (1988), *Popular Music of the Non-Western World: An Introductory Survey*, New York and Oxford: Oxford University Press.

Mao, Y. R. (1991), 'Music under Mao, its Background and Aftermath', *Asian Music* XXII (2): 97–125.

Melvin, S. and J. D. Cai (2004), *Rhapsody in Red: How Western Classical Music Became Chinese*, New York: Algora Publishing.

Ministry of Education, The People's Republic of China (2001), *Quanri Zhi Yiwu Jiaoyu: Yinyue*

Kecheng Biaozhun (Shiyan Gao) [*Full-time Voluntary Education: Standard of Music Curriculum (Experimental Version)*], Beijing: Beijing Normal University Publisher.

Ministry of Education, The People's Republic of China (2012), *Yiwu Jiaoyu Yinyue Kecheng Biaozhun* (*Curriculum Standards for Primary Education and Junior Secondary Education: Music*), Beijing: Beijing Normal University Press.

Reed, G. G. (1995), 'Moral/Political Education in the People's Republic of China: Learning through Role Models', *Journal of Moral Education* 24 (2): 99–111.

Rosen, S. (1985), 'Recentralization, Decentralization, and Rationalization: Deng Xiaoping's Bifurcated Educational Policy', *Modern China* 11 (3): 301–46.

Scott, A. C. (1963), *Literature and the Arts in Twentieth Century China*, Garden City, New York: Doubleday.

Shen, J. P. (1994), 'Educational Policy in the People's Republic of China: A Political Influence Perspective', *Journal of Education Policy* 9 (1): 1–13.

Song, J. (2007), 'How does a Music Teacher Face the Education of the New Century', *Journal of Xichang College* 21 (2): 101–3, 110.

Southcott, J. E. and A. H. C. Lee (2008), 'Missionaries and Tonic Sol-fa Music Pedagogy in 19th-century China', *International Journal of Music Education* 26 (3): 213–28.

Stevens, R. S. (2007), 'Tonic Sol-fa in Asia-Pacific Countries – the Missionary Legacy', *Asia-Pacific Journal for Arts Education* 5 (1): 52–76.

Teaching Resources Editing Group for High School Teachers (2001), *Zhongxue Yinyue Jiaoxuelun Jiaocheng* (*Theory of Secondary School Music Education*) (2nd edn), Beijing: People's Music Publishing Company.

Wang, Y. W. (2004), 'The Ethical Power of Music: Ancient Greek and Chinese Thoughts', *Journal of Aesthetic Education* 38 (1): 89–104.

Wang, Z. (2008), 'National Humiliation, History Education, and the Politics of Historical Memory: Patriotic Education Campaign in China', *International Studies Quarterly* 52: 783–806.

Wiant, B. (1966), *The Music of China,* Hong Kong: Chung Chi College, the Chinese University of Hong Kong.

Wong, I. K. F. (1984), 'Geming Gequ: Songs for the Education of the Masses' in B. S. McDougall (ed.), *Popular Chinese Literature and Performing*, London: University of California Press, pp. 112–43.

Xiu, H. L. (1998), 'Modern Music Education and Cai Yuanpei's Views on Chinese and Western Culture', *Musical Performance* 21 (2), 15–17.

Yao, S. Y. (1989), 'On the Construction and Development of China Schools' Musical Education', *People Music* (*Renmin Yinyue*) 10: 24–7.

Yao, S. Y. (2000), *Zhongguo Dangdai Xuexiao Xinyue Jiaoyu Wenxuan* (*Selected Papers for School Music Education in Contemporary China*), Shanghai: Shanghai Educational Publisher.

Yoshihara, M. (2007), *Musicians from a Different Shore: Asians and Asian Americans in Classical Music*, Philadelphia: Temple University Press.

Zhang, J. R. (1990), 'The development and investigation of contemporary China music education' in C. C. Liu (ed.), *History of New Music in China 1946–1976: Collected Essays*, Hong Kong: University of Hong Kong, pp. 439–56.

Zhang, L. Z. (2000), 'Cai Yuanpei (1868–1940)', *Prospects* XXIII (1/2): 147–57.

Zhang, Q. (1991), 'The History and Future of the Reception of Western Music by China in the 20th Century' in Y. Tokumaru, M. Ohmiya, M. Kanazawa, O. Yamaguti, T. Tukitani, A. Takamatu and M. Shimosako (eds), *Tradition and its Future in Music: Report of SIMS 1990 Osaka*, Tokyo: Mita Press, pp. 407–12.

Zhuang, Z. L. (2005), *Xuetang Chunqiu* (*Schools and Colleges in Old Shanghai*), Shanghai: Shanghai Cultural Publishing House.

Chapter 18

South Africa: Indigenous roots, cultural imposition and an emerging national identity

Robin Stevens and Eric Akrofi

Unlike the situation in European cultures, community-based systems of education have developed over millennia in African indigenous populations to prepare children for their role as adult members in their tribal communities. In most African cultures, such a system of education has utilized 'musical arts' – singing, drumming, dancing and other forms of music – as the principal means through which both rites of passage and more general life skills have been provided. Indeed, the role of music in indigenous African life, particularly within the South African context, has been an integral component of *ubuntu*. This is the notion based on the Zulu maxim *umuntu ngumuntu ngabantu* ('a person is only a person through their relationship to others') as well the Xhosa dictum *umntu ngumntu ngabantu* ('a person is a person because of other persons') that utilizes and supports the social reciprocity inherent in music. As Herbst, de Wet and Rijsdijk (2005: 262) put it: 'Indigenous sub-Saharan African musical arts performance and education require the total involvement of individuals as they express themselves through the instruments they play and the dances they perform. All these activities take place within the context of social norms.'

This chapter draws on the three-level schema identified by several authors including Thorsén (1997) and Campbell (2008). This schema includes, respectively:

- 'informal education' described as 'life-long learning within families, peer groups etc, often without pronounced educational objectives' (Thorsén 1997: 3), which is synonymous with 'natural learning' that is 'enculturative, occurring naturally, non-consciously and without direct instruction of any sort' (Campbell 2008: 41);

- 'non-formal' that involves 'private or non-government educational enterprise' (Thorsén ibid.) or learning that is 'only partly guided, occurring outside institutionalized settings through the prompting of occasional and nonconsecutive directives' (Campbell ibid.);

- 'formal' that is represented by 'the governmentally geared system from primary to tertiary education' (Thorsén ibid.) or learning that is 'occurring through a teacher's intervention in highly structured settings such as a school' (Campbell ibid.).

Despite differences in terminology and definitions, this schema allows the issue of music in compulsory schooling in South Africa – selected as perhaps the most well-documented example in the sub-Saharan African region of music in education – to be considered in a more culturally appropriate and relevant manner than considering it merely within the confines of an essentially European 'school-based' construct. In addition, this schema accommodates successive phases in the evolution of 'an education in and through music' in South Africa. Accordingly, this chapter will be arranged in three sections, which, broadly speaking, incorporate this three-level schema – namely music in indigenous learning, music in mission-based schooling and music in government schooling. In all these settings, one or other forms of education were an integral part of the experience of young people and therefore all settings incorporate some measure of compulsory or at least obligatory participation in the communal learning endeavour of their immediate social environment.

The introduction and nature of compulsory school education in South Africa have varied according to the prevailing socio-political circumstances. School attendance for children of the European population became compulsory around the turn of the nineteenth century in most provinces but, as far as the indigenous population was concerned, it was not until 1994 with the coming of the 'new' South Africa that school education could be said to be both universally provided and compulsory for children of primary and lower secondary school age.

Music in indigenous learning

According to Hauptfleisch (1997: 193), the original inhabitants of South Africa were probably the San, a hunter-gatherer people who occupied a wide area of southern Africa for thousands of years. About 2,000 years ago, some San communities (calling themselves Khoikhoi) intermingled with the Bantu-speaking black African people, who were establishing themselves within the borders of present-day South Africa.

There had always been an informal education system operating among the San and the black African peoples. However, a more formal type of education took place during periods of initiation, such as *ulwaluko* (circumcision) and *intonjane* (puberty rites) among the Xhosa-speaking people. Nzewi (2003, cited in Herbst et al. 2005) argues that, contrary to common belief, indigenous music learning has a philosophy and a systematic transmission or teaching procedure normally only associated with 'formal' training in a format different from that found in Western 'formal' institutionalized training. Although Nzewi's assertion convinced Herbst, de Wet and Rijsdijk (2005) to avoid using the terms 'formal', 'informal' and 'non-formal', the present authors have nevertheless utilized these within what is considered to be most appropriate schema with which to engage in the discourse for this chapter.

From the outset, music often formed part of schooling for children of all racial backgrounds in South Africa. Particularly in the case of indigenous schooling provided by missionary societies, the tonic sol-fa method became the mainstay of school music education, especially in Cape Province. However, the introduction of European music to indigenous communities has not been without its critics. Many African scholars have identified the imposition of a foreign musical genre on the indigenous population through school education as well as through evangelizing by Christian missionaries as representing a form of 'cultural imperialism'. Kruger (1999: 129, cited in Emberly and Davidson 2011: 73) maintains that 'the promotion of local culture was strongly oppressed by the church' and Primos (2003: 3, cited in Herbst et al. 2005: 262) points out that only hymns and other European songs were taught in mission schools. Thus, indigenous children attending weekday schools and Sunday schools were denied access to their own indigenous music.

Mngoma (1990: 122), in asserting that the cultural history and indigenous belief systems of African people are embedded in their communal musical arts practices, laments that European culture has influenced the cultural preferences of African learners and has inhibited their growth, experience, and ability to express themselves in music, thus alienating them from their cultural heritage. Indeed, according to Herbst, de Wet and Rijsdijk (2005: 61), policymakers and many teachers prior to 1994 have frequently and incorrectly assumed that music education in South Africa began with the arrival of the Dutch at the Cape of Good Hope in 1652 and have thus ignored the role of learning implicit in indigenous musical arts practised prior to colonization in Africa.

It is evident from these criticisms that indigenous African musical arts were regarded in the immediate post-apartheid period as having some way to go before gaining full recognition within the context of South African school music education. As Akrofi (1998: 46) summed up the situation in the late 1990s, '[T]o place traditional African music on an equal footing with Western music in the curriculum of South African schools is an uphill task ... African music plays second fiddle to Western music in the country's school music education programme.'

Music in mission-based schooling

European settlement at the Cape of Good Hope (or Cape Colony as it was known) began in 1652 when the Dutch East India Company established Cape Town as a 'refreshment' station on the sea route to the Far East. From 1679 the Cape was a Dutch colony. It was then occupied by the British from 1795 until 1803, before becoming part of the short-lived Batavian Republic (1803–6). The Cape Colony was re-occupied by the British in 1806 and in 1820 some 5,000 British settlers arrived. From about this time, groups of Boers, dissatisfied with British rule, migrated north across the Orange River on what became known as the 'Great Trek' (Ferguson and Immelman 1961: 7–8).

Aside from Dutch and British settlers, the other inhabitants of Cape Colony were the indigenous San (Khoikhoi) people. To the north, Transvaal became an independent Boer Republic (1852–99) and adopted Dutch as its language. Following the two Anglo-Boer wars, the Transvaal finally became a British colony in 1907 and, in 1910, Transvaal and the other self-governing colonies of the Cape, Natal and Orange Free State became provinces of the Union of South Africa (see Figure 18.1); note that the British High Commission Territories of Basutoland (now Lesotho), Bechuanaland (now Botswana) and Swaziland were excluded from the Union of South Africa. English and Dutch (replaced later by Afrikaans) became the dual official languages in South Africa.

Education during the early days of Dutch colonization was based almost solely on the need for literacy in order to read the Bible. The Dutch Reformed Church established schools where new communities developed and private farm schools were frequently set up to cater for children in rural areas. With the coming of British rule, Lord Charles Somerset, Governor of Cape Colony from 1814 to 1826, established a system of free and secular education along the lines of the English elementary school system. Typically, local communities established their own schools that were subsidized and inspected by education authorities, who also prescribed the school curriculum (with English as the language of instruction). Education authorities also certificated teachers, many of whom were recruited from Scotland. When Transvaal came under British rule the Dutch Reformed Church set up its own system of Christian national schools in which Dutch as well as English were the languages of instruction. This set the scene for the bilingual system of education in English and Afrikaans, which was adopted at the provincial level after the union (Dean, Hartmann and Katzen 1983: 23–4). Theoretically, with elementary education being free and secular, schooling was also available to the indigenous people

Figure 18.1 Provinces of the Union of South Africa, 1910 (Source: Grade 11 Resources, 'Boer War – South Africa 1899' at http://dt-ss.tripod.com/eleven-resources.html; adapted by the authors).

– the Khoikhoi in the south and the Xhosa people on the east coast. However, with a colour bar effectively in operation, schools operated by missionary organizations repre- sented the only avenue available for elementary education to non-European children.

The majority of missions established in South Africa during the nineteenth century were of either Anglican or nonconformist Protestant foundations.[1] Particularly at missions established by nonconformist Protestant denominations – Methodist (Wesleyan), Baptist, Presbyterian and Congregational – the tonic sol-fa method and notation were almost universally adopted as the means of promoting congregational singing. At mission schools of all denominations, music was not only employed as a means of inculcating moral and religious principles through the singing of hymns and other liturgical music, but was also formally taught as one of the 'subjects of instruction', as was frequently the case in colonial schools throughout the British Empire.

One of the first recorded instances of tonic sol-fa being introduced to mission schools was by an English dentist, Thomas Daines (1829–1880), at King William's Town (Henning 1979a: 307). Before leaving England, Daines had become acquainted with tonic sol-fa, and, when appointed to Grey's Hospital in King William's Town about 1860, offered classes in sight singing and part singing presumably to the European community. Two years later, in 1862, Daines was teaching tonic sol-fa to indigenous pupils at St Matthew's Mission School and to Bantu[2] choirs in King William's Town (ibid.).

Somewhat later, tonic sol-fa was widely used at mission stations in Basutoland, in Kaffraria[3] and around Port Elizabeth in the south (*Tonic Sol-fa Reporter* 1883: 145). One of the most prominent missions in educational work in Cape Colony was the Lovedale Missionary Institution, at which tonic sol-fa was widely promoted. Lovedale Mission was founded in the 1820s by the Glasgow Missionary Society near the inland town of Alice, west-north-west of East London in what is now known as Eastern Cape Province (Shepherd 1941). Aside from religious activity, the mission's principal objective was the education of the indigenous community – the Xhosa people. A school for boys was established as the Lovedale Institution in 1841, which later provided higher education for young Xhosa men, many of whom graduated as teachers (Gandhi 1905). An important means of supporting the education of local Xhosa people – and, indeed, of indigenous South Africans generally – was the establishment at Lovedale of a printing press, which, from 1823, produced evangelical and educational publications. The key figure at the Lovedale Institution during its heyday was Reverend Dr James Stewart (1831–1905), who joined Lovedale in 1867 and became its principal in 1870. The printing press at Lovedale enabled the production of music in tonic sol-fa notation and this led to the publication of music composed by indigenous South Africans including Reverend John Knox Bokwe (1855–1922) and Enoch Sontonga (c. 1873–1905), both of whom were students at Lovedale. Akrofi (2006: 5) notes that the first generation of black South African composers of choral music acquired their musical education through missionary institutions such as Lovedale, where they 'were taught the rudiments of music via Tonic Sol-fa' (Hansen 1968: 3).

Although Lovedale Training Institution was a major centre for tonic sol-fa teaching, there were many other missions, especially in the east of Cape Province in urban areas such as King William's Town, Fort Beaufort and Grahamstown, where the method was utilized not only in mission schools but also in the training of indigenous teachers. In urban areas, where the influence of missions was less apparent, music taught principally through tonic sol-fa also assumed an important role in public and other government-supported schools.

Music in government schooling

Provision of funding for free and secular public school education by the colonial government of Cape Colony had been in place since Lord Somerset's initiatives of the 1820s. Government free schools (also known as English free schools) were generally based on Lancaster's monitorial system and the medium of instruction was English. Although free schools were originally intended to be multi-racial, they essentially catered for children of European background, whereas mission-based schools catered almost exclusively for indigenous children (South African History Online 1999–2008).

In the early years, music in government schools was an optional subject, and its introduction to the school curriculum was entirely dependent on the initiative of individual teachers who had existing knowledge and skills in music and who recognized its educational value. One of the pioneer school music teachers in South Africa was Christopher Birkett, who came to Cape Colony about 1854. Birkett trained at the Westminster Training College with another key figure, Henry Nixon, during 1853–4 (*School Music Review* 1894: 74; hereinafter referred to as *Sch Mus Rev*). Although originally trained in Hullah's method at Westminster, both learned tonic sol-fa informally prior to emigrating (*Musical Herald* 1894: 263; hereinafter referred to as *Mus Her*). In South Africa, Birkett introduced tonic sol-fa to native weekday schools and to Sunday school choirs in Grahamstown, Cradock and Healdtown (Malan 1979a: 130). Other urban school teachers using tonic sol-fa during the early 1860s included John Wedderburn and George Kidd (Henning 1979b: 104).

Another pioneer was James H. Ashley (1824–98), who introduced tonic sol-fa to Cape Town during the 1860s (*Mus Her* 1894: 263). After some effort, Ashley and Henry Nixon were successful in having tonic sol-fa adopted for use in government schools. About 1882, the then Superintendent General of Education, Dr (later Sir) Langham Dale, introduced music to the syllabus of subjects for the public school teacher's certificate and appointed Nixon as Inspector of Music in Training Colleges and Schools for the Cape Colony (*Sch Mus Rev* 1894: 74; *Mus Her* 1894: 263). Dale was so impressed by Nixon's advocacy of tonic sol-fa that the system was put on an equal footing with staff notation for use in public schools (*Mus Her* 1894: 263).

Dale's successor as Superintendent General of Education in 1891 was Dr (later Sir) Thomas Muir, reportedly 'himself a lover of music' (*Sch Mus Rev* 1894: 74). Muir commissioned Nixon to report on the state of music in Cape schools and, as a result, two instructors – Arthur Lee and James Rodger – were appointed to teach tonic sol-fa at the male and female teacher training colleges in Cape Town (ibid.). All trainees were examined by Nixon and required to pass a sight singing test. For over twenty years, Nixon as inspector of school music appears to have propagated tonic sol-fa at every opportunity, including a period that he devoted to teaching singing to the Hottentot (Khoikhoi) people (ibid.).

By 1895 Arthur Lee, also an ardent tonic sol-fa advocate, had established a choir of 600 children from government schools in the Cape Town area. Examinations of the Tonic Sol-fa College appear to have been widely promoted in Cape Town schools as completion of the Junior Certificate examination was a prerequisite for choir membership (*Sch Mus Rev* 1895: 116). The following year, the choir numbers increased to 700 (*Sch Mus Rev* 1896: 137). The concert included an unrehearsed programme of hand-sign singing and sight reading introduced by Thomas Muir, who forthrightly encouraged the adoption of tonic sol-fa in schools. In other parts of Cape Colony – for example Uitenhage, near Port Elizabeth in the east – tonic sol-fa had been introduced to the indigenous population and, partly because of this and other prejudices, the method was apparently not as popular with the European community (*Mus Her* 1896: 55–6).

By 1897 Cape Colony had, for the purposes of school music at least, been divided into two 'circuits' that were inspected respectively by Frederick Farrington (eastern districts) and Arthur Lee (western districts), both of whom were tonic sol-fa advocates. Frederick Farrington (1869–1931) immigrated to South Africa in 1893 and the following year was appointed as Inspector of Music for the Cape Colony. With the division of the music inspectorate into two 'circuits', Farrington was based in the Port Elizabeth–Uitenhage area, and within a year of his arrival over 3,500 children were being taught singing by tonic sol-fa. Also in 1898, the first examinations of the Tonic Sol-fa College were held in Port Elizabeth (Henning 1979c: 56). Farrington also introduced school choir competitions, which survived in Port Elizabeth until 1912–13 (Malan 1979b: 98).

Arthur Lee was trained as a teacher at Westminster Training College and taught for a brief period in London before emigrating to South Africa (*Mus Her* 1898: 269). He was employed as a teacher in a government school in Cape Town before being appointed as Instructor and Inspector of Singing for the Western Province. After three years of working in the Cape Town area, Lee extended his promotion of singing by tonic sol-fa to the whole province, undertaking extensive tours to inspect rural farm schools and mission schools as well as schools in urban centres. Like Farrington, Lee actively promoted the certificate examinations of the Tonic Sol-fa College, particularly the School Teacher's Music Certificate (*Mus Her* 1914: 206).

Farrington reported that 'the powers of the natives are astonishing' and also remarked on 'the quickness of the native children' in mission schools, where 'it is not uncommon to find all the available blackboard space covered with hymns and anthems' (*Sch Mus Rev*, 1898: 23–4, 33). Both music inspectors reported on the examinations for Tonic Sol-fa

College; for the year 1899, 736 certificates were awarded in the eastern districts and 2,179 in western districts (*Sch Mus Rev*, 1899: 63–4, 102).

One of the traditions in school music established at Cape Town in 1897 was the Annual School Choir Competition (for the Challenge Shield), which was organized under the auspices of Thomas Muir as Inspector-General of Education (*Sch Mus Rev*, 1898: 118–19). Although open to all schools, those competing appear initially to have been confined to 'superior' European schools such as the Normal College School, Good Hope Seminary, Trinity Public School and Rondebosch Girls' High School. Similar school choir competitions were established elsewhere in Cape Colony, including the Municipal Challenge Shield at Port Elizabeth. However, at the 1898 Port Elizabeth choir competition there were entrants from 'mixed' schools, with mention being made in the *School Music Review* of the 'typical' indigenous teacher who conducts his choir 'never looking harassed, but smilingly happy' and who has frequently composed his own songs, both music and words (*Sch Mus Rev*, 1899: 111). By 1900 a choir of indigenous children from a mission school achieved second place in the Cape Town school choir competition (*Mus Her* 1901: 15).

Tonic sol-fa had a major impact not only on music in public schools in urban areas but also in mission schools, teacher training institutions and local communities. It had enabled a high degree of musical literacy among indigenous people and, although it could be claimed that tonic sol-fa was one of the 'instruments of cultural colonization', it nevertheless contributed to the enrichment of people's lives during the nineteenth century and indeed laid a strong foundation for the later development of a fine African choral music tradition.

By the close of the nineteenth century, provision for elementary education by the colonial government was being implemented through a system of direct support of or subsidies to various types of school. The type of school was largely determined by geographic location of the pupils – government town schools catered predominantly for European children and farm schools in rural areas for the children of the European settlers, whereas school education for the indigenous population continued to be provided almost exclusively by missionary societies. Indeed, even as late as the 1920s, the number of government schools for indigenous children was miniscule in comparison with mission schools. A case in point was in Cape Province in 1926, where there was only one government school providing education for indigenous children, whereas there were 1,625 mission schools (Horrell 1963, cited in Hlatshwayo 2000: 36). In contrast with government policy in the mid-twentieth century, the British colonial authorities seem to have avoided any deliberate segregation of the schools according to race. For example, in Natal, Lieutenant-Governor Sir G. Wolseley openly expressed the view in 1875 that schools should be open equally to children of both European and non-European background (Behr and Macmillan 1971: 116). Nevertheless, particularly in larger centres, the establishment of fee-charging (although government-subsidized) private schools effectively precluded non-European pupils from attending.

Compulsory primary education was introduced to Cape Colony in 1905 by the then Superintendent of Education Sir Thomas Muir (ibid.: 116). In Transvaal and Orange Free State – both of which were most affected by the 1899–1902 Anglo-Boer War – compulsory primary education was introduced in 1907 and 1895 respectively (ibid.: 124, 136). Natal became a self-governing colony in 1893 but it was not until 1910 that primary schooling became compulsory, although it was still not free, as parents were required to pay school fees (ibid.: 134). The compulsory nature of primary schooling at this time appears to have applied principally if not exclusively to the European population.

Nevertheless, in rural areas where there was particularly strong missionary influence, schooling at mission stations was effectively compulsory, particularly for boys. In other situations where missionary influence was weaker compulsory attendance was impossible to achieve (Pells 1938: 79). Because of the concentration of racially dominant populations in particular areas, schools tended to cater respectively for European, coloured (mixed race or Indian) and black (indigenous) children. It was not until well after the coming together of the South African colonies into the Union of South Africa in 1910 that responsibility for indigenous education became increasingly centralized and separated from the European school system. With the introduction by the Afrikaans National Party of the apartheid or 'own affairs' policy of segregated education in 1948, the education of the indigenous population came under the control of a single education department, the Department of Native Affairs, through the Bantu Education Act of 1953.

The Afrikaans National Party, while centralizing its control of education and mandating the use of Afrikaans for key subjects of the curriculum, decentralized its management to racially discrete systems of school administration. Education for the black and coloured (including Indian) communities was removed from provincial governments to the central government and separate school systems were imposed on blacks in 1953, coloureds in 1963 and Indians in 1965. The establishment of the Department of National Education (DNE) in 1984 to handle 'general education affairs' continued the trend towards centralizing school education (Hauptfleisch 1997: 195).

Between 1948 and 1994 (the period of apartheid), school music education became increasingly fragmented along racial and ethnic lines for white, coloured and black South Africans. Major challenges that faced non-European schools were that music syllabi and teaching approaches were predominantly Western in their orientation and therefore irrelevant to a large proportion of non-white pupils. Indeed, Oehrle (1990: 9) described the situation as follows: 'The total Western bias of music education being propagated at the southern-most tip of Africa is disturbing ...' In addition, many non-white students received little or no class music tuition for a variety of reasons – a lack of a timetable allocation for classroom music, a lack of trained music teachers, a lack of facilities including musical instruments and teaching materials, a lack of career opportunities for music teachers and the low status accorded to class music in schools.

Music education in the 'new' South Africa

After the first democratic election in 1994, the chief policy framework for education – the Reconstruction and Development Programme (RDP) – of the African National Congress (ANC)-led Government of National Unity was put into effect. The statement in Paragraph 3.4.8 of the RDP (ANC 1994: 71) was especially significant for music education, stating that 'Arts education should be an integral part of the national school curricula at primary, secondary and tertiary level, as well as in non-formal education. Urgent attention must be given to the creation of relevant arts curricula, teacher training, and provision of facilities for the arts within all schools' (quoted in Hauptfleisch 1997: 201).

Also during 1994, the Minister of Arts, Culture, Science and Technology appointed an Arts and Culture Task Group (ACTAG) to draw up a new Arts and Culture programme consistent with the new South African constitution. Among ACTAG's (1995) proposals were that arts education (including music) should start from pre-school, musics from southern Africa, as well as Europe, Asia and the Americas should be included in the curriculum, and music curricula must accommodate local or regional resources, needs and interests (Hauptfleisch 1997).

The new education system instituted after the fall of the apartheid system was deliberately outcomes-based, having been designed to 'overcome the curricular divisions of the past' (Department of Basic Education [DBE] 2011a: 2). The 1996 National Curriculum Framework (NCF) saw the integration of music and other subjects into an 'Arts and Culture Learning Area'. An attempt was also made to incorporate indigenous knowledge systems into the Arts and Culture Learning Area, fostering the idea that the classroom should be an extension of the community and should therefore reflect the *ubuntu* principle (Herbst, de Wet and Rijsdijk 2005: 263). However, teachers in the immediate post-apartheid decade were generally totally unprepared for implementing the Arts and Culture curriculum (Smit 2007). In addition, a number of historical factors were identified by Herbst, de Wet and Rijsdijk (2005: 264) as being problematic for school music in South Africa: the influence of colonialism generally, the assumption that music education was only introduced to Africa with the arrival of Europeans, the preference given to Western musical forms and acquiring written music literacy to the detriment of oral literacy, and the influence of racial segregation.

Furthermore, the Department of Education's rationalization programme severely reduced the number of teacher training colleges in the country. Many colleges were closed, while others were amalgamated with universities. The remaining colleges usually had only one or two music education lecturers who were unrealistically expected to prepare teacher education students to implement the syllabi for Arts and Culture in schools. In addition, there were no universities in South Africa at the time that specifically trained teaching specialists in the Arts and Culture area.

Interestingly, one of the legacies of the past that was acknowledged at this time was continued use of tonic sol-fa teaching and notation in some choral music settings

– indigenous community churches, choral festivals and schools.[4] Indeed, when the National Anthem of the new Republic of South Africa was officially published in October 1997, it included tonic sol-fa notation as well as staff notation (see Figure 18.2).

Curriculum reviews followed in 2002 and again in 2009, but the curriculum that guided music and arts education implementation in South African schools during the latter half of the 2000s was the Revised National Curriculum Statement (RNCS) Grades R[eception]–9 Arts and Culture (Department of Education 2005). The RNCS listed a total of ten arts to be covered – dance, drama, music, visual arts, craft, design, media and communication, arts management, arts technology and heritage. Music was therefore recognized as only one of several arts disciplines. Because this curriculum was formulated at the level of learning areas only, specific outcomes for music and other art forms were not stipulated. Nevertheless, as Emberly and Davidson (2011: 76) point out, 'The goals of the RNCS … shift the balance toward an integrative system that celebrates and encourages the study of music in local, national and global contexts.' These authors further point out that Kwami, Akrofi and Adams (2003: 269) have argued for more of an inter-cultural approach to the music curriculum that would enable musical pluralism

NATIONAL ANTHEM of SOUTH AFRICA

Figure 18.2 An example of dual staff and tonic sol-fa notation: '*Nkosi Sikelel' iAfrika*' ('God Bless South Africa'), melody by Enoch Sontonga. (Source: Republic of South Africa, 1997. Government Gazette, No. 18341 of 1997, p. 3. Pretoria: Government Printer.)

and diversity. Taking the argument even further, Emberly and Davidson (2011: 77) make the observation that 'people [in South Africa] still celebrate multiculturalism over a nationalistic agenda of a homogenized South African Identity'. They argue for a more homogenous South African identity rather than mere multiculturalism, which they – and others – see as the ultimate goal for education in the new South Africa.

In 2011–12, the 2005 curriculum was replaced by the National Curriculum Statement for Grades R–12 that specified the subjects of Basic Education as Home Language, First Additional Language, Mathematics and Life Skills (referred to in the advanced phases as Life Orientation). The latter subject at the Foundation Phase consisted of four study areas, one of which was Creative Arts, that in turn consisted of Performing Arts (Music, Dance and Drama) and Visual Arts. Creative Arts was allocated one hour per week for Grades R–2, two hours for Grades 3–9 and four hours in Grades 10–12, where individual arts subjects – including Music – were available as a Group B (i.e. elective) subject and allocated four hours per week for study (DBE 2011a, 2011b, 2011c, 2011d). The content included in these curriculum statements specified musical outcomes ranging from simple and general in the Foundation Phase (creative games and the skills of improvisation and interpretation) to complex and more specific (music performance and improvisation/arranging, music literacy, and general music knowledge and analysis) in the Further Education and Training Phase (Grades 10–12).

Many of the problems previously identified are likely to persist for some time – not least of which is a shortage of teachers who are both competent and confident to deliver music teaching, especially at the Foundation and Intermediate phases. However, an analysis of the content of the National Curriculum Statement Grades R–12 indicates that indigenous African music is far better represented than hitherto. For example, at the Intermediate Phase, there is reference to cultural dance, African folktale, African songs and cultural ritual or ceremony, with an even greater focus on indigenous and multicultural music at the Senior Phase. However, although students at Further Education and Training Phase (Grades 10–12) have three options – the Western Arts Music stream, the Jazz stream (at Grade 12 there is a concentration on African jazz) and the Indigenous African Music stream – they are presently required to choose only one of these streams, which, as Antoinette Hoek (2015) has pointed out, could be seen as a perpetuation of an essentially 'apartheid' approach rather than adoption of a culturally pluralistic approach. An additional problem, in common with National Curriculum Statements from other countries, is the overcrowding of the curriculum, which in South Africa has meant that music is subsumed within the Creative Arts area, which, in turn, is subsumed within Life Skills until it emerges as a subject in its own right at the Further Education and Training Phase.

Despite the obvious reforms introduced through the National Curriculum, music may still not be assured of universal implementation within the South African school system. A report by the Nelson Mandela Foundation in 2005 noted that 'the educational needs of children in rural areas of South Africa are still not being met' (Samuel 2005, quoted in Emberly and Davidson 2011: 75).

Accordingly, this chapter concludes with the assertion that music education under colonial rule achieved a degree of both recognition and implementation in European and to a lesser extent in indigenous schools, albeit with a high degree of cultural imposition through missionary influence of European music. Music education in indigenous schools declined during the latter half of the twentieth century under the apartheid regime, and it is only with the socio-political reforms of the post-apartheid government from 1994 that something of a renaissance in music education has begun, with a movement towards a broader multicultural basis. Nevertheless, as Emberly and Davidson (2011) point out, education – including an education in music – has yet to reflect a truly homogenized South African cultural identity.

Acknowledgement

I am indebted to Antoinette Hoek for reviewing this chapter, specifically in relation to recent curriculum developments in the South African National Curriculum.

Reflective questions

1 As we have seen, Mgoma (1990), Oehrle (1990), Akrofi (1998) and others have been critical of the promotion of European music by missionaries in South Africa as representing a form of cultural imperialism. If this is the case, what reasons might explain the enormous popularity among indigenous choirs even today of European choral repertoire such as Handel's *The Messiah*, Mendelssohn's *Elijah*, etc.? Are there parallels in any other former colonial countries, and, if so, do similar reasons explain them?

2 Given the strong missionary emphasis during the nineteenth and early twentieth centuries on providing indigenous communities with music education and on providing teacher training, music appears not to have been actively promoted in black South African schools during the apartheid era. What reasons might explain this situation?

3 Given that so many members of the indigenous community in present-day South Africa are familiar with tonic sol-fa and read music using its notation, what reasons might explain the method not being given any measure of recognition in the 2012 *National Curriculum Statement Grades R–12*?

4 To what extent has music education in its various forms – informal, non-formal and formal – since colonial intervention influenced the course of socio-political development of South Africa? Are there parallels in any other former colonial countries?

Notes

1. Roman Catholic missions in Africa flourished in the French, Italian and Portuguese colonies in east, central and west Africa, but not in Dutch, Boer and British colonies in southern Africa.
2. 'Bantu' was a widely used generic term referring to the indigenous peoples of South Africa and more particularly to their languages.
3. Kaffraria was the area immediately to the north of the Great Fish River on the east coast, which incorporated King William's Town and East London and northwards, including the area known as Transkei to the border of Natal. Kaffraria was annexed to Cape Colony in 1865.
4. See R. S. Stevens (2005), 'Tonic sol-fa in contemporary choral music practice: a South African case study' in P. de Vries (ed.), *Proceedings of the XXVIIth Annual Conference of the Australian Association for Research in Music Education*, Sydney: AARME, pp. 157–67.

References

African National Congress (1994), *Reconstruction and Development Programme*, Johannesburg: Umanyano.

Akrofi, E. A. (1998), 'Traditional African Music Education in Ghana and South Africa', *Legon Journal of the Humanities* 11, 39–47.

Akrofi, E. A. (2006), 'Composition in Tonic Sol-fa: An Exogenous Musical Practice in the Eastern Cape Province of South Africa', unpublished paper.

Behr, A. L. and R. G. Macmillan (1971), *Education in South Africa* (2nd edn), Pretoria: J. L. van Schaik.

Campbell, P. S. (2008), *Musician and Teacher: An Orientation to Music Education*, New York: W. W. Norton & Co.

Dean, E., P. Hartman and M. Katzen (1983), *History in Black and White: An Analysis of South Africa Schools History Textbooks*, Paris: UNESCO.

Department of Basic Education, Republic of South Africa (2011a), *Curriculum and Assessment Policy Statement Grades R–3: Life Skills*, Pretoria: Department of Basic Education.

Department of Basic Education, Republic of South Africa (2011b), *Curriculum and Assessment Policy Statement Grades 4–6: Life Skills*, Pretoria: Department of Basic Education.

Department of Basic Education, Republic of South Africa (2011c), *Curriculum and Assessment Policy Statement Grades 7–9: Life Skills*, Pretoria: Department of Basic Education.

Department of Basic Education, Republic of South Africa (2011d), *Curriculum and Assessment Policy Statement Grades 10–12: Music*, Pretoria: Department of Basic Education.

Department of Education, South Africa (1996), *National Curriculum Framework*, Pretoria: Department of Education.

Department of Education, South Africa (2005), *Revised National Curriculum Statement Grades R–9 Arts and Culture*, Pretoria: Department of Education.

Emberly, A. and J. Davidson (2011), 'From the Kraal to the Classroom: Shifting Musical Arts Practices from the Community to the School with Special Reference to Learning *tshigombela* in Limpopo, South Africa', *International Journal of Music Education* 29 (3): 265–82.

Ferguson, W. T. and R. F. M. Immelman (1961), *Sir John Herschel and Education at the Cape, 1843–1840*, Cape Town: Oxford University Press.

Gandhi, M. K. (1905), 'Education among the Kaffirs', *Indian Opinion* (30 December 1905), in *Complete Works of Mahatma Gandhi, Vol. 5*, http://mkgandhi.org/vol5/ ch045.htm (accessed 13 February 2009).

Hansen, D. (1968), 'The life and work of Benjamin Tyamzashe: a contemporary Xhosa composer', Occasional Paper No. 11, Grahamstown: Institute of Social and Economic Research, Rhodes University.

Hauptfleisch, S. (1997), 'Transforming South African music education: a systems view'
    (unpublished DMus thesis, University of Pretoria).
Henning, C. G. (1979a), 'Daines, Thomas' in J. P. Malan (ed.), *South African Music Encyclopedia,*
    vol. I, Cape Town: Oxford University Press.
Henning, C. G. (1979b), 'Graaff Reinet' in J. P. Malan (ed.), *South African Music Encyclopedia, vol.*
    II, Cape Town: Oxford University Press.
Henning, C. G. (1979c), 'Farrington, Frederick' in J. P. Malan (ed.), *South African Music*
    Encyclopedia, vol. II, Cape Town: Oxford University Press.
Herbst, A., de Wet, J. and S. Rijsdijk (2005), 'A Survey of Music Education in the Primary Schools
    of South Africa's Cape Peninsula', *Journal of Research in Music Education* 53 (3): 260–83.
Hlatshwayo, S. A. (2000), *Education and Independence: Education in South Africa, 1658–1988,*
    Westport, CT: Greenwood Press.
Hoek, A. (2015), Personal communication (21 February 2015).
Kruger, J. (1999), 'Singing Psalms with Owls: A Venda 20th Century Musical History', *African*
    Music 7 (4): 122–46.
Kwami, R. M., E. A. Akrofi and S. Adams (2003), 'Integrating Musical Arts Cultures' in A. Herbst,
    M. Nzewi and K. Agawu (eds), *Musical Arts in Africa,* Pretoria: Unisa Press, pp. 261–78.
Malan, J. P. (1979a), 'Grahamstown' in J. P. Malan (ed.), *South African Music Encyclopedia, vol. II,*
    Cape Town: Oxford University Press.
Malan, J. P. (1979b), 'Port Elizabeth, Music in (1820–1920)' in J. P. Malan (ed.), *South African*
    Music Encyclopedia, vol. IV, Cape Town: Oxford University Press.
Mngoma, K. (1990), 'The Teaching of Music in South Africa', *South African Journal of Musicology*
    10: 121–6.
Musical Herald (1892–1914), London: John Curwen & Sons.
Oehrle, E. (1990). 'Music Education in South Africa', *The Quarterly* 1 (4): 5–9.
Pells, E. G. (1938), *European, Coloured, and Native Education in South Africa, 1652–1938,* New
    York: AMS Press.
Samuel, J. (ed.) (2005), *Emerging Voices: A Report of Education in South African Rural*
    Communities, Human Sciences Research Council, Nelson Mandela Foundation; Educational
    Policy Corporation, Cape Town: HSRC Press.
School Music Review (1892–9), London: Novello & Co. Ltd.
Shepherd, R. H. W. (1941), *Lovedale, South Africa: The Story of a Century, 1841–1941,* Lovedale,
    Cape Province, South Africa: Lovedale Press.
Smit, M. (2007), 'Facilitating the Formation of Personal and Professional Identities of Arts
    and Culture Educators' in E. Akrofi, M. Smit and S-M. Thorsen (eds), *Music and Identity:*
    Transformation and Negotiation, Stellenbosch: African Sun Media, pp. 215–31.
South African History Online (1999–2008), 'The Amersfoort legacy: a history of education in
    South Africa' (Timeline 1800–1899), www.sahistory.org.za/class- room/education-350years/
    timeline1800s.html (accessed 19 February 2009).
Thorsén, S.-M. (1997), 'Music Education in South Africa – Striving for Unity and Diversity'
    [Swedish], *Schwedische Zeitschrift für Musikforschung* [*Swedish Journal for Musicology*]
    79 (1): 91–109, available in English at www.hsm.gu.se/digitalAssets/848/848801_Music_Educ_
    in_South_Africa_.pdf (accessed 11 September 2008).
Tonic Sol-fa Reporter (1883–91), London: John Curwen & Sons.

Conclusion

Gordon Cox and Robin Stevens

All of the essays in this volume have focused upon tracing the historical roots of music in compulsory schooling. In this Conclusion we attempt to draw together the threads of the intertwined areas of historical and political contexts, curriculum aims and content, teaching methods, training of teachers, experience of pupils, and reflections on the present state of music education in the light of past developments. We will briefly summarize common issues, referring in parentheses to specific countries (the subjects of foregoing chapters) whose history provides some mention of these matters. We will also draw upon some recent contributions to the literature that will serve to corroborate and extend the discussion.

Historical and political contexts

What is striking in the various accounts is the link between the state and compulsory mass schooling in the nineteenth century, which developed 'to include virtually all children, employing a standardized curriculum' (Ramirez and Boli, 1994: 10) and which frequently included music. In some instances these nation-states created empires with an educational dimension. As far as the teaching of music is concerned, it will have become apparent that influences of political ideologies, colonialism and imperialism have been profound, whether talking about authoritarian rule, or, stretching into the twentieth and twenty-first centuries, the subsequent reactions of colonized, occupied or defeated countries.

According to Lucy Green (2011), musical cultural imperialism or colonialism took place through the export of Western classical music as a status symbol and cultural icon, 'and along with this went the educational systems that were associated with this music' (ibid.: 20). In many countries what was threatened was the survival of a rich and highly diverse traditional or classical indigenous music. Such a process is illustrated by Kim's (2014a) exploration of imperialist control of music education during the Japanese colonial rule of Korea between 1910 and 1945. She states her uncompromising view of colonialism: 'Colonialism is the control or governing influence of a nation over a dependent country, territory or people. Fundamentally colonialism involves the economic exploitation of occupied territories' (ibid.: 27). Kim's (2014b) elderly informants testified that as school pupils they had sung songs praising the Japanese Emperor and Japan. They also performed Japanese military songs on the formal ceremonies when Korean adult males were drafted for compulsory military service to support the Japanese war effort. Decades later, some of her respondents still identified emotionally with Imperial Japan, even though they had been treated as second-class citizens. For Kim, there were no pedagogic benefits for music education through the colonial learning process – 'instead school children's musical and cultural identity were irrevocably distorted' (ibid.: 279).

On the other hand, Patricia Shehan Campbell (2004) concedes that school music programmes in North America, Europe, Australia and New Zealand, and in parts of Asia and Latin America, successfully developed Western-oriented musical skills and understandings through an effective pedagogy. However, she insists that this is but one model, 'and a colonial one', that fixes European music (and its staff notation) and its pedagogical processes highest in 'a hierarchy atop the musical expressions and instructional approaches of so many other rich traditions' (ibid.: xvi).

The implication is that music educators would do well to consider whether nineteenth- and twentieth-century European systems travel well in time and place, and what a twenty-first-century system actually means in practice (Fautley and Murphy 2015). One solution offered in the Canadian context by Juliet Hess (2015) calls for a 'decolonizing music education' and focuses upon 'a Comparative Music Model', which would refuse to recognize the 'exalted' status of Western music. It would consequently emphasize the interconnectedness between different musics and the contexts of musics. This, according to Hess, would bring the intersections of race, class, gender, dis/ability and nation to the forefront and focus on the way these categories related with each other.

Curriculum aims and content

It is hardly surprising considering the relationship between mass schooling and the nation-state that patriotic and nationalist sentiments have permeated many of the aims and much of the content of school music education. It was the struggle for political independence and the defence of national interests that particularly shaped what went on in schools. In music lessons school songs were frequently used to revive patriotic feeling (Argentina, Britain, France, Norway), to forge new national identities (Germany [Prussia], Israel), to act in concert with language revival movements (Ireland, Israel, Kosovo, Lithuania), to elevate national culture (Brazil) and inspire resistance (China, Kosovo, Lithuania).

The distinction between nationalism and internationalism is explored by Estelle Jorgensen (2013) in an editorial for *Philosophy of Music Education Review*. She helpfully clarifies the dilemma faced between those music educators who are increasingly aware of music cultures beyond particular societies and consequently want to engage with them in their teaching, and others who wish to foster nationalism and localism in the service of the nation-state by promoting a monoculture that epitomizes a unified culture. It is an age-old struggle, particularly acute in recent decades in the oppositions between globalism and localism, internationalism and nationalism, and cultural monism and multiculturalism.

In relation to pedagogy, Hebert and Kertz-Welzel (2012: 175) argue that to teach patriotic loyalty is 'an ethically questionable practice' because it denigrates music to a function as an ideological tool in educational settings. Moreover, it largely neglects the musical diversity of cultural minorities residing in most nations. In this respect they foster the hope that globalization and internationalism might eventually replace nationalism. They do, however, add a caveat that concerns some small nations, well represented in this collection, which have recently regained their democracy and are still recovering their cultural identity, largely through music. In this regard it is significant that for John Gray (2015: 31), a noted political philosopher, 'nationalism is an expression of enduring human needs for identity and recognition which shows no signs of fading away'.

From reading some of the chapters it is clear that there was no shortage of high-minded justifications for music in the curriculum. In the nineteenth century, religious motives predominated (Lithuania, Norway, USA). Later came the notion of music as a humanizing and civilizing force (Australia, Brazil, Britain), out of which developed the belief that music could help mould the future citizen (Israel, USA). Probably one of the most influential justifications was that music in schools had an effect on the formation of mind and personality (Germany), which connects with the notion that music is a powerful agent of moral culture (Britain), which could help to enhance social harmony (Brazil, China).

A fundamental problem with these justifications is that music is rarely incorporated into the curriculum for its own sake. If music merely exists as a means to an end, its fate is decided not on its own merits, but on that associated with other areas of learning, such as moral education. This makes for vulnerability. Geoffrey Baker (2014) expands on this point by reviewing many of the justifications for music education, starting with the Platonic idea of music as a moral influence, in which the middle classes sought to elevate the working classes while reproducing their own values. Behind this notion lay the assertion that music had the power to change society. However, it could be argued that for all its focus on the betterment of the poor, the drive for music education and expanded access to high culture was fundamentally conservative.

Such utilitarian arguments, Baker asserts, have been critiqued as 'scientifically weak, philosophically problematic and politically risky' (ibid.: 175). Fautley and Murphy (2015) agree. They point out that today, in this era of global austerity in the developed world, music educators are having to argue their case and 'fight their corner' by responding to questions like 'What are the purposes of music education?' But well-meaning responses, which point to the transferability of learning music to improvements in mathematics, literacy and social skills, are often based upon insecure foundations. Nevertheless, as Jorgensen (2008) conjectures, once public funds are involved, there is a tension between musicians (and music educators) who believe in the value of music for music's sake and those responsible for the disbursement of funds, who may require other arguments to justify the subject. Bowman (2012: 36) takes up this theme, noting that the significance of music's contribution to general education has become less and less apparent. His conclusion is that negative perceptions of music education and a reluctance to support it often stem from the failures of music educators to 'change with the changing time'. As a result, 'music education must be as concerned with changing itself as it is with winning the support of others' (ibid.: 37).

There is an unresolved tension here that persists throughout the later history of music education. Historically, it appears that those pioneers who introduced music into the curriculum subscribed to a common view that music related to the shared values of nation and community building. Today, that link is at risk.

Teaching methods

When it comes to considering the methods employed in teaching school music in the early days, it is remarkable that almost universally the focus was upon teaching the skill of singing at sight. Most of this teaching was based on solmization – the application of sol-fa syllables as a mnemonic or memory aid for reading pitch. This teaching technique goes back, in Western culture at least, to Guido d'Arezzo in the eleventh century. The broad outlines of early methods shared a striking unanimity. However, this apparent amity fractured when it came to deciding which rival system was best. The debate over the relative merits of the fixed-doh system, where 'doh' is always 'C' (Argentina, France, Lithuania, Spain), and the movable-doh system, where 'doh' is always the keynote (Australia, Britain, Canada, South Africa), has been well rehearsed in this book. It is clear that in some cases inappropriate adaptations were made, particularly of the fixed–doh method, with disastrous results (Australia, Britain, Ireland). Another significant method that is represented was cipher or numeral notation based upon the ideas of Jean-Jacques Rousseau (China, France, Norway, Prussia [Germany]).

Some later music education 'methods' that took a hold in the countries under consideration included those of Carl Orff (Argentina, Australia, Britain, Canada, Cuba, Kosovo, Lithuania, Spain, Turkey), Zoltan Kodály (Australia, Britain, Canada, Cuba, Kosovo, Lithuania, Turkey) and Émile Jaques-Dalcroze (Argentina, Australia, Cuba, Israel, Lithuania, Spain, Turkey). In connection with Orff, Kertz-Welzel (2015) considers *Orff Schulwerk* a successful example of borrowing and adapting an educational approach. Intended by Orff to be international, clearly, many countries have adopted and adapted it effectively, and have developed their own special versions.

A fascinating, if controversial, contemporary example of cultural transfer is the rapid international rise of the Venezuelan *El Sistema* movement, which by 2012 had spawned over sixty projects in North America and over twenty in Europe, as well as projects in South Africa, Australia and New Zealand (Hallam 2012). Essentially, *El Sistema* is based upon the idea that the symphony orchestra is a progressive pedagogical tool and motor of social justice. But for Geoffrey Baker (2014), the original model lacked support from rigorous objective research, and hence required critical scrutiny. Furthermore, he observed that rather than promising a major new model for music education, *El Sistema* was in effect 'a massification of old-fashioned "drills and skills" classical music education' (ibid.: 158). Sarah Hennessy (2015: 37) noted that 'the excitement and "glamour" of *El Sistema* had governments in many countries falling over themselves to set up projects with little regard, in some cases, for what already exists in the locality; and with an almost missionary zeal which tends to preclude critical evaluation'.

Undoubtedly, one of the key tasks of comparative education is 'to contemplate what might be borrowed from the foreign example elsewhere' (Ochs and Phillips 2004: 7). However, according to Kertz-Welzel (2014: 107), comparative music education has not yet critically reflected on the challenges and opportunities of educational transfer that is 'more than mere copying and pasting'. She notes the failure of Luther Whiting Mason in the 1880s to transfer the American music education system on to Japan in a way that would be useful for Japan, including Japanese musical and educational traditions, while the attempt by Lowell Mason to adopt Pestalozzian principles into American music education concerned just the method rather than the overall philosophy of teaching (see Gruhn 2001).

Finally, a salutary warning that could be applied to all these historical and contemporary ideas of cultural transfer is that 'we should not expect systems of education ... to be successfully transplanted wholesale into new territories without accommodating for local traditions and values' (Neilsen 2006: 13).

Teacher training

When we come to consider the issue of teacher training, it was expected in several countries during the pioneering days of mass education that classroom teachers would teach the subject of music, as there was no provision for specialist teachers. This training took a variety of forms, including special summer schools (Canada, USA), normal schools (Argentina, Spain), intensive in-service courses (Ireland), Pedagogical High Schools (Kosovo) and teacher training colleges (Britain). It was the task of teacher training courses to provide classroom teachers with the necessary musical skills, which comprised the ability to sing in tune, to sing at sight, and to possess an elementary knowledge of musical rudiments (Argentina, Britain, France, Germany). This made considerable demands on student teachers tackling the intricacies of *solfège* (Argentina, France) and learning a musical instrument to use in their teaching (Germany, Kosovo, Lithuania, Norway). Gradually, with the growth of secondary education, systems of subject-teaching specialists developed. Music specialists received their training in music conservatoires, music academies and universities.

It appears that the teaching of music in elementary schools is still largely in the hands of generalist teachers, although in the USA elementary schools are largely served by credentialed music teachers (also see Groulx 2013). But what emerges in most of the chapters is the need for education systems to support classroom teachers by providing them with a comprehensive training in music that ensures that they will possess the necessary skills, knowledge and confidence to implement an effective classroom music programme. One such attempt is presented in a recent paper by Biasutti et al. (2015). It deals with confidence development in non-music-specialist primary teachers who teach music. The focus is upon an eleven-day intensive workshop for twenty-three trainee primary teachers from Austria, Italy, The Netherlands and Slovenia. The sessions included singing and accompanying skills, workshops and project work, underpinned by the notion of teaching creatively and teaching for creativity. It was found through statistical analysis that there was a significant improvement in students' confidence by the end of the course. Two years later, this finding was consolidated with the teachers demonstrating 'a definite and stable acquisition of confidence in teaching music' (ibid.: 156).

Marie McCarthy (2012) notes that in those countries where music is taught by specialists, teachers frequently do not receive the kind of professional development that would help them to implement a curriculum based on state-of-the-art theory and practice in music education. Presumably, a contemporary trend in the training of teachers in England observed by Ruth Wright (2013) might not meet the demands of such a rigorous curriculum, as it promotes a model of teacher education similar to an apprenticeship, based primarily in schools, and following a competency-based mode of training rather than a model in which teachers are valued as researchers contributing to evidence-based educational policy. There is a historical resonance here with the early nineteenth-century development of a British pupil–teacher scheme, in which pupils were apprenticed at aged thirteen or more to carefully selected head teachers for a period of five years. Dent (1977: 21) points out drily that 'euphoria about pupil–teachers did not last very long'.

Experiences of pupils

When it comes to uncovering the experiences of children in making music at school, it must be admitted that describing what actually happened in nineteenth-century classrooms is a real challenge because of the absence of direct records, although the utilization of contemporary prints provides some unique insights into music teachers and their classrooms (Germany), as do school newspapers, reports of school concerts and photographs of children performing (Australia).

A noteworthy addition to the literature concerning pupil experiences of music education is, however, provided by Stephanie Pitts in *Chances and Choices: Exploring the Impact of Music Education* (2012). In this work, Pitts assembles retrospective accounts of formative musical experiences, and in particular focuses upon individuals' musical engagement once they leave school. She draws upon the experiences of over 100 adults from Britain and Italy, using in-depth life history research, and includes chronological slices of reminiscences of music in school between the 1930s and the 1990s. As Pitts observes, 'getting at the truth of what happened during a school day is no easy task' (ibid.: 3), but certainly her study supplies a model for uncovering in retrospect the traces that remain in individuals of their formal music education. Moreover, from a comparativist point of view, of particular interest is her Italian perspective, which acts as a case study of a distinctive music education system that has historically prioritized specialist training rather than the generalist approaches of the British curriculum.

Reflections on the present

Finally, we come to reflect on the present state of school music education in the light of past experiences. It will have become apparent that, while there have been many positive and innovative developments in the teaching of music in compulsory schooling, there are concerns that increasingly music becomes just one of a number of learning areas – many of them optional – under the generic title of 'artistic education' (Argentina, Australia, Brazil, France, Germany, Israel, South Africa, Spain). Similarly, there are a number of reports that concentration on the basic or core subjects – literacy, numeracy, science, languages etc. – has begun to squeeze music out of the curriculum (England [Britain], France, Norway, Spain). Much of the tension in these situations results from a top-down control over national educational standards (Britain, Turkey, USA). This control is also frequently in tandem with a broad devaluation of the arts in a market-driven system that regards education as a state investment from which there need to be tangible economic dividends. Consequently, in many countries, education now functions as a market in which schools as well as children must compete. This leads to non-negotiable standards and assessment regimes with high-stake testing and league tables (see Finney 2011; Horsley 2014).

Such profound changes in society contribute to what Marie McCarthy (2012) identifies as 'a crisis of identity' in which music educators are challenged by such matters as political ideology, expanding global consciousness, communications and technology, among others. The placement of music within broader 'arts education' is problematic, as music needs to maintain a separate curriculum status and disciplinary identity in an era of interdisciplinarity. She argues eloquently for international perspectives that:

> provide a vital lens for critiquing current practice and expanding philosophical viewpoints and pedagogical approaches. Comparative perspectives can also inspire music educators world-wide, knowing that what they do in the classroom is part of a global mission to establish and maintain a presence for music in general education and to sensitise young people to the humanity of music in their lives and cultures. (Ibid.: 41)

The goal for educational historians, including those who focus upon music education, is summed up succinctly by Emile Durkheim (1977: 9): 'it is only by carefully studying the past that we can come to anticipate the future and then to understand the present'. In the context of contemporary globalization, however, it may also be judicious to adopt 'an increasingly comparative approach and an internationalization that challenges the insularity of researchers who find their comfort zone in the single empirical case' (McCulloch, 2011: 114).

It was our intention that this volume should demonstrate something of the richness of international and comparative approaches to the history of music education, which not only relate to the past, but also to the present and the future. In turn, we hope that it will encourage our readers to grasp opportunities to contribute both in research and practice to a wider international understanding and awareness of the origins and foundations of music education.

References

Baker, G. (2014), *El Sistema: Orchestrating Venezuela's Youth*, Oxford: Oxford University Press.

Biasutti, M., S. Hennessy and E. de Vugt-Jansen (2015), 'Confidence Development in Non-specialist-music Trainee Primary Teachers after an Intensive Programme', *British Journal of Music Education* 32 (2): 143–61.

Bowman, W. (2012), 'Music's place in education' in G. E. McPherson and G. Welch (eds), *The Oxford Handbook of Music Education* Vol. 1, Oxford: Oxford University Press, pp. 21–39.

Campbell, P. S. (2004), *Teaching Music Globally*, New York: Oxford University Press.

Dent, H. C. (1977), *The Training of Teachers in England and Wales 1800–1975*, London: Hodder & Stoughton.

Durkheim, E. (1977), *The Evolution of Educational Thought: Lectures on the Formation and Development of Secondary Education in France*, London: Routledge & Kegan Paul.

Fautley, M. and R. Murphy (2015), 'Editorial: Difficult Questions in Music Education', *British Journal of Music Education* 32 (2): 119–22.

Finney, J. (2011), *Music Education in England, 1950–2010: The Child-Centred Progressive Tradition*, Farnham: Ashgate.

Gray, J. (2015), 'The politics of catastrophe', *New Statesman* 18–24 September, 29–35.

Green, L. (2011), 'Musical Identities – Learning and Education: Some Cross-cultural Issues' in B. Clausen (ed.) *Vergleich in der musikpädagogischen Forschung*, Essen: Die Blaue Eule, pp. 11–34.

Groulx, T. J. (2013), 'Three Nations, One Common Root: A Historical Comparison of Elementary Music Education in the United Kingdom, the United States and Australia', *Journal of Historical Research in Music Education* XXXIV (2): 137–53.

Gruhn, W. (2001), 'European "Methods" for American Nineteenth-century Singing Instruction: A Cross-cultural Perspective on Historical Research', *Journal of Historical Research in Music Education* 23 (1): 3–18.

Hallam, R. J. (2012), 'Sistema: Where Academic, Educational, Personal and Musical Development all Meet' in C. Harrison and S. Hennessy (eds), *Listen Out: International Perspectives on Music Education*, Solihull: National Association of Music Educators, pp. 104–15.

Hebert, D. and A. Kertz-Welsel (eds) (2012), *Patriotism and Nationalism in Music Education*, Farnham, UK: Ashgate.

Hennessy, S. (2015), 'O jardín o erial: contradicciones entre políticas educativas y prácticas escolares en educación musical' ['Garden or desert: the contradictions of policy and practice in music education'], *Revista internacional de Educatión musical* 3, 39–47

Hess, J. (2015), 'Decolonizing Music Education: Moving Beyond Tokenism', *International Journal of Music Education* 33 (3): 336–47.

Horsley, S. (2014), 'A Comparative Analysis of Neoliberal Education Reform and Music Education in England and Ontario, Canada', University of Western Ontario: Electronic Thesis and Dissertation Repository. Paper 1873.

Jorgensen, E. (2008), *The Art of Teaching Music*, Bloomington, IN: Indiana University Press.

Jorgensen, E. (2013), 'Editorial', *Philosophy of Music Education Review* 21 (1), 1–3.

Kertz-Welzel, A. (2014), 'The Policy of Educational Transfer in International Music Education' in P. Gonsonasis (ed.), *Policy and Media In and For a Diverse Global Community: Proceedings of the 17th Biennial International Seminar of the Commission on Music Policy – Culture, Education and Media*, Vancouver: ISME Commission on Music Policy: Culture, Education and Media, pp. 93–8.

Kertz-Welzel, A. (2015), 'Lessons from Elsewhere? Comparative Music Education in Times of Globalization', *Philosophy of Music Education Review* 23 (1): 48–66.

Kim, J. H. (2014a), 'Rethinking Colonialism: Korean Primary School Music Education during the Japanese Colonial rule of Korea, 1910–1945', *Journal of Historical Research in Music Education* XXXV (1), 23–42.

Kim, J. H. (2014b), 'Musical acculturation through primary school activities during Japanese colonial rule of Korea (1910–1945)', *British Journal of Music Education* 31 (3): 265–80.

McCarthy, M. (2012), 'International Perspectives' in G. E. McPherson and G. Welch (eds), *The Oxford Handbook of Music Education* Vol.1, Oxford: Oxford University Press, pp. 40–62.

McCulloch, G. (2011), *The Struggle for the History of Education*, London: Routledge.

Neilsen, F. N. (2006), 'A View of the Future of an International Philosophy of Education: A Plea for a Comparative Strategy', *Philosophy of Music Education Review* 14 (1): 7–14.

Ochs, K. and D. Phillips (2004), 'Processes of Educational Borrowing in Historical Context' in D. Phillips and K. Ochs (eds), *Educational Policy Borrowing: Historical perspectives*, Oxford: Symposium Books, pp. 7–23.

Pitts, S. E. (2012), *Chances and Choices: Exploring the Impact of Music Education*, Oxford: Oxford University Press.

Ramirez, F. O. and J. Boli (1994), 'The Political Institutionalization of Compulsory Education: The Rise of Compulsory Schooling in the Western Cultural Context' in J. A. Mangan (ed.), *A Significant Social Revolution: Cross-Cultural Aspects of the Evolution of Compulsory Education*, London: The Woburn Press, pp. 1–20.

Wright, R. (2013), 'Epilogue: Changing Music Education' in J. Finney and F. Laurence (eds), *Master Class in Music Education: Transforming Teaching and Learning*, London: Bloomsbury, 211–14.

Index

The letter *f* after an entry indicates a page that includes a figure.
The letter *t* after an entry indicates a page that includes a table.